Rachael Ray's
Book of 10

CLARKSON POTTER/PUBLISHERS

NEW YORK

Rachael Ray's
Book of 10

More Than 300 Recipes
to Cook Every Day

RACHAEL RAY

Copyright © 2009 by Rachael Ray

All rights reserved.
Published in the United States by Clarkson Potter/Publishers, an imprint
of the Crown Publishing Group, a division of Random House, Inc., New York.
www.crownpublishing.com
www.clarksonpotter.com

CLARKSON POTTER is a trademark and POTTER with colophon
is a registered trademark of Random House, Inc.

Much of the material in the work originally appeared in the following works
published by Clarkson Potter/Publishers: *Rachael Ray's 30-Minute Get Real
Meals*, copyright © 2005 by Rachael Ray, photographs © 2005 by Ben Fink,
Rachael Ray 365: No Repeats, copyright © 2005 by Rachael Ray, photographs
copyright © 2005 by Ben Fink; *Rachael Ray Express Lane Meals*, copyright
© 2006 by Rachael Ray, photographs copyright © 2006 by Ben Fink; *Rachael
Ray 2, 4, 6, 8*, copyright © 2006 by Rachael Ray, photographs copyright © 2006
by Ben Fink.

Library of Congress Cataloging-in-Publication Data
Ray, Rachael.
    Rachael Ray's book of 10 / Rachael Ray.—1st ed.
    Includes index.
    1. Quick and easy cookery.   I. Title.
TX833.5.R3893 2009
641.5'55—dc22   2009018696
ISBN 978-0-307-38320-4

Printed in the United States of America

Design by Stephanie Huntwork

10 9 8 7 6 5 4 3 2 1

First Edition

CONTENTS

THANK-YOUS

This collection of recipes wouldn't have been possible without the help of my editor, Emily Takoudes, and Peggy Paul, Amy Boorstein, Joanna Gryfe, Kate Tyler, and Lauren Shakely. A special thanks to Em, Andrew "Kappy" Kaplan, and Michelle Boxer for keeping it all together. Thank you to my family and friends for cooking and eating with me.

FOREWORD

When people meet me they are naturally quite curious about what it's like to be married to Rachael Ray. The most commonly asked question is "But is she really a good cook?" to which I invariably respond "Of course! They don't give away those TV cooking show jobs to just anyone!"

Beyond being an exemplary cooker of food (she avoids the label "chef" as she feels she's not worthy since she's not had the formal training required and subsequent diploma or "papers" as she calls them), she truly finds joy in cooking. Even after a long day at work, during which she would have cooked at least three to six full meals on camera, she can't wait to get home to unwind by—you guessed it—cooking. And drinking (typically an Italian red). And living, savoring, and slurping up every little nuance and big event in the lives of her friends and family.

Rachael's food reflects her taste for life—it is filled with flavors bold and familiar, subtle and haunting, and whether it's a cuisine comfortable or foreign to her, it is somehow always spot-on. Her food is filled with love and a family tradition of hard work and focus with the goal being a life surrounded by richness and beauty, the kind not reliant on financial wealth.

Most important, her food tastes of love and care. More than anything, Rach hates to disappoint and approaches the preparation of every meal as seriously as if it were the James Beard Awards—even if it's just some pasta at home with Isaboo and me.

While it is difficult for me to narrow all of her meals down to one single favorite, I can proudly brag that in a city of 20,000 restaurants I get the best food in town. Some (but not all) of my favorites are in this collection.

Mangia!

JOHN CUSIMANO

INTRODUCTION

I am a list type of girl. I make lists on the back of lists. You will find dozens of lists in my notebook. Lists of ingredients, lists of recipes, lists of ideas for recipes.

I am very excited to share this collection with you. For the first time, I've created LISTS OF TEN—so the faves and most requested recipes are bundled into your favorite categories. There are ten chapters, with three LISTS OF TEN in each (plus you get a bonus dessert list in the last chapter!). You'll find some all-time faves—yours, my family's, John's. These are recipes I've been making for years both at home and on my television shows. Now get cooking!

1

Let Me Entertain You

What's better than cooking a great meal and having family and friends over to enjoy it with you? Whether you're hosting a family get-together, dinner party, or movie night with friends, this chapter has just the right flavor for your evening.

OUR FAMILY'S FAVES

Mediterranean Chicken and Saffron Couscous
Italian-Style Garlic Shrimp with Cherry Tomatoes and
  Thin Spaghetti
BBQ Sloppy Chicken Pan Pizza
Lamb "Stew"
Grilled Chicken Caesar with Bacon-Herb-Parmesan "Croutons"
Smoky Black Bean and Rice Stoup
Mostly Green Curry Veggies and Tofu Over Coconut Jasmine Rice
French Onion Soup with an Italian Attitude
Spinach and Spicy Ham Pasta Bake
London Broil with Mushroom Vinaigrette

BEST DISHES TO SHOW OFF

Spinach-Stuffed Steaks with Sautéed Cremini Mushrooms
Seared Tuna Steaks on White Beans with Grape Tomatoes
  and Garlic Chips
Walnut-Parsley-Rosemary Pesto
Ham and Cheese Mini Frittatas
Korean Barbecued Flank Steak on Hot and Sour Slaw Salad
Seared Scallops with Lemon Scented Bread Crumbs and Fettuccine
  with Asparagus and Saffron Cream Sauce
Black Cherry–Black Pepper Lamb Chops with Sweet Pea Risotto
Spinach and Goat Cheese Chicken Rolls in a Pan Sauce
Sliced Steak Sensation
Roast Crispy Mushrooms and Grilled Tenderloin Steaks
  with Scallions

SUPER EASY

Grilled Kielbasa Reubens with Warm Mustard-Caraway Sauerkraut
Sweet Soy-Soaked Salmon Fillets Over Noodle-y Veggies
Prosciutto-Wrapped Endive and Radicchio with Balsamic-
  Fig Reduction
Brutus Salad
Mac 'n' Jack Salad
Roasted Mushroom Pasta with Prosciutto
Sicilian-Style Swordfish Rolls with Fennel and Radicchio Salad
Crispy Turkey Cutlets with Bacon-Cranberry Brussels Sprouts
Spring Chicken with Leeks and Peas Served with Lemon Rice
Indian Summer Turkey Chili

Mediterranean Chicken and Saffron Couscous

I'm sure your family will love this hearty dish as much as ours does.

4 SERVINGS

4 tablespoons **extra-virgin olive oil** (EVOO)

½ cup all-purpose **flour**

4 6-ounce boneless, skinless **chicken breast halves**

Salt and **freshly ground black pepper**

½ teaspoon **cayenne pepper**

3 cups **chicken stock**

1 pinch of **saffron**, or 1 single-use packet saffron powder (available at many fish markets)

4 **garlic cloves**, 1 crushed, 3 chopped

1 cup **couscous**

1 large **red onion**, chopped

1 tablespoon fresh **thyme** leaves, chopped (from 4 sprigs)

1 15-ounce can quartered **artichoke hearts**, drained

1 cup **dry white wine**

10 **kalamata olives**, pitted, cut in half

½ pint **grape** or **cherry tomatoes**

½ cup fresh **flat-leaf parsley** leaves, coarsely chopped

20 fresh **basil** leaves, coarsely chopped

Preheat a large skillet over medium-high heat with 2 tablespoons of the EVOO. Place the flour in a shallow dish, season the chicken breasts with salt, pepper, and the cayenne, then transfer the seasoned chicken to the dish with the flour, toss around in the flour, then shake off the excess. Add the chicken to the skillet and cook for 5 to 6 minutes on each side. While the chicken is cooking, make the saffron couscous.

In a sauce pot, bring 2 cups of the chicken stock up to a boil with the saffron, the crushed clove of garlic, salt, and pepper. When the stock is at a boil, add the couscous, cover with a lid, and turn the heat off. Let the couscous stand for 10 minutes.

Once the chicken is done, remove it from the pan and cover with a piece of aluminum foil to keep warm. Return the skillet to the heat and add the remaining 2 tablespoons of EVOO. Add the onion, the 3 cloves of chopped garlic, the thyme, salt, and pepper. Cook, stirring frequently, for 4 minutes. Add the artichokes and wine to the pan, bring up to a simmer, then add the remaining 1 cup of chicken stock, olives, and grape tomatoes. Return the liquids to a simmer and cook for 2 to 3 minutes, or until the grape tomatoes start to burst and the sauce has reduced by half. Give the sauce a taste to see if it needs more salt and pepper. Add the chicken back to the skillet and warm through.

Add the parsley and basil to the completed dish and stir to distribute the herbs.

To serve, fluff the couscous with a fork, remove and discard the crushed garlic clove, and transfer the couscous to serving plates. Serve the chicken whole or sliced on top of the saffron couscous. Top the chicken with some of the sauce and vegetables.

Italian-Style Garlic Shrimp with Cherry Tomatoes and Thin Spaghetti

My mama loves this one. Well . . . shrimp, tomatoes, and pasta . . . is there anything NOT to like? 4 SERVINGS

Coarse salt

1 pound thin **spaghetti**

1 pound small **shrimp**, deveined and peeled, tails removed

2 teaspoons **lemon zest** plus **the juice of** ¼ lemon

¼ cup **extra-virgin olive oil** (EVOO)

6 **garlic cloves**, minced

1 pint **cherry tomatoes**, halved

4 **scallions**, thinly sliced on an angle

¼ cup **white vermouth** or ⅓ cup dry white wine

2 handfuls fresh **flat-leaf parsley**, chopped

20 fresh **basil** leaves, torn or shredded

Coarse black pepper

Heat a large pot of water for the pasta. When the water boils, salt it and cook the pasta al dente.

Heat a large nonstick skillet over medium to medium-high heat. Season the shrimp with the lemon zest, lemon juice, and a little salt. Add the EVOO to the hot pan and then add the shrimp. Cook for a minute, then add the garlic, tomatoes, and scallions and toss, cooking for another minute or two until the shrimp are firm and pink. Add the white vermouth and the herbs. Turn off the heat. Drain the pasta well and add to the sauce. Toss and combine the sauce with pasta and season with salt and black pepper.

BBQ Sloppy Chicken Pan Pizza

This cornmeal crust is delicious! 4 SERVINGS, 2 SLICES EACH

2 boxes **corn muffin mix**, such as Jiffy brand, 8½ ounces each

2 **eggs**

4 tablespoons **unsalted butter**, melted

1½ cups **milk**

1 cup frozen **corn kernels**

Extra-virgin olive oil (EVOO)

TOPPING

2 tablespoons **EVOO**

1 pound **ground chicken breast**

3 **garlic cloves**, crushed from their skins and chopped

1 medium **yellow onion**, chopped

1 small **red bell pepper**, cored, seeded, and chopped

Coarse salt and **coarse black pepper**

1 tablespoon **chili powder**

1½ teaspoons **ground cumin**

2 teaspoons **hot sauce**

1 tablespoon **Worcestershire sauce**

1 cup **tomato sauce**

3 tablespoons **dark brown sugar**

1 sack (10 ounces) shredded **Cheddar cheese**

3 **scallions**, chopped

2 to 3 tablespoons chopped fresh **flat-leaf parsley** or cilantro, your preference

Preheat the oven to 400°F.

In a large bowl, combine the 2 packages of corn muffin mix with the eggs, melted butter, and milk. Stir in the corn. Drizzle some EVOO into a large nonstick skillet with an oven-safe handle and wipe it around the pan with a folded paper towel. (Wrap the handle in a double layer of foil if it has a plastic or rubber handle.) Pour in the batter, place the pan in the center of the preheated oven, and bake until the cornbread becomes light golden in color, 12 to 15 minutes.

Place a second skillet over medium-high heat and add the 2 tablespoons of EVOO. Add the chicken and break it up with a wooden spoon. Once the chicken has crumbled and begins to brown, add the garlic, onions, and bell peppers and season with salt and pepper, chili powder, cumin, and hot sauce. Cook for 5 minutes, then add the Worcestershire, tomato sauce, and brown sugar. Stir to combine and reduce the heat to low. Simmer until the cornbread sets up and begins to brown. Adjust the seasonings to taste.

Remove the cornbread from the oven and cover it with the sloppy chicken mixture, then sprinkle with the cheese. Put the pan back in the hot oven and cook for 5 minutes longer to set the toppings and melt the cheese. Top with the scallions and chopped parsley or cilantro and serve from the skillet, cutting the pizza into 8 wedges.

Lamb "Stew"

Calling all lamb lovers, these chops are served atop a vegetable stew.

4 SERVINGS

2 tablespoons **extra-virgin olive oil** (EVOO)

1 large **yellow onion**, chopped

6 medium **red bliss potatoes**, cut in half and then sliced

1 tablespoon chopped fresh **thyme** (from 3 to 4 sprigs)

3 **garlic cloves**, chopped

1 **bay leaf**, fresh or dried

Salt and **freshly ground black pepper**

2 large **carrots**, peeled and thinly sliced

2 **celery ribs**, chopped into 1-inch pieces

2 rounded tablespoons **tomato paste**

2 tablespoons all-purpose **flour**

½ cup **dry red wine**

2½ cups **chicken stock** (eyeball it: just over half a quart-size carton)

12 **rib lamb chops** (3 chops per person)

¼ cup fresh **flat-leaf parsley** leaves (a generous handful), chopped

Preheat the broiler.

To make the "stew," preheat a large skillet over medium-high heat with the EVOO; add the onions, potatoes, thyme, garlic, bay leaf, salt, and pepper. Cook until the onions start to brown, about 6 to 7 minutes. Add the carrots, celery, and tomato paste and continue to cook for 2 to 3 minutes. Sprinkle with the flour, cook for 1 more minute, and then whisk in the red wine. Cook for 1 minute, then add the chicken stock and bring the mixture up to a bubble. Turn the heat down to medium low and simmer for 10 minutes.

While the "stew" is simmering, start the lamb chops. Arrange the chops on a broiler pan and season both sides with salt and pepper. Broil the chops for 3 to 4 minutes on each side for medium rare, up to 5 minutes on each side for medium well.

To serve, add the parsley to the "stew," remove and discard the bay leaf, taste, and adjust the seasoning with salt and pepper. Divide the stew among 4 shallow serving bowls and arrange 3 chops atop each portion.

Grilled Chicken Caesar with Bacon-Herb-Parmesan "Croutons"

My family just loves this salad.   4 SERVINGS

½ cup **extra-virgin olive oil** (EVOO)

2 slices **bacon**, finely chopped

1½ cups grated **Parmigiano-Reggiano**

2 tablespoons fresh **flat-leaf parsley** (a handful), chopped

4 **garlic cloves**, chopped

Juice of 2 lemons

Salt and **freshly ground black pepper**

8 thin **chicken breast cutlets** (about 1¼ pounds)

2 tablespoons **Dijon mustard**

1 tablespoon **Worcestershire sauce**

3 **romaine lettuce** hearts, roughly chopped

3 **hard-boiled eggs**, chopped (see Tidbit)

Preheat the oven to 400°F. Preheat a charcoal grill or grill pan to high.

Heat a small skillet over medium-high heat with 1 tablespoon of the EVOO (once around the pan). Add the chopped bacon and cook until really crispy, 2 to 3 minutes. Remove the bacon to a plate lined with a paper towel to drain and cool.

In a small bowl combine 1 cup of the grated cheese with the chopped parsley and cooled bacon. Mix to distribute the bacon and parsley evenly. Line a baking sheet with a piece of parchment paper. Pour the cheese mixture out onto the center of the baking sheet and with your fingers, spread out the cheese in an even and very thin layer. Give the pan a little shake to help you even it out. This way you will have a lacy web when the cheese melts. Place the baking sheet in the oven for 3 to 4 minutes, turning the pan midway through the cooking. If your oven has hot spots, you will have to turn it more often than just once to ensure even browning. Once the cheese has melted and is nice and golden brown, remove it from the oven to cool completely.

While the cheese is baking, prepare the chicken and the Caesar dressing. (But a little heads up: Don't forget about the Parmesan "croutons" because they go from golden brown to black in a blink of your eye.) Like I was saying, for the chicken, in a shallow dish combine half of the chopped garlic, half of the lemon juice, salt, pepper, and a generous drizzle of the EVOO. Add the chicken cutlets and toss to completely coat. Place the chicken on the hot grill and cook on each side for 3 to 4 minutes. Remove from the grill.

While the chicken is cooking, in a mixing bowl combine the remaining chopped garlic, the Dijon mustard, the Worcestershire sauce, the remaining lemon juice, and lots of freshly ground pepper. Whisk in about ⅓ cup of the EVOO. Add the remaining ½ cup of Parmigiano and stir to combine. In a salad bowl combine the romaine lettuce and the hard-boiled eggs. Dress with the Caesar dressing.

To serve, slice the cooled chicken into thin strips and divide among 4 plates. Top the chicken with the dressed romaine and hard-boiled egg. Gingerly remove the baked Parmesan from the pan, pulling on one of the corners of the parchment paper to help you lift it up and out. With your hands, crack the baked cheese into "croutons" or asymmetrical 1- to 2-inch pieces. Garnish the salad with the "croutons" and serve.

tidbit >> Place eggs in a small sauce pot and add enough water to cover them. Place over high heat. Once the eggs are at a simmer, turn the heat off, cover the pot, and let the eggs sit for 10 minutes. Drain off the hot water then shake the pan aggressively to crack the eggshells. Run the eggs under cold water, then peel.

Smoky Black Bean and Rice Stoup

This is a chop, drop, and open recipe. Place your cutting board next to the stove, heat up the pots, chop everything on the board, drop it into the pan, then open up your cans. As soon as the stoup bubbles, dinner is done.   4 SERVINGS

2 tablespoons **EVOO** (extra-virgin olive oil)

3 **bacon slices,** chopped

1 **bay leaf**

2 **celery ribs,** chopped

1 medium **onion,** chopped

4 **garlic cloves,** chopped

1 cup **frozen corn kernels**

2 15-ounce cans **black beans**

1 tablespoon **ground coriander**

1 tablespoon **chili powder**

1½ teaspoons **ground cumin**

1 tablespoon **Worcestershire sauce**

2 teaspoons **hot sauce**

Coarse salt and **coarse black pepper**

1 15-ounce can diced **fire-roasted tomatoes,** such as Muir Glen

1 8-ounce can **tomato sauce**

1 quart **chicken stock**

1 cup **white rice**

Heat a medium soup pot over medium-high heat. Add the EVOO, then add the bacon and cook for 3 to 4 minutes to render the fat. Add the bay leaf, celery, onions, and garlic and cook for 3 to 4 minutes to soften the veggies. Add the corn and 1 can of black beans and their juice. Drain the other can, then add half the can of beans. Mash the remaining beans in the can with a fork to make a paste out of them, then scrape them into the soup pot—this will make the stoup souper-thick! Season the veggies and beans with the coriander, chili, ground cumin, Worcestershire, and hot sauce. Season the mixture with salt and pepper to taste. Stir in the tomatoes, tomato sauce, and stock, then cover the pot and raise the heat to bring the stoup to a boil. Add the rice and cook the stoup over a rolling simmer until the rice is tender but has a little bite left to it, 15 minutes. Adjust the seasonings and serve.

Mostly Green Curry Veggies and Tofu Over Coconut Jasmine Rice

Do you think tofu is bland? Think again. Try this tofu combined with the bold flavor of curry, served over sweet coconut rice. Delish!

4 SERVINGS

1½ cups **vegetable stock**

1 13½-ounce can **coconut milk**

1 cup **jasmine rice**

3 tablespoons **vegetable** or **canola oil**

1 14-ounce container **firm tofu**, cut into 1½- to 2-inch pieces, patted dry

Salt and **freshly ground black pepper**

1 **green bell pepper**, cored, seeded, and thinly sliced

1 medium **yellow onion**, thinly sliced

3 large **garlic cloves**, chopped

1 small **jalapeño pepper**, cut in half and seeded

3-inch piece of fresh **ginger**, peeled and finely grated

2 cups **broccoli florets**

Zest and juice of 1 lime

¼ cup fresh **cilantro** leaves (a handful), chopped

3 **scallions**, thinly sliced

½ cup fresh **flat-leaf parsley** leaves (a couple of handfuls), chopped

1 cup frozen **peas**

Hot sauce, such as Tabasco, to taste (optional)

In a sauce pot, combine 1 cup of the vegetable stock, 4 ounces (½ cup) of the coconut milk, and the jasmine rice. Bring to a simmer, cover, and cook for 15 to 18 minutes. Turn the heat off and keep the rice covered until ready to serve.

While the coconut jasmine rice is cooking, preheat a large nonstick skillet over high heat with about 2 tablespoons of the vegetable oil. Season the tofu pieces with salt and pepper. Add the tofu pieces, spreading them evenly across the pan, and brown the tofu on all sides, about 3 to 4 minutes. Remove the browned tofu to a plate and reserve. Add the last tablespoon of vegetable oil to the pan. Add the green bell peppers, onions, garlic, jalapeños, ginger, and broccoli florets. Cook, stirring frequently, for 3 to 4 minutes, or until the veggies start to wilt. To the skillet add the remaining coconut milk and ½ cup vegetable stock. Bring the mixture to a boil, then reduce the heat and simmer for 4 to 5 minutes. Add the tofu back to the skillet, and return it to a simmer for about 2 more minutes. Add the lime zest, lime juice, cilantro, scallions, parsley, and frozen peas. Stir to thoroughly combine. Simmer a minute more to heat the peas, taste, and adjust the seasoning. Add more salt or some hot sauce, if you like heat. Serve over the coconut jasmine rice.

French Onion Soup with an Italian Attitude

It takes a Sicilian attitude to think one could improve on a French classic, especially in 30 minutes. Well, this Sicilian says "Bring it on."

4 SERVINGS

---

1 tablespoon **EVOO** (extra-virgin olive oil)

2 tablespoons **butter**

6 medium **onions**, thinly sliced

Salt and **black pepper**

Leaves from 1 sprig of **rosemary**, finely chopped

½ pint **grape tomatoes**, halved

½ cup fresh **basil**, about 10 leaves, torn into pieces

¼ cup shredded or grated **Parmigiano-Reggiano** cheese

4 thick slices **crusty bread**

1 **garlic clove**, crushed

1 tablespoon **balsamic vinegar**

½ cup **white wine**, a couple of good glugs

6 cups **beef stock**

8 slices **fresh mozzarella** cheese

Preheat the broiler to high.

Heat a deep pot over medium to medium-high heat. Add the EVOO and butter to the pot. When the butter melts, start adding the onions as you slice them. Season the onions with salt, pepper, and the rosemary. Cook the onions for 15 to 18 minutes, until tender, sweet, and caramel colored, stirring frequently. If you find that the onions are burning in spots before browning all over, add a splash of water and stir now and then, scraping the bottom of the pot.

While the onions are cooking, make the topping. In a small bowl, combine the grape tomatoes, basil, grated cheese, salt, and pepper. Under the broiler or toaster oven, toast the crusty bread until golden; rub each side of the golden toast with the crushed garlic clove.

Once the onions are done, add the balsamic vinegar and white wine, stirring up all the brown bits from the bottom of the pot. Add the stock and cover the pot to bring the soup up to a quick boil.

Arrange 4 small, deep soup bowls or crocks on a cookie sheet. Once the soup reaches a boil, ladle it into the bowls. Float a toasted bread slice on each serving and cover each toast with a mound of the grape tomato mixture. Top with 2 slices of the mozzarella cheese. Slide the cookie sheet under the hot broiler until the cheese melts and bubbles.

Spinach and Spicy Ham Pasta Bake

Who doesn't like a baked pasta dish? Leafy greens and ham make this one a real crowd pleaser. *4 SERVINGS AMONG BIG EATERS LIKE ME AND MY FAMILY*

Coarse salt

1 pound **cavatappi** (ridged corkscrew pasta) or ridged macaroni

3 tablespoons **extra-virgin olive oil** (EVOO)

2 tablespoons **unsalted butter**

1 medium **onion**, chopped

Coarse black pepper

3 tablespoons all-purpose **flour**

1½ cups whole or 2-percent **milk**

½ pound sliced **capocollo** (spicy ham), halved, then sliced into thin ribbons

1 10-ounce box frozen **chopped spinach**, defrosted and wrung out in a clean kitchen towel

1 cup grated **Parmigiano-Reggiano**

½ teaspoon **ground** or **freshly grated nutmeg**

¼ teaspoon **ground cayenne pepper**

1-pound ball of **fresh mozzarella** (buy a piece wrapped, not packed in water, then cut into ½-inch cubes)

1 cup **plain** or **Italian-style bread crumbs**

Preheat the broiler.

Bring a large pot of water to a boil over high heat. Salt the water, add the pasta, and cook al dente, with a bite.

While the water is coming up to a boil for the pasta, heat a medium, deep skillet over medium heat. Add 1 tablespoon of the EVOO (once around the pan), and the butter. When the butter melts into the oil, add the onions and season with salt and pepper. Cook, stirring frequently, for 2 minutes, then dust the onions with the flour and continue to cook for 1 minute. Slowly whisk in the milk. Gently bring the milk to a bubble, allow the mixture to thicken a bit, then stir in the capocollo, spinach, and ½ cup of the grated Parmigiano. Season the sauce with nutmeg and cayenne and remove from the heat. Taste and add a little salt, if you like.

Combine the cooked pasta and the cubed mozzarella with the sauce, then stir to coat completely by turning over and over. Transfer the dressed pasta to a baking dish.

To make the bread-crumb topping, in a small bowl, combine the bread crumbs, the remaining 2 tablespoons of EVOO, and the remaining ½ cup of Parmigiano. Sprinkle the bread-crumb mixture over the top to cover the pasta from edge to edge. Transfer the baking dish under the broiler and broil until golden brown and crispy. What a gut-buster! Yum-o!

London Broil with Mushroom Vinaigrette

Serve with baby spinach salad dressed with oil and vinegar or blue cheese dressing, your choice.   4 SERVINGS

2-pound boneless **shoulder steak** or top round steak

3 tablespoons **Worcestershire sauce**

5 tablespoons **extra-virgin olive oil** (EVOO), plus some for drizzling

Salt and **freshly ground black pepper**

1 10-ounce package **cremini (baby portobello) mushrooms**, brushed clean, quartered

1 large **yellow onion**, chopped

3 **garlic cloves**, chopped

1 tablespoon fresh **thyme** leaves, chopped (from 4 sprigs)

¼ cup **sherry vinegar**

2 heaping tablespoons **Dijon mustard**

½ cup fresh **flat-leaf parsley** leaves (2 generous handfuls), chopped

Preheat the broiler on high and set the rack closest to the flame.

Coat the steak with the Worcestershire sauce, a drizzle of EVOO, salt, and pepper. Marinate the steak for 5 minutes. Transfer the marinated steak to a broiler pan and broil for 6 minutes per side. Remove from the broiler and allow the meat to rest for 5 minutes, tented loosely with a piece of aluminum foil.

While the steak is working, heat a large skillet over medium-high heat with 2 tablespoons of the EVOO (twice around the pan). Add the mushrooms and brown for 5 minutes, stirring every now and then. Turn the heat down to medium and add the onions, garlic, and thyme and season with salt and pepper. Cook for 3 to 4 minutes, or until the onions become tender and translucent. Add the sherry vinegar and mustard and stir to combine. Turn off the heat. Some liquid will evaporate. Whisk in about 3 tablespoons more of EVOO, add the parsley, and reserve the vinaigrette while you slice the steak.

Slice the rested steak very thin, against the grain and on an angle. Serve the sliced meat topped with some of the mushroom vinaigrette.

tidbit >> Shoulder steak is often labeled as "London broil" in the meat case.

Spinach-Stuffed Steaks with Sautéed Cremini Mushrooms

A side order of spinach is a staple at every good steakhouse across America. So why not put the spinach inside your steak? That's what I've done here and it's a real pleaser at the table! When this dish is paired with another classic steak sidekick, mushrooms, you have a Michelin 3-star meal on one plate! 4 SERVINGS

1 10-ounce box **frozen chopped spinach**

4 tablespoons **extra-virgin olive oil** (EVOO)

3 **garlic cloves**, chopped

½ small **yellow onion**, chopped

½ small **red bell pepper**, ¼ chopped and ¼ cut into thin strips for garnish

2 ounces **prosciutto di Parma**, chopped

½ cup grated **Parmigiano-Reggiano**

Freshly ground black pepper

2 pounds **eye round roast**, strings cut off

Coarse salt

Large **plastic food storage bag**

SAUTÉED CREMINI MUSHROOMS

1 tablespoon **extra-virgin olive oil** (EVOO)

2 tablespoons **butter**

1½ pounds **cremini mushrooms**, brushed clean with damp towel

Salt and freshly ground black pepper

3 tablespoons **fresh thyme**, chopped

1 pint **grape tomatoes**

½ cup **dry red wine**

2 tablespoons chopped fresh **flat-leaf parsley**

Defrost the spinach in the microwave, then wrap in a clean kitchen towel and twist to wring dry.

Heat a large skillet over medium-high heat. Add 2 tablespoons of the EVOO (twice around the pan), then the garlic, onion, and chopped bell pepper, and cook for 1 minute. Add the spinach and stir to incorporate it. Add the prosciutto and incorporate it. Add the cheese and black pepper and stir. Remove the stuffing from the heat and let it sit until cool enough to handle.

To create a cavity for the stuffing, use a long, sharp knife, such as a boning knife, and cut into each end of the meat. Turn the knife to create a 2-inch hole through the center of the meat, meeting the incisions at the middle of the roast. Twist the handle of a wooden spoon into the hole to loosen and widen the cavity, making the hole even for its entire length. Season the roast with the coarse salt.

Put the stuffing into a plastic food storage bag and cut a 1-inch hole in one bottom corner. Gather the bag, like a pastry bag, forcing the stuffing to that side. Stand the

recipe continued

roast on its end and fill half the roast with stuffing. Turn on the opposite end and finish filling the cavity by piping in the stuffing. You might need to push it along with your fingers to make sure it goes all the way through.

Preheat a large nonstick skillet over medium-high heat. Cut the roast into eight 1-inch-thick slices. Add the remaining 2 tablespoons of EVOO to the pan (2 turns of the pan). Add the meat and cook for 2 minutes, flip, cook 2 minutes more, then reduce heat to medium low and cook for 4 minutes more. Prepare the mushrooms while the meat cooks.

Heat a second large skillet over medium-high heat. Add the EVOO and butter. When the butter melts into the EVOO, add the mushrooms. Brown the mushrooms for 5 minutes, then season with salt, pepper, and thyme. Add the tomatoes and cook for 2 to 3 minutes more, until the tomatoes start to burst, then add the red wine and deglaze the pan. Finish with the parsley and turn off the heat.

Transfer 2 pieces of stuffed steak onto each of 4 dinner plates and garnish with the thinly sliced red bell pepper. Serve with a few spoonfuls of mushrooms alongside the steak.

Seared Tuna Steaks on White Beans with Grape Tomatoes and Garlic Chips

Tuna lovers, you're going to love this Mediterranean-style dish.
4 SERVINGS

4 tablespoons **EVOO** (extra-virgin olive oil), plus some for drizzling

5 large **garlic cloves**, very thinly sliced—just do your best

1 large **onion**, sliced

3 **celery ribs**, finely chopped

1 large pinch **red pepper flakes**

Salt and **black pepper**

4 6-ounce **tuna steaks**, about 1½ inches thick

¾ cup **white wine**, a few good glugs

1¼ cups **chicken stock**

2 14-ounce cans **cannellini beans**, rinsed and drained

1 pint **grape tomatoes**

½ cup fresh **flat-leaf parsley**, a couple of generous handfuls, chopped

Juice of ½ lemon

Place a medium skillet on the stovetop with the 4 tablespoons of EVOO. Add the sliced garlic and spread it out in one layer in the oil. Turn the heat on to medium low to slowly brown the garlic, about 2 to 3 minutes. With a slotted spoon, remove the garlic chips to a paper-towel-lined plate, leaving the oil in the skillet. Turn the heat up to medium high; add the onions, celery, red pepper flakes, salt, and pepper. Cook for 5 minutes, until the onions take on some color and become tender.

While the onions are browning, place a large non-stick skillet over high heat. Pat the tuna steaks dry and drizzle with a little EVOO, coating the steaks evenly. Season the steaks with salt and pepper. When the pan is very hot, add the tuna steaks. Sear and brown the steaks on one side for 2 minutes, then turn and immediately reduce the heat to medium. Loosely tent the pan with aluminum foil and cook the steaks 5 minutes for rare, 7 minutes for medium. The steaks should be firm but have a little give, with some pink at the center.

While the tuna is cooking, add the white wine and chicken stock to the onions and celery. Bring up to a bubble and continue to cook for about 3 minutes. Add the cannellini beans and grape tomatoes and continue to cook until they are warmed through, about 2 minutes. Finish the beans with the parsley, garlic chips, and lemon juice and stir to distribute.

To serve, pile a serving of beans on each dinner plate and top with a tuna steak.

Walnut-Parsley-Rosemary Pesto

This is also good with scrod or haddock broiled with lemon and EVOO.

4 SERVINGS

Coarse salt

1 pound **penne rigate**

1 cup **walnuts**

About ½ cup **extra-virgin olive oil** (EVOO)

½ head of **cauliflower**, florets sectioned and cut into ½-inch slices

4 **garlic cloves**, chopped

Coarse black pepper

1 cup fresh **flat-leaf parsley** leaves (a few generous handfuls)

3 tablespoons fresh **rosemary** leaves (from 4 sprigs)

¼ to ⅓ cup grated **Romano** (an overflowing handful), plus some to pass at the table

Zest of 1 orange

Heat a pot of water to boil for the pasta. When it boils, salt the water and add the pasta, cooking al dente, with a bite to it.

Heat a deep skillet over medium heat. Add the walnuts and toast for 5 minutes to develop their flavor. Remove the nuts from the pan and cool. Bring an inch of salted water to a boil in a small pot, add the cauliflower, and cook for 2 to 3 minutes. Drain. Return the skillet to the stove over medium-high heat. Add 2 tablespoons of the EVOO (twice around the pan), then the cauliflower and garlic. Season the cauliflower with salt and pepper and cook, stirring frequently, for 2 minutes.

While the cauliflower cooks, grind half the nuts with the parsley, rosemary, cheese, and orange zest in a food processor. Stream in about ⅓ cup of the EVOO and process until a paste forms, then season with salt and pepper.

Drain the pasta. Add the pesto to the cauliflower. Add the pasta to the pesto and toss to coat evenly, then toss in the remaining whole toasted nuts. Adjust the seasonings and grated cheese and transfer to a serving platter or plates. Pass more cheese at the table.

Ham and Cheese Mini Frittatas

Quiche—hold the crust and the work!   12 MINI FRITTATAS

3 tablespoons **melted butter**

¼ pound deli-sliced **Swiss cheese**, finely chopped

¼ pound **ham steak** or Canadian bacon, finely chopped

A splash of **milk** or half-and-half

3 tablespoons snipped or chopped fresh **chives**

Salt and **freshly ground black pepper**

A few drops of **hot sauce**

8 large **eggs**, well beaten

Preheat the oven to 375°F.

Brush a 12-muffin tin liberally with the butter. Divide the chopped cheese and ham evenly among the muffin cups. Add the milk, chives, salt and pepper, and hot sauce to the eggs and fill the cups up to just below the rim with the egg mixture. Bake the frittatas until golden and puffy, 10 to 12 minutes. Remove to a plate with a small spatula and serve.

Alternative fillings: You can also try defrosted chopped frozen broccoli and shredded Cheddar, or chopped cooked bacon with shredded smoked Gouda and sautéed mushrooms.

Korean Barbecued Flank Steak on Hot and Sour Slaw Salad

Here's a new take on flank steak—Korean style! This one is cheap to make and really tasty.   4 SERVINGS

1 tablespoon **grill seasoning,** such as McCormick's Montreal Steak Seasoning

¼ cup **tamari** (dark aged soy sauce)

2 tablespoons **honey**

2 teaspoons **red pepper flakes**

4 large **garlic cloves,** chopped

2 teaspoons **dark sesame oil**

2 **scallions,** finely chopped

Vegetable oil, for drizzling, plus 2 tablespoons

2 pounds **flank steak**

1 pound **bok choy** or napa cabbage, trimmed and shredded with a knife

½ **red bell pepper,** cored, seeded, and thinly sliced

Salt

1 cup **sauerkraut** (it will taste like kim chee when combined with red pepper flakes)

In a shallow dish, combine the grill seasoning, tamari, 1 tablespoon of the honey, 1 teaspoon of the red pepper flakes, half of the chopped garlic, the sesame oil, scallions, and a drizzle of vegetable oil. Coat the flank steak in the mixture and let it stand for 10 minutes.

Preheat an indoor electric grill, a stovetop grill pan, or an outdoor grill to medium high. When the grill pan or grill is screaming hot, add the meat and cook for 5 minutes on each side for medium rare, 7 to 8 minutes on each side for medium well.

Heat a large skillet over high heat. Add 2 tablespoons of the vegetable oil, the cabbage, and the bell pepper. Season with salt and stir-fry for 2 or 3 minutes. Add a drizzle of honey (the remaining tablespoon), the remaining red pepper flakes, and the remaining garlic and toss to combine with the cabbage. Add the sauerkraut and mix in, heating it through for 1 minute. Turn off the heat.

To serve, let the meat rest for 5 minutes for juices to redistribute. Thinly slice the meat on a heavy angle against the grain (the lines in the meat). Pile up the slaw, top with the sliced Korean steak, and serve.

Seared Scallops with Lemon-Scented Bread Crumbs and Fettuccine with Asparagus and Saffron Cream Sauce

Saffron adds a subtle flavor and mellow yellow color to this recipe, which will put plain old Fettucine Alfredo to shame! 4 SERVINGS

Salt

1 pound **asparagus tips**

1 pound **fettuccine**

2 tablespoons **EVOO** (extra-virgin olive oil), plus some for drizzling

2 **garlic cloves**, chopped

1 **shallot**, thinly sliced

½ cup **dry white wine**

½ cup **chicken stock**

1 14-ounce can **crushed tomatoes**

Pinch of **saffron** or 1 packet saffron powder (available in many markets on the spice aisle)

¼ cup **heavy cream**

Black pepper

2 tablespoons **butter**

1 cup **bread crumbs**

Zest of 1 lemon

Handful of fresh **flat-leaf parsley** leaves, finely chopped

16 **sea scallops**, trimmed

Bring an inch of water to a boil in a large skillet and bring a large covered pot of water to a boil for the pasta. When the water in the skillet comes to a boil, add salt and the asparagus and blanch for 2 minutes. Drain the asparagus and reserve. When the pasta water comes to a boil, salt it and cook the fettuccine to al dente.

In the pan that you blanched the asparagus in, heat the 2 tablespoons of EVOO, twice around the pan, over medium heat. Add the garlic and shallots and sauté for 4 to 5 minutes. Deglaze the pan with the wine, then cook for 30 seconds to reduce it slightly. Add the stock, tomatoes, and saffron and simmer for 10 minutes. Stir in the cream, then season the sauce with salt and pepper.

While the sauce cooks, heat a skillet over medium-low heat. Melt the butter and toast the bread crumbs. Stir in salt and pepper, the lemon zest, and parsley, then scrape into a bowl. Wipe the pan clean and return the skillet to medium-high heat and preheat until it's very hot. Drizzle the scallops with EVOO and add them to the hot pan to brown and caramelize on each side, 3 minutes on the first side and 2 minutes on the second.

Chop the asparagus into 1-inch pieces and add to the sauce. Drain the pasta and toss with the asparagus and sauce. Serve with the seared scallops, 4 per person, alongside, and top the scallops with the lemon-scented bread crumbs.

Black Cherry–Black Pepper Lamb Chops with Sweet Pea Risotto

This is a great date meal for your Lamb Chop, Sweet Pea, or Honey Pie.

2 SERVINGS

1 quart **chicken stock**

2 tablespoons **butter**

2 tablespoons **EVOO** (extra-virgin olive oil), plus some for drizzling

1 small **onion,** chopped

2 **garlic cloves,** chopped

1 cup **Arborio rice**

½ cup **white wine**

1 cup **frozen green peas**

4 **loin lamb chops,** each 1½ inches thick

1 **shallot,** thinly sliced

½ cup **black cherry all-fruit preserves**

3 tablespoons **balsamic vinegar**

½ teaspoon **cracked black pepper**

Salt

½ cup grated **Parmigiano-Reggiano** cheese

2 tablespoons chopped fresh **mint,** plus a few sprigs for garnish

A handful of fresh **flat-leaf parsley,** chopped

Place the stock in a medium pot and warm it up over medium-low heat.

Place an oven rack 8 inches from the broiler and preheat the broiler to high.

In a medium skillet over medium to medium-high heat, melt a tablespoon of the butter with a tablespoon of the EVOO. When the pan is hot, add the onions and garlic and cook for 2 to 3 minutes, then add the Arborio and cook for a minute more. Add the wine and cook it all away, 1 minute. Add a few ladles of warm stock and let the rice absorb it, stirring occasionally. Add a ladle of broth as each addition is absorbed, until the risotto is starchy, creamy, and cooked to al dente. The risotto will take 22 minutes to cook. Add the peas when the risotto is just about al dente.

When the risotto is half cooked, 10 minutes from being done, drizzle the lamb chops with EVOO and put on a slotted broiler pan. Place the chops under the hot broiler and cook for 8 to 10 minutes for medium rare. Place a tiny pan on the stove over medium heat. Add the remaining tablespoon of EVOO and the shallots to the pan. Cook the shallots for 2 minutes, then add the preserves and whisk them together with the balsamic vinegar and black pepper. Heat to a bubble, then remove from the heat and whisk the remaining tablespoon of butter into the sauce.

Season the risotto with salt to taste. Place a generous serving of risotto into shallow dinner plates. Arrange 2 chops on each plate alongside the risotto and drizzle the black cherry–black pepper glaze over the chops. Add the cheese, chopped mint, and parsley just before serving. Garnish with extra sprigs of mint.

Spinach and Goat Cheese Chicken Rolls in a Pan Sauce

Serve with buttered and parslied orzo or small potatoes or with lots of crusty bread.   4 SERVINGS

4 6-ounce boneless, skinless **chicken breast halves**

1 10-ounce box **frozen chopped spinach**, defrosted

½ cup crumbled **goat cheese or goat cheese with herbs**, or crumbled **Boursin** (garlic and herb cow's-milk cheese)

Zest and juice of 1 lemon

Salt and **freshly ground black pepper**

Toothpicks

3 tablespoons **sesame seeds**

All-purpose **flour**, for dredging, plus 1 tablespoon

4 tablespoons **extra-virgin olive oil** (EVOO)

3 **garlic cloves**

1 small **yellow onion**, finely chopped

1 tablespoon fresh **thyme** leaves, chopped (from 4 sprigs)

½ teaspoon **red pepper flakes**

2 cups **chicken stock** or broth

¼ cup fresh **flat-leaf parsley** leaves (a generous handful), chopped

3 tablespoons diced **roasted red peppers**

Preheat the oven to 325°F.

Sprinkle a little water in four food storage bags. Place 1 chicken breast in each bag, and seal it up, pushing out excess air. Using a mallet or a small, heavy pot or pan, pound each breast until flat and just shy of busting out of the bag.

Wring the spinach dry in a kitchen towel. Separate it and add it to a bowl. Add the goat cheese and the lemon zest, season with salt and pepper, and mix until combined.

Lay the 4 pounded chicken breasts out on a cutting board. Season them with salt and pepper. Place one fourth of the spinach-goat cheese filling on each breast, along one long edge of the cutlet. Roll the chicken breast to enclose the filling, creating a cigar shape, and secure with toothpicks. Season the outside of the chicken with salt and pepper and then dredge in the sesame seeds and flour.

Preheat a large skillet over medium to medium-high heat with 2 tablespoons of the EVOO. Shake the excess flour from the chicken and then add to the hot skillet and sauté on all sides for about 5 minutes, or until golden brown all over. Transfer to a rimmed cookie sheet and place in the oven to finish cooking through, another 5 to 7 minutes, until the juices run clear.

Place the skillet back over medium-high heat, add the remaining 2 tablespoons of EVOO, and add the garlic, onions, thyme, red pepper flakes, and some salt. Cook for about 3 minutes, then sprinkle the mixture with 1 table-

recipe continued

spoon flour and continue to cook for about 1 minute. Whisk in the chicken stock and thicken the sauce, 3 to 4 minutes. Finish the sauce with the lemon juice, the parsley, and the diced roasted peppers.

Ladle some sauce onto each dinner plate. Slice the chicken rolls on an angle, and serve atop the sauce.

tidbit >> Use this method of pounding chicken portions in plastic storage bags to store the meat as well. You can transfer the food bags to the freezer and have single-portion servings of chicken cutlets for quick defrosting, anytime.

Sliced Steak Sensation

The trick to serving London broil is to let it rest, then slice it super thin and against the grain. Use a very sharp knife.   4 SERVINGS

3 tablespoons **Worcestershire sauce**

2 teaspoons **hot sauce**

1 tablespoon **white wine vinegar**

2 tablespoons **EVOO** (extra-virgin olive oil)

Salt and **freshly ground black pepper**

1 **top round steak** (also labeled London broil), 1 to 1½ inches thick, about 2 pounds

Preheat the broiler on high.

Combine the Worcestershire, hot sauce, vinegar, EVOO, and some salt and pepper and coat the steak with the mixture. Put the steak on a broiler pan and situate the pan on the rack closest to the flame; broil for 6 minutes per side. Remove the steak from the broiler and allow it to rest for 5 minutes, tented with a piece of aluminum foil. Then slice it very thin against the grain to serve.

Roast Crispy Mushrooms and Grilled Tenderloin Steaks with Scallions

In France, I had some cèpes (wild mushrooms) cooked in duck fat— yum-o! I make these mushrooms with EVOO at home.   4 SERVINGS

8 **portobello mushroom caps,** cut into large chunks

8 large **garlic cloves,** cracked from the skins

½ cup fresh **flat-leaf parsley** leaves (a couple of generous handfuls)

½ cup **extra-virgin olive oil** (EVOO), plus some for drizzling

Sea salt and **coarse black pepper**

4 1½-inch-thick **beef tenderloin steaks**

8 **scallions,** split lengthwise

Crusty bread

Preheat the oven to 500°F. Preheat a grill pan or outdoor grill to high.

Place the mushroom chunks in a large bowl. Combine the garlic and parsley in a food processor and finely chop. Add the garlic and parsley to the mushrooms.

Pour about ½ cup EVOO over the bowl and toss vigorously to coat the mushrooms with oil and garlic. Arrange the mushrooms in a single layer on a rimmed cookie sheet and roast for 20 minutes, or until crisp, dry, and dark brown. RESIST the devil on your shoulder that wants you to open the oven because things smell good in there. If you let the heat out, the 'shrooms will not crisp.

Also, season with salt and pepper *after* removing from the oven—salting too soon will cause the mushrooms to give off their juices and not crisp.

Grill the steaks for 4 minutes on each side for medium rare, 5 to 6 minutes for medium to medium well. Season the steaks with salt and pepper and let them rest for 5 to 10 minutes for the juices to redistribute. Coat the scallions in EVOO and season with salt and pepper. Grill to mark, 2 minutes on each side.

Serve the steaks with grilled scallions on top and crispy mushrooms on the side. Low-carbers can skip the bread.

Grilled Kielbasa Reubens with Warm Mustard-Caraway Sauerkraut

This meal is a touchdown whether you eat it while watching the NFL or after playing a little light-tackle with your buddies.　4 SERVINGS

1 teaspoon **caraway seeds**

1 (1-pound sack) of **sauerkraut**, drained

1 cup **beer or apple cider**

¼ cup **spicy brown, grainy mustard**

2 sticks or 1 long folded **link kielbasa** or turkey kielbasa, 1¼ pounds

2 tablespoons **butter**, softened

8 slices **marble rye bread**

8 deli slices **Emmentaler** or other Swiss cheese

½ cup **sweet red pepper relish**

Preheat a griddle pan to medium high.

Heat a medium skillet over medium heat. Toast the seeds for a couple of minutes, then stir in the sauerkraut, beer or cider, and mustard and simmer for 10 minutes.

Cut the kielbasa into 4 portions and split the sausage pieces lengthwise, opening them like a book. Grill the sausages on the hot griddle until they are crispy on both sides, 7 to 8 minutes total. Wipe some of the grease off the griddle and turn the heat down to low.

Lightly butter 1 side of each slice of bread. With the buttered sides out, build sandwiches of grilled kielbasa, sauerkraut, and 2 slices of cheese; spread the top slice of bread with red pepper relish before setting in place. Cook the sandwiches on the griddle until they are crispy, lightly pressing with a spatula to set the layers. Cut and serve.

Sweet Soy-Soaked Salmon Fillets Over Noodle-y Veggies

Guilt-free pasta? Just add fresh fish and lots of veggies   4 SERVINGS

Salt

½ pound of the thinnest **long-cut pasta** you have on hand

6 tablespoons **tamari** (dark aged soy sauce)

3-inch piece **fresh ginger,** peeled and grated

Juice of 1 **lime,** plus more to taste

¼ teaspoon **red pepper flakes**

4 **salmon fillets**

1 large bundle **broccolini**

1 large **carrot**

4 to 5 **garlic cloves**

1 large **red bell pepper**

4 **scallions,** trimmed

4 tablespoons **vegetable oil**

2 teaspoons **sugar**

¾ cup **chicken stock**

Place a large pot of water with a tight-fitting lid over high heat and bring to a boil. Once it comes up to a boil, add salt and pasta. Cook the pasta according to package directions to al dente. Drain thoroughly.

While the pasta works, in a shallow dish combine the tamari, ginger, lime juice, and the red pepper flakes. Add the salmon fillets, turn to coat, and marinate for about 5 minutes.

Trim the broccolini ends. Place 2 to 3 inches of water in a large nonstick skillet; add salt to the water along with the trimmed broccolini. Cover with a lid or some aluminum foil and bring up to a bubble; simmer for 4 to 5 minutes, until tender.

While the broccolini is cooking, chop up the rest of the veggies and reserve them on your cutting board or on a plate: peel and grate the carrot, finely chop the garlic, seed and thinly slice the red bell pepper. Thinly slice both the white and green parts of the scallions down to the roots and reserve separately.

Drain the broccolini and reserve. Return the skillet to the stove over medium-high heat and add 2 tablespoons of the vegetable oil, twice around the pan. Remove the salmon fillets from the marinade, reserving the marinade, and add the salmon to the hot skillet, skin side down. Cook the salmon until it has just cooked through, about 3 to 4 minutes on each side.

Remove the salmon to a plate and cover it with a piece of aluminum foil to keep it warm. Wipe the skillet out and return it to the stove over medium-high heat; add

recipe continued

the remaining 2 tablespoons of oil. Add the garlic, bell pepper, and grated carrots, and cook for about 2 minutes, stirring frequently. Add the sugar to the reserved salmon marinade, stir it to combine, then add it to the skillet. Add the cooked broccolini and the chicken stock, bring the liquids up to a bubble, and let them simmer for 1 minute. Add the cooked, drained pasta and the scallions and toss to combine. Taste for seasoning and add more tamari and lime juice to taste if the flavor is not strong enough for you.

To serve, divide the noodles and veggies among 4 serving plates and top with the salmon.

Prosciutto-Wrapped Endive and Radicchio with Balsamic-Fig Reduction

Salty prosciutto, bitter endive, sweet balsamic. Does it get any better than this for a gourmet dinner?　4 SERVINGS

2 heads **Belgian endive**, quartered lengthwise

2 small heads **radicchio**, quartered lengthwise

Salt and **freshly ground black pepper**

¼ pound sliced **prosciutto**, slices cut in half on an angle across the center

Extra-virgin olive oil (EVOO), for brushing

2 **dried figs**, finely chopped

½ cup **balsamic vinegar**

Preheat a grill pan over medium-high heat.

Season the endive and radicchio with salt and pepper. Wrap each quarter with a half slice of prosciutto. Brush the bundles with EVOO and grill for 7 to 8 minutes, turning occasionally, until the prosciutto is crispy and the greens are tender. Transfer to a platter.

Place the figs and vinegar in a pot and bring to a boil, then reduce the heat to a simmer. Reduce the vinegar down to a few tablespoons, until the fig pieces are soft and the vinegar is thick, 5 minutes. Drizzle back and forth over the grilled bundles.

Brutus Salad

This is one of my classic 30-Minute Meals—beefy Brutus Salad, a Caesar-style salad with Italian thin cut steak! Why should chicken have all the fun?   4 SERVINGS

1½ pounds very thin cut, ½-inch thick, **shell steak** (2 large, thin steaks)

EVOO (extra-virgin olive oil) for drizzling, plus ⅓ cup

1 tablespoons finely chopped **rosemary**, a few sprigs

1 tablespoon (a palmful) **grill seasoning** such as McCormick's Montreal Steak Seasoning

A large crusty **semolina roll** or ½ small semolina loaf

2 **garlic cloves**, cracked away from skin

Black pepper

Juice of 1 lemon

2 teaspoons **Dijon mustard**

2 teaspoons **Worcestershire sauce**

1 teaspoon **hot sauce**, such as Tabasco

2 teaspoons **anchovy paste** (a must for me, optional for you)

3 **hearts of romaine**, chopped

1 cup grated **Parmigiano-Reggiano** or Pecorino Romano cheese (a few generous handfuls)

Preheat the broiler.

Set the meat out on the counter to get the chill off it from the fridge while you heat a grill pan over high heat. Drizzle the steak with EVOO and rub it with the rosemary and grill seasoning. Grill for 3 minutes on each side—these steaks are really thin—then transfer the meat to a plate and let it rest to allow the juices to redistribute.

Toast the split roll or bread under the broiler until deeply golden, then rub with one clove of cracked, split garlic. Drizzle EVOO over the bread and season with a little pepper, then chop the bread into cubes.

Rub the inside of a bowl with the remaining cracked clove of garlic, then mince up the garlic and add it to the bowl. Whisk in the lemon juice, mustard, Worcestershire, hot sauce, and anchovy paste, then whisk in ⅓ cup of EVOO. Add the greens and bread to the bowl and toss to coat with the dressing. Add the cheese to the salad and toss again, then season with black pepper to taste. Top servings of the salad with slices of steak or serve the meat alongside.

Mac 'n' Jack Salad

I grew up in the country, which means I've been to my share of fairs. You can picture the scene: bandstand music, cotton candy, livestock and tractors, whirly-twirling machines that make you dizzy—what fun!

This mac 'n' Jack salad is tasty after a long day at the office, but it always makes me think of the fairgrounds. 8 SERVINGS

Salt

1 pound **elbow macaroni** or cavatappi (hollow corkscrew pasta)

1 10-ounce box **frozen corn**, defrosted

1 **red bell pepper**, seeded and chopped

1 **red onion**, chopped

4 **celery ribs**, chopped

1 8-ounce brick of **Monterey Pepper Jack** cheese, diced

Black pepper

3 tablespoons **red wine vinegar**

⅓ cup **EVOO** (extra-virgin olive oil)

1½ cups store-bought **tomatillo salsa** (mild, green) or chipotle salsa (hot, smoky red)

3 tablespoons fresh **cilantro** or flat-leaf parsley leaves, chopped

Bring a large covered pot of water to a boil. Salt it and add the pasta. Cook until al dente.

While the pasta is working, combine the corn, bell peppers, onions, and celery in a bowl with the cheese. Season with salt and pepper.

Drain the pasta and run it under cold water to cool it; drain it well again. Add the pasta to the vegetables and cheese.

Place the vinegar in a small bowl and whisk in the EVOO. Fold in the salsa. Pour the sauce over the salad and toss to coat evenly. Garnish with cilantro or parsley and serve.

Roasted Mushroom Pasta with Prosciutto

When I'm having a crowd over, my oven often gets a workout. Roast up extra mushrooms and some tomatoes for a truly delicious appetizer.
6 SERVINGS

Salt

1½ pounds **bow-tie pasta** (farfalle)

6 large **portobello mushroom** caps

¼ cup **EVOO** (extra-virgin olive oil), plus some for drizzling

Black pepper

5 large **garlic cloves**, thinly sliced

½ cup **white wine**

3 tablespoons cold **butter**

1 cup fresh **flat-leaf parsley** leaves, 4 generous handfuls, chopped

12 slices **prosciutto di Parma**, cut into strips

1 cup grated **Parmigiano-Reggiano**, 3 overflowing handfuls, plus more to pass at the table

Preheat the oven to 450°F.

Bring a large covered pot of water to a boil over high heat for the pasta. Once it's boiling, salt the water, add the pasta, and cook the pasta to al dente. Reserve 1 cup of the pasta cooking water, then drain the pasta.

While the water is heating, place the portobello mushrooms on a cookie sheet and drizzle both sides with a little EVOO. Roast the mushrooms for 10 minutes, or until they are tender. Remove them from the oven, season them with salt and pepper, slice, and reserve.

Drain the pasta and return the pasta pot to the stove over medium-high heat. Add the ¼ cup of EVOO and the garlic and cook until the garlic is golden. Add the wine and the reserved pasta cooking liquid, a little salt, and a lot of freshly ground black pepper. Return the pasta to the pot along with the sliced roasted mushrooms and stir to combine them. Turn the heat off, add the butter, parsley, prosciutto, and grated cheese, and stir it until the butter has melted and the parsley and prosciutto are distributed through the pasta. Serve immediately, with more cheese to pass at the table.

Sicilian-Style Swordfish Rolls with Fennel and Radicchio Salad

I love the combination of a warm breaded cutlet with cool salad.

4 SERVINGS

---

2 pounds very thin **swordfish steaks**

Coarse salt

2 cups **Italian bread crumbs**

½ cup fresh **flat-leaf parsley** leaves

4 large **garlic cloves**

1 **lemon**, zested, then cut into wedges

1 small **red onion**, thinly sliced

1 large **navel orange**, peeled and cut into thin half-moons

2 fresh **fennel** bulbs, trimmed of tops, quartered, cored, and thinly sliced lengthwise

2 medium heads of **radicchio**, shredded

2 tablespoons **red wine vinegar**

6 to 7 tablespoons **extra-virgin olive oil** (EVOO)

Coarse black pepper

2 tablespoons chopped fresh **oregano** (optional)

Pat the swordfish steaks dry and trim off the skin and dark connective tissue. Place the fish between sheets of wax paper and pound with a small skillet or a mallet, as you would chicken or veal cutlets, to a ¼-inch thickness. Cut the thin slices into several rectangular strips, about 2 inches by 4 to 5 inches. Season the fish strips with coarse salt.

Place the bread crumbs in a shallow dish. Pile a handful of the parsley, the garlic, lemon zest, and a little coarse salt on a cutting board. Finely chop the lemon-garlic mixture, then combine it with the bread crumbs. Gently press the fish slices into the bread-crumb mixture, coating both sides. Roll the coated fish strips tightly into small bundles.

For the salad, combine the onions, oranges, fennel, and radicchio in a bowl. Coarsely chop the remaining parsley and add to the salad. Dress the salad with the vinegar and about 3 tablespoons of the EVOO; just eyeball the amounts. Season with salt, pepper, and oregano, if using.

Preheat a medium nonstick skillet over moderate heat and add 3 to 4 tablespoons of EVOO (3 to 4 times around the pan). Cook the rolls gently, 3 to 4 minutes on each side, until deep golden and firm. Remove from the pan and serve the swordfish rolls with lemon wedges and the fennel and radicchio salad.

Crispy Turkey Cutlets with Bacon-Cranberry Brussels Sprouts

This colorful dish is great for company—and a cinch to make.

4 SERVINGS

2 tablespoons **vegetable oil**, plus some for shallow frying

5 slices **bacon**, chopped

1 large **onion**, chopped

1 tablespoon fresh **thyme** leaves, chopped (from 4 sprigs)

Salt and **freshly ground black pepper**

2 pounds **turkey breast cutlets**

½ tablespoon **poultry seasoning**

3 to 4 tablespoons all-purpose **flour**

2 cups **plain bread crumbs**

1 **lemon, zested**, then cut into wedges

2 **eggs**

2 10-ounce boxes frozen **Brussels sprouts**, defrosted

½ cup **dried cranberries**

¾ cup **chicken stock** or broth

½ cup fresh **flat-leaf parsley** leaves chopped

Start the bacon-cranberry Brussels sprouts by preheating a nonstick skillet over medium-high heat with the 2 tablespoons of vegetable oil. Add the chopped bacon and cook until crispy, about 2 to 3 minutes. Add the onions and thyme, season with salt and pepper, and cook for 3 to 4 more minutes.

While the onions are cooking with the bacon, season the cutlets with the poultry seasoning, salt, and pepper on both sides, and dredge in the flour. Combine the bread crumbs and lemon zest in a shallow dish. Beat the eggs in a separate shallow dish with a splash of water.

Heat ½ inch of vegetable oil in a large skillet over medium to medium-high heat. Coat the cutlets in eggs, then in breading, and add to the hot oil. Cook the cutlets in a single layer, in 2 batches if necessary, for about 3 or 4 minutes on each side, until their juices run clear and the breading is evenly browned.

While the first batch of cutlets is cooking, add the defrosted Brussels sprouts to the bacon and onions, toss, and stir to combine. Add the dried cranberries and the chicken stock to the pan and continue to cook for 3 to 4 minutes, or until the Brussels sprouts are heated through and the cranberries have plumped. Finish the sprouts with the chopped parsley.

Serve the turkey cutlets alongside the bacon-cranberry Brussels sprouts. Pass the lemon wedges; squeeze the juice over the cutlets at the table.

Spring Chicken with Leeks and Peas Served with Lemon Rice

You can make this dish in all four seasons. I call it "Spring Chicken" because it tastes light and crisp, like spring air.   4 SERVINGS

2 cups **chicken stock** or broth

1 cup **white rice**

Zest and juice of 1 lemon

3 tablespoons **extra-virgin olive oil** (EVOO)

1 tablespoon **unsalted butter,** cut into small pieces

1½ to 2 pounds **chicken tenders,** cut into large bite-size pieces, about 2 inches

2 medium **leeks,** trimmed of tough tops and roots

½ cup **dry white wine,** or substitute chicken stock if you do not have wine on hand

1 10-ounce box frozen tender **green peas**

Salt and **freshly ground black pepper**

A handful of fresh **flat-leaf parsley** leaves, finely chopped

Bring the chicken stock to a boil in a small pot. Stir in the rice, lemon zest, and 1 tablespoon of the EVOO (eyeball it). Return to a boil, then reduce the heat to a simmer and cover the pot. Cook for 17 to 18 minutes, until tender.

Heat a large nonstick skillet over medium-high heat. Add the remaining 2 tablespoons of EVOO (twice around the pan), and the butter. When the butter melts into the oil, add the chicken to the pan and sauté until lightly golden on both sides, 4 minutes.

Cut the leeks in half lengthwise, then slice into ½-inch half-moons. Place the leeks in a colander and wash under cold running water, separating the layers and releasing all the grit. You can also place the sliced leeks in a large bowl of cold water and swish them around like a washing machine. The grit will fall to the bottom of the bowl. Drain the leeks well and add them to the chicken.

Cook the leeks with the chicken until they wilt down, 3 minutes or so. Add the white wine to the pan and scrape up any pan drippings. Add the peas and heat through, another minute or two. Turn off the heat and season with salt and pepper. Drizzle the lemon juice over the chicken and leeks. (Juice the fruit with the cut side facing up, keeping the seeds with the lemon rather than in the chicken.)

Fluff the rice with a fork. The zest in the cooking liquid will have infused the rice with lemon flavor. Add the parsley and toss the rice to combine.

Pile the chicken and leeks on dinner plates and top with a small mound of lemon rice.

Indian Summer Turkey Chili

Choose any or all of the toppers for your chili.　4 SERVINGS

2 tablespoons **extra-virgin olive oil** (EVOO)

1¼ pounds **ground turkey breast** (99% lean) (average weight of 1 package)

3 tablespoons **dark chili powder**

1 tablespoon **grill seasoning**, such as McCormick's Montreal Steak Seasoning

1 tablespoon **ground cumin**

2 tablespoons **Worcestershire sauce**

2 tablespoons **hot sauce**

1 large **yellow onion**, quartered

2 **bell peppers**, any colors, cored, seeded, and cut in ¼-inch dice

¾ cup (½ bottle) **beer** (the alcohol cooks out)

1 28-ounce can **tomato sauce** or tomato purée

½ cup **smoky barbecue sauce**

1 cup **frozen corn kernels**

TOPPERS

Shredded cheeses: smoked white sharp Cheddar, Pepper Jack, chipotle Cheddar, five-peppercorn Cheddar, Monterey Jack

Sliced canned jalapeños, drained

Salsas

Sour cream

Chopped green olives and pimientos

Chopped fresh cilantro

Heat a pot over medium to medium-high heat. Add the EVOO and the ground turkey. Season the meat with the chili powder, grill seasoning, cumin, Worcestershire, and hot sauce. Break up the meat with the back of a wooden spoon into small crumbles.

Chop the onion, reserving one quarter of it for topping the chili. (Chop the reserved onion extra-fine.) Brown the meat for 5 minutes, then add the onion and bell peppers and cook 10 minutes more. Add the beer and deglaze the pan, scraping up the drippings and cooking off the alcohol. Add the tomato sauce or purée, barbecue sauce, and corn and bring the chili to a bubble. Let the chili simmer for 10 minutes. Adjust the seasonings and heat level to your taste. Remove from the heat and serve with your choice of toppers.

tidbit >> To make a double batch, heat two pots and make one batch in each pot, rather than using one massive pot that is hard to control.

2

Stretch-a-Buck Meals

My mom taught me that good meals don't have to break the bank. Here are our top ten Family Faves, Most Requested recipes, and Great Rollovers that will have you eating like royalty . . . even if you don't want to spend a lot of dough.

FAMILY FAVES

Walnuts, Ham, and Cheese . . . Oh, My!
Zucchini and Bow Ties
Chicken and Egg Sammies Deluxe
Mikey from Philly Cheese Steaks
Sausage, Pepper, and Onion Subs
Wingless Buffalo Chicken Pizza
Fresh Tomato and Basil Chicken Over Super Creamy Polenta
Mighty Migas
Steak Niçoise
Black Forest Reubens

MOST REQUESTED

Tomato Basil Pasta Nests
Good Fennels Pasta
Sweet and Spicy Pineapple Pork
Sautéed Salmon with Spicy Fresh Mango-Pineapple Chutney
Mini Meatball Burgers on Antipasto Salad
Grilled Chicken Posole Salad
Not-sagna Pasta Toss
Chicken Francese and Wilted Spinach
Smoky Chipotle–Chicken Corn Chowder with Salsa Salad
Ginger-Orange Roasted Carrot Soup with Spicy Shrimp

GREAT ROLLOVERS

My Mom's 15-Minute Tomato and Bean Stoup
*Veal Polpette with Thin Spaghetti and Light Tomato
    and Basil Sauce*
*Smoked Paprika Chicken with Egg Noodles and Buttered
    Warm Radishes*
Cider-Sauced Chicken Breasts
Everything Lo Mein
Smoky Turkey Shepherd's Pie
Thai-Style Steak Salad
Shrimp Po'Boys
Italian Tuna Melts with White Beans and Provolone
Paco's Fish Tacos in Lettuce Wraps

Walnuts, Ham, and Cheese . . . Oh, My!

This is one of those dinners that came to me after a long, hard stare into what looked like an empty fridge.   4 SERVINGS

Salt

1 pound **bow-tie pasta** (farfalle)

½ cup **walnuts**, finely chopped

3 tablespoons **EVOO** (extra-virgin olive oil)

10 slices **Canadian bacon** or breakfast ham, cut into thin strips

2 large **garlic cloves**, chopped

½ teaspoon **red pepper flakes**

Juice of 1 lemon

¾ cup fresh **flat-leaf parsley** leaves, 3 generous handfuls, chopped

2 tablespoons **butter**

1 cup grated **Parmigiano-Reggiano**, plus some to pass at the table

Place a large covered pot of water over high heat and bring it up to a boil for the pasta. Once the water boils, salt it and cook the pasta to al dente. Note: Right before draining the pasta, you'll want to remove and reserve 1 cup of the pasta cooking water.

Place a large skillet over medium-high heat, add the chopped walnuts, and toast them, stirring every now and then, until they are golden and smell toasty—a couple of minutes. Remove the nuts from the skillet and reserve. When the pasta is nearly done, return the skillet you cooked the walnuts in to the stovetop over medium-high heat with the EVOO, 3 times around the pan. Once the EVOO is hot, add the Canadian bacon and cook it for 2 to 3 minutes, or until it starts to lightly brown. Add the garlic and red pepper flakes and cook for another minute. Add the reserved pasta cooking liquid and cook it until the liquid has reduced by half. Add the drained pasta, toasted walnuts, lemon juice, and parsley to the skillet, toss it to coat the noodles, and continue to cook until the pasta has soaked up almost all of the liquid. Turn the heat off, add the butter and grated cheese, and toss until the butter has melted. Serve with extra Parmigiano to pass at the table.

Zucchini and Bow Ties

This is a simple, light, healthy meal for the family.   4 SERVINGS

Coarse salt

1 pound **bow-tie pasta** (farfalle)

¼ cup **extra-virgin olive oil** (EVOO)

6 **garlic cloves**, minced

2 medium **zucchini**, cut into matchsticks

Coarse black pepper

1 cup grated **Parmigiano-Reggiano** or Romano cheese

1 cup fresh **basil** leaves, torn or shredded (20 leaves)

Bring a large pot of water to a boil and salt it. Cook the bow ties al dente, with a bite. Heads up: You will need a couple of ladles of starchy cooking water.

Heat a large, deep skillet over medium heat. Add the EVOO and the garlic. Cook for 2 minutes, then add the zucchini. Cook gently for 8 to 10 minutes. Season with salt and pepper and add a couple of ladles of cooking water. Drain the pasta and add to the zucchini. Toss with the cheese and turn off the heat. Toss for 2 minutes, until the liquids are absorbed. Serve in shallow bowls with lots of shredded basil on top.

Chicken and Egg Sammies Deluxe

I dunno who came first, but I'm glad they met up in my sandwich! This simple sammie supper stacks together cutlets, egg, cheese, and greens, all in one bun.   4 SERVINGS

1½ pounds **chicken breast cutlets**

2 teaspoons **smoked paprika**

Salt and **black pepper**

4 tablespoons **EVOO** (extra-virgin olive oil)

4 large **eggs**

2 tablespoons **milk** or half-and-half, whichever you keep on hand for coffee

2 **jarred roasted red peppers**, patted dry and chopped

A handful of fresh **flat-leaf parsley**, chopped

4 **crusty rolls**, split

4 slices **smoked Gouda** cheese

2 cups chopped **watercress** (from 1 bunch)

Preheat the broiler.

Season the chicken breast cutlets evenly with smoked paprika, salt, and pepper. Heat 2 tablespoons of the EVOO, twice around the pan, in a large nonstick skillet over medium-high heat. Add the chicken to the pan and cook for 2 to 3 minutes on each side. Remove the chicken from the skillet and let it rest, tented with foil. Wipe out the pan and add the remaining 2 tablespoons of EVOO. In a small bowl, beat the eggs with salt, pepper, and milk or half-and-half. Add the roasted peppers and parsley to the skillet and cook for 30 seconds, then add the eggs and scramble to your desired doneness with a wooden spoon or spatula.

While the eggs cook, toast the rolls under the broiler, 1 minute, then remove them to a work surface. Keep the broiler on.

To assemble, slice the chicken and pile it on the roll bottoms. Top each sammy with one quarter of the eggs and a slice of cheese. Place the sammies back under the broiler for 30 seconds to melt the cheese. Reserve the tops. When the cheese has melted, transfer the sammies to plates and top them with a pile of watercress, then set the roll tops in place.

Mikey from Philly Cheese Steaks

This is my make-at-home version of one of my favorite brunch items at Union Square Cafe in New York City. Chef Michael Romano makes a mean Italian-style hoagie with sliced steak, tomato sauce, and capers—yum-o! When I'm up at my cabin, out in the sticks, I make these knock-offs all the time.   4 SERVINGS

1½ pounds **thick-cut sirloin**

4 tablespoons **EVOO** (extra-virgin olive oil), plus some for drizzling

Coarse salt and **coarse black pepper**

1 **red bell pepper**, seeded and sliced

1 large **onion**, quartered and sliced

5 **garlic cloves**, 3 chopped, 2 cracked from the skin

1 large loaf **ciabatta bread** or other chewy Italian loaf, split

½ cup grated **Pecorino Romano** cheese, a couple of generous handfuls

½ cup **dry red wine**

½ cup **beef stock**

1 cup **tomato sauce** or crushed tomatoes

3 tablespoons **capers**, drained and coarsely chopped

A fistful of fresh **flat-leaf parsley**, coarsely chopped

8-ounce chunk **sharp provolone cheese**

Slice the meat very thin with a sharp knife, working against the grain.

Heat 2 tablespoons of the EVOO in a large nonstick pan over high heat. When the oil ripples, add the meat slices and sear them for a minute or two to caramelize evenly all over—keep the meat moving with tongs. Season the meat slices with salt and pepper, remove to a platter, and tent loosely with foil. Go 2 more times around the pan with the EVOO and reduce the heat to medium high. Add the peppers, onions, and chopped garlic, season with salt and pepper, and cook, stirring frequently, for 5 minutes.

Preheat the broiler to high and place the rack on the second highest position. Arrange the bread on a broiler pan and toast until golden. Once toasted, rub the bread with the garlic, drizzle with EVOO, and top with grated Pecorino Romano and some black pepper. Slide the bread back under the broiler to melt the cheese, 45 seconds. Remove the bread and reserve, keeping the broiler on.

Add the wine to the vegetables and cook down for 1 minute. Add the stock, then the tomatoes, capers, and parsley and bring to a bubble. Slide the meat and any juices back into the pan to heat through for 2 to 3 minutes.

Shred the provolone with a box grater or slice thin. Pile the meat and vegetables evenly over the loaf of bread and cover with the provolone. Place the gi-gundo-size sandwiches under the broiler to melt the cheese until bubbly. Cut each open-faced sammy into 4 sections, transfer 2 to each plate with a large spatula, and serve.

Sausage, Pepper, and Onion Subs

I'm famous for my sausage sandwiches . . . my homemade relish is the secret that makes them great. Double the relish recipe and use it on any Italian cold cut sandwich. Either traditional Italian chicken or hot pork sausage will work fine in this.   MAKES 4 SUBS

4 **fresh Italian chicken sausages** (or hot pork sausages)

3 tablespoons **EVOO** (extra-virgin olive oil)

⅓ cup **chicken stock** or dry white wine, a generous douse

1 **cubanelle pepper**, seeded and sliced

1 **red bell pepper**, seeded and sliced

1 large **onion**, thinly sliced

3 **garlic cloves**, chopped

Salt and **black pepper**

1 cup **giardiniera** (Italian pickled vegetable salad; see Tidbit)

A handful of fresh **flat-leaf parsley**

½ cup fresh **basil**, 10 leaves

Zest of ½ lemon

4 crusty **sub rolls**, split

Place the sausages in a large skillet and add 1 inch of water. Prick the sausages. Add 1 tablespoon of the EVOO to the skillet, once around the pan. Bring the water to a boil, then reduce the heat a little. Allow all the liquid to cook away, then brown and crisp the casings, 10 to 12 minutes total. Deglaze the pan with the stock or wine and cook it off, 1 minute. Remove the sausages to a platter.

Add the remaining 2 tablespoons of EVOO to the skillet. Add the peppers, onions, and garlic, season with salt and pepper, and cook for 10 minutes, or until tender.

Place the giardiniera, parsley, basil, and lemon zest in a food processor and grind them into a relish.

Slice the sausages on an angle. Fill each roll with a little relish, then peppers and onions, then the sliced sausages.

tidbit >> Giardiniera is a mixture of pickled hot peppers, cauliflower, carrots, and celery. It's available in jars on the Italian foods aisle or in bulk bins near the olives.

Wingless Buffalo Chicken Pizza

I am always trying to make the foods that are bad for my figure less of a guilty pleasure. Case in point: Buffalo chicken wings. The chicken here is all white meat; it's not fried; and as an added attraction, it's sitting on top of a pizza. Put a game on or pop a movie in and enjoy. Wings away!

4 SERVINGS

¾ pound **chicken breast cutlets**

EVOO (extra-virgin olive oil), for drizzling

2 teaspoons **grill seasoning**, such as McCormick's Montreal Steak Seasoning

1 **pizza dough**, store-bought or from your favorite pizzeria

Cornmeal or flour, for dusting

2 tablespoons **butter**

1 tablespoon **Worcestershire sauce**

2 to 3 tablespoons **hot sauce**, to taste

½ cup **tomato sauce**

1 cup shredded **Monterey Jack cheese**, 4 generous handfuls

½ cup **crumbled blue cheese**

3 **scallions**, thinly sliced

Preheat the oven to 425°F. Preheat a grill pan over high heat.

Place the chicken on a plate and drizzle with EVOO. Season it with the grill seasoning. When the grill pan is hot, cook the chicken for about 3 minutes on each side, until it is cooked through.

Stretch the dough to form a pizza, using cornmeal or flour to help you handle it. If you let it rest and warm up for a few minutes, it will handle more easily. Set the pizza on a pizza pan to the side.

In a medium skillet over medium heat, melt the butter and stir in the Worcestershire, hot sauce, and tomato sauce.

Remove the chicken from the grill pan and slice it thin. Add the chicken to the sauce and stir to coat. Cover the pizza dough with the saucy Buffalo chicken, cheeses, and scallions. Bake for 18 minutes, or until crisp.

Fresh Tomato and Basil Chicken Over Super Creamy Polenta

Pour yourself a glass of Chianti and you'll think you are sitting in the Italian countryside with these classic flavors. Molto bene!   4 SERVINGS

---

4 cups **chicken stock** or broth

2 tablespoons **extra-virgin olive oil** (EVOO)

4 6-ounce boneless, skinless **chicken breast halves**

Salt and **freshly ground black pepper**

¼ teaspoon **red pepper flakes**

1 large **red onion**, thinly sliced

5 **garlic cloves**, chopped

1 cup **quick-cooking polenta** (found in Italian or specialty foods aisles)

½ cup **mascarpone cheese**

¼ cup grated **Parmigiano-Reggiano** (a handful)

½ pint **yellow grape tomatoes**

½ pint **red grape tomatoes**

20 fresh **basil** leaves, chopped or torn

For the super creamy polenta, bring 3 cups of the chicken stock to a boil in a sauce pot. If the chicken stock is at a boil before you are ready to add the polenta, just turn it down to low and let it wait for you.

While the stock is coming to a boil, start the fresh tomato and basil chicken. Heat a large nonstick skillet over medium-high heat with the EVOO. Season the chicken with salt, pepper, and red pepper flakes, add to the hot skillet, and cook for about 3 to 4 minutes, or until the chicken is lightly browned. Scoot the chicken over to the edges of the skillet, then add the onions and garlic, continuing to cook for 3 minutes more. Add the remaining cup of chicken stock and cook until reduced by half, another 3 to 4 minutes.

While the sauce is reducing, whisk the quick-cooking polenta into the boiling chicken stock in the sauce pot until it masses. Stir in the mascarpone cheese and the Parmigiano and season with salt and pepper. You want the polenta to be slightly loose. If it gets too tight, stir in some more stock to loosen it up a little.

To finish the chicken, add the yellow and red grape tomatoes, stir to combine, and continue to cook for about 1 to 2 minutes, or until the tomatoes are heated through and starting to burst. Add the basil and toss with the chicken and tomatoes.

Serve the polenta in shallow bowls and top with the fresh tomato and basil chicken.

Mighty Migas

This one is a B, L, D: good for breakfast, lunch, or dinner. It's easy to adjust to make a single serving; I often opt for eggs if I am cooking for just myself. Migas in soft tortillas is a favorite dish in Austin, Texas, and now it's a favorite of mine. When I am home alone I put Bob Schneider, my favorite Austin musician, on my stereo and invite him to sit down to share my migas. I end up eating his, since my imaginary boyfriends eat light!   4 SERVINGS

3 tablespoons **EVOO** (extra-virgin olive oil)

2 **jalapeño peppers**, seeded and chopped

1 small **red or green bell pepper**, cored, seeded, and chopped

1 small **white onion**, chopped

Salt and **black pepper**

2 **plum tomatoes**, seeded and diced

8 large **eggs**, beaten

1 cup crushed **tortilla chips**

1 10-ounce sack (2 cups) shredded **Monterey Jack** or Cheddar cheese

8 6-inch **flour tortillas** (soft taco size)

1 cup **tomato sauce**

1 to 2 **chipotle chiles in adobo**, medium to extra hot, finely chopped

A handful of fresh **cilantro**, finely chopped

Heat a large skillet over medium-high heat. Add the EVOO. Add the jalapeños, bell peppers, and onions and season them with salt and pepper. Cook for 2 to 3 minutes, then add the tomatoes and cook a minute more. Beat the eggs with a pinch of salt and pepper and add to the veggies. Reduce the heat to medium low. Scramble the eggs not quite halfway, so they are still nice and wet. Add the crushed tortilla chips and scramble them in. Cover the eggs with the cheese and turn off the heat. Cover the pan loosely with foil to melt the cheese and set aside for a minute.

Heat a second, dry skillet over high heat. Add the tortillas one at a time and sear for 30 seconds on each side to blister them.

In a small bowl, stir together the tomato sauce and the chopped chipotle. Stir in the cilantro.

Place a mound of the *migas* on each flour tortilla and dot with the sauce. Serve immediately, two per person.

Steak Niçoise

Hey, why should tuna have all the fun? Try this even-heartier rendition.

4 SERVINGS

---

3 tablespoons **Worcestershire sauce**

2 **garlic cloves**, finely chopped

2 teaspoons **hot sauce**

7 tablespoons **EVOO** (extra-virgin olive oil)

Black pepper

2 pounds **boneless shoulder** or top round steak

2 pounds white or red **boiling potatoes**, halved

Salt

4 **eggs**

1 pound trimmed **fresh green beans**

2 large **shallots**, finely chopped

A couple of **anchovy fillets**, finely chopped (optional)

1 heaping tablespoon **Dijon mustard**

3 tablespoons **red wine vinegar**

1 tablespoon **capers**

6 cups **mixed greens**, multiple large handfuls

1 cup fresh **basil**, 20 leaves, chopped or torn

½ cup **pitted kalamata olives**

¼ cup fresh **flat-leaf parsley**, a generous handful, chopped

2 **vine-ripe tomatoes**, cut into 8 wedges each

Preheat the broiler and place the rack in the highest position.

In a shallow dish, combine the Worcestershire sauce, garlic, hot sauce, 3 tablespoons of the EVOO, and a good amount of black pepper. Add the meat and coat it thoroughly. Let the meat hang out and marinate while you get the potatoes, eggs, and green beans going.

Place the halved potatoes in a pot. Cover them with water and bring them to a boil over high heat. When the water boils, add 2 big pinches of salt and boil the potatoes for 10 minutes, or until tender. Drain and spread them out on a cookie sheet to cool.

While the potatoes cook, place the eggs in a small sauce pot and add enough water to cover. Bring them up to a simmer over high heat and then turn the heat off, cover them with a lid, and let them sit for 10 minutes. Drain the eggs, then aggressively shake the pan to crack the shells. Run the eggs under cold water until they cool down a little. Peel the eggs and then cut them into quarters.

Fill a large skillet with 1 inch of water, place it over high heat, and bring it up to a boil. Add a large pinch of salt and the green beans. Cook the green beans for 1 minute, drain, and run them under cold water to stop the cooking process.

Once the potatoes, eggs, and water for the beans are going, put the steak on a broiler pan, season it with some salt, and broil for 6 minutes per side. Remove it from the broiler and allow the meat to rest for 5 minutes, tented with a piece of aluminum foil.

For the dressing, in a mixing bowl combine the shallots, anchovies (if using), mustard, vinegar, and capers with some salt and pepper. In a slow steady stream, whisk in the remaining 4 tablespoons (¼ cup) of EVOO.

On a platter toss together the cooled green beans, mixed greens, basil, olives, and parsley. Arrange the quartered hard-boiled eggs, tomato wedges, and cooled potatoes around the platter. Slice the rested steak very thin, against the grain and on a slight angle, and arrange the steak slices on top of the greens. Drizzle the dressing over the entire salad.

tidbit >> Many markets sell trimmed raw green beans in packages in the fresh produce department; if your market doesn't, just snap off the stem end of the beans.

Black Forest Reubens

When is a sammie not just a sammie? When it's a meal! Try wrapping your mouth around this riff on a Reuben.   4 SERVINGS

8 slices **pumpernickel bread**

4 tablespoons (½ stick) **butter**, softened

3 tablespoonfuls **dill pickle relish**

1 **shallot**, finely chopped

1 tablespoon capers, chopped

4 tablespoonfuls **spicy brown mustard**

16 deli slices **Swiss cheese**

¾ pound deli-sliced **corned beef**

¾ pound deli-sliced **Black Forest ham**

1 jar cooked red cabbage

4 large **half-sour** or **garlic pickles**

Gourmet potato chips

Spread one side of each bread slice with softened butter. In a small bowl, mix together the relish, shallots, capers, and mustard. Build the sandwiches with buttered sides of the bread facing out: slather a liberal amount of the mustard mixture on 4 slices, then top with a slice of Swiss, one fourth of the corned beef, one fourth of the ham, a small mound of drained red cabbage or sauerkraut, another slice of cheese, and finally another slice of bread.

Heat a nonstick skillet over medium heat. Toast the Reubens for 5 to 6 minutes on each side until the cheese melts. Cut the sammies in half and serve with pickles and chips.

Tomato-Basil Pasta Nests

When I worked in a commercial kitchen, making different items for the prepared food counter, there were a few items that always "sold out." The best sellers, day to day, month to month, no matter the season, were apricot chicken tenders, sesame noodles, and pasta nests.   4 SERVINGS

MOST REQUESTED

Coarse salt

1 pound **angel hair pasta**

3 tablespoons **extra-virgin olive oil** (EVOO)

5 **garlic cloves**, minced

1 medium **yellow onion**, finely chopped

1 28-ounce can **crushed tomatoes** (look for San Marzano Italian tomatoes; when not available, use any brand)

Coarse black pepper

20 fresh **basil** leaves, shredded (chiffonade) or torn

3 rounded tablespoonfuls prepared, refrigerated **pesto sauce**

1 cup grated **Parmigiano-Reggiano** or Romano cheese

Crusty bread, to pass at the table

Bring a large pot of water to a boil for the pasta. Salt the water and cook the pasta al dente, with a bite to it.

While the water is heating, begin the sauce by heating a large, deep skillet over medium heat. Add the EVOO, garlic, and onions. Sauté for 8 to 10 minutes; reduce the heat a bit if the onions begin to brown. You want them to become sweet and soft, but not to caramelize.

Stir in the tomatoes and heat through. Season the sauce with salt and pepper. Wilt in the basil and turn off the heat. Stir in the pesto sauce.

Drain the pasta and add to the sauce. Toss in the pan to distribute. Sprinkle in the cheese, tossing to combine. Grab a meat fork. Stick the fork into the pasta and bring up a heaping forkful. Turn and twist the pasta, using your palm to guide the pasta a bit, to form a nest. The recipe should yield 8 small nests, 4 inches wide and 5 to 6 inches long.

Serve 2 nests per person with a small salad and crusty bread.

Good Fennels Pasta

I make this one when I watch GoodFellas. Shave the garlic nice and thin, like Paulie would, but don't use a razor blade like he does in the movie. A sharp knife is fine.   4 SERVINGS

Salt

1 pound **bucatini** (hollow fat spaghetti) or other long-cut pasta

3 tablespoons **EVOO** (extra-virgin olive oil)

1 pound **bulk sweet Italian sausage**

4 **garlic cloves**, very thinly sliced

1 medium **onion**, very thinly sliced

1 **fennel bulb**, trimmed, quartered, cored, and very thinly sliced

2 **cubanelle peppers**, seeded and very thinly sliced

Black pepper

1 cup **dry white wine** or stock

1 28-ounce can **crushed tomatoes**, such as San Marzano

½ cup grated **Parmigiano-Reggiano** cheese, plus some to pass at the table

1 cup fresh **basil**, 20 leaves, shredded or torn

Crusty bread, for mopping

Place a large pot of water on to boil for the pasta. Salt the water and add the bucatini and cook it to al dente.

While the water comes to a boil and the pasta cooks, make the sauce. Heat a large, deep nonstick skillet over medium-high heat. Add 1 tablespoon of the EVOO. Add the sausage to the skillet and break up the sausage into small bits. Brown the sausage all over, then transfer it to a paper-towel-lined plate. Return the pan to the heat and add the remaining 2 tablespoons of EVOO, the garlic, onions, fennel, and peppers. Season the vegetables with salt and pepper. Cook, turning frequently, 7 to 8 minutes, until tender, but do not allow the fennel and onions to brown. Reduce the heat a bit if they begin to burn. Add the wine or stock next and reduce for 2 minutes. Stir in the tomatoes and slide the sausage back into the pan. Reduce the heat to a simmer and cook until the pasta is done.

Drain the pasta very well and add it to the sauce. Sprinkle the pasta with ½ cup cheese (a couple of handfuls), then toss the pasta with the thick sauce to combine. Transfer the pasta to a large shallow platter and cover the pasta with basil leaves. Serve it with extra cheese and pass crusty bread at the table to mop up the plates.

Sweet and Spicy Pineapple Pork

Serve with white or flavored rice, cooked according to the package directions, or with sweet rolls.　4 SERVINGS

---

3 tablespoons **extra-virgin olive oil** (EVOO)

4 1½-inch-thick boneless center-cut **pork chops**

Salt and **freshly ground black pepper**

1 large **red onion**, chopped

2 **garlic cloves**, chopped

1 **red bell pepper**, cored, seeded, and chopped

1 **jalapeño pepper**, seeds removed, finely chopped

1 8-ounce can **pineapple chunks** in juice

½ cup **chicken stock** or broth

¼ cup fresh **flat-leaf parsley** leaves (a generous handful)

Preheat the oven to 375°F.

Heat a large skillet over medium-high to high heat with 2 tablespoons of the EVOO (twice around the pan). Season the chops with salt and pepper. Place the chops in the skillet and sear for about 2 minutes on each side to caramelize. Transfer the chops to a rimmed cookie sheet and place in the oven to finish off, 8 to 10 minutes, until the meat is firm to the touch, but not tough. Remove from the oven and let the chops rest, covered with a piece of aluminum foil, for a few minutes.

While the chops are in the oven, return the skillet to medium-high heat and add the remaining tablespoon of EVOO. Add the onions, garlic, bell peppers, jalapeños, salt, and pepper and cook for 3 to 4 minutes or until the veggies start to wilt. Add the chunked pineapple and its juice and the chicken stock. Continue to cook the sauce for 3 to 4 minutes. Add the parsley and stir to combine, then pour the sweet and spicy pineapple sauce over the pork chops.

Sautéed Salmon with Spicy Fresh Mango-Pineapple Chutney

Serve with steamed asparagus, snap peas, or green beans.   4 SERVINGS

3 tablespoons **vegetable oil**

1 small **red onion**, chopped

1 large **jalapeño pepper**, seeded and chopped

Salt and **freshly ground black pepper**

1 8-ounce can **pineapple chunks** in juice, drained

2 tablespoons **honey** (a couple of good drizzles)

4 6-ounce **salmon fillets**

1 tablespoon **ground coriander**

1 ripe **mango**, peeled and diced

Juice of 1 lime

¼ cup fresh **flat-leaf parsley** leaves (a generous handful), chopped

¼ cup fresh **cilantro** (a generous handful), chopped

Heat a sauce pot over medium-high heat with 1 table-spoon of vegetable oil (once around the pan). Add the red onions and jalapeños and season with a little salt and pepper; cook for 3 to 4 minutes, or until the onions are slightly wilted. Add the pineapple, honey, and 1 cup water, turn the heat down to medium low, and gently simmer for about 5 minutes.

While the chutney is cooking, preheat a medium nonstick skillet over medium-high heat with the remaining 2 tablespoons of vegetable oil. Season the salmon with the coriander, salt, and pepper. Add the seasoned salmon to the hot pan and cook until just cooked through, about 3 to 4 minutes on each side.

While the salmon is cooking, finish the chutney: Add the mango, lime juice, parsley, and cilantro, stir to combine, and then turn off the heat.

Transfer the sautéed salmon to 4 serving plates and top each portion with some of the spicy mango-pineapple chutney.

Mini Meatball Burgers on Antipasto Salad

The first time I made this, I knew it was a winner—and I think you'll agree. It's a new take on the meatball, served over classic antipasto salad. 4 SERVINGS, 3 MINI BURGERS EACH

1½ pounds **ground sirloin** or ground beef, pork, and veal, combined

Salt and **freshly ground black pepper**

1 **egg yolk**, beaten

½ cup grated **Parmigiano-Reggiano** (a couple of handfuls)

2 tablespoons **tomato paste**

A handful of chopped fresh **flat-leaf parsley**

2 **garlic cloves**, finely chopped

½ to 1 teaspoon **red pepper flakes**

Extra-virgin olive oil (EVOO) for drizzling, plus about ¼ cup for dressing salad

2 **romaine lettuce** hearts, chopped

1 15-ounce can quartered **artichoke hearts**, drained

1 jarred **roasted red pepper**, drained and chopped

4 or 5 **pepperoncini peppers**, chopped, or ¼ cup hot banana pepper rings, drained

½ cup pitted good-quality **olives**, green or black, drained

3 **celery ribs**, chopped

¼ pound **Genoa salami** or slicing pepperoni, chopped

¼ pound deli-sliced **provolone cheese**, chopped

3 tablespoons **red wine vinegar**

½ pound fresh **mozzarella** or fresh smoked mozzarella, diced

2 **vine-ripe tomatoes**, seeded and diced

1 cup **basil leaves**, torn or shredded

Preheat a grill pan or large nonstick skillet over medium-high or prepare an outdoor grill.

Place the meat in a bowl and season with salt and pepper. Add the egg yolk, Parmigiano, tomato paste, parsley, garlic, and red pepper flakes. Mix the meat and form 12 large meatballs, 2 to 2½ inches each. Flatten the meatballs and form patties. Drizzle the patties with EVOO and add them to the hot pan or grill. Cook for 3 minutes on each side. Hold the cooked patties on a plate under foil.

On a large platter or in a salad bowl, combine the romaine with the quartered artichoke hearts, roasted red pepper, hot peppers, olives, celery, salami, and provolone. Toss the salad with vinegar first, about 3 tablespoons, then toss with EVOO—up to ¼ cup to your taste. (Just eyeball the amounts.) Season the salad with salt and pepper to taste. Scatter the chopped mozzarella, tomatoes, and basil across the salad. Arrange the cooked mini meatball burgers on top of the arranged antipasto salad.

Grilled Chicken Posole Salad

Picnics are a birthright for us all. Eating outside, on a big blanket, amidst the grass and trees, the birds—hold the bees! Dress it up. Pack real plates and silver, along with some chilled rosé and pretty glassware. This is a picnic-perfect spicy salad, made mayo-free. Bring along some chips and salsa.   4 SERVINGS

---

4 6-ounce boneless, skinless **chicken breasts**

3 tablespoons **EVOO** (extra-virgin olive oil), plus some for drizzling

1 tablespoon **grill seasoning**

2 teaspoons ground **cumin**, ⅔ palmful

1 teaspoon ground **thyme** or poultry seasoning, ⅓ palmful

3 **garlic cloves**, chopped

1 medium **onion**, chopped

12 **tomatillos**, husks removed, rinsed and dried, then coarsely chopped

4 Spanish **piquillo peppers** or 2 roasted red peppers, drained and chopped

3 **celery ribs**, with green tops, chopped

½ cup **green olives** with pimientos, drained and chopped

1 15-ounce can **hominy**, drained

1 tablespoon **hot sauce**

Juice of 2 limes

Salt and **black pepper**

2 cups lightly crushed **tortilla chips**, any color or variety

Preheat a grill pan or outdoor grill to high. Coat the chicken with a generous drizzle of EVOO. Combine the grill seasoning with the cumin and ground thyme and sprinkle it evenly over the chicken. Grill for 5 to 6 minutes on each side. Remove the chicken from the heat and set aside until cool enough to handle.

Heat a skillet over medium-high heat. Add 1 tablespoon of the EVOO, the garlic, and the onions and cook them together for a few minutes. Add the tomatillos and cook for 3 to 4 minutes just to take the bitter edge off the tomatillos. Remove the skillet from the heat.

In a large bowl, combine the chopped peppers, celery, olives, and hominy. Dice and add the chicken. Add the hot sauce and lime juice to the salad and dress it with the remaining 2 tablespoons of EVOO. Toss the salad, then add the tomatillo mixture and combine. Season the salad with salt and pepper and garnish with crushed tortilla chips.

> **tidbit** >> Hominy, the key ingredient in posole, is hulled corn kernels. You can find it in the Latin food section.

Not-sagna Pasta Toss

Easier than lasagna, because it's not lasagna, this pasta, meat sauce, and ricotta toss-up is just as hearty and comforting as the layered Italian fave, but it's ready in a fraction of the time and with much less effort. Serve with a simple green salad dressed with oil and vinegar.

4 SERVINGS

Coarse salt

1 pound curly **short-cut pasta,** such as campanelle or cavatappi

2 tablespoons **EVOO** (extra-virgin olive oil)

1 pound **ground sirloin**

1 medium **onion,** finely chopped

4 **garlic cloves,** chopped

½ teaspoon **red pepper flakes**

Black pepper

½ teaspoon **ground allspice**

1 teaspoon **Worcestershire sauce**

½ cup **dry red wine**

½ cup **beef stock**

1 28-ounce can **crushed tomatoes**

1½ cups **part-skim ricotta cheese**

½ cup grated **Parmigiano-Reggiano** cheese, plus some to pass

1 cup fresh **basil,** about 20 leaves

Bring a large pot of water to a boil. Salt the water and cook the pasta to al dente. You will need to add a ladle of the cooking water to the sauce before you drain the pasta.

Heat a deep nonstick skillet over medium-high heat. Add the EVOO, then the meat. Break it up into small bits and cook for 4 to 5 minutes, or until the meat has good color to it. Add the onions, garlic, and red pepper flakes and season with salt, pepper, the allspice, and the Worcestershire sauce. Cook for another 5 minutes, deglaze the meat and onions with the red wine, cook off a minute, then stir the stock into the meat. Stir in the tomatoes and bring it to a bubble. Reduce the heat to medium low and simmer for 5 minutes.

Place the ricotta in the bottom of a shallow bowl. Add a ladleful of boiling pasta water to the ricotta and stir to combine them. Add a couple of handfuls of grated Parm cheese to the ricotta and mix it in.

Drain the pasta and toss it with the cheeses. Add half of the thick meat sauce to the pasta bowl and toss again to combine. Tear the basil and add it to the meat and pasta, then toss again. Taste to adjust the salt and pepper. Serve bowlfuls of Not-sagna with extra sauce on top and more Parm to pass at the table.

THAI CHICKEN PIZZA >> (page 284)

ABOVE: **GRILLED MOROCCAN-SPICED TURKEY BURGERS** >> (page 86); **VEGGIE CHICKPEA AND COUSCOUS SALAD WITH YOGURT DRESSING** >> (page 229)

OPPOSITE: **SHRIMP MARTINIS AND MANHATTAN STEAKS** >> (pages 339–40)

ABOVE: **LIME-AND-HONEY GLAZED SALMON WITH WARM BLACK BEAN AND CORN SALAD** ›› (page 194)

OPPOSITE: **SWEDISH MEATBALLS ON NOODLES** ›› (page 315)

ABOVE: **HONEY NUT CHICKEN STICKS** >> (page 265)

OPPOSITE: **CREAM OF CHEDDAR SOUP AND LIME CHICKEN AVOCADO SALAD** >> (page 248)

ABOVE: **DRUNKEN TUSCAN PASTA** >> (page 172)

OPPOSITE: **MEDITERRANEAN CHICKEN AND SAFFRON COUSCOUS** >> (pages 14–15); **PRETZEL-CRUSTED CHICKEN BREASTS WITH A CHEDDAR-MUSTARD SAUCE** >> (page 276); **CHIPOTLE CHICKEN ROLLS WITH AVOCADO DIPPING SAUCE** >> (pages 272–73)

ABOVE: **STEAKS WITH TANGY CORN RELISH AND SMASHED SPUDS** >> (pages 302–03)

OPPOSITE: **BIG BIRD: JUMBO CHICKEN BURGER** >> (page 117); **SUPER TUSCAN BURGER** >> (page 98); **BIG BISTRO BURGER** >> (page 305)

ABOVE: CHORIZO-COD-POTATO STEW >> (page 212); BLACK FOREST REUBENS >> (page 57)

OPPOSITE: GRILLED KIELBASA REUBENS WITH WARM MUSTARD-CARAWAY SAUERKRAUT >> (page 36); SMOKED PAPRIKA O-RINGS >> (page 140)

ABOVE: MASCARPONE PARFAIT WITH CITRUS SALAD>> (page 372)

Chicken Francese and Wilted Spinach

I like to pair this with an Italian liqueur called limoncello, a lemon vodka concoction that is sweet and citrusy and too easy to drink! One night out, Mama was spied enjoying encores of limoncello and ever since that night, Mama has been referred to as Mamacello. Limoncello is very affordable and is available in most liquor stores.   4 SERVINGS

1½ pounds **chicken breast cutlets**

Salt and **freshly ground black pepper**

2 teaspoons **poultry seasoning** (half a palmful)

½ cup all-purpose **flour**

2 large **eggs** plus 1 **egg yolk**

A splash of **milk** or half-and-half

4 tablespoons **extra-virgin olive oil** (EVOO)

3 tablespoons **unsalted butter**

3 **garlic cloves**, 1 crushed, 2 chopped

½ cup **dry white wine** (a couple of glugs)

A handful of fresh **flat-leaf parsley**, finely chopped

1 pound triple-washed **spinach**, tough stems removed, coarsely chopped

¼ teaspoon **grated nutmeg**

Preheat a large nonstick skillet over medium to medium-high heat. Season the chicken cutlets with salt and pepper and poultry seasoning. Dredge the chicken in flour. In a small bowl, beat the eggs and egg yolk with milk or half-and-half and season with a little salt. Add 2 tablespoons of the EVOO to the skillet (twice around the pan), then add 2 tablespoons of the butter, cut into small pieces. When the butter melts into the oil, add the crushed clove of garlic to the skillet. When the garlic speaks by sizzling in the oil, coat the chicken in the egg mixture, then add to the hot pan. Cook the chicken on both sides until just golden, 6 to 7 minutes total. Transfer the chicken to a plate and tent loosely with foil to retain the heat. Add the wine to the pan and deglaze by whisking up the drippings. Reduce the wine for 1 minute, then add the remaining tablespoon of butter and the parsley to the pan. Pour the sauce over the chicken.

Return the skillet to the heat. Add the remaining 2 tablespoons of EVOO, then add the chopped garlic and let it come to a sizzle. Wilt in the spinach, turning it to coat in the EVOO, and season it with salt, pepper, and nutmeg. Serve the spinach alongside the chicken francese. Pass crusty bread to mop up the sauce.

Smoky Chipotle–Chicken Corn Chowder with Salsa Salad

East Coast meets West Coast in this dish. Chowder plus Tex-Mex equals a really good idea!   4 SERVINGS

5 tablespoons **EVOO** (extra-virgin olive oil)

1 large **onion**, chopped

3 large **garlic cloves**, chopped

1 **chipotle chile in adobo**, chopped

2 **celery ribs**, finely chopped

1 teaspoon **ground coriander**, ⅓ handful

½ teaspoon **ground cumin**

Salt and **black pepper**

20 white or yellow **tortilla chips**, plus some for garnish

1 quart **chicken stock**

3 boneless, skinless **chicken breasts**, cut in half lengthwise, then cut into small bite-size pieces

2 10-ounce boxes **frozen corn kernels**

Juice of 2 limes

1 tablespoon **Dijon mustard**

2 ripe **Hass avocados**

1 pint **grape tomatoes**

2 tablespoons fresh **cilantro leaves**, a palmful, chopped

1 small head **romaine lettuce**, washed and coarsely chopped

½ small **red onion**, finely chopped

¼ cup fresh **flat-leaf parsley**, a generous handful, chopped

Preheat a soup pot over medium-high heat with 2 tablespoons of the EVOO, twice around the pan. Add the onions, garlic, chipotle, celery, coriander, cumin, and a little salt and pepper. Cook for about 3 minutes or until the onions are slightly tender, stirring frequently.

While the onions are cooking, in a food processor grind the tortilla chips until they are pretty fine. If you don't have a food processor, put the chips in a resealable plastic bag and smash them up using a rolling pin until you don't feel like doing it anymore. They might not be ground as fine as they would be in the machine, but it won't matter in the end. You need about 1 cup of ground chips; since different brands of chips come in different sizes, adjust the amount you grind accordingly. Add the ground chips to the onions, stir to combine, then add the chicken stock, bring it up to a bubble, and simmer for 8 to 10 minutes. Add the chicken and frozen corn and continue to cook it for 5 minutes, or until the chicken is cooked through.

While the soup is cooking, prepare the salsa salad. To make the dressing, in a small mixing bowl combine the juice of 1 lime, the mustard, and a little salt and pepper. In a slow steady stream whisk in the remaining 3 tablespoons of EVOO. Reserve the dressing.

Cut all around the circumference of the avocados, lengthwise and down to the pit. Twist and separate the halved fruit. Remove the pit with a spoon, then scoop the flesh out in one piece from both halves, chop it into bite-size pieces, and transfer it to a salad bowl. Cut the grape tomatoes in half and add them to the avocados along with the cilantro, chopped romaine lettuce, and chopped red onion. Pour the dressing over the salad and toss it to coat and combine.

If the soup becomes too thick, adjust it by adding a little more stock, and if it is too thin, let it continue to cook and reduce until it is to your liking. Taste and check for seasoning, adjust with a little salt and pepper, and if you want more heat, you have that adobo sauce on hand, so use it. Add the parsley and serve the soup with the salsa salad alongside. Garnish each bowl of soup with a chip or two.

Ginger-Orange Roasted Carrot Soup with Spicy Shrimp

The roasted carrots make this soup extra delicious.   4 SERVINGS

1 pound **carrots**, peeled and sliced into ¼-inch-thick disks

5 tablespoons **EVOO** (extra-virgin olive oil), plus some for drizzling

Salt and **black pepper**

1 **orange**

1 teaspoon **hot sauce**

12 **large shrimp**, shelled, deveined, and butterflied (see Tidbit)

2 medium **onions**, thinly sliced

2-inch piece **fresh ginger**, peeled and chopped

2 large **garlic cloves**, chopped

1 teaspoon **curry powder**, ⅓ palmful

1 quart **chicken stock**

¼ cup fresh **flat-leaf parsley**, a generous handful, chopped

Preheat the oven to 450°F.

Put the carrot disks on a cookie sheet, drizzle them with a little EVOO, and season them with salt and pepper. Toss the carrots around to make sure they are well coated. Spread in an even layer then roast them for 15 minutes, or until they are tender and the bottoms are browned. Stir the carrots at least twice while they roast so they cook evenly. Zest the orange and reserve.

In a shallow dish, combine the juice of half of the orange with the hot sauce, 2 tablespoons of the EVOO, and a little salt. Add the shrimp and toss to coat; set aside for a few minutes.

Preheat a soup pot over medium-high heat with 2 tablespoons of the EVOO, twice around the pan. Add the onions, ginger, garlic, curry powder, and salt and pepper to the pot and cook until the onions are tender and lightly colored, about 5 minutes, stirring frequently. If you find the onions are browning before they are getting tender, add a splash of water. Transfer the cooked onions to a blender or food processor, where they can wait for the carrots to finish roasting. Return the soup pot to the cooktop, add the chicken stock, and bring it up to a simmer.

When the carrots are roasted, transfer them to the blender or food processor where the onions are patiently waiting. Add a little ladle of the hot chicken stock and puree until the vegetables are smooth. Start by pulse-grinding the mixture to get it going and then let 'er rip. Add more hot stock, bit by bit, until it incorporates. Careful, sometimes when blending hot things the blender or food processor top is not tight enough and you can get splashed: Put a kitchen towel over the lid for extra safety. (Hot carrot puree is not a home facial technique!) Add the carrot-onion puree to the bubbling stock and stir to combine, then let the soup gently simmer while you cook the shrimp.

Preheat a large skillet over medium-high heat with the remaining tablespoon of EVOO. Drain the shrimp and cook them on each side for 2 to 3 minutes, or until cooked through. Add the parsley and toss.

Check the soup consistency. If you want it thicker, let it simmer a little bit longer; if you want it less thick, add a couple splashes of chicken stock to thin it out. Add the orange zest, stir it to combine, then taste and check for seasoning and adjust with salt and pepper.

Ladle some soup into shallow serving bowls and arrange 3 shrimp in the center of each bowl, standing up if you can manage it.

tidbit >> To butterfly the shrimp, using a paring knife run your knife lengthwise along where the vein was removed, just shy of cutting through. Once cooked, the shrimp will open like a butterfuly and be able to sit upright in the soup.

My Mom's 15-Minute Tomato and Bean Stoup

This recipe is good for 4 soulful bowlfuls, 2 servings with seconds, or enough for 1 stay-in-bed day.   4 SERVINGS

2 tablespoons **EVOO** (extra-virgin olive oil)

3 **garlic cloves**, chopped

½ teaspoon **red pepper flakes**

1 medium **onion**, chopped

2 **carrots**, peeled and thinly sliced

2 **celery ribs**, chopped

1 small **zucchini**, sliced

2 cups **vegetable or chicken stock**

1 15-ounce can **diced tomatoes**

1 15-ounce can **tomato sauce**

1 15-ounce can **small white beans** or cannellini beans

1 10-ounce box **frozen cut green beans**

Salt and **black pepper**

1 cup fresh **basil leaves**, torn or shredded

Grated **Parmigiano-Reggiano or Romano cheese**, for topping

Crusty bread, for mopping

Add the EVOO to a large pot. Add the garlic and red pepper flakes, stir, then add the onions, carrots, celery, and zucchini. Cook for 10 minutes, then add the stock, tomatoes, tomato sauce, and both kinds of beans. Bring the stoup up to a bubble and season it with salt and pepper to taste. Simmer for 5 minutes. Turn off the heat and wilt the basil into the stoup. Ladle up the stoup and serve it with lots of grated cheese and bread.

Veal Polpette with Thin Spaghetti and Light Tomato and Basil Sauce

Polpette are baby meatballs and these are stuffed with a pine nut (buttery, slightly crunchy surprise) and a currant or raisin (to keep the meat moist). 4 SERVINGS

Coarse salt

¾ pound **thin spaghetti** (vermicelli)

1 pound **ground veal**

4 **garlic cloves,** 2 cloves minced, 2 cloves chopped

1 **egg**

½ to ⅔ cup **Italian-style bread crumbs** (a couple of overflowing handfuls)

½ cup grated **Parmigiano Reggiano,** plus some to pass at the table

¼ teaspoon **freshly grated or ground nutmeg**

Coarse black pepper

3 tablespoons **extra-virgin olive oil** (EVOO), plus some for drizzling

¼ cup **pine nuts** (a handful)

¼ cup small **raisins** or currants

1 small to medium **yellow onion,** finely chopped

½ cup **dry white wine** (a couple of glugs)

1 28-ounce can **diced tomatoes,** San Marzano variety if available

1 8-ounce can **tomato sauce**

20 fresh **basil** leaves, torn

Preheat the oven to 400°F. Heat a large pot of water to a boil. When it boils, salt it and add the pasta.

While the water boils, in a large bowl, mix the meat with the minced garlic, egg, bread crumbs, cheese, nutmeg, salt, pepper, and a generous drizzle of EVOO. Roll small meatballs with a pine nut and raisin in the center of each, and arrange them on a rimmed nonstick cookie sheet. Bake the meatballs for 10 minutes, or until cooked through.

Heat a deep skillet over medium heat. Add the 3 tablespoons of EVOO (3 times around the pan). Add the chopped garlic and the onions and cook for 5 minutes, or until soft and sweet. Add the wine, reduce for a minute, then stir in the diced tomatoes and tomato sauce and simmer for 5 minutes. Fold in the basil to wilt it.

Cook the pasta al dente, drain, and toss with half of the sauce. Take the meatballs from the oven and carefully loosen them from the cookie sheet with a thin spatula, then add them to the remaining sauce to coat.

Top the pasta with the polpette and serve with extra grated cheese to pass at the table and a green salad.

Smoked Paprika Chicken with Egg Noodles and Buttered Warm Radishes

Just like Grandma might have made for you, if she were Hungarian.

4 SERVINGS

Salt

8 ounces **extra-wide egg noodles**

2 tablespoons **EVOO** (extra-virgin olive oil), twice around the pan

1½ pounds **chicken tenders**, cut into bite-size pieces

1 medium **onion**, thinly sliced

2 **garlic cloves**, chopped

1½ teaspoons **smoked sweet paprika**, ½ palmful

Black pepper

½ cup **chicken stock**

2 tablespoons **butter**, cut into small pieces

1 pound large **radishes**, trimmed and halved

½ cup **sour cream** or reduced-fat sour cream

2 tablespoons chopped or snipped **chives**

¼ cup fresh **flat-leaf parsley**, a generous handful, chopped

Bring a pot of water to a boil for the egg noodles. Salt the water and cook the noodles for 6 minutes, or until tender but with a little bite left to them.

Heat a large skillet over medium-high heat. Add the EVOO and then the chicken. Lightly brown the meat on all sides for 3 to 4 minutes. Add the onions and garlic and cook it for a few minutes more. Season the chicken mixture with the smoked paprika, salt, and pepper, then stir in the chicken stock and reduce the heat to low.

Heat a small skillet over medium to medium-high heat. Add a tablespoon of the butter and melt it. Add the radishes and cook for 3 to 4 minutes to warm through.

Stir the sour cream into the chicken and turn the heat off. Add the chives to the radishes and turn the heat off under this pan as well. Drain the noodles and return them to the warm pot. Add the remaining tablespoon of butter and toss to coat the noodles. Add half the parsley to the noodles. Divide them among 4 dinner plates. Top with the chicken and sauce and garnish with the remaining parsley. Serve the radishes alongside the chicken and noodles.

Cider-Sauced Chicken Breasts

Where I come from, we'll walk a country mile for apple-anything. In this menu, the bite of apple cider vinegar makes a great flavor partner for the sweet apple cider. You are in store for a simply elegant dinner.
6 SERVINGS

3 tablespoons **EVOO** (extra-virgin olive oil)

6 6-ounce boneless, skinless **chicken breasts**

Salt and **black pepper**

1 large **onion**, finely chopped

6 fresh **thyme sprigs**, leaves removed and coarsely chopped

3 **garlic cloves**, chopped

1 **Gala apple**, peeled, cored, and cut into thin wedges

2 tablespoons **dark brown sugar**

½ cup **apple cider**

3 tablespoons **apple cider vinegar**

2 cups **chicken stock**

3 tablespoons cold **butter**

½ cup fresh **flat-leaf parsley** leaves, 2 generous handfuls, chopped

Preheat the oven to 500° F.

You'll need an extra-large oven-safe skillet that will fit 6 chicken breasts without overcrowding. (If you don't have one that big, use the largest one you have for 4 of the chicken breasts and a medium one for the remaining 2 breasts.) Preheat the skillet over medium-high heat with the EVOO, 3 times around the pan. Season the chicken breasts liberally with salt and pepper, add them to the skillet, and brown them on both sides, about 6 minutes total. Remove the chicken to a baking pan or rimmed baking sheet and transfer them to the oven to cook for 10 minutes more, or until their juices run clear when pierced with a sharp knife.

Return the skillet to the stovetop over medium-high heat and add the onions, thyme, garlic, apples, and brown sugar. (If you used 2 skillets do this step in the larger of the skillets.) Cook, stirring frequently, for 4 to 5 minutes. Add the apple cider and vinegar and cook for about 2 minutes. Add the chicken stock, turn the heat up to high, and simmer until the liquid is reduced by about half, or until it is slightly thickened. Turn the heat off, add the butter and parsley, and stir until the butter is incorporated. Serve the apple cider sauce over the chicken breasts.

Everything Lo Mein

Make your own take-out. When you do, you control the salt, fat, and quality of ingredients. This dish is not only healthful, but you also don't have to make any decisions like whether you want chicken or pork. This recipe has got everything in it but the kitchen sink.

4 SERVINGS

3 rounded tablespoons **hoisin sauce**

3 tablespoons **tamari** (dark aged soy sauce)

2 teaspoons **hot sauce**

Salt

1 pound **spaghetti**

4 tablespoons **vegetable oil**

2 large **eggs**, beaten

3 **chicken breast cutlets**, sliced into thin strips

3 thin-cut **pork chops**, sliced into thin strips

Black pepper

2 teaspoons **ground coriander**

4 **garlic cloves**, finely chopped

2-inch piece **fresh ginger**, peeled and finely chopped or grated

6 **scallions**, cut into 3-inch lengths, then sliced lengthwise

½ pound fresh **shiitake mushrooms**, stemmed and chopped

1 **red bell pepper**, cut into quarters, seeded, then sliced

1 small can sliced **water chestnuts**, chopped

2 cups fresh **bean sprouts**, 4 generous handfuls, or ½ pound packaged shredded cabbage

Mix together the hoisin, tamari, hot sauce, and about 3 tablespoons of water in a small bowl and reserve.

Bring a big pot of water to a boil for the pasta. Salt the water, add the pasta, and cook to al dente.

While the pasta cooks, heat 1 tablespoon of the vegetable oil, once around the pan, in a large, nonstick skillet over high heat. When the oil ripples, add the beaten eggs and scramble them to light golden brown. Remove to a plate and reserve.

Season the meat strips with salt, pepper, and the coriander. Heat the remaining 3 tablespoons of vegetable oil to a ripple over high heat, then add the meat and stir-fry for 4 minutes. Push the meat to the sides of the skillet and add the garlic, ginger, scallions, shiitakes, bell peppers, water chestnuts, and bean sprouts or cabbage. Stir-fry the veggies for 2 minutes, then add the drained pasta and the eggs to the skillet. Pour the reserved sauce over the lo mein and toss it to combine. Turn off the heat. Toss for 30 seconds and let the pasta absorb all of the liquids. Taste it to adjust the seasonings. Yum-o! You're not getting this off of any take-out menu!

Smoky Turkey Shepherd's Pie

Shepherd's pie started as a good way for using up leftover meat, but today it's a staple of American comfort food. This healthy version uses lean turkey to remove fat and rev up flavor!   4 SERVINGS

Coarse salt

3 large Idaho **potatoes**, peeled and cubed

2 tablespoons **extra-virgin olive oil** (EVOO)

¼ pound **bacon** or turkey bacon, chopped

1 package (about 1⅓ pounds) **ground turkey**

1 tablespoon **smoked paprika**, or substitute 1½ teaspoons each of sweet paprika and cumin, plus a sprinkle

Coarse black pepper

2 tablespoons fresh **thyme** leaves (from 5 or 6 sprigs)

1 medium **onion**, chopped

2 **carrots**, diced

3 **celery ribs** from the heart, chopped

1 small **red bell pepper**, cored, seeded, and chopped

2 cups frozen **peas**

2 tablespoons all-purpose **flour**

2 cups **chicken stock** or broth

1 cup **sour cream**

1 large **egg**, beaten

3 tablespoons **unsalted butter**

10 to 12 fresh **chives**, chopped or snipped

Bring a medium pot of water to a boil, salt it, and cook the potatoes while you make the turkey filling.

Heat a deep, large skillet over medium-high heat. Add the EVOO to the skillet, then add the bacon and brown it up. Drain off the excess fat, then add the turkey to the pan and break it up with a wooden spoon. Season the turkey with the smoked paprika, salt, pepper, and thyme. When the turkey is browned, add the onions, carrots, and celery. Season the veggies with salt and pepper. Cook for 5 minutes, stirring occasionally, then add the red bell peppers and peas and cook for another 2 minutes. Stir in the flour and cook for 2 minutes. Add the stock and combine. Stir in ½ cup of the sour cream and simmer the mixture over low heat.

Preheat the broiler to high.

When the potatoes are tender (10 to 12 minutes), stir a ladle of the cooking water into the egg, then drain the potatoes. Return the potatoes to the warm pot to dry them out a little. Add the remaining ½ cup of sour cream, the butter, and salt and pepper. Smash and mash the potatoes, mashing in the beaten, tempered egg. If the potatoes are too tight, mix in a splash of milk.

Pour the turkey mixture into a medium casserole dish. Top with the smashed potatoes and spread evenly. Place the casserole 5 inches from the hot broiler. Broil until the potatoes are golden at the edges. Garnish the casserole with the chives and a sprinkle of smoked paprika.

Thai-Style Steak Salad

I LOVE Thai food, and anytime I get the chance to create the flavors at home, I Thai it—HA, get it?!   4 SERVINGS

3 **garlic cloves**, chopped

2-inch piece of **fresh ginger**, peeled and grated

2 tablespoons **tamari** (dark aged soy sauce, found on the international aisle)

2 teaspoons **hot sauce**, such as Tabasco

6 tablespoons **vegetable oil**

2 pounds **flank steak**

1 cup **sweetened shredded coconut**

1 tablespoon **sugar**

3 tablespoons **rice wine vinegar**

Salt and **freshly ground black pepper**

½ **English** or **seedless cucumber**, thinly sliced

1 **red bell pepper**, cored, seeded, and thinly sliced

5 **radishes**, thinly sliced

2 cups shredded **carrots** (available in pouches in the produce department)

½ small **red onion**, thinly sliced

10 fresh **mint** leaves, chopped

¼ cup fresh **cilantro** leaves (a generous handful), chopped

10 fresh **basil** leaves, chopped or torn

1 sack (12 ounces) **baby spinach** or ¾ pound from bulk bins, washed and patted dry

¼ cup **unsalted roasted peanuts**, chopped

Heat a grill pan or outdoor grill to high heat.

In a small bowl, mix the garlic, three fourths of the grated ginger, the tamari, and hot sauce. Whisk in about 3 tablespoons of the vegetable oil. Place the meat in a shallow dish and coat it evenly in marinade. Let stand for 10 minutes.

In a small skillet, toast the shredded coconut until lightly golden, about 2 to 3 minutes. Keep an eye on it; the coconut can go from golden brown to burnt quickly. Remove the toasted coconut from the skillet and reserve.

In a small bowl, whisk together the remaining ginger, the sugar, rice wine vinegar, salt, and pepper. Whisk in the remaining 3 tablespoons of vegetable oil in a slow, steady stream.

In a salad bowl, combine the cucumbers, bell peppers, radishes, shredded carrots, onions, mint, cilantro, and basil. Pour the dressing over the veggies, toss to coat, and let sit while you cook the steak.

Grill the flank steak for 6 to 7 minutes on each side. Remove the flank steak from the grill and let the juices redistribute before slicing, 5 to 10 minutes. Thinly slice the meat on an angle, cutting the meat against the grain. To the dressed veggies, add the spinach, sliced steak, toasted coconut, and chopped peanuts, toss thoroughly, and serve.

Shrimp Po'Boys

I live near Saratoga Springs, New York, home of SPAC, a performing-arts center. Every summer a huge jazz fest is held here. I like to have my own jazz fest at home, with plenty of New Orleans–style food and drink to enjoy with the music. Load up the stereo with your favorite music and whip up your Po'boys.   4 SERVINGS

Vegetable or peanut oil, for frying

1 large **egg**

1 cup **milk**

Salt

1½ pounds **large shrimp**, peeled and deveined, tails removed

½ cup all-purpose **flour**

1 cup **cornmeal or plain bread crumbs**

2 tablespoons **Old Bay** or other seafood seasoning, a couple palmfuls

8 leaves **Bibb or butter lettuce**

1 **beefsteak tomato**, thinly sliced

4 **soft club rolls** or sub rolls, split

1 **lemon,** cut into wedges

¼ cup **sweet pickle relish**

½ cup **spicy, grainy mustard**

Preheat an inch of oil in a deep skillet over medium to medium-high heat.

Beat the egg and milk together in a large bowl. Salt the shrimp, then set them in the milk batter. Before you begin breading the shrimp, cover a plate with plastic wrap for easy cleanup, then mix together the flour, cornmeal or bread crumbs, and seafood seasoning on the plate. Using tongs, remove a few shrimp at a time from the batter and coat in the breading. Add the breaded shrimp to the hot oil and fry them for 5 to 6 minutes, or until they are firm and deeply golden all over. Repeat until all the shrimp are fried, draining them on paper towels.

Pile lettuce and tomatoes on the roll bottoms, top with the shrimp, and douse the shrimp with a little lemon juice. Mix the relish and mustard and dot the roll tops with spoonfuls of the sauce before setting them into place.

Italian Tuna Melts with White Beans and Provolone

I love tuna salad, but I always hold the mayo! In my family, EVOO was used to dress or cook almost any food, so I still make my tuna salads with lemon and oil, rather than mayo. You're good to go with this all-in-one meal.   2 SERVINGS

---

1 15-ounce can **white beans**, rinsed and drained

1 can **tuna in water or oil**, drained and flaked

¼ **red onion**, chopped

2 tablespoons **capers**, drained

2 **celery ribs**, finely chopped

Handful of pitted **kalamata olives**, chopped

2 to 3 fresh **rosemary** sprigs, finely chopped

Juice of 1 lemon

2 1-inch-thick slices of **crusty bread**

1 **garlic clove**, peeled and halved

3 tablespoons **EVOO** (extra-virgin olive oil), plus more for drizzling

1 cup **arugula**, chopped

Salt and **black pepper**

4 deli slices mild or sharp **provolone cheese**

Preheat the broiler.

Place half of the beans in a mixing bowl and mash them with a fork. Add the rest of the beans to the bowl along with the tuna, onions, capers, celery, olives, rosemary, and lemon juice. Char the bread on both sides under the broiler, rub it with the cut garlic, and drizzle with EVOO. Dress the arugula with the 3 tablespoons of EVOO, then mix and season with salt and pepper. Pile the arugula on the bread, divide the tuna between the two slices, and top each with a couple pieces of cheese. Melt the cheese under the broiler until bubbly.

Paco's Fish Tacos in Lettuce Wraps

Better than burritos and tacos, these wraps have crunch and the lettuce lets the flavors of the fillings shine through.   4 SERVINGS

Cooking spray

2 pounds **halibut or grouper** fillets

Salt and **freshly ground black pepper**

Bibb or green leaf lettuce leaves, for wrapping

1 **jalapeño pepper,** seeded and chopped

1 cup fresh **cilantro leaves** (stems removed)

3 sprigs **fresh mint**

3 tablespoons **grainy mustard**

2 tablespoons **red wine vinegar**

¼ cup **extra-virgin olive oil** (EVOO)

1 **lime**

Hot sauce, such as Tabasco

½ **red onion,** finely chopped

Heat a grill pan or nonstick skillet over high heat. Spray the pan with cooking spray. Place the fish on the grill pan, season with salt and pepper, and cook for 5 minutes on each side, or until opaque. Transfer to a serving plate.

Arrange the lettuce leaves on a platter. Place the jalapeño in a food processor with the cilantro, mint, mustard, and vinegar. Turn on the processor and stream in the EVOO, then season the sauce with salt and pepper.

Break the fish into chunks and squeeze lime juice over the fish. Add a few dashes of hot sauce.

Pile the fish in lettuce leaves and top each "taco" with the jalapeño cilantro sauce and chopped red onions.

Burgers

Over the years, I have made tons of burgers. Beef burgers, salmon burgers, veggie burgers, turkey burgers . . . I can go on and on, but I'd rather get grilling. There's a burger here for every mood, appetite, and season.

FIGURE-FRIENDLY FAVES

Chicken Burgers with Chowchow and Cold Sesame Noodle Salad
Paella Burgers and Spanish Fries with Pimiento Mayonnaise
Grilled Moroccan-Spiced Turkey Burgers
Lamb Mini Burgers on Mixed Salad with Fennel
Ginger-Garlic Tuna Burgers on Cucumber Salad
Chicken Caesar Burgers
Five-Spice Burgers with Warm Mu Shu Slaw Topping and Pineapple
Mini Cheeseburger Salad with Yellow Mustard Vinaigrette
Salmon Burgers with Ginger-Wasabi Mayo and French Fries
Lamb Patties with Garlic and Mint Over Mediterranean Salad

JOHN'S FAVES

BBQ Chicken Burgers Topped with Honey Slaw
Open-Face Blue Moon Burgers with 'Shrooms
Super Tuscan Burgers and Potato Salad with Capers and Celery
BLT Turkey Burger Clubs
Gyro Burgers with Greek Salad
Beef and Chicken Fajita Burgers with Seared Peppers
Ricotta-Smothered Mushroom "Burgers" with Prosciutto
Bacon Bit Burgers with Smoked Gouda and Onions
Cubano Pork Burgers and Sweet Orange Warm Slaw
Jambalaya Burgers and Cajun Corn and Red Beans

GUT-BUSTERS

Bacon and Creamy Ranch Chicken Burgers with Scallion "Sticks"
Cheddar-Studded Chili Turkey Burgers with Cilantro Cream
Chicken Kiev Burgers and Russian-Style Slaw Salad
Hungry-Man Bloody-Mary Burgers and Spicy Broccoli
Bacon-Wrapped Meatloaf Patties with Smashed Potatoes
Cajun-Style Meatloaf Patties with Glazed String Beans
Big Bird: Jumbo Chicken, Spinach, and Herb Burgers
Burly-Man-Size Chicken-Cheddar Barbecued Burgers
Chili Dog Bacon Cheeseburgers and Fiery Fries
The T2: Turkey Chili-Topped Turkey Chili Burgers

Chicken Burgers with Chowchow and Cold Sesame Noodle Salad

Some nights at my house, we can't decide between burgers and take-out. This menu seals the deal. **2 SERVINGS**

Salt

½ pound **perciatelli** or spaghetti

½ pound **Savoy cabbage,** half coarsely chopped, half shredded

½ **red onion**, chopped

1 **celery rib**, chopped

1 small **red bell pepper**, chopped

1 large **unripe or green tomato**, chopped

¼ cup **cider vinegar**

¼ cup **sugar**

½ teaspoon **five-spice powder**

½ teaspoon **cayenne pepper**

½ teaspoon ground **turmeric**

Black pepper

¾ pound **ground chicken**

2 **garlic cloves**, chopped

2 tablespoons peeled and grated **fresh ginger**

2 tablespoons finely chopped fresh **cilantro** or flat-leaf parsley leaves

¼ cup plus 2 tablespoons **tamari** (dark aged soy sauce)

2 tablespoons **vegetable oil**

¼ cup **smooth peanut butter**

1 teaspoon **dark sesame oil**

4 **scallions**, cut into thirds then shredded into grass-like threads

2 tablespoons **toasted sesame seeds**

2 crusty **cornmeal kaiser rolls**, split

4 pieces of **leaf or Bibb lettuce**

Bring a large covered pot of water to a boil. Add salt and the pasta and cook to al dente. Drain the pasta and run it under cold running water until it's cool.

While the water is coming to a boil, place the chopped cabbage in a food processor. Pulse the processor to finely chop the cabbage, then transfer to a medium sauce pot. Add the red onions, celery, red bell peppers, and tomatoes to the processor and pulse to finely chop. Add the veggies to the pot with the cabbage, then add the vinegar, sugar, five-spice powder, ¼ teaspoon of the cayenne pepper, the turmeric, salt, and pepper. Bring the relish to a boil, then cook over medium heat for 10 to 12 minutes. Adjust the seasonings.

While the chowchow works, mix the meat with the garlic, ginger, cilantro, 2 tablespoons of the tamari, a little salt, and lots of black pepper. Form 2 large, inch-thick patties—they'll hang off the bun! Add the oil to a skillet and get it screaming hot over medium-high heat. Add the patties and cook them for 5 to 6 minutes on each side.

In a small pot, melt the peanut butter over low heat and whisk in the remaining ¼ cup tamari, the sesame oil, and the remaining ¼ teaspoon cayenne pepper. Pour the sauce over the cold noodles and toss them with the shredded Savoy cabbage, the scallions, and sesame seeds.

Place the burgers on the rolls and top them with lots of chowchow and lettuce, set the roll tops in place, and serve with the noodle salad.

tidbit >> You can make the chowchow in a double batch and save it in the fridge for a couple of weeks to use on sammies or dogs.

Paella Burgers and Spanish Fries with Pimiento Mayonnaise

Paella is a delicious rustic dish, and I've found a way to make it even better! I've taken the flavors and ingredients straight out of this Spanish classic and piled them into one mouthwatering burger. With ground chicken breast, chorizo, and shrimp in the mix, you'll never go back to fast-food patties again.   4 SERVINGS

---

1 16- to 18-ounce sack **extra-crispy-style frozen fries**

1½ pounds **ground chicken breast**

1 cup fresh **flat-leaf parsley** leaves (3 or 4 handfuls)

7 **garlic cloves**, finely chopped

1 small **yellow onion**, finely chopped

4 teaspoons **sweet paprika**

4 teaspoons **hot sauce**

Zest of 2 **lemons**, 1 lemon cut into wedges after zesting

2½ tablespoons **grill seasoning**, such as McCormick's Montreal Steak Seasoning

Extra-virgin olive oil (EVOO), for drizzling

½ pound **chorizo**, casings removed, cut into 4 3-inch pieces and butterflied (see Tidbit)

4 **jumbo shrimp** (8 count per pound), peeled, deveined, and butterflied

Coarse salt

4 **Portuguese rolls** (slightly sweet rectangular crusty rolls), or other crusty bread or roll, split

1 cup **pimiento peppers**, jarred or canned, drained well

1 cup **mayonnaise**

3 tablespoons **unsalted butter**

2 cups chopped **romaine lettuce**

Preheat the oven and prepare the fries according to the package directions.

Preheat a large griddle or nonstick skillet over medium-high to high heat.

Place the chicken in a bowl. Set aside a handful of whole parsley leaves and finely chop the rest. Add half of the chopped parsley and a little less than half of the chopped garlic to the bowl with the chicken. Next, add the chopped onions, 2 teaspoons (⅔ palmful) of the paprika, about 2 teaspoons of the hot sauce, the zest of 1 lemon, and the grill seasoning. Pour a healthy drizzle of EVOO around the outside of the bowl. Combine the mixture and form 4 patties. Place the patties on the griddle and cook for 5 minutes on each side.

Place the chorizo on the griddle alongside the burgers. Try to weight down the chorizo to keep it from curling up by placing a plate or small skillet on the sausage and adding something heavy from your pantry, such as canned goods, to weight it down. Cook for just 2 or 3 minutes on each side. The chorizo is already fully cooked; you're just crisping the edges and heating it through. Transfer to a platter and keep warm.

Squeeze about 1 tablespoon of the lemon juice over the shrimp, then season them with a little coarse salt and drizzle them with EVOO. Grill the butterflied shrimp alongside the burgers, 2 minutes on each side, weighting them as you did the chorizo.

Remove the patties and shrimp and add to the chorizo, loosely tenting to keep warm. Drizzle the rolls with EVOO and place cut side down on grill. Weight the rolls down and press to toast and char them on both sides.

Place the pimiento peppers and mayo in a food processor and add the reserved whole parsley leaves, the zest of the second lemon, the remaining 2 teaspoons of hot sauce, and a few pinches of salt. Process together until the dressing is smooth.

Melt the butter together with the remaining chopped garlic over low heat until the garlic sizzles in the butter. Remove the fries from the oven and place in a large bowl. Add the remaining chopped parsley to the bowl and pour the melted garlic butter over the fries, then season with salt and toss.

Mound some chopped lettuce on the roll bottoms, then top with chorizo, chicken patties, and shrimp. Slather the bun top with pimiento mayo and set in place. Serve extra mayo with the fries for dipping.

tidbit >> To butterfly the chorizo chunks, cut into and across but not all the way through the sausage, then spread the meat, like wings. For the shrimp, cut along the incision used to devein the shrimp, then spread it open.

Grilled Moroccan-Spiced Turkey Burgers

I'm always trying to figure out cool and easy new ways to put turkey burgers together. This one is particularly easy since the dry spices will be doing the heavy lifting. I love inviting a crowd over on burger night. Entertaining with casual food is a great rule to follow: people are more relaxed around relaxed food.   8 SERVINGS

3½ to 4 pounds **ground turkey breast**

2 tablespoons **ground cumin**

1 teaspoon **ground turmeric**

2 teaspoons **sweet or smoked sweet paprika**

1 tablespoon **ground coriander**

1 teaspoon **cayenne pepper**

1 tablespoon **curry powder**

1 small **onion**, grated

3 **garlic cloves** chopped

¼ cup fresh **cilantro** or flat-leaf parsley leaves, a handful, chopped

Zest and juice of 1 lemon

Salt and **black pepper**

EVOO (extra-virgin olive oil), for drizzling

½ cup prepared **mango chutney**

¼ cup **plain yogurt** (eyeball it; look for thick, creamy Greek style yogurt)

1 16-ounce sack of **shredded cabbage mix**

8 **pita breads**, any flavor or variety

Preheat an outdoor grill or grill pan to medium high.

Combine the turkey, cumin, turmeric, paprika, coriander, cayenne, curry powder, onions, garlic, cilantro or parsley, lemon zest, salt, and pepper in a bowl and mix well to distribute the spices. Form the mixture into 8 large patties about 1 inch thick. Drizzle the patties with EVOO and grill them for 6 minutes on each side, or until cooked through.

While the burgers are grilling, chop up the mango chutney, breaking up any large chunks. (This may not be necessary depending on the brand you buy.) Transfer the chutney to a bowl and mix with the lemon juice and yogurt. Add the cabbage mix and a little salt and pepper and toss to combine.

When the turkey burgers are done, put the pitas on the grill and heat on each side just to warm them up. Open up the pocket in each pita, nestle a turkey burger inside each, and spoon in some of the mango chutney slaw.

Lamb Mini Burgers on Mixed Salad with Fennel

How cute is this?! Little mini burgers served over a salad. This one is fast and nutritious.   4 SERVINGS, 3 MINI BURGERS EACH

1½ pounds **ground lamb**

2 to 3 tablespoons chopped **fresh rosemary**

1 large **navel orange**, zested, then peeled and sectioned or sliced into disks

½ **red onion**, ¼ finely chopped, ¼ sliced

Salt and **freshly ground black pepper**

1 **romaine lettuce** heart, chopped

1 head **radicchio**, chopped

1 bulb **fennel**, trimmed of fronds and tops and quartered lengthwise

¼ cup chopped fresh **flat-leaf parsley**

2 tablespoons **red wine vinegar**

¼ cup **extra-virgin olive oil** (EVOO)

Preheat a grill pan over medium-high heat or preheat the broiler to high. Combine the lamb, rosemary, orange zest, chopped red onion, salt, and pepper. Make 12 balls and flatten them into patties. Grill for 2 to 3 minutes on each side. Hold the cooked patties on a plate under foil.

Combine the lettuces in a shallow bowl with the sliced onion. Cut the core out of the fennel pieces and thinly slice, then add to the salad. Scatter the oranges and parsley around the salad and dress with the vinegar, oil, salt, and pepper, to your taste. Top portions of the salad with 3 mini lamb patties and serve.

Ginger-Garlic Tuna Burgers on Cucumber Salad

This is one of the first tuna burgers I ever made and it's a good one. Instead of fries, I serve it with edamame . . . Who misses fries? (Well, okay, they're good too, but soy beans are actually good for you as well!)

4 SERVINGS

1¾ to 2 pounds **ahi tuna**, cut into cubes

3-inch piece **fresh ginger**, peeled and grated

4 **garlic cloves**, finely chopped

3 to 4 tablespoons **tamari** (dark aged soy sauce)

2 teaspoons **coarse black pepper**

2 **scallions**, finely chopped

2 tablespoons finely chopped fresh **cilantro**

Vegetable oil, for drizzling, plus some for the salad

1 **romaine lettuce** heart, chopped

2 cups fresh **bean sprouts** or pea shoots

½ **English (seedless) cucumber** (the one wrapped in plastic), cut into ¼-inch dice

Zest and juice of 1 lime

Coarse salt

1 pound **edamame** (soybeans in pods available in freezer section of market)

Heat a grill pan or large skillet over high heat.

Place the fish in a food processor and pulse until the fish is the consistency of ground beef. Transfer the ground ahi to a bowl and mix with the ginger, garlic, tamari, black pepper, scallions, and cilantro. Form 4 equal patties and drizzle them with vegetable oil. Place the tuna burgers in the screaming hot pan and cook for 1 minute on each side for very rare, 2 minutes on each side for medium rare, 3 to 4 minutes on each side to cook through. Hold the cooked patties on a plate under foil.

In a medium bowl combine the lettuce, sprouts, and cucumber. Dress the salad with the lime zest and juice, salt, and vegetable oil to your taste.

Place the edamame in a microwaveable bowl and cover with plastic wrap. Pop a small hole in the top of the wrap and microwave on High for 5 minutes. When the time is up, sprinkle the edamame with 2 teaspoons of coarse salt and toss.

Pile the salad up equally onto 4 plates. Top the salad with tuna patties. Pile the edamame alongside the burgers. To enjoy the edamame, shimmy the soybeans free from their pods in your mouth.

Chicken Caesar Burgers

Wade, my good friend and coworker for many years, joined me at a fancy restaurant in Las Vegas in honor of our friend Lucky's birthday. He saw me cringe as he politely asked our server to request that the chef prepare a "Chicken Caesar" for him. Chef Eric Klein at SW at the Wynn Las Vegas Hotel made Wade a fabulous free-range roast chicken Caesar salad. Wade, this burger is for you. Viva Chicken Caesar!   4 SERVINGS

1½ pounds **ground chicken breast**

3 garlic cloves, 2 finely chopped, 1 cracked from the skin

4 anchovies, finely chopped (optional—but recommended)

A couple of handfuls of grated **Parmigiano-Reggiano** or **Pecorino Romano cheese**

Salt and **coarse black pepper**

1 tablespoon **Worcestershire sauce**

A handful of fresh **flat-leaf parsley**, chopped

Zest of 1 lemon plus juice of ½ **lemon**

4 tablespoons **EVOO** (extra-virgin olive oil), plus some for drizzling

4 crusty rolls, split

1 teaspoon **Dijon mustard**

1 **romaine lettuce** heart, chopped

2 **plum tomatoes**, thinly sliced

Gourmet potato chips

In a bowl, combine the ground chicken, finely chopped garlic, anchovies, a handful of the cheese, a pinch of salt, a generous amount of pepper, the Worcestershire, parsley, and lemon zest. Score the mixture and form 4 oval, rather than round, patties.

Heat a large nonstick skillet with 1 tablespoon of the EVOO, once around the pan, over medium-high heat. When hot, add the chicken patties and cook for 3 to 4 minutes on each side.

Preheat the broiler and toast the rolls on a cookie sheet or broiler pan. When they are lightly golden in color, remove the sheet from the oven and rub the breads with the cracked garlic clove. Drizzle the bread with EVOO and sprinkle with the remaining handful of cheese. Return the sheet to the broiler for another 30 seconds, then remove it and let it stand.

In a large bowl, combine the Dijon, lemon juice, and the remaining 3 tablespoons of EVOO with salt and pepper. Toss the romaine in the dressing.

Place the patties on the roll bottoms and top them with a pile of dressed romaine, sliced tomatoes, and the roll tops. Serve the burgers with chips alongside.

Five-Spice Burgers with Warm Mu Shu Slaw Topping and Pineapple

Just a few key Asian ingredients transform your conventional burger, coleslaw, and chips into an exotic delight! You'll never miss Chinese takeout with these Asian-inspired patties.   4 SERVINGS

1½ pounds **ground chicken** or pork

2 teaspoons **Chinese five-spice powder** (⅔ palmful)

1 tablespoon **grill seasoning,** such as McCormick's Montreal Steak Seasoning (a palmful)

2 **garlic cloves,** minced

1-inch piece of **fresh ginger,** peeled and minced

5 **scallions,** 2 finely chopped, 3 cut into thirds then thinly sliced lengthwise

3 tablespoons **tamari** (dark aged soy sauce)

2 tablespoons **vegetable oil,** plus more for drizzling

12 **shiitake mushrooms,** stems removed and thinly sliced

½ pound shredded **cabbage** (or buy a bag of cole slaw mix in the produce department)

3 tablespoons **hoisin sauce**

4 cornmeal-dusted or sesame **kaiser rolls,** split and toasted

1 fresh **pineapple,** cored into chunks

1 package **vegetable chips**

Heat a nonstick skillet or grill pan over medium-high heat. In a medium bowl, combine the meat with the five-spice powder, grill seasoning, garlic, ginger, finely chopped scallions, tamari, and a drizzle of vegetable oil. Mix and score the meat into quarters, then form 4 patties, 1 inch thick. Cook the burgers for 6 minutes on each side.

Heat a nonstick skillet over high heat. Add the 2 tablespoons of vegetable oil. Cook the shiitakes for 2 minutes, add the cabbage, and stir-fry for 3 minutes more. Add the sliced scallions and hoisin sauce, toss to combine, and remove from the heat.

Serve the burgers on the buns piled high with mu shu slaw on top. Serve with chunks of fresh pineapple and vegetable chips alongside the burgers.

Mini Cheeseburger Salad with Yellow Mustard Vinaigrette

There are many flavors of sharp Cheddar to choose from, so go plain or go wild! Among the choices are five-peppercorn, smoked, dill, garlic and herb, roasted garlic, horseradish, chipotle, habanero, and jalapeño.

4 SERVINGS, 3 MINI BURGERS EACH

---

2 pounds **ground sirloin**

½ cup finely chopped white or yellow **onion** (1 small onion)

2 tablespoons **Worcestershire sauce**

1 rounded tablespoon **grill seasoning,** such as McCormick's Montreal Steak Seasoning, or coarse salt and freshly ground black pepper

Extra-virgin olive oil (EVOO), for drizzling

12-ounce brick of sharp **Cheddar cheese,** such as Cabot brand or Cracker Barrel brand, any flavor you like

3 **romaine lettuce** hearts

1 cup sliced **pickles,** drained (choose from sweet, half-sour, or dill varieties)

1 cup **cherry or grape tomatoes,** halved

DRESSING

3 tablespoons **yellow mustard,** such as French's brand

2 tablespoons **apple cider vinegar**

½ cup **extra-virgin olive oil (EVOO)**

2 to 3 tablespoons finely chopped fresh **chives**

3 tablespoons drained **salad pimientos,** or ¼ red bell pepper, finely chopped

Preheat a grill pan or a large nonstick skillet over medium-high heat or preheat an outdoor grill.

Combine the meat with the onion, Worcestershire, and steak seasoning or salt and pepper. Form 12 large meatballs. Flatten the balls into small patties. Drizzle the formed mini patties with EVOO to keep them from sticking to the cooking surface.

Slice the brick of cheese into ¼-inch pieces. Grill or panfry the mini burgers for 3 minutes on each side, then add the cheese to melt over the burgers, closing the lid of your grill to melt the cheese or tenting the mini cheeseburgers loosely with foil.

Coarsely chop the romaine and combine with the sliced pickles and halved tomatoes. Whisk together the mustard and vinegar, then stream in the EVOO. Add the chives and pimientos to the dressing and stir.

Arrange the mini cheeseburgers on the salad and drizzle the yellow mustard dressing over the completed dish.

Salmon Burgers with Ginger-Wasabi Mayo and French Fries

I am the queen of ground meat, or, in this case . . . salmon. Classic Japanese flavors are mixed into this salmon to make a tasty burger.

4 SERVINGS

---

1 16- to 18-ounce sack **crispy-style frozen French fries**

4 tablespoons **sesame seeds**

1½ pounds fresh **salmon fillet,** pin bones and skin removed

2 **garlic cloves,** chopped

3-inch piece of **fresh ginger,** minced or grated

3 tablespoons **tamari** (dark aged soy sauce, found on the international aisle)

2 **scallions,** white and green parts, chopped

½ small **red bell pepper,** cored, seeded, and finely chopped

2 teaspoons **sesame oil**

2 teaspoons **grill seasoning,** such as McCormick's Montreal Steak Seasoning, or 1 teaspoon coarse black pepper and ½ teaspoon coarse salt

Coarse black pepper

1 tablespoon **light-in-color oil,** such as canola, safflower, or peanut oil

½ to ¾ cup **mayonnaise**

2 tablespoons **wasabi paste**

Juice of 1 lime

4 **sesame kaiser rolls,** split and toasted

Red leaf lettuce, for garnish

Preheat the oven according to the package directions for the fries.

Spread the French fries out on a cookie sheet and cook according to the package directions. Three minutes before the fries are finished cooking, remove them from the oven, sprinkle with the sesame seeds, toss with a spatula to coat, and return to the oven to finish cooking and to toast the sesame seeds.

Cube the salmon into bite-size pieces and place in a food processor. Pulse the processor to coarse-grind the salmon; it should take on the consistency of ground beef or turkey. Transfer the salmon to a bowl and combine with the garlic, three fourths of the ginger, the tamari, scallions, red bell peppers, sesame oil, grill seasoning, and black pepper. Form 4 large patties, 1½ inches thick. Drizzle the patties on both sides with the oil. Preheat a nonstick skillet over medium-high heat, add the salmon burgers, and cook for 5 to 6 minutes on each side for well done.

While the salmon burgers are cooking, prepare the ginger-wasabi mayo. In a bowl, combine the mayonnaise, wasabi paste, lime juice, and the remaining ginger.

Spread the ginger-wasabi mayonnaise on the buns. Top with a salmon burger and red leaf lettuce and set the bun tops in place. Serve with the sesame-crusted French fries.

tidbit >> Get your juices flowing! To get lots of juice from your lemons and limes, heat them in a microwave for 10 seconds on High before you juice them. When you are juicing lemons, remember to hold them cut side up when you squeeze them so the pits remain with the lemon and not in your recipe.

Lamb Patties with Garlic and Mint Over Mediterranean Salad

Hop on board, we're heading to the Greek Islands with these spiced-up lamb patties served over warm pita.   4 SERVINGS

¾ cup fresh **flat-leaf parsley** leaves, divided

1¾ pounds **ground lamb**

5 to 6 **garlic cloves**, chopped

1 large **shallot**, chopped

¼ cup fresh **mint** leaves (a generous handful), finely chopped

2 teaspoons to 1 tablespoon **grill seasoning**

2 teaspoons to 1 tablespoon **ground cumin** (half a palmful)

3 tablespoons **extra-virgin olive oil** (EVOO), plus some for drizzling

½ seedless **cucumber**, chopped

1 **green bell pepper**, cored, seeded, and chopped

1 small **red onion**, chopped

3 **plum tomatoes**, chopped

1 cup pitted **kalamata olives**

1 cup **feta cheese crumbles** (⅓ pound)

8 **pepperoncini peppers**, chopped

Juice of 2 lemons

Salt and **freshly ground black pepper**

4 **pita breads**, any flavor or brand, warmed in the oven or toaster oven, then cut into halves or quarters

Coarsely chop the parsley. Set aside two thirds and finely chop the rest.

Heat a grill pan or a large nonstick skillet to medium-high heat. Place the ground lamb in a bowl with the garlic, shallots, mint, finely chopped parsley, grill seasoning, cumin, and a generous drizzle of EVOO. Mix the meat and score it into 8 portions. Form 8 patties, each 3 inches across and 1 inch thick. Add the patties to the skillet. Cook for 3 minutes on each side.

While the meat cooks, combine all the vegetables with the reserved coarsely chopped parsley, the olives, cheese, and hot peppers. Dress the salad with the juice of 2 lemons and about 3 tablespoons EVOO (3 times around the bowl). Season the salad with salt and pepper. Serve the salad with 2 lamb patties on top and warm pita bread alongside.

BBQ Chicken Burgers Topped with Honey Slaw

John appreciates a really good BBQ chicken. I created this burger for him and topped it with a sweet honey slaw. He loved it!   8 SERVINGS

2 tablespoons **butter**, cut into pieces

1 medium **red onion**, ½ finely chopped, ½ thinly sliced

2 **garlic cloves**, finely chopped

3 tablespoons **tomato paste**

2 teaspoons **sugar**

2 tablespoons **Worcestershire sauce**

1 tablespoon **hot sauce**

2 pounds **ground chicken**

2 tablespoons **grill seasoning**, such as McCormick's Montreal Steak Seasoning, a couple of palmfuls

5 tablespoons **EVOO** (extra-virgin olive oil)

3 tablespoons **honey**

Juice of 1 lemon

3 rounded tablespoons **sweet pickle relish**

4 cups **shredded cabbage mix**

Salt and **black pepper**

8 cornmeal **kaiser rolls**, split

In a small skillet, melt the butter over medium heat. Add the chopped onions, garlic, and tomato paste and sweat them for 5 minutes to soften and sweeten. Sprinkle the mixture with the sugar and transfer to a bowl to cool for 5 minutes. Add the Worcestershire and hot sauce and combine. Add the chicken and grill seasoning and combine well to distribute the flavors evenly. Form the mixture into 8 patties. Wash up.

Heat 1 tablespoon of the EVOO, 1 time around the pan, in a nonstick skillet over medium-high heat. Cook the patties 4 at a time, for 5 minutes on each side.

Combine the honey, lemon juice, and the remaining 4 tablespoons of EVOO in a bowl. Add the relish, cabbage mix, and sliced onions and season with salt and pepper. Toss the slaw to coat.

Serve the burgers on the buns topped with some of the slaw.

Open-Face Blue Moon Burgers with 'Shrooms

Here's another one of my great burgers. This one comes out looking so impressive.   4 SERVINGS

2 pounds **ground sirloin**

1 tablespoon **Worcestershire sauce**

1 **shallot**, finely chopped

Salt and **black pepper**

2 tablespoons **EVOO** (extra-virgin olive oil), plus some for drizzling

2 tablespoons **butter**

½ pound **button mushrooms**, trimmed and thinly sliced

½ pound **cremini mushrooms**, trimmed and thinly sliced

½ small **onion**, finely chopped

2 large **garlic cloves**, chopped

½ cup **chicken stock**

¼ cup fresh **flat-leaf parsley**, chopped, a generous handful

4 thick slices country-style **crusty bread**

10 fresh **basil leaves**, about ½ cup

1 small bunch **arugula**, washed and thick stems removed

1 **red beefsteak tomato**, cut into 4 thick slices

1 **yellow beefsteak tomato**, cut into 4 thick slices

4 ounces good-quality **blue cheese**, crumbled

In a mixing bowl, combine the ground sirloin, Worcestershire sauce, and chopped shallot. Mix thoroughly. Score the meat with your hand, marking 4 equal portions. Form each portion into a large 1-inch-thick patty. Preheat a nonstick skillet over medium-high heat. Season the patties liberally with some salt and pepper and then drizzle the patties with a little EVOO and place in the hot skillet. Cook for 5 to 6 minutes per side, or until the patties are firm to the touch and cooked through.

Preheat the broiler.

While the burgers are cooking, preheat a second large skillet over medium-high heat with the 2 tablespoons of EVOO, twice around the pan, and the butter. Add the mushrooms to the skillet and spread them out in an even layer, resisting the temptation to stir for a few minutes to let the mushrooms start to brown. Once brown, go ahead and stir, continuing to cook for 2 minutes, then add the onions and garlic and season with salt and pepper. Continue to cook, stirring every now and then, for about 3 minutes, or until the onions start to look tender. Add the chicken stock, bring it up to a bubble, and simmer for about 2 minutes. Add the parsley and stir to combine; taste and adjust the seasoning with salt and pepper.

While the burgers and the mushrooms are working, toast the bread slices under the broiler until they are golden on both sides.

Coarsely chop the basil and arugula.

Place a piece of toast on each serving plate. Top each piece of toast with 1 slice of red tomato and 1 slice of yellow tomato and season the tomatoes with a little salt and pepper. Sprinkle the tomatoes with the arugula-basil mixture and put a cooked burger on top of that. Add the blue cheese crumbles to the mushrooms, stir to combine, and top each burger with the mushroom–blue cheese mixture. Grab a fork and a knife and dig in.

Super Tuscan Burgers and Potato Salad with Capers and Celery

Now, I don't know if this is one of John's faves because he gets to drink a big glass of Tuscan wine, or because he actually likes the burger. Either way, this is a tasty one!   4 SERVINGS

4 large Idaho **potatoes**

Coarse salt

¾ pound **ground pork**

¾ pound **ground veal**

½ cup **dry Italian red wine**

¼ medium **yellow onion**, finely chopped

3 tablespoons chopped fresh **sage** leaves (from 5 or 6 sprigs)

4 **garlic cloves**, chopped

Coarse black pepper

4 to 5 tablespoons **extra-virgin olive oil** (EVOO)

½ pound **cremini (baby portobello) mushrooms**, sliced

4 **crusty rolls**, split

8 ounces Italian **sheep's-milk cheese**, sliced

1 cup **arugula** leaves, trimmed of stems

3 tablespoons **capers**

4 **celery ribs** and their greens, from the heart of the stalk, chopped

½ medium **red onion**, finely chopped

Zest and juice of 1 lemon

2 tablespoons **red wine vinegar**

Bring a medium pot of water to a boil while you peel and dice the potatoes. Add the potatoes to the boiling water and salt the water liberally. Boil the potatoes until tender, 12 to 15 minutes.

While the potatoes cook, prepare the burgers. Combine the pork and veal in a bowl with ¼ cup of the red wine (eyeball it), the yellow onions, sage, and garlic; and salt and pepper to taste. Form 4 large patties.

Preheat a large nonstick skillet over medium-high heat. Add a tablespoon of the EVOO, once around the pan, and set the burgers into the skillet, leaving a space in the center of the pan to pile in the mushrooms. Add the sliced mushrooms to the skillet with the burgers. Flip the burgers after 6 minutes and toss the mushrooms around as they brown at the center of the skillet. After the mushrooms begin to brown, season them with salt and pepper. (The color will be deeper and the mushrooms will remain firmer if you wait for them to brown before salting.) Cook the burgers for 5 minutes on the second side, then remove them from the pan and place them onto the bottom halves of the rolls and arrange on a serving plate. Place the sliced cheese on the burgers, then spoon the hot mushrooms over the cheese. Cover the plate loosely with foil to slightly melt the cheese. Add the remaining ¼ cup of wine to the skillet and loosen the pan drippings. Dip the top halves of the rolls into the pan drippings to soak them up. Pile arugula on each burger, then set the top halves in place.

When the potatoes are cooked, drain them and return them to the warm pot to dry them out. Take the pot over to your cutting board and add the capers, celery, red onions, lemon zest and juice, red wine vinegar, and 3 or 4 tablespoons of the EVOO to the pot. Toss to combine the salad, then season the salad with salt and pepper. Transfer the salad to a serving dish. The potato salad can be served warm or cold.

BLT Turkey Burger Clubs

Gotta love a good burger. All the flavors of a Turkey BLT, in the form of a burger.　2 SERVINGS

2 tablespoons **EVOO** (extra-virgin olive oil), plus some for drizzling

5 slices **smoky bacon**

1 small **leek**

¾ pound **ground turkey breast**

1 tablespoon **grill seasoning**, such as McCormick's Montreal Steak Seasoning

6 to 8 soft **sun-dried tomatoes**, chopped (available in pouches or bulk bins in the produce department)

1 **vine-ripe tomato**, thinly sliced

Salt

6 slices **white sandwich bread**

½ cup **herbed cheese** such as Alouette or Boursin

¼ cup **cream** or half-and-half

Black pepper

4 leaves **green leaf or Bibb lettuce**

Heat a medium nonstick skillet with a drizzle of EVOO over medium to medium-high heat. Chop one slice of the bacon and add it to the pan. While the bacon cooks, trim the tough green tops from the leek, halve the leek lengthwise, and thinly slice it into half-moons. Place the slices in a colander and rinse vigorously with running water, separating the layers to release the grit. Dry the leeks on a clean kitchen towel and add them to the browned chopped bacon. Wilt the leeks for 2 or 3 minutes, then transfer them and the bacon pieces to a plate to cool. Return the skillet to the stove over low heat and add the 2 tablespoons of EVOO.

Place the turkey in a bowl and add the grill seasoning, sun-dried tomatoes, and cooled-to-handle leeks and bacon. Mix the meat and other ingredients, then form 2 very large patties no thicker than 1 inch. The patties will hang just off the sides of the bread once cooked.

Raise the heat under the EVOO and add the burgers. Cook them for 6 minutes on each side.

Preheat the broiler.

Heat a second skillet over medium-high heat and add the remaining 4 slices of bacon. Cook the bacon until it is crisp and transfer it to a paper-towel-lined plate to drain. (Don't pour the fat down the drain; it'll cause a clog. Cool the fat and discard it in the garbage.)

Season the sliced tomatoes with salt.

Place the sliced bread under the broiler and toast for 1 minute on each side.

In a blender or food processor, combine the herbed cheese, cream or half-and-half, and pepper.

Assemble the clubs: bread, burger, herbed-cheese sauce, bread, bacon, lettuce, tomatoes, herbed-cheese sauce, and bread.

Gyro Burgers with Greek Salad

John loves a great big gyro on pita. I made this burger for him with all of the flavors of that sandwich—I think I passed the test.

4 SERVINGS, 2 SMALL BURGERS EACH

1½ pounds **ground chicken** or ground lamb

1 cup full-fat plain **yogurt**

A handful of fresh **flat-leaf parsley**, chopped

2 **garlic cloves**, finely chopped

1 tablespoon **ground cumin** (a palmful)

1½ teaspoons **dried oregano** (half a palmful)

1½ teaspoons **sweet paprika** (half a palmful)

1 tablespoon **grill seasoning** (such as McCormick's Montreal Steak Seasoning; a palmful)

Extra-virgin olive oil (EVOO) for drizzling, plus about 3 tablespoons for dressing

1 **English (seedless) cucumber**, diced into bite-size pieces

1 **red or green bell pepper**, cored, seeded, and diced into bite-size pieces

4 **celery ribs** with leafy greens intact, chopped

½ large **red onion**, chopped

2 vine-ripe **tomatoes**, seeded and diced

½ pound **feta**, crumbled

½ cup pitted **kalamata olives**, coarsely chopped

6 **pepperoncini** (pickled hot, light green peppers), chopped

Juice of 2 lemons

Several drops of **hot sauce**, such as Tabasco

Coarse salt

Pita bread, warmed and cut in half

Preheat a grill pan, large nonstick skillet, or outdoor grill to medium-high heat.

In a large bowl combine the ground meat with the yogurt, parsley, garlic, spices, and seasonings. Form 8 thin 3-inch patties. Drizzle the patties with EVOO and cook for 3 minutes on each side in 2 batches. Hold the cooked patties on a plate under foil.

In a large, shallow serving bowl combine the cucumber, bell pepper, celery, red onion, tomatoes, feta, olives, and pepperoncini. Dress the salad with lemon juice, hot sauce, and salt. Toss, add about 3 tablespoons EVOO, and toss again. Taste to adjust seasonings. Top the salad with the patties and serve with pita bread.

Beef and Chicken Fajita Burgers with Seared Peppers

Have one of each! Serve with spicy refried beans.

4 SERVINGS, 1 BEEF AND 1 CHICKEN BURGER PER PERSON

BEEF FAJITA BURGERS

1⅓ pounds **ground sirloin**

2 tablespoons **Worcestershire sauce**

1 tablespoon **chili powder**

1½ teaspoons **ground cumin**

2 to 3 tablespoons fresh **thyme** leaves (from several sprigs)

Several drops of **hot sauce**

1 tablespoon **grill seasoning**, such as McCormick's Montreal Steak Seasoning

Extra-virgin olive oil (EVOO), for drizzling

CHICKEN FAJITA BURGERS

1⅓ pounds **ground chicken**

1 tablespoon **ground chipotle powder**

2 to 3 tablespoons chopped fresh **cilantro**

Several drops of **hot sauce**

1 tablespoon **grill seasoning**, such as McCormick's Montreal Steak Seasoning

EVOO, for drizzling

SEARED PEPPERS AND ONIONS

1 tablespoon **EVOO**

2 **red** and/or **green bell peppers**, cored, seeded, and thinly sliced lengthwise

1 medium **yellow onion**, thinly sliced lengthwise

2 **garlic cloves**, smashed out of the skin and chopped

1 **jalapeño** or **serrano pepper**, seeded and chopped

2 cups prepared **tomatillo salsa** or chipotle-tomato salsa

8 **crusty rolls**, split

Heat a grill pan or large skillet over medium-high heat.

For the beef fajita burgers: In a large bowl, combine the ground meat, Worcestershire, chili powder, cumin, thyme, hot sauce, and grill seasoning. Divide the mixture into 4 portions and make 4 patties, 1 inch thick. Drizzle with EVOO. Cook the patties for 4 minutes on each side for medium, or until desired doneness.

For the chicken fajita burgers: In a large bowl, combine the ground chicken, chipotle powder, cilantro, hot sauce, and grill seasoning. Divide the meat into 4 portions and form 4 big patties, 1 inch thick. Drizzle the patties with EVOO and cook for 6 minutes on each side, or until the burgers are firm and cooked through.

To make the peppers and onions, heat a medium skillet over high heat. Add EVOO and the bell peppers and onions. Stir-fry the veggies, tossing them with tongs, to sear them at the edges. Add the garlic and jalapeños. Toss and turn the mixture for about 3 minutes, then add the salsa and toss for a minute longer. Place the burgers on each bun bottom and top with ⅛ of the pepper and onion mixture and bun top.

Ricotta-Smothered Mushroom "Burgers" with Prosciutto

Portobellos take the place of the meat on these hearty "burgers."

4 SERVINGS

¼ cup **balsamic vinegar**

4 tablespoons **extra-virgin olive oil (EVOO)**

Salt and freshly ground black pepper

4 large **portobello mushroom caps**

1 large **red onion**, thinly sliced

2 large **garlic cloves**, chopped

1 rounded tablespoon **tomato paste**

1½ cups whole-milk **ricotta cheese**

3 tablespoons store-bought **pesto sauce**

½ cup **chicken stock** or broth

⅓ cup (a couple of handfuls) pitted **kalamata olives**, chopped

4 crusty **kaiser rolls**, split in half, toasted or not—it's up to you

8 thin slices **prosciutto di Parma** (optional)

1 small bunch of **arugula**, washed and trimmed of any thick stems

Preheat the oven to 450°F.

In a shallow bowl, combine the balsamic vinegar, about 2 tablespoons of the EVOO, salt, and pepper. Add the portobello mushrooms and toss to coat. Arrange the mushrooms on a cookie sheet, gill side up. Roast the mushrooms for 12 minutes or until tender and cooked through. While the mushrooms are roasting, prepare the caramelized onion topping.

Heat a medium skillet over medium-high heat with the remaining 2 tablespoons of EVOO. Add the sliced red onions, garlic, tomato paste, salt, and pepper. Cook the onions, stirring frequently, for about 8 minutes, or until nice and brown. While the onions are caramelizing, prepare the ricotta cheese topping for the mushrooms.

In a bowl, thoroughly combine the ricotta cheese and the pesto. Once the mushrooms have roasted for 12 minutes, remove them from the oven and divide the ricotta mixture evenly among the 4 mushrooms, spreading it onto the gill side of the mushrooms with the back of a spoon. Return to the oven for about a minute, just to heat the cheese.

Add the chicken stock and chopped olives to the onions. Turn the heat to high and continue to cook until the stock has reduced almost completely.

Arrange one cheese-topped mushroom on the bottom of each split roll. Top the cheese with some of the caramelized onions. Top that with 2 slices of prosciutto and some arugula. Finish it off with a roll top. Eat and enjoy!

Bacon Bit Burgers with Smoked Gouda and Onions

Bacon—what's not to like? It's smoky flavored salt and fat! Yum-o! In fact, the only way to improve on bacon is to wrap it up with beef and top it with cheese, then open wide! You gotta be more hungry than tired for this one!   4 SERVINGS

6 **smoky bacon slices,** chopped into ½-inch pieces

6 tablespoons **EVOO** (extra-virgin olive oil), plus more for for drizzling

2 **yellow onions,** ¼ finely chopped, 1¾ thinly sliced

1½ pounds **ground sirloin**

2 teaspoons **Worcestershire sauce**

1 teaspoon **hot sauce,** eyeball it

1 heaping tablespoon **grill seasoning,** such as McCormick's Montreal Steak Seasoning (a rounded palmful)

4 crusty **kaiser rolls,** poppy seed or plain, split

4 slices **smoked Gouda**

¼ cup plus 1 tablespoon **steak sauce,** such as A1 or Lea and Perrins

1 tablespoon **balsamic vinegar**

1 sack washed **baby spinach leaves**

Salt and **black pepper**

Preheat the broiler and place a medium nonstick skillet over medium-high heat.

Add the bacon and a drizzle of EVOO to the hot skillet and cook until crisp, 4 to 5 minutes. Transfer the bacon to a paper towel–lined plate and drain off all but 1 tablespoon or so of the fat from the skillet. Return the pan to medium-low heat and add the finely chopped onions to sweat out in the remaining fat, 2 to 3 minutes.

Preheat a second medium nonstick skillet with 2 tablespoons of the EVOO, 2 times around the pan, over medium heat. When the oil is hot, add all the thinly sliced onions and top them with a plate that can fit inside the skillet. Top the plate with a heavy can and smother the onions for 10 minutes, stirring occasionally. Lift the plate with tongs; it'll be hot!

Place the beef in a bowl and top with the Worcestershire, hot sauce, and grill seasoning.

Remove the chopped onions to the plate with the bacon to cool. Turn off the heat and reserve the pan. Once the onions are cool, add them and the bacon to the ground sirloin and combine well. Score the meat into 4 even sections and form 4 large patties. Add 1 tablespoon of EVOO to the skillet and reheat it over medium-high heat. Add the burgers and cook for 4 minutes on each side for medium rare, 6 minutes on each side for medium well.

Toast the split rolls under the hot broiler until golden. Place the burgers on the bun bottoms and top with the smoked Gouda. Remove the bun tops from the broiler pan. Return the burgers to the broiler just to melt the cheese, about 30 seconds.

Stir ¼ cup of the steak sauce into the smothered onions. Top the burgers with the onions and set the bun tops in place.

Place the remaining tablespoon of steak sauce in a small salad bowl. Add about 1 tablespoon of balsamic vinegar and whisk in about 3 tablespoons of EVOO. Toss with the spinach, season with salt and pepper, and serve alongside the burgers.

Cubano Pork Burgers and Sweet Orange Warm Slaw

Cubanos are traditionally served on a sweet roll. The orange juice and honey are used to hit that sweet note here.   4 SERVINGS

1¾ pounds **ground pork**

4 **garlic cloves**, chopped

Zest and juice of 2 navel oranges

1 tablespoon **ground cumin**

1½ teaspoons **coriander**

3 tablespoons **yellow mustard**, such as French's brand

Several drops of **hot sauce**, such as Tabasco

Salt and **freshly ground black pepper**

¼ cup **vegetable oil**

12 **pickle slices**, dill, garlic, or sour

4 deli slices **baked or boiled ham**

4 deli slices **Swiss cheese**

1 small **red onion**, thinly sliced

¼ cup **red wine vinegar**

1 tablespoon **honey** (a good drizzle)

1 16-ounce sack of **coleslaw mix** (found on the produce aisle)

1 small **red bell pepper**, seeded and thinly sliced

A handful of fresh **cilantro leaves**, chopped

A handful of fresh **flat-leaf parsley** leaves, chopped

4 **Portuguese rolls**, split

In a bowl combine the ground pork, half of the chopped garlic, half of the orange zest, the cumin, coriander, mustard, hot sauce, salt, and pepper. Score the meat into 4 sections and then form 4 large patties about 1 inch thick.

Preheat a medium skillet with 2 tablespoons of the vegetable oil (twice around the pan), over medium-high heat. Add the patties to the hot skillet and cook on the first side for 6 minutes. Flip and top each patty with three pickles, a slice of ham, and a slice of Swiss. Cook the patties for another 5 to 6 minutes. Place a foil tent over the pan for the last 2 minutes or so to ensure that the cheese melts and the fixings heat up.

While the patties are cooking, make the sweet orange warm slaw. Preheat a large skillet with the remaining vegetable oil. Add the remaining garlic and the sliced onion to the hot oil and cook for 1 minute. Add the remaining orange zest, the orange juice, red wine vinegar, and honey. Continue cooking the dressing for 1 minute. Turn the heat off and add the coleslaw mix, red bell pepper, cilantro, parsley, and salt and pepper, tossing to coat in the warm dressing.

Serve your Cubano burgers on Portuguese rolls with the sweet orange warm slaw both on top of the burger and alongside.

Jambalaya Burgers and Cajun Corn and Red Beans

Y'all are gonna love this New Orleans—inspired burger.   4 SERVINGS

---

1 package (1⅓ pounds) **ground chicken** or ground turkey breast

½ pound **Cajun andouille sausage**, casing removed, diced

3 **celery ribs** and their greens, finely chopped

1 **green bell pepper**, cored, seeded, and finely chopped

1 small **onion**, finely chopped

4 **garlic cloves**, finely chopped

3 tablespoons fresh **thyme** (5 or 6 sprigs), chopped

2 tablespoons **hot sauce**, such as Tabasco

Salt and **freshly ground black pepper**

4 tablespoons **extra-virgin olive oil** (EVOO), plus more for drizzling

Kernels cut from 3 ears of fresh **corn**, or 1 10-ounce box frozen corn kernels, defrosted

4 **scallions**, chopped

1 15-ounce can **red beans**, drained

1 cup **chili sauce**, divided

½ cup **mayonnaise**

¼ cup **grainy mustard**

4 jumbo **shrimp**, peeled, deveined, and butterflied (cut almost all the way through)

1 tablespoon **Old Bay Seasoning**, at the seafood counter or on the spice aisle

4 **crusty rolls**, split

4 **green leaf lettuce** leaves

1 large **beefsteak tomato**, sliced

Preheat a grill pan or large nonstick skillet over medium-high heat.

Place the chicken or turkey in a bowl. Add the sausage, half the chopped celery, half the chopped green bell peppers, the onions, half the garlic, the thyme, hot sauce, salt, pepper, and about 2 tablespoons of the EVOO. Combine the mixture and form 4 patties. Grill for 5 minutes on each side.

Heat a skillet over medium-high heat. Add 2 tablespoons of the EVOO, the remaining bell peppers, remaining garlic, and the corn kernels, and season with salt and pepper. Cook the corn and peppers, stirring frequently, for 3 or 4 minutes, then add the scallions and red beans to the pan and heat through, 2 or 3 minutes. Add ½ cup of the chili sauce and cook for 1 minute. Turn off the heat and let stand.

Combine the remaining chili sauce with the remaining celery, the mayo, and the mustard and reserve.

Coat the shrimp with a little EVOO and the Old Bay Seasoning, salt, and pepper. Grill alongside the burgers, pressing down with a small heavy skillet to prevent the shrimp from curling. Cook for 2 minutes on each side.

Place the roll bottoms on plates and top with burgers, shrimp, lettuce, and tomato slices. Slather the bun tops with chili-mayo-mustard sauce and set in place. Serve the Cajun corn and beans alongside.

Bacon and Creamy Ranch Chicken Burgers with Scallion "Sticks"

Wow! Is this one a looker!   4 SERVINGS

8 **bacon slices**

1½ pounds **ground chicken breast**

2 **garlic cloves**, finely chopped

½ small **onion**, grated

¼ cup fresh **flat-leaf parsley**, a generous handful, chopped

¼ pound **dill havarti cheese**, cut into ¼-inch dice (see Tidbit)

2 teaspoons **poultry seasoning**, ⅔ palmful

2 **lemons**

Salt and **black pepper**

Vegetable oil, for frying and for drizzling

2 cups **buttermilk**

1 teaspoon **paprika**, ⅓ palmful

All-purpose flour, for dredging

16 to 18 **scallions**, trimmed of roots

4 sandwich-size **English muffins**, split

Creamy ranch dressing, for slathering toasted muffins

1 **beefsteak tomato**, cut into 8 slices

Cook the bacon in a large nonstick skillet over medium-high heat until it is crisp.

While the bacon cooks, in a large bowl combine the ground chicken, garlic, onion, parsley, dill havarti chunks, poultry seasoning, the zest and juice of ½ lemon, salt, and pepper. Divide the mixture into 4 equal mounds, then form the meat into large, thin patties, about 1 inch thick. Drizzle them with vegetable oil to coat.

Remove the crispy bacon from the skillet to a paper-towel-lined plate and reserve. Wipe the excess grease from the skillet and return it to the cooktop over medium-high heat; add the burgers to the skillet, and cook them for 5 to 6 minutes on each side, or until they are cooked through.

While the burgers are cooking, put together the scallion "sticks." Heat 1½ inches of the vegetable oil in a deep-sided skillet over medium heat. In a wide mixing bowl, combine the buttermilk, paprika, and the zest of the remaining 1½ lemons. Place the flour in a second wide mixing bowl. Before you go at it, take one of the scallions and hold it up next to the skillet containing the heating oil. If needed, trim off some of the green tops to allow it to fit in the skillet easily.

Line a plate with a few paper towels and set it near the stovetop. Add a 1-inch cube of bread to the hot oil. If it turns deep golden brown in color after a count of 40, the oil is ready. If the bread cube browns too quickly, turn down the heat and wait a few minutes for it to cool.

Working in 2 to 3 batches, dip some of the scallions in the buttermilk, then into the flour, coating thoroughly. Put them back into the buttermilk and then into the flour again. Fry the coated scallions in the hot oil for about 1 minute on each side, or until golden brown. Transfer to the paper-towel-lined plate and immediately season them with a little salt. Repeat the process until all the scallion "sticks" are fried up.

Toast the English muffins and slather both sides with the ranch dressing. Arrange the cooked Ranch burgers on the English muffin bottoms, top each burger with 2 slices of the crispy bacon and 2 slices of tomato, and finish them with the English muffin tops. Serve them alongside the crispy scallion "sticks."

tidbit >> The colder the cheese, the easier it is to dice. Pop it in the freezer while you prep everything else and you will find that dicing it will be a breeze.

Cheddar-Studded Chili Turkey Burgers with Cilantro Cream

Being the burger queen that I am, I think I hit the nail on the head with this Cheddar-studded burger.　4 SERVINGS

1⅓ pounds **ground turkey breast** (the average weight of 1 package)

1 medium **red onion**, half finely chopped, half diced

¼ pound **sharp Cheddar cheese**, cut into ¼-inch dice

1 rounded tablespoon **chili powder**

2 teaspoons **ground cumin**

1 **jalapeño or serrano pepper**, seeded and finely chopped

2 **garlic cloves**, chopped

Salt and **freshly ground black pepper**

3 tablespoons **extra-virgin olive oil** (EVOO), plus some for drizzling

½ cup **sour cream**

A handful of fresh **cilantro leaves**, chopped

½ head **iceberg lettuce**, chopped

1 ripe **mango**, peeled and diced

1 small **red bell pepper**, cored, seeded, and cut into thin strips

1 ripe **Hass avocado**

2 **limes**

4 **corn** toaster cakes, any brand, toasted

Preheat a large nonstick skillet, indoor grill pan, or table-top grill to medium-high heat.

In a medium bowl combine the ground turkey, the finely chopped onion, the Cheddar, chili powder, cumin, jalapeño, garlic, salt, and pepper. Form the meat into 4 large patties no more than 1 inch thick. Drizzle EVOO on the patties and place them in the hot skillet or on the hot grill. Cook for 5 to 6 minutes on each side, or until the turkey is cooked through.

While the burgers are cooking, prepare the rest of the meal. For the cilantro cream, in a small bowl combine the sour cream, chopped cilantro, and salt and pepper to taste.

Next, in a salad bowl combine the chopped iceberg, mango, red bell pepper, and the diced onion. Cut the avocado in half lengthwise and remove the pit, then scoop the flesh out in one piece from both halves. Chop the avocado into bite-size pieces and add them to the salad. Squeeze the juice of 2 limes over the salad and drizzle with about 3 tablespoons of EVOO, season with salt and pepper, and toss to coat.

Serve the Cheddar-studded turkey burgers topped with a little of the cilantro cream on toaster cakes and a mound of the iceberg salad alongside.

Chicken Kiev Burgers and Russian-Style Slaw Salad

The herbed butter in the center of the burger adds great flavor and tons of moisture and is a good-time, exploding centerpiece to this fast and simple meal.   4 SERVINGS

¼ cup fresh **flat-leaf parsley**, chopped

2 tablespoons chopped fresh **chives**

1 tablespoon fresh **thyme leaves**, chopped (a few sprigs, stripped)

4 tablespoon-size tabs of cold **butter** (½ stick cut in 4 thick slices)

2 pounds **ground chicken**

3 tablespoons **Worcestershire sauce**

3 tablespoons **Dijon mustard**, divided

Salt and **freshly ground black pepper**

Extra-virgin olive oil (EVOO), for drizzling

4 rounded tablespoons **sour cream**

Juice of 1 lemon

4 to 5 tablespoons chopped **fresh dill**

1 tablespoon **prepared horseradish**

8 **radishes**, sliced

½ small **red onion**, thinly sliced

2 cups **shredded carrots**

1 **English (seedless) cucumber** (the one wrapped in plastic), cut in half lengthwise, then thinly sliced into half-moons

3 **celery ribs**, thinly sliced

2 cups **coleslaw mix**

4 slices of **rye bread** or marble rye, toasted

Preheat a large nonstick skillet, indoor grill pan, or tabletop grill to medium-high heat.

On your cutting board, combine 2 tablespoons of the chopped parsley, the chopped chives, and the chopped thyme. Dip the tabs of cold butter into the herbs one at a time, pressing the herbs into the butter to coat them completely.

In a medium bowl combine the ground chicken, Worcestershire sauce, 2 tablespoons of the mustard, salt, and pepper. Form the mixture into 4 large patties no more than 1 inch thick. Nest 1 herb-coated cold butter tab into the center of each patty and gently form the patty around the butter. Drizzle EVOO over the patties and place them in the hot skillet or on the hot grill. Cook for 5 to 6 minutes on each side.

While the burgers are cooking, in a mixing bowl thoroughly combine the sour cream, lemon juice, dill, horseradish, and the remaining tablespoon of mustard. Add the radishes, red onion, carrots, cucumber, celery, coleslaw mix, the remaining 2 tablespoons of chopped parsley, and salt and pepper to taste. Toss to combine. Serve the burgers open-faced on a slice of toast with the salad alongside.

Hungry-Man Bloody-Mary Burgers and Spicy Broccoli

A friend recommended that I add a little fresh dill and lime juice to my regular Bloody Mary concoction. I gave it a shot and it was great! The dill and lime punched up all the flavors without taking them over. I've applied that trick to these burgers.   4 SERVINGS

¼ cup **EVOO** (extra-virgin olive oil), plus some for drizzling

4 to 5 **garlic cloves**, finely chopped

1 tablespoon **chili powder**

Salt and **black pepper**

1 large head **broccoli**, cut into thin, long spears

2 **celery ribs**, finely chopped

½ pint **grape tomatoes**, halved

3 to 4 sprigs **fresh dill**, chopped

¼ cup fresh **flat-leaf parsley**, a generous handful, chopped

Juice of 1 lime

3 tablespoons **mayonnaise**

2 pounds **ground sirloin**

2 tablespoons **prepared horseradish**

1½ teaspoons **celery salt**

2 tablespoons **Worcestershire sauce**

2 teaspoons **hot sauce**

4 sandwich-size **English muffins**

Preheat the oven to 425°F.

Place the ¼ cup of EVOO, the garlic, chili powder, and a little salt and pepper in the bottom of a large bowl and add the broccoli spears. Toss to coat the broccoli evenly, then transfer to a large nonstick baking sheet. Roast the broccoli until the ends are crisp and brown and the stalks are tender, 17 to 20 minutes.

To make the burger topping, in a bowl combine the chopped celery and the grape tomato halves with the dill, parsley, lime juice, and mayonnaise. Use the back of a fork to smash up the tomatoes while you incorporate them into the sauce.

In a mixing bowl, combine the ground sirloin, horseradish, celery salt, Worcestershire sauce, hot sauce, and a little pepper. Mix thoroughly. Score the meat with your hand marking 4 equal portions. Form each portion into a large, 1-inch-thick patty. Preheat a nonstick skillet over medium-high heat. Drizzle EVOO over the patties and place them into the hot skillet. Cook for 5 to 6 minutes per side, until the patties become firm to the touch and are cooked through.

While the burgers are cooking, toast the English muffins. Remove the burgers to the bottoms of the toasted English muffins, add some of the celery-tomato topping, and then cover with the muffin tops. Serve the spicy garlic broccoli alongside.

Bacon-Wrapped Meatloaf Patties with Smashed Potatoes

Serve this with steamed broccoli or asparagus.   4 SERVINGS

2 pounds small **red-skinned potatoes**, quartered

1½ pounds **ground sirloin** (90-percent lean ground beef)

¼ cup **plain bread crumbs**

½ cup **milk**, plus a splash

1 **egg**

2 teaspoons **grill seasoning**, such as McCormick's Montreal Steak Seasoning, or coarse salt and black pepper combined

½ teaspoon **ground allspice**

1 rounded tablespoon **tomato paste**

1 medium **onion**, finely chopped (reserve one fourth)

8 slices **bacon**

2 tablespoons **extra-virgin olive oil** (EVOO)

3 tablespoons **unsalted butter**

2 rounded tablespoons **sour cream**

Salt and **freshly ground black pepper**

2 **plum tomatoes**, seeded and chopped

2 tablespoons all-purpose **flour**

1 to 1½ cups **chicken stock** or broth

1 rounded teaspoon **spicy brown mustard**

1 tablespoon **Worcestershire sauce**

¼ cup fresh **flat-leaf parsley** (a generous handful), chopped

Cover the potatoes in water in a medium saucepan. Bring the water to a boil and cook the potatoes for 10 minutes, or until fork tender.

Place the meat in a large mixing bowl and create a well in the center of the meat. Fill the well with the bread crumbs and dampen them with a splash of milk. Add the egg, grill seasoning, allspice, tomato paste, and three quarters of the onions to the bowl. Combine the mixture and form into 4 large ¾-inch-thick oval patties. Arrange 2 slices of bacon in an X on a cutting board; repeat with the other 6 slices of bacon so that you have a total of 4 X's. Place a meatloaf patty on the center of each X. Fold the bacon around each patty. Preheat a large nonstick skillet over medium-high heat with the EVOO. Transfer the bacon-wrapped patties, bacon seam side down, to the hot skillet. Fry the meatloaf patties for 7 minutes on each side under a loose aluminum-foil tent. The tent will reflect heat and allow steam to escape the pan.

Check on the potatoes. When they are tender, turn the heat off; drain the potatoes and return them to the hot pan and warm stovetop to dry them out. Add 2 tablespoons of the butter, the sour cream, and the ½ cup of milk to the potatoes and smash to the desired consistency. Season the potatoes with salt and pepper, then fold in the chopped

recipe continued

plum tomatoes. Cover the potatoes to keep warm until you are ready to serve.

Remove the meatloaf patties to a platter and return the pan to the heat. Reduce the heat to medium and add the remaining tablespoon of butter and the remaining onions to the skillet. Cook the onions for 2 minutes and sprinkle the pan with the flour. Cook the flour for 1 minute, then whisk in 1 cup of the chicken stock. Bring the broth to a bubble. If the gravy is too thick, thin with additional stock. Stir in the mustard, Worcestershire sauce, and parsley and taste to see if the sauce needs salt and pepper.

Drizzle the bacon-wrapped meatloaf patties with the gravy. Pile smashed potatoes alongside and make a well in the center for extra sour cream or gravy.

Cajun-Style Meatloaf Patties with Glazed String Beans

Mom's old-fashioned meatloaf meal gets jazzed up for this gut-busting fave.   4 SERVINGS

---

1 pound **ground sirloin** (90-percent lean ground beef)

⅓ pound **ground pork**

¼ cup **plain bread crumbs**

⅛ cup **milk** (a generous splash)

1 **egg**, lightly beaten

Salt and **freshly ground black pepper**

3 tablespoons **Worcestershire sauce**

¼ teaspoon **ground** or **freshly grated nutmeg**

1 rounded tablespoon **tomato paste**

1 **green bell pepper**, cored, seeded, and finely chopped

1 large **garlic clove**, finely chopped

5 **scallions**, white and green parts, thinly sliced

2 tablespoons **vegetable oil**

½ cup **pecan halves**, chopped

1¾ cups **chicken stock** or broth

1½ pounds **green beans**, stem ends removed

4 tablespoons **unsalted butter**

¼ cup **maple syrup**

1 small **onion**, finely chopped

¼ teaspoon **red pepper flakes**

2 tablespoons all-purpose **flour**

¼ cup **heavy cream**

¼ cup fresh **flat-leaf parsley leaves** (a generous handful), chopped

Place the meat in a large mixing bowl and create a well in the center of the meat. Fill the well with the bread crumbs and dampen them with the milk. Pour the egg over the bread crumbs and then add salt, pepper, the Worcestershire, nutmeg, tomato paste, green peppers, garlic, and scallions. Mix together and form into 4 large oval patties, ¾ inch thick. Preheat a large nonstick skillet over medium-high heat with the vegetable oil. Fry the meatloaf patties for 7 minutes on each side.

Preheat another large skillet over medium-high heat. Add the chopped pecans and toast them, stirring frequently, for about 3 minutes. Remove the toasted pecans from the pan and reserve. Return the skillet to the heat and add ¾ cup of the chicken stock; bring it up to a simmer. Add the trimmed string beans and spread out in an even layer. Cook the beans for about 3 minutes, or until almost tender. Add 2 tablespoons of the butter, the maple syrup, salt, and pepper to the skillet with the beans, turn the heat up to high, and cook until the liquid has evaporated and the beans are shiny and glazed, 2 to 3 minutes. Toss with the pecans.

Remove the meatloaf patties to a platter, tent with foil, and return the pan to the heat. Reduce the heat to

recipe continued

medium and add the remaining 2 tablespoons of butter, the onions, and the red pepper flakes. Cook for about 2 minutes and then sprinkle the onions with the flour. Cook the flour for 1 minute and then whisk in the remaining cup of chicken stock and the heavy cream. Bring the gravy to a bubble. If the gravy is too thick, thin with additional stock. Taste and season with salt and pepper. Stir in the parsley and remove the gravy from the heat.

Slice the meatloaf patties and smother with the gravy. Serve with a pile of maple pecan–glazed string beans.

Big Bird: Jumbo Chicken, Spinach, and Herb Burgers

This is a serious gut-buster!   4 SERVINGS

1 10-ounce box **frozen chopped spinach**, defrosted

2 pounds **ground chicken breast**

1 **shallot**, finely chopped

2 tablespoons **Dijon mustard**, plus some for slathering on the rolls

10 leaves of fresh **basil**, shredded or torn

3 tablespoons fresh **flat-leaf parsley** (a handful), chopped

Salt and **freshly ground black pepper**

2 tablespoons **extra-virgin olive oil** (EVOO), plus some for drizzling

20 **white button mushrooms**, thinly sliced

2 **garlic cloves**, chopped

½ cup **dry white wine** or chicken stock

4 slices **Swiss cheese**, from the deli counter

4 **kaiser rolls** or sandwich-size sourdough English muffins, split and toasted

4 **red** or **green leaf lettuce** leaves

1 vine-ripe **tomato**, thinly sliced

Preheat a large nonstick skillet over medium-high heat.

Arrange the defrosted chopped spinach in the center of a kitchen towel. Wrap the towel around the spinach and squeeze out the excess liquid. Put the spinach in a mixing bowl and combine with the chicken, shallots, 2 tablespoons of Dijon mustard, basil, parsley, salt, and pepper. Score the meat with the side of your hand to separate into 4 equal portions. Make 4 large patties, ¾ to 1 inch thick. Drizzle the patties with EVOO and place them in the hot skillet. Cook for 6 to 7 minutes on each side, until the chicken is cooked through.

Preheat a second medium-size skillet over medium-high heat with 2 tablespoons of EVOO, twice around the pan. Add the sliced mushrooms and garlic and cook, stirring occasionally, for 4 to 5 minutes, or until the mushrooms are nice and brown. Season the 'shrooms with salt and pepper. Add the wine or stock and cook until the pan is almost dry, about 2 minutes.

Top the big-bird burgers with the mushroom topping and the Swiss cheese. Fold each slice of cheese in half to fit the burger, if necessary. Cover loosely with aluminum foil. Turn off the pan and let the cheese melt, about 2 minutes.

Slather the tops of the rolls or English muffins with a little mustard. Place the burgers on the roll bottoms and top with lettuce and tomato. Put the roll or muffin tops in place.

Burly-Man-Size Chicken-Cheddar Barbecued Burgers

Serve with waffle-cut frozen fries, cooked to package directions, or fancy specialty chips.   4 SERVINGS

1 cup **mayonnaise**, plain yogurt, or prepared ranch-style dressing—your pick

1 tablespoon **hot sauce**, such as Tabasco

Juice of 1 lime

½ cup fresh **flat-leaf parsley** leaves (a couple of generous handfuls), chopped

¼ cup fresh **cilantro** leaves (a generous handful), chopped

Salt and **freshly ground black pepper**

½ small **red cabbage**, halved, cored, then thinly sliced

1 **red bell pepper**, cored, seeded, and thinly sliced

6 **scallions**, thinly sliced

2 pounds **ground chicken**

½ cup of your favorite prepared **barbecue sauce**

⅓ pound **sharp Cheddar cheese**, cut into ¼-inch dice

Extra-virgin olive oil (EVOO), for drizzling

4 **kaiser rolls**, split

For the spicy coleslaw, in a bowl combine the mayonnaise, hot sauce, lime juice, parsley, cilantro, salt, and pepper. Add the sliced cabbage, red bell peppers, and half of the scallions, stir to coat the cabbage, and reserve the spicy slaw for topping the burgers.

In a mixing bowl, combine the ground chicken, barbecue sauce, Cheddar dice, reserved scallions, salt, and pepper. Mix thoroughly. Score the meat with your hand to mark 4 equal portions. Form each portion into a 1-inch-thick patty. Preheat a nonstick skillet over medium-high heat. Drizzle EVOO over the patties and place them in the hot skillet. Cook for 5 to 6 minutes per side, or until the patties are firm to the touch and cooked through.

While the burgers are cooking, toast the kaiser rolls. Transfer the burgers to the bottoms of the toasted rolls, pile some spicy coleslaw on top, and then replace the roll tops.

Chili Dog Bacon Cheeseburgers and Fiery Fries

Serve this burger with veggie sticks or oil-and-vinegar-dressed slaw.

4 SERVINGS

8 slices center-cut or other lean, thick-cut **smoky bacon**

1 16- to 20-ounce sack **crispy-style frozen French fries**

1 pound **lean ground beef**

2 beef or pork **hot dogs**, diced

2 tablespoons **chili powder** (2 palmfuls)

1 tablespoon **grill seasoning**, such as McCormick's Montreal Steak Seasoning

2 teaspoons **Worcestershire sauce**

1 tablespoon plus 1 teaspoon **hot sauce**

2 tablespoons **ketchup**

Vegetable oil, for drizzling

4 slices deli-sliced **Cheddar cheese**

2 tablespoons **unsalted butter**

3 **garlic cloves**, finely chopped

3 tablespoons chopped **chives** (a handful)

Coarse salt, to taste

½ cup **chili sauce**

4 **kaiser rolls**, split

Preheat the broiler to high.

Place the bacon on a slotted broiler pan. Cook the bacon 10 inches from the heat for 3 to 4 minutes on each side, until crisp, and remove to a plate. Adjust the oven to bake, setting at the temperature recommended on the package of fries, and bake the fries.

While the fries cook, make the burgers. Preheat a large nonstick skillet over medium-high heat. Mix the beef with the chopped hot dogs, chili powder, grill seasoning, Worcestershire, 1 teaspoon of the hot sauce, and the ketchup. Form 4 large patties. Add a drizzle of oil, once around the skillet, and add the patties. Cook the burgers for 6 minutes on each side, then top each with 2 slices of bacon and 1 slice of Cheddar. Turn the heat off, cover the pan with a loose foil tent, and let the cheese melt for a minute or two.

When the fries are extra crisp remove them from the oven. Place the butter, the remaining tablespoon of hot sauce, and the garlic in a small dish and microwave on High for 20 seconds, then transfer the fries to a large bowl. Toss the fries with the butter mixture and chives and season with salt.

Slather chili sauce on the tops of the split kaiser rolls. Place the bacon-chili-cheeseburgers on the roll bottoms and set the tops in place. Pile fries alongside and serve.

The T2: Turkey Chili-Topped Turkey Chili Burgers

One helping is never enough at my dinner table, and that's why I decided to put two servings of turkey chili into one giant burger! With chili on the inside, and chili on the outside, you better make sure you save enough room for the spicy pepper slaw and funky fries.

4 SERVINGS

1 16- to 20-ounces sack **extra-crispy-style frozen French fries**

¼ cup **chili powder** (3 palmfuls)

2 tablespoons **ground cumin**

2 tablespoons **grill seasoning**, such as McCormick's Montreal Steak Seasoning (a palmful)

2 tablespoons **vegetable oil**

2 packages (2 to 2⅔ pounds total) **ground turkey breast**

1 medium **onion**, finely chopped

2 tablespoons **Worcestershire sauce**

1 8-ounce can **tomato sauce**

3 **red bell peppers**, ¼ of 1 pepper finely chopped, remaining peppers thinly sliced

4 **garlic cloves**, chopped

2 tablespoons **hot sauce**, such as Tabasco

6 ounces **Cheddar** or smoked Cheddar, cut into ¼-inch dice

3 tablespoons **red wine vinegar**

1 tablespoon **sugar**

2 teaspoons **coarse salt**

1 16-ounce sack shredded **red cabbage** (available in the produce department)

1 small **red onion**, thinly sliced

Coarse black pepper, to taste

3 tablespoons **unsalted butter**, cut into chunks

¼ cup finely chopped **curly parsley**

4 soft **burger rolls**

Preheat the oven to the temperature listed on the sack of fries.

Preheat a medium nonstick skillet over medium-high heat. Combine the chili powder, cumin, and grill seasoning in a small bowl. To the skillet add a tablespoon of the vegetable oil, once around the pan, and half of the turkey. Break up the turkey with the back of a wooden spoon, then season with half of the spice mixture. Combine to break up and brown the turkey for a couple of minutes, then add half of the chopped onions and cook for another couple of minutes. When the onions are translucent, add the Worcestershire sauce and tomato sauce; adjust the seasonings and simmer the chili sauce over low heat until ready to serve.

While the chili sauce is working, make the burgers. Place the remaining turkey in a bowl and add the remaining spice mixture, half of the remaining chopped onions, the finely chopped bell peppers, half the chopped garlic, and about a tablespoon of hot sauce. Mix well with your hands, then incorporate the diced cheese. Form the mixture into 4 1-inch-thick patties. Heat a second nonstick skillet over medium-high heat. Add a tablespoon of vegetable oil (once around the pan) and when hot, add the burgers. Cook the burgers for 6 minutes on each side.

When you place the burgers in the pan, the timing is right to add the fries to the preheated oven.

While everything is moving forward, throw together the slaw salad. In the bottom of a medium bowl, combine 1 tablespoon hot sauce—just eyeball it—with the vinegar, sugar, and 1 teaspoon of the salt. Add the red cabbage, red pepper strips, and red onions to the bowl and toss to combine. Season with black pepper.

On your cutting board add about a teaspoon of salt to the remaining chopped garlic and, using the flat of your knife blade, mash the garlic and salt into a paste. Scrape the paste into a small bowl with the butter and microwave on High for 20 seconds or so. Remove the fries from the oven and toss with the melted butter and the chopped parsley. Adjust seasoning to taste.

To serve, pile the chili-cheese burgers onto the buns, top with scoops of chili sauce, and a spoonful of the remaining chopped onions. Serve the burgers with piles of red pepper slaw and funky fries.

Vegetarian

Time and time again I am asked to write more vegetarian recipes. Although I am many things, a vegetarian I am not. But that's not to say I don't crave a hearty black bean chili in the winter, or a big salad in the summer. Here you'll find some of my all-time veggie faves.

COMFORT FOODS

Spinach-Artichoke Ravioli-Lasagna
Roasted Asparagus
Lemon, Garlic, and Cilantro Baked Stuffed Tomatoes
Fall Minestrone
Creamy Polenta with Veggie Ragu
Wilted Spinach with Garlic Chips
Giambotta—Eat Your Vegetables Stew
Roasted Baby Vegetables with Rosemary
Mushroom Lovers' French Bread Pizzas
Smoked Gouda Fondue with Almonds

SPICY PICKS

Indian Spiced Vegetables
Salsa Stoup and Double-Decker Baked Quesadillas
Vegetable Portobello Pizzas
Ginger Noodles
Chipotle Potato Salad
Warm Cinnamon-Chipotle Tomato Salsa
Garlicky Guacamole and Chips
Smoked Paprika O-Rings
Indian-Spiced Chickpea and Fire-Roasted Tomato Soup
Spicy Sweet Potato Pancakes with Holiday Guacamole

SAMMIES

Grilled Eggplant Roll-Ups
Grilled Cheese and Watercress Sandwiches
Tuscan Calzones with "The Works"
Roasted Portobello Burgers with Rosemary
  Garlic Oven Fries
Meatless Muffaletta Panini
Fontina, Olive, and Roasted Red Pepper Paninis
Spinach and Artichoke Calzones
Mushroom-Veggie Sloppy Sandwiches
Hummus-Topped Pit-Zas
Baked Sesame Eggplant Subs with Fire-Roasted Tomato
  and Red Pepper Sauce

Spinach-Artichoke Ravioli-Lasagna

This is a great dinner for anyone, but, if you have a friend not in need but rather in new-born, this would be a really cool gift. It takes only 30 minutes to make and it will feed the new parents for a couple of days—unless you decide to steal a portion or two for yourself before giving it away.   8 SERVINGS

2 10-ounce boxes **frozen chopped spinach**

2 tablespoons **butter**, cut into pieces

¼ cup all-purpose **flour**

1 quart **milk**

Freshly grated or ground **nutmeg**

Salt and **black pepper**

2 15-ounce cans **artichoke hearts in water**, drained and thinly sliced

4 packages **large fresh ravioli** (cheese, wild mush-room, or spinach varieties)

3 cups **ricotta cheese**

1 tablespoon **lemon zest**

4 **garlic cloves**, minced

1½ cups grated **Parmigiano-Reggiano cheese**

Bring a large covered pot of water to a boil for the pasta.

Place the oven rack in the middle of the oven and preheat the broiler. Defrost the spinach in the microwave for 6 or 7 minutes on high; check the spinach and micro-wave for another 2 or 3 minutes if not fully defrosted.

While the spinach defrosts, melt the butter in a medium sauce pot over medium heat. Whisk in the flour and cook it for a minute or two, then whisk in the milk. Bring the sauce to a bubble and, as it begins to thicken, drop the heat to low and season it with nutmeg, salt, and pepper to taste. Remove from the heat.

Wring the spinach completely dry in a kitchen towel. Open the towel and separate the clumps of spinach with your fingers. Pile up the sliced artichokes on your cutting board.

When the water comes to a boil, salt it, add the ravi-oli, and cook to al dente, 5 minutes. The ravioli will float to the top when they are close to done. Drain the ravioli.

Warm the ricotta in the microwave for 2 minutes on high. Season it with salt and pepper, the lemon zest, and garlic; cover and reserve it.

Ladle just enough of the white sauce into the bot-tom of a lasagna dish to coat it lightly. Top the sauce with one third of the ravioli. Top the pasta with half of the ricotta cheese dotted with half of the spinach and arti-chokes. Thinly cover the veggies with more white sauce, then top it liberally with grated cheese. Repeat these lay-ers, then top your lasagna with the remaining third of the cooked ravioli and the last of the white sauce and grated cheese.

Place the lasagna under the hot broiler until the sauce browns and bubbles, 3 minutes.

tidbit >> The size of the ravioli will vary a lot depending on the brand, but don't worry, the size doesn't matter, really. If you use small ravs the layers will be more pasta than cheese, and if the ravs are big it will be cheesier.

Roasted Asparagus

I'll find any excuse to add asparagus to my plate, especially in the spring!

¾ pound **asparagus**, ends trimmed (fat stems should be peeled down a bit as well)

2 tablespoons **EVOO** (extra-virgin olive oil), plus extra for liberal drizzling

Salt

Preheat the oven to 425°F. Spread the asparagus on a small baking sheet, dress it with a liberal drizzle of EVOO, and season it with salt. Roast the spears until they are tender and the ends are crisp and slightly brown at the edges, 10 to 12 minutes. The asparagus should remain bright green.

Lemon, Garlic, and Cilantro Baked Stuffed Tomatoes

This dish is great any time of year.   4 SERVINGS

2 **beefsteak tomatoes**

Salt and **freshly ground black pepper**

1 cup **whole-milk ricotta cheese**

Zest of 1 large lemon (2 tablespoons)

¼ cup fresh **cilantro leaves,** chopped

¾ cup fresh **flat-leaf parsley,** chopped

2 **garlic cloves**, chopped

2 **scallions**, finely chopped

⅓ cup grated **Parmigiano-Reggiano**

1 **egg yolk**

Extra-virgin olive oil (EVOO), for drizzling

Preheat the oven to 450°F.

For the baked stuffed tomatoes you will need to make 4 tomato cups out of your 2 tomatoes. To do so, cut a very thin slice off both ends of each of the tomatoes to create 4 flat bottoms. Then cut each tomato in half, across, making 4 tomato cups.

To create a cavity, use a melon-ball scoop to remove the seeds and guts from the wide, fleshy side of each tomato cup. You don't have to be too fussy about this. You are just trying to create enough room to hold the filling. When scooping, take some care not to rip through the bottoms of the cups. (If you do rip one, don't worry, it is not the end of the world, just keep moving forward. That tomato will just be tricky to transfer to the plate.) Season the inside of the tomato cavities with salt and pepper. Reserve the seasoned tomato cups while you make the filling.

In a small mixing bowl combine the ricotta cheese, lemon zest, cilantro, parsley, garlic, scallions, and Parmigiano cheese, then season with salt and pepper. Taste the mixture. This is your last chance to adjust the seasoning. Once you're happy with the flavor, add the egg yolk and mix thoroughly. Divide the filling among the 4 tomato cups, pushing it into the cavity with a rubber spatula or spoon. Drizzle EVOO into a baking dish. Arrange the stuffed tomatoes in the dish and bake for 15 to 17 minutes, until lightly brown and cooked through.

Fall Minestrone

More like fall-in-love-with soup.   4 SERVINGS

2 tablespoons **extra-virgin olive oil** (EVOO)

½ teaspoon **red pepper flakes**

4 **garlic cloves**, chopped

3 **portobello mushroom caps**, chopped

2 medium **onions**, chopped

2 medium **carrots**, peeled and diced

2 **celery ribs**, chopped with greens

Salt and **freshly ground black pepper**

2 stems of fresh **rosemary**

8 fresh **sage** leaves, thinly sliced

1 medium **zucchini**, diced

1 small bunch of **kale** or chard, trimmed of tough ends and veins and coarsely chopped (4 to 5 cups)

1 15-ounce can **cannellini beans**, drained

1 14-ounce can petite **diced tomatoes** or chunky-style crushed tomatoes

1 quart **vegetable stock** plus 2 cups

A piece of rind of **Parmigiano cheese**—buy a hunk that has a piece of rind attached to it, cut from the outside of the wheel

1 cup **ditalini** pasta

Grated **Parmigiano-Reggiano**, to pass at the table

Crusty bread, for mopping

Heat a medium soup pot over medium-high heat and add the EVOO. Add the red pepper flakes, garlic, mushrooms, onions, carrots, and celery. Cook for 5 to 6 minutes, until the mushrooms are lightly browned. Season with salt and pepper and add the rosemary stems and the sage to the pot. Add the zucchini and chopped greens and stir them into the pot until all the greens wilt down, 2 to 3 minutes.

Add the beans, tomatoes, stock, and cheese rind, then place a lid on the pot and bring the soup to a boil. Uncover and add the ditalini pasta. Cook the soup for 7 to 8 minutes at a rolling simmer, uncovered, until the pasta is al dente, with a bite to it. Remove the pot from the heat. Remove the rind and the now bare rosemary stems (the leaves fall off into the soup as it cooks). Adjust the salt and pepper to taste.

Ladle the soup into shallow bowls and top with grated cheese. Pass the crusty bread at the table.

tidbit >> You can now find vegetable stock in cartons on the soup aisle next to the boxes of beef and chicken broth.

Creamy Polenta with Veggie Ragù

Rarely has going veggie tasted so satisfying as with the help of creamy polenta.   6 SERVINGS

---

1 large head of **cauliflower**, about 2 pounds, cut into bite-size florets

3 tablespoons **EVOO** (extra-virgin olive oil; eyeball it), plus some for drizzling

Salt and **black pepper**

6 cups **vegetable stock**

2 cups **milk**

1 large **fennel bulb**, cored and thinly sliced

1 large **onion**, thinly sliced

4 large **garlic cloves**, chopped

2 **red bell peppers**, seeded and sliced

½ teaspoon **red pepper flakes**

½ cup **golden raisins**, 1 over-flowing handful

2 cups **quick-cooking polenta**, found in the Italian or specialty foods aisles

1 head of **escarole**, washed and coarsely chopped

2 tablespoons **butter**

½ cup grated **Parmigiano-Reggiano**, a couple of generous handfuls, plus more to pass at the table

½ cup fresh **flat-leaf parsley** leaves, 2 generous handfuls, chopped

Preheat the oven to 450°F.

Arrange the cauliflower on a rimmed baking sheet, drizzle it generously with EVOO, then season it with salt and pepper, tossing it around to make sure all of it is coated. Roast the cauliflower for 15 minutes, or until it's lightly browned and tender but still has a bit of a bite.

While the cauliflower is roasting, combine 4 cups of the vegetable stock and the milk in a sauce pot. Add salt and pepper and bring it up to a simmer, then turn the heat down until you are ready to add the polenta.

Place a large skillet over medium-high heat with the 3 tablespoons of EVOO. Add the fennel, onions, garlic, bell peppers, and red pepper flakes and season them with a little salt and black pepper. Cook, stirring frequently, for about 5 minutes, or until the veggies are approaching being tender. Add the remaining 2 cups of vegetable stock and bring it up to a simmer, then continue to cook for 4 or 5 minutes.

Add the roasted cauliflower and the raisins, toss them to combine, and continue to cook them for 3 to 4 minutes, or until the liquids have reduced by half.

Once you've added the cauliflower to the skillet, finish the polenta. Using a whisk, add the polenta to the simmering stock and milk mixture; cook, stirring constantly, for about 5 minutes. Be careful; the closest you'll probably ever come to having hot lava in your kitchen is a pot of bubbling polenta. Once the polenta is cooked, add the chopped escarole to the skillet with the cauliflower and cook it until the escarole wilts, a couple of minutes.

Add the butter and cheese to the polenta, and stir them to melt in. If the polenta thickens too much, add a little more stock or milk to loosen it up.

Add the parsley to the skillet with the cauliflower and combine. To serve, place a helping of the polenta in the bottom of 6 shallow serving dishes and top it with some of the veggie ragù. Serve it along with a little more cheese to pass at the table.

Wilted Spinach with Garlic Chips

I'm always down for another way to prepare spinach. Here, the garlic chips add a new element to your basic spinach side dish.   4 SERVINGS

¼ cup **extra-virgin olive oil** (EVOO)

4 large **garlic** cloves, carefully peeled and very thinly sliced into chips

2 pounds triple-washed **spinach**, stems removed

½ teaspoon **grated nutmeg**

Coarse salt and **coarse black pepper**

Place a large skillet on the stove and add the oil and garlic chips. Turn heat onto low and let the garlic chips fry up until golden, flipping them around from time to time, about 5 minutes. Remove the crisp garlic chips with a slotted spoon and reserve. Add the spinach to the pan, turning with tongs to wilt it all in. Season the spinach with the nutmeg, salt, and pepper. Serve immediately, garnished with the garlic chips.

Giambotta—Eat Your Vegetables Stew

You'll have your veggies for the day all in this dish.   8 SERVINGS

¼ cup **EVOO** (extra-virgin olive oil), plus some to drizzle

1 **bay leaf**, fresh or dried

6 **garlic cloves**, 2 cracked from their skins and halved, 4 thinly sliced

2 **onions**, sliced

3 large **Idaho potatoes**, peeled and chopped

1 **eggplant**, chopped

2 medium **zucchini**, chopped

1 **red bell pepper**, seeded and chopped

1 **cubanelle pepper**, seeded and chopped

Salt and **black pepper**

2 28-ounce cans **fire-roasted diced tomatoes**

2 cups **vegetable stock**

1 cup fresh **basil**, 20 leaves, torn or chopped

1 loaf **whole-grain crusty bread**, split lengthwise

1 cup grated **Pecorino Romano cheese**

Heat a large soup pot over medium-high heat. Add the ¼ cup of EVOO, the bay leaf, chopped garlic, and onions and let them sweat while you prepare the rest of the veggies. Work next to the stove and drop as you chop, in this order: potatoes, eggplant, zucchini, and peppers. Season the veggies with salt and black pepper, cover the pot, and cook for 15 minutes, stirring the stew occasionally. Uncover the pot and add the tomatoes and stock and cook for 5 minutes more, to heat through. Turn the heat off and stir in the basil.

While the stew cooks, preheat the broiler. Char the bread under the broiler and rub it with the cracked garlic, then drizzle it with EVOO. Top the bread with the cheese and return it to the broiler for 30 seconds to brown the cheese.

Serve hunks of cheesy whole-grain bread alongside bowlfuls of vegetable stew for mopping.

Roasted Baby Vegetables with Rosemary

There's nothing quite as good—or as easy—as roasted veggies. They make the perfect side dish for any meal, and the rosemary will leave your kitchen smelling heavenly.   4 SERVINGS

2½ pounds total weight of **mixed baby vegetables**, your choice: tiny **zucchini**, halved lengthwise; **pattypan squash**, halved across; **baby eggplant**, cut into 1-inch wedges lengthwise; whole **baby carrots** with tops, trimmed, peeled, and halved lengthwise; **cipollini baby onions**

5 to 6 **garlic cloves**, smashed

¼ cup **extra-virgin olive oil (EVOO)**

3 tablespoons finely chopped **fresh rosemary** (a handful of leaves)

Salt and **freshly ground black pepper**

Preheat the oven to 500°F.

Combine the veggies on a large baking sheet and toss with the garlic, EVOO, rosemary, salt, and pepper. Roast for 15 minutes. Remove from the oven. Let stand for 5 minutes, then serve.

Mushroom Lovers' French Bread Pizzas

Mushrooms are beefy and delicious. This is a great quick supper for meat-free-ers and meat eaters alike because it is so hearty.

MAKES 4 12-INCH FRENCH BREAD PIZZAS

8 large **portobello mushroom caps**

1 pound **button mushrooms,** stems trimmed

½ pound fresh **shiitake mushrooms,** stems discarded

3 tablespoons **EVOO** (extra-virgin olive oil)

2 tablespoons **butter,** cut into pieces

1 **bay leaf**

4 large **garlic cloves,** finely chopped

Salt and **black pepper**

½ cup **dry white wine,** eyeball it

1 teaspoon **red wine vinegar**

1 tablespoon chopped fresh **thyme leaves,** 4 sprigs stripped and chopped

1 24-inch loaf of **crusty French bread**

3 cups shredded **Gruyère** or **Swiss cheese**

Preheat the broiler.

Wipe the mushrooms clean with a damp towel and slice them. Heat the EVOO and butter in a deep skillet over medium heat. When the butter melts into the oil, add the bay leaf, garlic, and sliced mushrooms. Cook until the mushrooms are dark and tender, 12 to 15 minutes. Season the mushrooms with salt and pepper and add the wine, stirring the skillet with a wooden spoon to deglaze. Shake the pan and add the vinegar and thyme. Turn off the heat.

Split the loaf first lengthwise and then across. Pull out and discard a bit of the soft insides. Toast the bread lightly under the broiler then fill each section of bread evenly with mushrooms. Top liberally with the cheese. Return the bread sections to the broiler until the cheese browns and bubbles then remove the pizzas from the oven and serve.

Smoked Gouda Fondue with Almonds

Fondue aficionados, you're going to love this version with smoked gouda and almonds. 4 SERVINGS

8 ounces **Gruyère cheese**, shredded

⅓ pound (about 6 ounces) **smoked Gouda**, shredded

1 rounded tablespoon **flour**

1 large **garlic clove**, smashed out of its skin

¾ cup **dry white wine**

2 teaspoons fresh **lemon juice**

½ cup **smoked almonds** (I like Diamond brand), coarsely chopped

SERVE WITH . . .

Blanched bite-size pieces of cauliflower, white asparagus, parsnip

Cornichon pickles

Red pears, slightly underripe

Combine the cheeses in a bowl with the flour. Rub the inside of a small pot with the smashed garlic, then discard the garlic. Add the wine and lemon juice to the pot and bring up to a bubble over medium heat. Reduce the heat to simmer and add the cheese mixture in handfuls. Stir constantly in a figure-eight pattern with a wooden spoon, melting the cheese in batches. Transfer the fondue to a fondue pot and top with smoked nuts.

Indian Spiced Vegetables

This is a great spice blend to know how to make. Enjoy this healthy dish with a kick!   4 SERVINGS

SPICE BLEND

1½ teaspoons **turmeric**

1 teaspoon **ground coriander**

1 teaspoon **cumin seeds**

1 tablespoon **curry powder**

½ teaspoon **cayenne pepper**

2 pinches of **ground cinnamon**

3 large waxy **white potatoes**, peeled and diced

Coarse salt

1 head of **cauliflower**, cut into small florets

1 tablespoon **vegetable oil**, plus some for drizzling

2 tablespoons **unsalted butter**, cut into pieces

1 medium **onion**, chopped

3 **garlic cloves**, chopped

1 15-ounce can **chickpeas**, drained

1 cup **vegetable stock**

1 cup frozen **green peas**

1 small head of **iceberg lettuce**, shredded

¼ cup sliced or slivered **almonds**

4 **radishes**, thinly sliced

3 tablespoons chopped fresh **mint**

3 tablespoons chopped fresh **flat-leaf parsley** or cilantro, your choice

Juice of 1 lemon

Combine the ingredients for the spice blend and reserve.

Place the potatoes in a pot and cover them with water. Cover the pot with a lid and bring to a boil. Take off the lid and add salt. Boil the potatoes for 6 to 7 minutes, then add the cauliflower to the same pot. Cook for 2 to 3 minutes longer, then drain. The potatoes and cauliflower should still be a little undercooked.

Heat a large skillet over medium heat. Add the vegetable oil, then the butter. When the butter melts into the oil, add in the onions and garlic and sauté for 5 minutes. Add the drained potatoes and cauliflower and the chickpeas and combine. Stir the reserved spices into the vegetables and cook for a minute or two to develop the flavors. Stir in the stock and turn the vegetables to evenly distribute. The dish will turn a bright yellow. Cook over medium-low heat for 2 to 3 minutes longer. Add the peas and turn off the heat. The carry-over heat will warm them through. Taste to adjust the salt in the dish.

In a large bowl, combine the shredded lettuce with the almonds, radishes, mint, and parsley or cilantro. Dress the salad with the lemon juice, a drizzle of vegetable oil, and some salt. Pile the salad on plates, top with the hot vegetables, and serve.

Salsa Stoup and Double-Decker Baked Quesadillas

This spicy meal fills you up without filling you out!   4 SERVINGS

2 tablespoons **vegetable oil,** plus some for brushing the tortillas

2 **jalapeño peppers,** seeded and chopped

1 **green bell pepper,** cored, seeded, and chopped

1 large **onion,** chopped

3 **celery ribs,** chopped with greens

3 **garlic cloves,** chopped

Salt and **freshly ground black pepper**

1 28-ounce can **stewed tomatoes**

1 28-ounce can **crushed tomatoes**

2 cups **vegetable stock**

3 tablespoons chopped fresh **cilantro**

6 6- to 8-inch **flour tortillas**

1 cup shredded **Cheddar**

3 **scallions,** chopped

1 cup shredded **Pepper Jack**

Sour cream, for garnish

Preheat the oven to 300°F.

Heat a medium soup pot over medium-high heat. Add the vegetable oil and the jalapeños, bell peppers, onions, celery, and garlic. Season with salt and pepper, then sauté the veggies for 5 minutes. Add all the tomatoes and stock and bring to a bubble. Reduce the heat to a simmer and stir in the cilantro.

Paint one side of 2 tortillas with oil and place them, oiled side down, on a large cookie sheet. Mix the Cheddar with the scallions and divide between the tortillas evenly. Top with another tortilla and top each of those with equal amounts of Pepper Jack cheese. Set the last tortillas on top and brush the tops with oil. Bake the quesadillas for 10 minutes, then cool for 5 minutes to set. Cut each into 6 wedges.

Serve each bowl of stoup with 3 wedges of quesadilla alongside and sour cream for topping either.

Vegetable Portobello Pizzas

Mini pizzas, hold the bread, built on roasted portobellos instead!

1 SERVING, 2 MINI PIZZAS

2 large **portobello mushroom caps**, stems removed

Extra-virgin olive oil (EVOO), for drizzling

4 pieces jarred **grilled eggplant** or marinated eggplant (available on Italian food aisle), drained

1 jarred **roasted red pepper**, drained and sliced

4 water-packed **artichoke hearts**, drained and sliced

3 tablespoons chopped fresh **flat-leaf parsley** or basil

½ cup **arugula** or baby spinach

¼ cup finely chopped **onion** or shallot

Salt and **freshly ground black pepper**

4 slices deli **provolone cheese**, or ¼ pound Italian Fontina cheese, sliced

Red pepper flakes

Italian dried seasoning or dried oregano

Preheat the oven or toaster oven to 450°F. Place the mushroom caps gill side up on a baking sheet and drizzle with EVOO. Roast for 12 minutes, or until tender. Layer the caps with the grilled eggplant, sliced roasted red pepper, sliced artichokes, parsley or basil, and arugula or spinach. Drizzle the tops with a little more EVOO, and sprinkle with finely chopped onion or shallot and salt and pepper. Top the mushrooms with 2 slices provolone or fontina each in even layers, then return the pizzas to the oven. Bake for 5 minutes to set the vegetables and melt the cheese. Add a pinch of red pepper flakes and Italian dried seasoning or oregano to the top of each portobello mini pizza and transfer to a plate.

Ginger Noodles

Enjoy this version of an old favorite at home. And don't forget the fortune cookies.   8 SERVINGS

Salt

1½ pounds **perciatelli** or bucatini pasta—they boil up big!

2 tablespoons **vegetable oil**

4-inch piece of **fresh ginger**, peeled and grated

3 large **garlic cloves**, chopped

1½ cups **vegetable stock**

½ cup **tamari** (dark aged soy sauce; eyeball it)

6 **scallions**, thinly sliced

Fill your largest pot with water, cover, and bring to a boil over high heat. Once it reaches a boil, add some salt and the pasta and cook to al dente.

Once you've dropped the pasta in the boiling water, preheat a large skillet over medium heat with the oil, 2 times around the pan. Add the ginger and garlic and cook, stirring frequently, for 2 to 3 minutes. Add the stock and tamari and bring up to a simmer. Let it continue to simmer while you wait for the pasta to finish cooking. Drain the pasta thoroughly and add to the skillet. Toss to coat and continue to cook until the pasta has soaked up most of the liquid in the skillet. (If you don't think your skillet is big enough for all the pasta, then transfer the sauce to the pot you cooked the pasta in and combine and cook it in there.) Turn the heat off and add the scallions.

Chipotle Potato Salad

I love the smokiness of chipotle peppers, and I'm always looking for a new way to incorporate them into a dish. Here, they take potato salad from ordinary to extraordinary.　4 SERVINGS

4 large **Russet potatoes**, about 2½ pounds, peeled and thinly sliced

Salt

2 **chipotles in adobo**, chopped, plus 2 tablespoons of the adobo sauce

3 tablespoons **orange marmalade**

3 tablespoons **orange juice**

3 tablespoons **red wine vinegar**

3 tablespoons **EVOO** (extra-virgin olive oil)

1 small **red onion** or ½ large red onion, chopped

2 tablespoons chopped **fresh cilantro**, a handful

A couple **fresh oregano** sprigs, finely chopped, or a couple pinches of dried

Black pepper

Place the potatoes in a pot and cover them with water. Bring the water to a boil and season liberally with salt, then cook the potatoes until they are just fork tender, 8 to 9 minutes.

Combine the chipotles and adobo sauce, marmalade, orange juice, and vinegar in a bowl, then whisk in the EVOO.

Drain the potatoes well, return them to the hot pot to let the water evaporate, then add them immediately to the dressing. (The dressing will be better absorbed by warm taters.) Toss them with the onions and herbs and season the salad with salt and pepper. Serve it warm or chilled. Drizzle with a little more EVOO if the salad gets dry.

Warm Cinnamon-Chipotle Tomato Salsa

Serve this one at your next party and people will be wondering what that sweet kick in the background is. It's cinnamon, but shhh . . . it's our secret.   2 SERVINGS

1 or 2 **chipotles in adobo**, medium to extra-hot, finely chopped, plus 2 tablespoons of the adobo sauce

2 pinches ground **cinnamon**

1 15-ounce can crushed **fire-roasted tomatoes**

In a small sauce pot over medium heat, combine the chipotles, adobo sauce, cinnamon, and fire-roasted tomatoes. When the salsa bubbles, reduce the heat to low, and simmer for 2 to 3 minutes.

Transfer the salsa to a small bowl and serve with tortilla chips.

Garlicky Guacamole and Chips

Guacamole is always sure to please, and this version gets kicked up with some serious garlic action.   2 SERVINGS

1 ripe Hass **avocado**

1 small **jalapeño pepper**, seeded and finely chopped

¼ small **onion**, finely chopped

1 **garlic clove**, cracked

1 teaspoon coarse **salt**

Juice of 1 lemon

Tortilla chips, any variety

Halve the avocado and discard the pit. Scoop the flesh into a small bowl and add the jalapeños and onions. On a cutting board, chop the garlic then sprinkle it with salt. Using the side of your knife and applying pressure with the heel of your hand, mash the garlic and salt into a paste. Add the salty garlic paste and lemon juice to the avocado and mash the guacamole with a fork until it's fairly smooth. Scoop it into a serving dish and surround it with a few handfuls of good-quality tortilla chips.

Smoked Paprika O-Rings

I love the smokiness that paprika adds to any food, but onion rings . . .
ridiculous! 4 SERVINGS

About 6 cups **vegetable oil**,
for frying

1 large **Vidalia onion**, sliced
into rings about ¼ inch thick

3 cups **buttermilk**

1½ cups all-purpose **flour**

1½ cups **cornmeal**

2 tablespoons **smoked sweet
paprika**, a couple palmfuls

1 tablespoon **chili powder**,
a palmful

1 tablespoon **ground cumin**,
a palmful

1 tablespoon **salt**

1½ cups **sour cream**

2 **pimiento peppers** or
1 roasted red pepper,
patted dry and chopped

3 tablespoons chopped
fresh **dill**

Heat a couple inches of oil in a deep pot over medium to
medium-high heat. When it's hot enough, 10 minutes or
so, a piece of bread dropped into the oil should brown in
a count of 20.

Separate the onion rings and toss them in the buttermilk. Cover a large, deep plate with plastic wrap for easy
cleanup. Combine the flour, cornmeal, spices, and salt on
the plate. Toss one third of the rings in the breading at a
time, coating them evenly, then fry them in the hot oil for
3 to 4 minutes, or until they are deep golden. Drain them
on a paper-towel-lined plate. Repeat with the remaining
onion rings.

Combine the sour cream with the peppers and dill
in a food processor and process them to make a smooth
sauce. Transfer the sauce to a dish for dipping, surround it
with o-rings, and serve.

Indian-Spiced Chickpea and Fire-Roasted Tomato Soup

One of my favorite restaurants in New York City is Tamarind, my personal Mecca for savory Indian delights, whether I eat there or order take-out. When I am at home in the country, though, there's no Tamarind to dial up, so I make my own take-out. This is my latest Bollywood night soup. Enjoy it with a great Indian flick.   2 SERVINGS

¼ cup **EVOO** (extra-virgin olive oil)

2 **garlic cloves**, chopped

1 15-ounce can **chickpeas**, drained

½ small **onion**, coarsely chopped

1 teaspoon ground **cumin**, ⅓ palmful

½ teaspoon ground **cardamom**

½ teaspoon ground **turmeric**

Salt and **black pepper**

1 cup **vegetable stock**

1 28-ounce can **fire-roasted tomatoes**

¼ cup **plain yogurt**

Heat the EVOO in a medium pot over medium heat. Add the garlic and cook for 2 to 3 minutes. Combine the chickpeas and onions in a food processor and process until finely chopped. Add them to the pot and cook for 5 minutes to sweeten the onions. Season the chickpeas with the cumin, cardamom, turmeric, salt, and pepper. Stir in the stock, then the tomatoes, and simmer the soup for 5 to 10 minutes to combine the flavors. Serve it with a dollop of yogurt on top.

Spicy Sweet Potato Pancakes with Holiday Guacamole

Traditionally, potato pancakes are served alongside sour cream or applesauce, but this version cranks up the volume by pairing sweet potatoes and guacamole for a treat that is just delish! These certainly aren't your Bubby's latkes!   8 SERVINGS

Light olive oil or peanut oil, for frying

1 large **Idaho potato**, peeled and shredded

2 medium **sweet potatoes**, peeled and shredded

1 small **onion**, peeled

1 **egg**, beaten

3 tablespoons all-purpose **flour**, cracker meal, or matzo meal

1 tablespoon **chili powder**, a palmful

2 teaspoons **smoked sweet paprika**, ⅔ palmful

2 teaspoons **ground cumin**, ⅔ palmful

2 teaspoons **ground coriander**, ⅔ palmful

Salt

¾ cup **pomegranate juice**

2 **Hass avocados**

Juice of 1 lemon

½ medium **red onion**, finely chopped

1 small **garlic clove**, pasted up with some salt

2 **jalapeño peppers**, seeded and finely chopped

Heat about ⅓ cup of the oil over medium to medium-high heat.

Drain the shredded potatoes and sweet potatoes, pressing them down in a colander to get as much moisture out as possible. Place the potatoes in a bowl and, using a box grater, grate the onion directly into the potatoes so that the onion juices fall into the bowl as well. Add the egg and flour or meal to the bowl, then season with the chili powder, paprika, cumin, coriander, and salt. Drop the batter into the hot oil to make 2½-inch pancakes. Fry the cakes in batches, adding more oil as needed, until deeply golden on both sides. Drain on paper towels. You will get about 16 pancakes.

Pour the pomegranate juice into a small saucepan. Bring to a boil and cook until it's reduced to a syrup. Cut the avocados in half, all the way around the pit. Remove the pit with a spoon, then scoop the flesh into a bowl. Add the lemon juice, red onions, garlic, jalapeños, and a generous amount of salt. Mash the guacamole until smooth.

Arrange the potato pancakes on a platter and top them with heaping spoonfuls of guacamole. Drizzle with the pomegranate syrup.

Grilled Eggplant Roll-Ups

You won't miss the pasta when you make this cannelloni-style dish with grilled eggplant!   6 SERVINGS

1 large, firm **eggplant**

½ cup **EVOO** (extra-virgin olive oil; eyeball it)

Grill seasoning, such as McCormick's Montreal Steak Seasoning

2 cups **Alouette** or other soft garlic-and-herb cheese

6 to 8 soft **sun-dried tomatoes**, chopped (tender sun-dried tomatoes are available in small pouches in the produce department)

2 cups **arugula leaves**, chopped

1 cup fresh **basil**, about 20 leaves, chopped

Heat a grill pan over high heat. Thinly slice the eggplant; you should have a minimum of 18 slices. Brush the slices on both sides with the EVOO and season them with grill seasoning. Grill the thin slices to mark and tenderize the eggplant, 2 to 3 minutes on each side. Top each slice of cooked eggplant with a dab of cheese, sprinkle on sun-dried tomatoes and some arugula and basil, then roll them up. The eggplant roll-ups should have a few greens sticking out of each end.

Grilled Cheese and Watercress Sandwiches

Try this variation on classic grilled cheese—it's golden!   4 SERVINGS

8 slices **pumpernickel** or marble rye bread

½ pound your choice of **Muenster, Havarti with dill, or Leyden cheese** (Gouda with cumin seeds), thinly sliced

1 cup **watercress leaves**, shredded or chopped

2 tablespoons **dill pickle relish** or sweet red pepper relish

4 tablespoons (½ stick) **butter**, softened

Preheat a griddle or large skillet over medium-low heat. Make 4 sandwiches of sliced cheese, chopped greens, and relish, distributing the ingredients evenly among them. Butter the outsides of the sammies with softened butter and cook them in the preheated pan until they are golden and the cheese has melted.

Tuscan Calzones with "The Works"

These calzones are meat-free, super hearty, and super healthy. Eat up, chow down, and enjoy.   4 SERVINGS

1 sack (1 pound) **pizza dough**

A little **flour** to dust your hands with

4 tablespoons **EVOO** (extra-virgin olive oil), plus some for drizzling

4 **portobello mushroom caps**, thinly sliced

3 **garlic cloves**, chopped

2 tablespoons chopped fresh **rosemary**

Salt and **black pepper**

1 10-ounce box **frozen chopped spinach**

1 15-ounce can **cannellini beans**, drained

2 cups **shredded provolone** or mozzarella cheese

1 15-ounce can **pizza sauce**

¼ cup **kalamata or oil-cured olives**, pitted and finely chopped

Preheat a medium nonstick skillet.

Preheat the oven to 400°F. Cut the dough into 4 equal portions. Dust your hands with flour and spread the dough into 4 rounds, 8 to 10 inches in diameter.

To the hot skillet, add 2 tablespoons of the EVOO, twice around the pan, then add the sliced mushrooms and two thirds of the chopped garlic. Cook the mushrooms until they are dark and tender, 10 minutes, then season with rosemary, salt, and pepper.

While the mushrooms cook, microwave the frozen spinach on high for 6 minutes. Place the defrosted spinach in a clean kitchen towel and wring dry. Separate the spinach as you transfer it to a bowl with the drained beans. Mash the beans with the spinach and remaining chopped garlic, a drizzle of EVOO, and salt and pepper to taste.

Spread half of each dough round with one fourth of the bean mixture. Top with one fourth of the mushrooms and then about ½ cup of cheese. Fold the dough over and seal the calzones. Brush a cookie sheet with EVOO, arrange the calzones on the sheet, and brush the remaining EVOO lightly over each calzone. Bake the calzones until golden all over, 15 minutes.

Heat the pizza sauce over low heat in a small pot. Stir in the chopped olives and remove it from the heat.

Serve the calzones with small ramekins of black-olive pizza sauce for dipping.

Roasted Portobello Burgers with Rosemary Garlic Oven Fries

This sammie is so hearty you won't think to ask "where's the beef?"

4 SERVINGS

2 to 2½ pounds red or white **boiling potatoes**, washed

3 tablespoons **EVOO** (extra-virgin olive oil), plus some for drizzling

2 fresh **rosemary** sprigs, leaves finely chopped

Salt and **black pepper**

2 tablespoons finely **chopped garlic**

8 large **portobello mushrooms**, stems removed

2 tablespoons **balsamic vinegar**

4 cups **arugula leaves**, washed

2 **jarred roasted red peppers**, seeded

4 slices fresh **mozzarella cheese**

Preheat the oven to 450°F.

Cut the potatoes into wedges and drop them onto a cookie sheet. Drizzle the potatoes with about 3 tablespoons of EVOO and toss to coat them thoroughly in the oil. Season the potatoes with the rosemary, salt, and pepper. Roast them for 25 minutes in all. Halfway through the roasting add the garlic, stir to distribute, and flip the potatoes, then continue to roast. The potatoes should be brown and tender.

While the potatoes roast, place the portobello mushroom caps on a cookie sheet. Season them with salt and pepper and arrange the mushrooms gill side up. Drizzle the gill side with a little EVOO and the balsamic vinegar. Transfer them to the oven and roast for 12 minutes, or until they are cooked through. Don't turn off the oven.

While the mushrooms are roasting, coarsely chop the arugula and roasted red peppers and combine them in a bowl. Season them with a little salt and pepper.

Top 4 of the cooked mushroom caps with a mound of the arugula and roasted pepper mixture, and a slice of mozzarella. Return the mushrooms to the oven to melt the cheese, about 2 to 3 minutes. Once the cheese has melted, remove the mushrooms from the oven and top each one with a second roasted mushroom cap to make a sandwich. Serve the roasted portobello burgers with the rosemary garlic oven fries. It's easiest to eat these burgers with a fork and knife.

Meatless Muffaletta Panini

It may be a mouthful to say, but trust me, once you get a mouthful of it, you won't put it down! The classic muffaletta originated in New Orleans and I've re-created it for the vegheads.   4 SERVINGS

2 handfuls of good-quality **pitted green and black olives**

1 cup **giardiniera** (pickled cauliflower, carrot, and hot pepper mix), drained

4 sesame or cornmeal **kaiser rolls**, split

8 deli slices sharp **provolone cheese**

1 15-ounce can **artichoke hearts in water**, drained and thinly sliced

2 **roasted red peppers**, drained and thinly sliced

Preheat a griddle or a grill pan over medium-high heat, or prepare a panini press.

Place the olives and pickled veggies in a food processor and pulse or chop them into a relish. Divide the relish among the bottom halves of the sandwich rolls and top it with a single slice of cheese. Layer the sliced artichokes and peppers onto the cheese, then add another slice of provolone to each sandwich and press the tops in place.

Place the sandwiches on the griddle or grill pan and press them with a heavy skillet weighted down with cans, or place them in the panini press. Press the sammies for a few minutes on each side, then cut into halves and serve.

Fontina, Olive, and Roasted Red Pepper Paninis

I'm crazy for these paninis. I used to pile cheese and peppers on olive bread and press them, but once when the bakery counter was sold out of the bread, I had to come up with a makeshift substitute. A hot panini is so good when dunked into a steaming bowl of soup. Yum-o!

2 SERVINGS

1 **roasted red pepper**

¼ cup **pitted kalamata olives**

A small handful of fresh **flat-leaf parsley** leaves

A couple pinches of **red pepper flakes**

4 slices **Fontina cheese**, 4 to 6 ounces total

4 slices good-quality **crusty bread**

Preheat a panini press, medium skillet, or grill pan over medium heat.

Slice the roasted red pepper into strips, then pile them together on a cutting board with the olives and parsley leaves. Run your knife through the mixture to coarsely chop them together. Season the mixture with some red pepper flakes.

Place a slice of Fontina cheese on each of 2 bread slices, then top each sandwich with an equal amount of the red pepper and olive mixture. Cover with a second slice of cheese and top with the remaining bread slices.

If you are using a sandwich press, place the sammies in the machine and press. For the skillet or grill-pan method, add the paninis to the pan, place a piece of foil on top of the sandwiches, and press with a full tea kettle, another pan weighted with cans, or a garden brick. Brown and crust the sandwiches, about 2 minutes on each side; cut and serve.

Spinach and Artichoke Calzones

A handheld version of everyone's favority party dip!   4 SERVINGS

Coarse salt

4 ounces **walnut pieces**, toasted (about ⅓ cup)

1 15-ounce can **artichoke hearts**, drained

2 large **garlic cloves**, cracked away from the skin

Zest of 1 lemon

A handful of fresh **flat-leaf parsley** leaves

½ cup grated **Parmigiano-Reggiano**

Coarse black pepper

¼ teaspoon **grated or ground nutmeg**

⅓ cup **extra-virgin olive oil (EVOO)**

4 cups **ricotta cheese**

2 10-ounce boxes **frozen chopped spinach**, defrosted in the microwave and wrung completely dry in a clean kitchen towel

2 balls or tubs of fresh **pizza dough**, any variety or brand

A sprinkle of **flour**, to dust hands for handling the dough

1 sack (10 ounces) **shredded Italian cheese blend**, shredded provolone, or shredded mozzarella, your choice

A dab of **EVOO** to brush on the dough before baking

Preheat the oven to 400°F.

In the bowl of a food processor, combine the nuts, artichoke hearts, garlic, lemon zest, parsley, cheese, some pepper, and nutmeg and pulse the ingredients until chopped. Turn the processor on and stream in the EVOO in a slow stream until the pesto forms. It should be thick and pastelike in consistency.

In a large bowl, combine the pesto and the ricotta. Add the spinach, pulling it apart as you add it to the bowl, then mix it through the ricotta and pesto. Taste the filling to adjust the salt and pepper.

Cut each ball of dough in half and with each half, dust your hands with flour and form a 6- to 7-inch round crust. Pile one fourth of the ricotta filling on half of the round dough. Top with one fourth of the shredded cheese. Fold the dough over and seal at the edges. Brush the calzone lightly with EVOO and place it on a cookie sheet. You should be able to fit all 4 on a large nonstick sheet. Bake for 15 to 18 minutes, until the calzones are evenly deep golden and crisp.

Mushroom-Veggie Sloppy Sandwiches

Not only do cooked mushrooms provide nutrients, minerals, and fiber, but they also boast a deliciously meaty flavor, which makes them a great replacement for beef. This savory swap-out makes this sammie just as healthy and tasty as it is messy!   4 SERVINGS

---

4 **portobello mushrooms**, stems removed

Coarse salt and freshly ground **black pepper**

2 **limes**

4 tablespoons **vegetable oil**

5 **garlic cloves**, chopped

3 tablespoons **chili powder**

1 medium **yellow onion**, chopped

1 large **red bell pepper**, cored, seeded, and chopped

1 large **jalapeño pepper**, seeded and chopped

1 small **zucchini** or yellow squash, cut in half lengthwise, then sliced into half-moons

1 tablespoon **ground cumin**

1 tablespoon **hot pepper sauce**

1 cup **pale beer** or vegetable stock or broth

1 15-ounce can **crushed tomatoes**

1 14-ounce can **dark red kidney beans**, rinsed and drained

1 cup **spicy vegetarian refried beans**

¼ cup fresh **cilantro** leaves (a generous handful), chopped

4 sandwich-size **English muffins**

1 ripe **avocado**

2 cups (8 to 10 ounces) shredded **spicy Monterey Jack** or smoked Cheddar cheese

Preheat the oven to 450°F.

Place the portobello mushrooms on a rimmed cookie sheet. Season the mushrooms with salt, pepper, the juice of 1 lime, about 2 tablespoons of the vegetable oil, half the chopped garlic, and 1 tablespoon of the chili powder, tossing them around in the seasonings to coat thoroughly. Arrange the mushrooms gill side up. Put them in the oven and roast for 12 minutes, or until cooked through. Remove from the oven and cover with foil to keep warm.

Preheat a large soup pot over medium-high heat and add the remaining 2 tablespoons of vegetable oil. Add the onions, bell peppers, jalapeños, zucchini or yellow squash, and the remaining garlic. Season the veggies with the cumin, the remaining 2 tablespoons of chili powder, the hot pepper sauce, and 1 teaspoon of salt and sauté for 5 to 6 minutes, to soften and lightly brown the vegetables. Deglaze the pan with the beer or stock. Add the tomatoes and red kidney beans to the vegetable chili and stir to combine. Thicken the chili by stirring in the refried beans. Simmer over low heat for about 10 minutes longer. Finish with the cilantro.

While the sloppy chili is simmering, toast the English muffins.

Prepare the avocado: Cut all around the circumfer-

recipe continued

ence of the ripe avocado, lengthwise and down to the pit. Twist and separate the halved fruit. Remove the pit with a spoon, then scoop the flesh out in one piece from both halves and slice the flesh lengthwise. Squeeze the juice of the second lime over the avocado to season it and prevent it from discoloring. Place 1 roasted mushroom on the bottom half of each muffin. Place a large helping of chili on top of the mushroom, sprinkle with the shredded cheese, and arrange some of the slices of avocado on top of that. Finish with the English muffin tops. Live on the edge and eat it with your hands. Have napkins handy.

Hummus-Topped Pit-Zas

Who doesn't love hummus? Here's a healthy sammie that will transport you to the Mediterranean.　6 SERVINGS

6 6-inch **pitas**

1 15-ounce can **chickpeas**, drained

2 whole **roasted red peppers**, drained

1 **garlic clove**, crushed from its skin

Juice of ½ lemon

1 tablespoon chopped fresh **rosemary leaves**, from a couple small sprigs

Salt

¼ cup **EVOO** (extra-virgin olive oil)

3 cups **shredded provolone** or mozzarella cheese, or a combination of the two

TOPPINGS (CHOOSE ONE OR ALL)

½ cup **pepperoncini** (pickled hot green peppers), chopped

1 can **artichoke hearts** in water, drained well and chopped

A generous handful of **pitted kalamata olives**, chopped

A handful of fresh **flat-leaf parsley leaves, chopped**

Preheat the oven to 400°F.

Arrange the pitas on baking sheets. In a food processor, combine the chickpeas, roasted red peppers, garlic, lemon juice, rosemary, and salt and turn the processor on. Stream the EVOO into the processor and process the hummus until it's smooth. Spread the hummus on the pitas and top them with the cheese, as you would a pizza. Cover the cheese with toppings of your choice: pepperoncini, artichokes, and/or olives. Bake them for 10 to 12 minutes to melt the cheese and crisp the pitas. Cut the pit-zas into wedges and garnish them with the parsley.

Baked Sesame Eggplant Subs with Fire-Roasted Tomato and Red Pepper Sauce

You won't be sharing these spicy and bold subs with anyone.

4 SERVINGS

1 cup **Italian-style bread crumbs** (3 overflowing handfuls)

½ cup grated **Parmigiano-Reggiano** (a couple of overflowing handfuls)

3 tablespoons **sesame seeds**

4 tablespoons **extra-virgin olive oil** (EVOO)

1 large firm **eggplant**, thinly sliced

½ cup all-purpose **flour**

2 **eggs**, beaten with a splash of water

2 **garlic cloves**, chopped

1 16-ounce jar **roasted red peppers**, drained

1 15-ounce can diced **fire-roasted tomatoes**, such as Muir Glen brand

Salt and **freshly ground black pepper**

4 **crusty sub rolls**, tops split

1 pound **smoked fresh mozzarella** cheese, thinly sliced

Preheat the oven to 400°F. In a shallow bowl, combine the bread crumbs, Parmigiano, sesame seeds, and 2 tablespoons of the EVOO.

Dust the eggplant slices in the flour, then dip in the eggs and press into the breadcrumb mixture. Arrange the eggplant on a large nonstick cookie sheet and bake in the center of the oven until deep golden all over, 15 to 17 minutes.

While the eggplant cooks, in a medium sauce pot over medium heat, sauté the garlic in the remaining 2 tablespoons of EVOO. Puree the roasted peppers in a food processor. Add the peppers and tomatoes to the garlic, season with salt and pepper, and heat through.

Turn the oven from bake to broil. Fill the sub rolls with sauce, breaded sesame eggplant, and smoked mozzarella, then place the subs under the broiler. Brown the cheese until it bubbles, then serve up the subs nice and hot.

30 Days No Repeat Pasta

I'm Italian. I was bred to love pasta. Enjoy making (and eating!) these delicious pastas. There are enough here for days on end, plus there are tons more throughout the book.

VEGETARIAN

Big Fat Spicy Saté Noodles
Lemon Spaghetti
Boo's Butternut Squash Mac-n-Cheese
Ricotta Pasta with Grape Tomatoes, Peas, and Basil
Whole-Wheat Penne with Cauliflower Sauce
Cabbage and Straw Pasta
MOP-It-Up Pasta with Mushrooms, Onions, and Peppers
Spinach-Artichoke Cheesy Tortellini
Three-Vegetable Penne with Tarragon-Basil Pesto
Creamed Mushroom Sauté with Artichoke Hearts, Spinach, and Penne

MOST REQUESTED

Spaghetti con Aglio e Olio with Tomato and Onion Salad
Mexican Pasta with Tomatillo Sauce and Meatballs
Toasted Ravioli
Bel Aria Chicken and Pasta
Pasta with Broccoli and Sausage with a Ricotta Surprise
Christmas Pasta
Drunken Tuscan Pasta
Deviled Fritatta and Heavenly Angel Hair Pasta
Pasta with Bacon, Tomatoes, and Cheese
Pesce Spada Pasta

FAMILY FAVES

Broccoli Rabe and Orecchiette
Shrimp Primavera Pasta with Asparagus, Peas, and Leeks
Ground Turkey Paprika-Goulash with Macaroni
White Beans, Pancetta, and Pasta
Cowboy Spaghetti
Cacio e Pepe (Cheese and Pepper Pasta) and Spinach with White Beans
Mega Meat-Stuffed Shells
Mac-n-Cheddar with Broccoli
Southwestern Pasta Bake
Eggplant and Wild Mushroom Pasta with Ricotta Salata

Big Fat Spicy Saté Noodles

When I make this, I've been known to reserve a little serving of it in a bowl and hide it way in the back of the refrigerator, concealed behind the milk, mustard, and jellies. They are mighty good cold the next day and I'm not afraid to eat them for breakfast.   4 SERVINGS

Salt

1 pound **bucatini** pasta

2 tablespoons **vegetable oil**

3-inch piece of **fresh ginger**, peeled and grated

3 large **garlic cloves**, chopped

1 teaspoon **red pepper flakes**, ⅓ palmful

1 cup **vegetable stock**

⅓ cup **tamari** (dark aged soy sauce)

½ cup **smooth peanut butter**

Juice of 2 limes

1 cup **unsalted roasted peanuts**

A generous handful of fresh **cilantro** or fresh flat-leaf parsley leaves, chopped

Bring a large covered pot of water to a boil for the pasta. Add some salt and the pasta and cook the pasta to al dente. Right before you drain it, remove and reserve 1 cup of the pasta cooking liquid. Drain the noodles and reserve.

Return the pot to the stove-top over medium-high heat; add the vegetable oil, 2 times around the pan. Add the ginger, garlic, and red pepper flakes and cook for 2 minutes. Add ½ cup of the reserved pasta cooking liquid, the vegetable stock, and tamari and bring it up to a bubble over high heat. Cook for 2 to 3 minutes. Turn the heat off, add the peanut butter, and whisk to combine. If the sauce gets too thick, add a couple more splashes of the reserved pasta cooking liquid. Add the lime juice and the drained noodles, toss to coat the noodles, then add the chopped peanuts and cilantro and toss again.

Lemon Spaghetti

On the Amalfi coast of Italy, lemons the size of melons grow from the edge of the sea to the top of the sky on the rocky cliffs that disappear up into the clouds. This is a menu that takes me back there, to my lemon heaven.   6 SERVINGS

Salt

1 pound **spaghetti**

3 tablespoons **EVOO** (extra-virgin olive oil)

4 **garlic cloves**, finely chopped

½ teaspoon **red pepper flakes**

Zest and juice of 2 lemons

¾ cup **heavy cream**

1 cup grated **Parmigiano-Reggiano cheese**

Handful of fresh **flat-leaf parsley** leaves, finely chopped

½ cup fresh **basil** leaves, 10 or 12 leaves, shredded

Bring a large covered pot of water to a boil. Salt the water and drop the spaghetti into the pot.

Heat a large, deep skillet over low heat. Add the EVOO, garlic, red pepper flakes, and lemon zest.

When the pasta has been cooking for about 5 minutes, to the garlic mixture add the lemon juice, a ladle of the cooking water from the pasta, and the cream. Raise the heat a bit to bring the sauce to a bubble.

Drain the pasta when it still has a good bite to it. Add the pasta to the skillet and turn off the heat. Add half the cheese to the pasta and toss the pasta with the sauce for a minute or two, allowing it time to soak up the sauce. Add the parsley and toss. Use tongs or a meat fork to gather one sixth of the pasta and twist it to form a bundle, or pasta nest. Top each serving with a sprinkle of the remaining cheese and lots of shredded basil.

Boo's Butternut Squash Mac-n-Cheese

I know it sounds odd, but my girl LOVED butternut squash! This dog might even go for it before a steak, especially if there were also pasta and cheese involved in the deal.   5 SERVINGS; BOO COUNTED FOR 2

Coarse salt

1 pound **macaroni** with ridges, such as tubettini or mini penne rigate

1 tablespoon **extra-virgin olive oil** (EVOO)

2 tablespoons **unsalted butter**

2 tablespoons chopped fresh **thyme**, plus a few sprigs for garnish

½ medium **onion**

3 tablespoons all-purpose **flour**

2 cups **vegetable stock**

1 10-ounce box **frozen cooked butternut squash**, defrosted

1 cup **cream** or half-and-half

2 cups (8 ounces) grated **sharp Cheddar cheese**

½ cup grated **Parmigiano-Reggiano** (a couple of handfuls)

¼ teaspoon **nutmeg**

Freshly ground black pepper, to taste

Heat a pot of water to boil for the pasta. Salt the water, then add the pasta and cook al dente, or with a bite to it.

While the pasta cooks, heat a medium heavy-bottomed pot over medium heat. Add the EVOO and butter. When the butter melts into the oil, add the thyme and grate the onion directly into the pot with a hand-held grater or Microplane. Cook the grated onions for a minute or 2, then add the flour and cook together for a minute or 2 more. Whisk in the stock, then add the butternut squash and cook until warmed through and smooth. Stir in the cream and bring the sauce to a bubble. Stir in the cheeses in a figure-eight motion and season the completed sauce with salt, nutmeg, and pepper. Taste to adjust seasonings.

Drain the cooked pasta well and combine with the sauce. Serve alongside chicken sammies or all on its own with a green salad. Garnish with thyme leaves. (Boo would also have a little extra sprinkle of that cheese, please!)

boo food >> Boo was my dog, my friend, and my test-kitchen eater for twelve years (eighty-four, to her) and about 2,700 recipes. These recipes are a tribute to all the flavors and foods Boo loved best. I was the luckiest girl in the world to share my life and so much good food with Miss Boo. When you make this meal, have a bite for her or for the special animal in your life.

Ricotta Pasta with Grape Tomatoes, Peas, and Basil

This dish can be made 100 ways. It's one of the first dishes you eat as an Italian kid: macaroni with butter and ricotta cheese. Once you grow up, you add stuff in, but the base remains the same.   4 SERVINGS

1 pound **penne** or ziti rigate

Coarse salt

2 cups **ricotta cheese**

2 tablespoons **unsalted butter,** cut into small pieces

½ cup **Parmigiano-Reggiano** or Romano cheese (a couple of handfuls)

2 tablespoons **extra-virgin olive oil** (EVOO)

1 medium **onion,** finely chopped

1 cup frozen **green peas**

A generous handful of fresh **flat-leaf parsley,** finely chopped

Coarse black pepper

20 fresh **basil** leaves, shredded or torn

1 cup halved **grape tomatoes** (½ pint)

Bring a large pot of water to a boil. Add the pasta and salt the water. Cook the pasta al dente, with a bite to it.

Place the ricotta, butter, and Parmigiano or Romano in a large bowl.

Heat a small skillet over medium heat. Add the EVOO and onions and cook for 5 minutes. Add the peas and parsley and cook for 2 minutes. Turn off the heat.

Drain the pasta. Add to the bowl with the cheeses. Toss to melt the butter and evenly coat the pasta with cheeses, then season with salt and pepper. Top the pasta with the peas, basil, and halved grape tomatoes. Season with a little salt. Toss and serve at the table.

Whole-Wheat Penne with Cauliflower Sauce

Whole grains have a rich, chewy texture that is nicely complemented by a creamy, hearty cauliflower sauce.   4 SERVINGS

Salt

1 pound **whole-wheat penne rigate**

¼ cup **EVOO** (extra-virgin olive oil)

3 **garlic cloves**, sliced

1 **red onion**, finely chopped

1 head of **cauliflower**, stemmed and chopped

1 cup **vegetable stock**

Leaves from 4 fresh **rosemary** sprigs, finely chopped

¾ cup grated **Romano cheese**, 3 handfuls

Black pepper

Bring a large covered pot of water to a boil for the pasta. Add the salt and pasta and cook to al dente. Heads up: you'll need some of the pasta cooking water before you drain the pasta.

While the water is coming up to a boil and the pasta cooks, make the sauce. Heat the EVOO in a deep skillet over medium heat. Add the garlic and cook for 3 minutes, then discard the garlic. Add the onions and cook for 5 minutes, then add the cauliflower, stock, and rosemary. Cover the pan and cook for 15 minutes. Uncover the sauce, add a ladle or two of the hot pasta water, and mash the cauliflower with the back of a wooden spoon or potato masher. Drain the pasta and add it to the cauliflower. Add the cheese and toss to combine with the pasta and the sauce. Season the dish with salt and pepper and serve.

Cabbage and Straw Pasta

This meal is fast to prepare but eating it will slow you way down. Wide noodles prepared with cabbage, potatoes, and sage make up the classic Genoa comfort food called pizzoccheri. Have a pillow handy.

6 SERVINGS

Salt

2 **Idaho potatoes**, peeled and cut into ½-inch dice

1 pound **fettuccine** or pappardelle pasta

1 small head of **Savoy cabbage**, quartered, cored, and finely shredded

½ cup (1 stick) **butter**, cut into pieces

3 to 4 **garlic cloves**, crushed from their skins and halved

16 fresh **sage leaves**, 6 left whole, 10 thinly sliced

1 teaspoon **coarse black pepper**

1½ to 2 cups grated **Romano cheese**

Bring a large covered pot of water to a boil and salt it. Add the potatoes and cook them for 7 minutes. Add the pasta and cook it for 2 minutes, then stir in the cabbage and cook it for 5 minutes longer.

While the potatoes and pasta cook, in a large, deep skillet, melt the butter over medium heat and add the garlic and 6 whole sage leaves. Cook for 3 to 4 minutes, remove the garlic and whole leaves (reserve the leaves), then add the sliced sage leaves and the black pepper. Just before draining the pasta and cabbage, add 2 ladles of starchy cooking water to the skillet.

Drain the potatoes, pasta, and cabbage and add them to the butter and sage. Toss the pasta to combine it with the sage butter, adding lots of cheese as you work. Toss it for 1 or 2 minutes to form a cheesy, buttery coating on the pasta and cabbage, then adjust the salt and serve. Use the reserved whole sage leaves to garnish the pasta.

MOP-It-Up Pasta with Mushrooms, Onions, and Peppers

This dish combines fresh and pickled veggies. It tastes awesome hot or cold.   4 SERVINGS

Salt

½ pound **cavatappi (hollow corkscrew pasta)**, or other shaped pasta

2 tablespoons **extra-virgin olive oil (EVOO)**

1 pound **cremini (baby portobello) mushrooms**, sliced

4 **garlic cloves**, chopped

1 large **yellow onion**, quartered and thinly sliced

1 **red bell pepper**, cored, seeded, quartered, and thinly sliced

1 **cubanelle** (long, light green mild Italian pepper), seeded and thinly sliced

Freshly ground black pepper

¼ cup jarred **hot banana or hot cherry pepper rings**, drained and chopped, plus a splash of their brine

1 cup jarred **marinated mushrooms**, drained and chopped

½ cup fresh **flat-leaf parsley**, coarsely chopped

⅓ cup grated **Parmigiano-Reggiano** (a couple handfuls)

Heat a pot of water to a boil for pasta. Season the water with some salt and add pasta. Cook the pasta al dente, or with a bite to it.

Preheat a large, deep skillet over medium-high heat. Add the EVOO and cremini mushrooms. Sauté until they start to become tender, 3 to 4 minutes, then add the garlic, stir for 30 seconds, and add the onion and fresh peppers. Season the MOP (mushrooms, onions, and peppers) with salt and pepper and cook 5 minutes more. Add the chopped hot peppers and a splash of their juice from the jar. Add the marinated mushrooms next and toss to combine.

Drain pasta and add to the MOP. Toss the whole thing together with the parsley and cheese and serve immediately.

ABOVE: HAZELNUT-CRUSTED CHICKEN WITH GORGONZOLA SAUCE >> (page 356); PROSCIUTTO-WRAPPED ENDIVE AND RADICCHIO WITH BALSAMIC-FIG REDUCTION >> (page 38)

ABOVE: CAUTION-FLAG CHILI WITH FLAT-TIRE CORN AND BLACK BEAN TOPPERS >> (page 254); FIRED-UP PEACHES AND CREAM >> (page 375)

OPPOSITE: CRISPY TURKEY CUTLETS WITH BACON–CRANBERRY BRUSSELS SPROUTS >> (page 43)

ABOVE: MONTALCINO CHICKEN WITH FIGS AND BUTTERED GNOCCHI WITH NUTMEG >> (pages 288–89)

OPPOSITE: SALSA STOUP AND DOUBLE-DECKER BAKED QUESADILLAS >> (page 135)

ABOVE: BACON AND CREAMY RANCH CHICKEN BURGERS WITH CRISPY SCALLION "STICKS" >> (pages 108–09); HUNGRY-MAN BLOODY-MARY BURGERS AND SPICY BROCCOLI >> (page 112)

OPPOSITE: TOASTED RAVIOLI >> (page 166); PEPPER-CRUSTED TENDERLOINS WITH MUSHROOM MARSALA CREAM >> (page 359); ROASTED ASPARAGUS >> (page 125)

ABOVE: SPANISH PORK CHOPS WITH LINGUICA CORN STUFFING AND WINE GRAVY >> (pages 298–99)

OPPOSITE: HEARTY SAUSAGE AND MUSHROOM STEW OVER POLENTA >> (pages 226–27)

ABOVE LEFT: CACIO E PEPE SPAGHETTI SQUASH >> (page 232); PORK LOIN CHOPS WITH SWEET AND HOT PEPPERS >> (page 313); WILTED SPINACH WITH GARLIC CHIPS >> (page 129)

ABOVE RIGHT: GINGER-GARLIC TUNA BURGERS ON CUCUMBER SALAD >> (page 88)

OPPOSITE: WARM CINNAMON-CHIPOTLE TOMATO SALSA >> (page 139); GARLICKY GUACAMOLE >> (page 139); SERRANO-WRAPPED HALIBUT WITH TORTILLAS AND SAVOY CABBAGE >> (page 211)

ABOVE LEFT: LEMON, GARLIC, AND CILANTRO BAKED STUFFED TOMATOES >> (page 126)

ABOVE RIGHT: MEXICAN FONDUE >> (page 228)

OPPOSITE: PUMPKIN-PEANUT CURRY NOODLES WITH FIVE-SPICE SEARED SCALLOPS AND SHRIMP >> (page 200);
LOOKING FOR MR. GOODBAR SUNDAES >> (page 375)

ABOVE LEFT: SESAME-CRUSTED RED SNAPPER WITH GINGER-DRESSED SNAPPY VEGGIES >> (page 192)

ABOVE RIGHT: GINGER-POACHED PEARS WITH RICOTTA AND BLUEBERRIES >> (page 374)

OPPOSITE: ITALIAN CHICKEN POT PIE FROM THE BOOT >> (pages 233–34); BOOZY BERRIES AND BISCUITS >> (page 370)

ABOVE: VERY BERRY CRUMBLE>> (page 373)

Spinach-Artichoke Cheesy Tortellini

If you like those spinach and artichoke dips you get on the appetizer menu in restaurants, you're gonna LOVE this! 4 SERVINGS

1 10-ounce box **frozen spinach**

2 tablespoons **EVOO** (extra-virgin olive oil)

1 tablespoon **unsalted butter**

3 **garlic cloves**, chopped

1 small **onion**, peeled and halved

2 tablespoons **all-purpose flour**

1 cup **vegetable stock**

1 cup **heavy cream**

⅛ teaspoon freshly grated **nutmeg**

1 14-ounce can **artichoke hearts** in water, drained and chopped

A couple of handfuls grated **Parmigiano-Reggiano** or Pecorino Romano cheese

Salt and **black pepper**

1 pound **cheese tortellini** or flavored tortellini, such as wild mushroom

Bring a large pot of water to a boil to cook the pasta. Microwave the spinach on high for 6 minutes to defrost.

Heat a deep skillet over medium heat with the EVOO and butter. When the butter melts and is hot, add the garlic. Using a box grater, grate the onion directly into the skillet. Sauté the onions and garlic for 5 minutes. Sprinkle the flour into the skillet and cook for 1 minute. Whisk in the stock, then the cream, and bring the sauce to a bubble. Season the sauce with nutmeg and reduce the heat to low.

Place the defrosted spinach in a clean kitchen towel and wring it dry. Separate it as you add it to the sauce. Stir in the chopped artichokes and a couple handfuls of cheese, then season the spinach-artichoke sauce with salt and pepper.

Salt the boiling water and cook the tortellini according to package directions, about 3 to 5 minutes. Drain it well and toss with the spinach-artichoke sauce. Serve immediately.

Three-Vegetable Penne with Tarragon-Basil Pesto

With veggies and pasta in one dish, there's no need to make any sides—plus, you only have to wash one pot!   4 SERVINGS

Salt

1 pound **penne rigate** (ridged) pasta

½ pound **asparagus**, tough ends trimmed

1 small **zucchini**

¼ pound **haricots verts** (thin green beans) or regular green beans, stem ends trimmed

¼ cup **pine nuts**

1 cup fresh **basil**, about 20 leaves

½ cup fresh **tarragon**, leaves stripped from 10 to 12 stems

A handful of fresh **flat-leaf parsley**

Zest of 1 lemon

1 **garlic clove**, peeled

½ cup grated **Parmigiano-Reggiano** cheese, a couple of handfuls, plus more to pass at the table

Coarse black pepper

⅓ cup **EVOO** (extra-virgin olive oil; eyeball it)

Bring a large pot of water to a boil for the pasta. Salt the water, add the pasta, and cook to al dente; it should still have a bite to it. Cut the asparagus spears on an angle into 2-inch pieces. Cut the zucchini into matchsticks. Cut the haricots verts or green beans on an angle into 2-inch pieces. Add the vegetables to the pot with the pasta after the penne has been cooking for about 5 minutes. Boil the veggies and pasta together for 2 minutes.

While the pasta is working, toast the pine nuts in a small dry skillet until golden, then cool. Place the nuts, basil, tarragon, parsley, lemon zest, garlic, ½ cup of cheese, and a little salt and pepper in a food processor. Turn the processor on and stream in the EVOO until a thick sauce forms.

Scrape the pesto into a large, shallow serving dish. Add a ladle of hot, starchy pasta water to the pesto. Drain the penne and veggies and immediately add them to the pesto. Toss to coat the pasta and vegetables evenly. Adjust the salt and pepper to taste. Serve with extra grated cheese to pass at the table.

Creamed Mushroom Sauté with Artichoke Hearts, Spinach, and Penne

Everyone's favorite party dip makes another appearance . . . in pasta! This vegetarian dish gets beefed up with mushrooms, which won't leave you missing the meat.   4 SERVINGS

1 pound **penne pasta**

2 tablespoons **extra-virgin olive oil (EVOO)**

2 tablespoons **unsalted butter,** cut into pieces

4 **garlic cloves,** finely chopped

2 **shallots,** thinly sliced

1½ pounds assorted **mushrooms,** such as cremini (baby portobello), portobello, shiitake, or fresh porcini, thinly sliced

2 tablespoons chopped fresh **thyme,** plus a few sprigs for garnish

Salt and **freshly ground black pepper**

3 tablespoons all-purpose **flour**

½ cup **dry white wine**

1 cup **vegetable stock**

½ cup **cream** or half-and-half

1 15-ounce can quartered **artichoke hearts,** drained well

1 10-ounce box **frozen chopped spinach,** defrosted and wrung dry in a kitchen towel

¼ teaspoon **grated** or **ground nutmeg**

½ cup grated **Parmigiano-Reggiano** (a couple of handfuls)

Bring a large pot of water to a boil. Add the pasta and salt and cook until al dente.

Heat a large nonstick skillet over medium to medium-high heat. Add the EVOO and butter. When the butter melts, add the garlic and shallots and swish around for 30 seconds, then add the mushrooms and combine. Sprinkle the chopped thyme over the mushrooms. Cook the mushrooms, stirring frequently, until they brown. Add salt and pepper to taste. (Do not season mushrooms before they brown. Salt draws out liquid and will make the mushrooms wet and as a result, they will actually take longer to brown.) Sprinkle the flour over the mushrooms and cook for 1 to 2 minutes more, stirring to evenly distribute. Whisk the white wine into the pan first and cook it off for a minute, then whisk in the stock. Thicken the broth for a minute, then add the cream and simmer over low heat for 5 minutes.

Stir the artichoke hearts into the sauce. Break up the spinach and add to the sauce. Stir to heat through and add the nutmeg. Adjust the salt and pepper to taste. Add the drained penne and cheese to the pan and toss to combine.

Spaghetti con Aglio e Olio with Tomato and Onion Salad

This is a classic. I simply could not have you (or me) live through a whole year without making this dish. Enjoy this oldie-but-oh-so-goodie!

4 SERVINGS

Coarse salt

1 pound **spaghetti**

Crusty bread, to pass at the table

⅓ cup **extra-virgin olive oil (EVOO)**, plus some for drizzling

8 **garlic cloves**, chopped

1 teaspoon **red pepper flakes**

8 to 10 **flat anchovy fillets**

1 cup fresh **flat-leaf parsley** leaves

4 vine-ripe **tomatoes** or 6 Roma tomatoes, cut lengthwise, lightly seeded, then sliced into thin half-moons

1 small **white** or **yellow onion**, quartered lengthwise, then thinly sliced

Coarse black pepper

Preheat the oven to 200°F.

Heat a large pot of water to boil for the pasta. Salt the water and cook the pasta until al dente, 6 to 7 minutes or so.

Place the bread in the oven to warm and crust it up.

While the pasta cooks, place a large, deep, nonstick heavy-bottomed skillet over medium-low heat. When the pan is warm, add the ⅓ cup of EVOO, the garlic, red pepper flakes, and anchovies.

While the sauce and pasta work, chop a fistful of the parsley and combine it with the tomatoes and onions in a shallow bowl. Dress the salad with a liberal drizzle of EVOO and season with salt and pepper. Finely chop the remaining parsley and set aside.

Drain the spaghetti really well but do not rinse it; rinsing will wash off the starch, and the starch helps the oil stick to the pasta. Pour the hot spaghetti into the skillet. Add the reserved parsley and toss the pasta together with the anchovies, garlic, and oil to coat evenly. Season the completed dish liberally with salt and pepper.

Serve the pasta with the tomato and onion salad and crusty bread alongside.

> **tidbit** >> If you think you don't like anchovies, just try them here. Once they melt into oil, the anchovies will no longer taste like fish but like salted, toasted nuts in garlic oil.

MOST REQUESTED

Mexican Pasta with Tomatillo Sauce and Meatballs

Tomatillos look like green tomatoes, but they're not. They are related to gooseberries and they are sour to taste. This dish is a funky, fun twist on spaghetti and meatballs. It's crazy—crazy good!   4 SERVINGS

Coarse salt

1 pound **fettuccine**

MEATBALLS

Extra-virgin olive oil (EVOO), for drizzling

1 pound **ground pork** or chicken

1 **egg**

½ cup **plain bread crumbs**

2 tablespoons fresh **cilantro**, finely chopped

2 tablespoons finely chopped fresh **thyme** (from 5 to 6 sprigs)

3 **scallions**, finely chopped

1 teaspoon **allspice**

A few dashes of **hot sauce**

Coarse black pepper

SAUCE

2 tablespoons **EVOO**

4 **garlic cloves**, crushed

1 large **yellow onion**, finely chopped

2 **jalapeño peppers**, fully seeded and very thinly sliced

1 cup **Mexican beer** or chicken stock

20 **tomatillos**, peeled and coarsely chopped

2 tablespoons fresh **cilantro**, finely chopped

Salt and freshly ground black pepper

1 cup grated **Manchego cheese**

Crusty bread

Preheat the oven to 400°F. Bring a large pot of water to a boil for the pasta. Salt the water and cook the pasta al dente.

While the pasta works, add a generous drizzle of EVOO to a mixing bowl. Place the meat in the bowl. Add the egg, bread crumbs, cilantro, the thyme, scallions, allspice, hot sauce, salt, and pepper, and mix to combine. Form 2-inch meatballs and arrange on a rimmed nonstick cookie sheet. Bake for 15 minutes.

While the meatballs bake, make the sauce. Heat a deep-sided skillet over medium-high heat. Add the 2 tablespoons of EVOO (twice around the pan), the garlic, onions, and jalapeños. Cook for 5 minutes, add the beer or stock, and cook for 1 minute. Add the tomatillos and the cilantro, season with salt and pepper, and cook until tender and saucy, about 10 minutes.

To serve, toss the drained pasta with the sauce and meatballs and the Manchego cheese. Olé! Pass crusty bread for mopping.

Toasted Ravioli

This dish is good for a special night: Congratulations! Happy Anniversary! I'm sorry. I love you. Thank you for everything. Take your pick and say it with food.   2 SERVINGS

---

2 **eggs**

A splash of **milk** or half-and-half

Salt and **black pepper**

1½ cups **Italian-style bread crumbs**

½ cup grated **Parmigiano-Reggiano cheese**, 2 generous handfuls

A handful of finely chopped fresh **flat-leaf parsley** leaves

12 large fresh **spinach and cheese ravioli** (1 package, about ¾ pound)

5 tablespoons **EVOO** (extra-virgin olive oil)

3 **garlic cloves**, finely chopped

A couple pinches of **red pepper flakes**

2 **roasted red peppers**, drained

1 14-ounce can **crushed tomatoes**

A handful of fresh **basil** leaves, thinly sliced

Beat the eggs and the splash of milk in a shallow dish and season with salt and pepper. Combine the bread crumbs with the cheese and parsley in a second dish. Dip the fresh ravioli in the eggs, then coat with the bread crumbs. Heat 3 tablespoons of the EVOO over medium heat in a large skillet, then toast the ravioli until deep golden, 3 to 4 minutes on each side.

In a small sauce pot, heat the remaining 2 tablespoons of EVOO with the garlic and red pepper flakes over medium-low heat. Grind the roasted peppers in a food processor and add them to the garlic after it has cooked for a couple of minutes. Stir in the tomatoes and season the sauce with salt and pepper. Heat through, then wilt in the basil and transfer the sauce to a small bowl. Surround the sauce with the toasted ravioli for dipping and serve.

Bel Aria Chicken and Pasta

This dish is my at-home version of a chicken dish prepared at a fabulous opera café in New York City called Caffe Taci—the same café where my mama earned her nickname. The flavors are as big as Pavarotti's voice and it will have you, too, singing for an encore plateful!

4 SERVINGS

Coarse salt

1 pound **rigatoni** pasta

3 tablespoons **extra-virgin olive oil** (EVOO)

3 tablespoons **unsalted butter**

1⅓ to 1½ pounds **chicken tenders,** cut into large bite-size pieces

Coarse black pepper

½ pound **cremini (baby portobello) mushroom caps,** thinly sliced, or 4 portobello caps, gills scraped out, halved and thinly sliced

4 **garlic cloves,** chopped

4 Italian **hot red cherry peppers,** drained and chopped, plus a splash of the pickling juices from the jar

½ cup **dry white wine**

½ cup grated **Parmigiano-Reggiano** (a couple of handfuls), plus more to pass at the table

A handful of fresh **flat-leaf parsley,** chopped

Crusty bread, to pass at the table

Bring a large pot of water to a boil for the pasta. When it comes to a boil, salt it and add the rigatoni. Heads up! Two ladles of the cooking water will be added to the sauce just before the pasta is drained.

While the pasta is working, heat a big, deep skillet over medium-high heat. Add 2 tablespoons of the EVOO (twice around the pan) and 1½ tablespoons of the butter. When the butter melts into the oil, add the chicken to the skillet, season with salt and pepper, and brown for 2 to 3 minutes on each side. Transfer the chicken to a plate. It will finish cooking through when added back to the sauce later.

Return the pan to the heat and add another table-spoon of EVOO, the remaining butter, then the mush-rooms and garlic. Cook until the mushrooms are tender, 10 to 15 minutes. Salt and pepper the mushrooms after they brown. (If you salt them when they are first added to the skillet, the salt will draw out the liquids and slow the browning process.) Next, add the hot peppers and a splash of the pickling liquid to the pan. Add the white wine and scrape up the pan drippings with a wooden spoon. Cook the wine down for a minute, then slide the chicken back into the pan. Cook together for another couple of minutes to finish cooking the chicken through.

Just before you drain the pasta, add 2 ladles of starchy water to the skillet. The starchy water will help

recipe continued

the sauce form and adhere to the pasta. Drain the pasta while it still has a strong bite to it, a little shy of al dente. It will continue to cook a little once it is combined with the sauce. Drain the rigatoni well and add it to the skillet. Turn off the heat and toss the chicken, mushrooms, and pasta together for a minute or two, sprinkling in 2 or 3 handfuls of grated Parmigiano cheese as you go, to allow the pasta to soak up the sauce and flavors. Garnish the pasta with lots of chopped parsley and pass extra cheese and crusty bread at the table.

tidbit >> If you want to add a salad, try *insalata tre colore* (three-color salad), a combination of chopped radicchio, endive, and romaine lettuce, dressed simply with balsamic vinegar or lemon juice, EVOO, salt, and pepper.

Pasta with Broccoli and Sausage with a Ricotta Surprise

Pasta with butter, ricotta, and Parm cheese is an Italian children's standard. Add a little broccoli—we grown-ups need our fiber—then be a kid again and enjoy. 4 SERVINGS

Salt

1 pound **short-cut pasta, such as** penne

1 cup **ricotta cheese**

Zest and juice of 1 lemon

Freshly ground **black pepper**

1 tablespoon **EVOO** (extra-virgin olive oil)

1 pound **bulk sweet Italian sausage**

1 large head **broccoli**

1 medium **onion**, chopped

4 large **garlic cloves**, chopped

¼ teaspoon **red pepper flakes**

1½ cups **chicken stock**

½ cup fresh **flat-leaf parsley**, a couple of generous handfuls, chopped

½ cup grated **Parmigiano-Reggiano** or Pecorino Romano cheese, plus some to pass at the table

Place a large pot of water with a tight-fitting lid over high heat and bring to a boil. Once it comes to a boil, add some salt and the pasta. Cook according to package directions until al dente. Heads up: You will need to use about ½ cup of the starchy cooking liquid for the sauce before you drain the pasta.

In a small mixing bowl, combine the ricotta cheese, lemon zest, salt, and a lot of freshly ground black pepper. Reserve the ricotta mixture on the countertop and let it come to room temp. The flavors of the cheese and lemon will develop as the cheese warms up.

Preheat a large skillet over medium-high heat with the EVOO. Add the sausage and break it up with the back of a wooden spoon into small bite-size pieces. Really go at breaking the meat up; it will make a big difference in the end. Cook the meat until brown, about 4 to 5 minutes. While the sausage is browning, prepare the broccoli. Cut the broccoli tops into small florets. Remove the fibrous outer layer of the stem (just square it off using your knife), then thinly slice the tender center portion of the stem.

Once the sausage is brown, remove it to a paper-towel-lined plate. Return the skillet to the heat and add all of the broccoli and the chopped onion. Spread the veggies out in an even layer in the pan, season with some salt and pepper, and let the broccoli brown up a bit before stirring, about 2 minutes. Add the garlic and red pepper flakes

recipe continued

and continue to cook 2 minutes more. Add the sausage back to the skillet along with the chicken stock. Ladle in some cooking water from the pasta and bring up to a simmer. Cook until the broccoli is tender and the liquids have reduced slightly, about 2 minutes. Add the lemon juice, parsley, and cooked, well-drained pasta. Toss to combine and simmer 1 last minute to allow the pasta to soak in the sauce and flavors. Turn the heat off, add the grated cheese, and toss to combine.

To serve, place a large dollop of the pepper-lemon-ricotta mixture into each of 4 shallow bowls and bury it with hot pasta. Once you are at the table, mix it up with a fork to distribute the ricotta cheese. Serve with extra grated cheese.

Christmas Pasta

I make this dinner every Christmas and cannot finish any year without it. This dish, with four different meats in it, is especially nice on Christmas night. Serve with tomato, basil, and mozzarella salad (the colors of the season and the Italian flag).   6 SERVINGS

Salt

1 pound **rigatoni**

2 tablespoons **extra-virgin olive oil** (EVOO)

¼ pound **pancetta**, chopped

¼ pound bulk **hot Italian sausage** (No bulk? Split a link open)

¼ pound bulk **sweet Italian sausage**

½ pound **ground sirloin**

½ pound **ground veal**

½ teaspoon **allspice**

Coarse black pepper

1 **carrot**, peeled and finely chopped

1 medium **yellow onion**, peeled and finely chopped

4 **garlic cloves**, crushed

½ cup **dry red wine**, a couple of glugs

1 cup **beef stock** or broth

1 28-ounce can **crushed tomatoes**

¼ cup **flat-leaf parsley** (a generous handful), finely chopped

½ cup grated **Romano cheese** (a couple of handfuls), plus some to pass at the table

Bring a large pot of water to a boil and salt it. Add the pasta and cook to al dente, with a bite to it.

While the water and pasta work, heat a large nonstick skillet over medium-high heat. Add 1 tablespoon EVOO. Add the pancetta to one half of the pan and all the sausage to the other. Break up the sausage into bits and brown while the pancetta renders, then combine and cook together another minute or so. Remove to a plate with a slotted spoon. Add the remaining tablespoon of EVOO, then the beef and veal. Brown and crumble the meat into tiny bits and season with allspice, salt, and pepper. Add the carrots, onions, and garlic and cook another 5 to 6 minutes to soften, then return the sausage and pancetta to the pan, draining away some of the fat. Deglaze the pan with the wine, scraping up all the good bits with a wooden spoon. Stir in the stock, then the tomatoes. Check the seasoning. Simmer over low heat until ready to serve, at least 10 minutes. Stir in half the parsley to finish.

Drain the pasta and add back to the hot pot. Ladle a few spoonfuls of the sauce over the pasta and add a couple of handfuls of cheese to the pot. Stir to coat the pasta evenly. Transfer to a large serving dish or individual bowls and top with the remaining sauce and parsley. Pass plenty of extra cheese at the table.

Drunken Tuscan Pasta

Pasta stewed up in red wine is a Tuscan invention: my kinda people!
I toss it together with other usual suspects from the region: wild
mushrooms, rosemary, and dark greens.   4 SERVINGS

1 bottle **Tuscan red table wine** such as Rosso di Montalcino or Chianti

Coarse salt

1 pound **perciatelli**, bucatini, or spaghetti (dried long-cut pasta)

3 tablespoons **EVOO** (extra-virgin olive oil)

¼ pound deli-sliced **pancetta** (see Tidbit)

3 **portobello mushroom caps**, thinly sliced

2 to 3 sprigs fresh **rosemary**, leaves finely chopped

4 **garlic cloves**, chopped

2 pinches of **red pepper flakes**

4 to 5 cups **chopped dark greens**, your choice of chard, escarole, spinach, or kale

Black pepper, to taste

¼ teaspoon freshly grated **nutmeg**

Grated **Parmigiano-Reggiano** cheese, a handful plus some to pass at the table

Pour the entire bottle of wine into a large pot. Add water and fill the pot up as you would to cook pasta. Bring the wine and water to a boil over high heat. When the liquids boil, add salt and the pasta and cook to al dente. Heads up: You will ladle out some cooking liquid for the pasta sauce before draining the pasta.

Heat a large nonstick skillet over medium heat. Add 2 tablespoons of the EVOO, then chop and add the pancetta. Brown the pieces until they are golden at the edges and transfer them to a paper-towel-lined plate. Add the mushrooms to the EVOO in the same skillet, season with the chopped rosemary, and cook until deeply golden, 6 to 8 minutes. Push the mushrooms to the sides of the pan and add the remaining tablespoon of EVOO to the center of the skillet. Add the garlic and red pepper flakes to the EVOO and cook them for a minute or so, then toss the mushrooms together with the garlic. Add the greens to the pan and season them with salt, pepper, and the nutmeg. When the greens have wilted down, add a couple of ladles of the pasta cooking liquid to the pan and cook for a minute to reduce.

Drain the pasta well and add it to the skillet. Add the pancetta and a handful of cheese to the pan. Toss the pasta for a minute or so to allow it to absorb the remaining liquid. Adjust the seasonings and serve. Pass the extra cheese at the table.

tidbit >> Three bacon slices may be substituted for the pancetta. They are similar in that both are cured pork, the difference being that bacon is also smoked.

Deviled Frittata and Heavenly Angel Hair Pasta

This pairs a mayo-free, warm, spicy take on deviled eggs with a pasta favorite from Trattoria Garga in Florence. The original "Pasta Magnifico," on which the Heavenly Angel Hair Pasta is based, is richer, with more cream and liquor. This lighter version is molto bene for brunch or a late-night bite. Your pick—it's always brunch time somewhere.   8 SERVINGS

Salt

1 pound **angel hair pasta**

5 tablespoons **EVOO** (extra-virgin olive oil)

1 medium **onion**, finely chopped

2 **celery ribs** from the heart, with greens, finely chopped

1 teaspoon **sweet paprika**

Black pepper

2 **garlic cloves**, finely chopped

¼ cup **green olives** with pimiento, finely chopped

1 tablespoon **hot sauce**

1 rounded teaspoon **Dijon mustard**

16 large **eggs**

1 cup **heavy cream**

A generous handful of fresh **flat-leaf parsley** leaves, finely chopped

2 **shallots**, thinly sliced

1 nip or 2 healthy shots **cognac**

Zest of 1 orange

Zest of 1 lemon

¾ cup grated **Pecorino Romano**, a few generous handfuls

1 cup fresh **basil**, 20 leaves, torn or shredded

Preheat the oven to 400°F.

Bring a large covered pot of water to a boil for the pasta. When it comes to a boil, salt the water, add the pasta, and cook it to al dente, 5 minutes. Before you drain the pasta, measure 2 ladles of starchy cooking water and reserve.

Heat 3 tablespoons of the EVOO, 3 times around the pan, in a large, oven-safe nonstick skillet over medium-low heat. Add the onions and cook them gently for 5 minutes. Do not caramelize the onions, just let them get translucent and sweet. Add the celery and season it with the paprika, salt, and pepper. Stir in the garlic, olives, hot sauce, and mustard. Beat together the eggs and ½ cup of the cream (eyeball it) and pour the mixture into the skillet. Stir in the parsley, then let the eggs settle and form a foundation, as you would for an omelet. Transfer the pan to the oven and bake the frittata until golden, 15 to 17 minutes.

recipe continued

Heat the remaining 2 tablespoons of EVOO in a deep skillet over medium heat. Add the shallots and cook for 5 minutes. Add the cognac, then stir in the remaining ½ cup of cream and reduce for 2 minutes. Add the zests and reduce for a minute or so more. Add the reserved pasta cooking water. Toss the drained pasta with the cheese and season it with salt and pepper. Transfer the pasta to a bowl and garnish it with an obscene amount of fresh basil. Yum-o!

Pasta with Bacon, Tomatoes, and Cheese

The ingredients list is the whole sales pitch. Need I say more?
4 SERVINGS

Salt

1 pound **short-cut pasta**

1 tablespoon **EVOO** (extra-virgin olive oil), once around the pan, plus more for the **greens**

4 **bacon** slices, chopped

1 large **onion**, chopped

4 large **garlic cloves**, chopped

¼ teaspoon **red pepper flakes**

Black pepper

½ cup **white wine**, a couple of good glugs

½ cup **chicken stock**

1 pint **grape tomatoes**

1 ball **fresh mozzarella**, cut into ¼-inch dice

1 bunch fresh **chives**, chopped

15 fresh **basil leaves**, chopped or torn, about ¾ cup

½ cup grated **Parmigiano-Reggiano** or Pecorino Romano cheese, plus some to pass at the table

6 cups **mixed greens**

Vinegar for the greens

Place a large pot of water with a tight-fitting lid over high heat and bring to a boil. Once it comes to a boil, add some salt and the pasta. Cook according to the package directions until al dente. Heads up: You need to reserve ½ cup of the cooking liquid before you drain the pasta.

While the pasta is cooking, start the sauce. Preheat a large skillet over medium-high heat; add the EVOO. Add the chopped bacon and cook, stirring every now and then, until crispy, about 2 to 3 minutes. Add the onions, garlic, red pepper flakes, and a little salt and pepper. Cook, stirring frequently, for about 5 minutes, or until the onions start to brown. Add the white wine and cook for 1 minute. Add the chicken stock and reserved pasta cooking liquid, then bring up to a bubble and simmer for 2 minutes. Add the grape tomatoes and cook them for about 30 seconds, just to start getting them hot and ready to burst. Add the cooked drained pasta, toss to coat in the sauce, and let some of the sauce soak in, about 1 minute. Turn the heat off and add the diced mozzarella, the chives, basil, grated cheese, and black pepper to taste. Dress the greens with oil and vinegar and serve with the pasta.

Pesce Spada Pasta

Try this pasta dish with swordfish steaks. It's a popular one!

4 SERVINGS

Coarse salt

1 pound medium **shell pasta**

1¼ to 1½ pounds **swordfish steak**, trimmed of skin and dark connective tissue

¼ cup **extra-virgin olive oil** (EVOO)

4 to 6 **garlic cloves**, chopped

1 medium **zucchini**, cut into short, thick matchsticks

1 pint **grape tomatoes**

6 **scallions**, chopped

¼ cup chopped fresh **mint** leaves (a handful)

¼ cup chopped fresh **flat-leaf parsley** (a handful)

½ cup **dry white wine**

Freshly ground black pepper

Bring a large pot of water to a boil. Add a couple of teaspoons of coarse salt to the boiling water, then add the pasta and cook for 8 or 9 minutes, until al dente.

Cut the swordfish into bite-size cubes.

Heat a large, deep skillet over medium-high heat. Add the EVOO, then the swordfish. Cook the fish until lightly browned on all sides. Remove with a slotted spoon to a plate, and cover loosely with foil to keep the fish warm.

Add the garlic, zucchini, and tomatoes to the pan and season with salt. Keep the veggies moving and cook for 3 minutes. Add the scallions. Cook for 2 minutes more to get the skins of the tomatoes to pop. Add the swordfish back to the pan and toss in the herbs. Douse the pan with the wine and scrape with a wooden spoon to lift the pan drippings. Add the hot drained starchy pasta and toss. Season with pepper and adjust the salt to taste, then transfer to a huge serving bowl or platter and serve.

Broccoli Rabe and Orecchiette

Add up to 1 pound of Italian hot or sweet bulk sausage, browned and crumbled, to make this dish stick to your ribs even more.   4 SERVINGS

Salt

½ pound **orecchiette** (little ear-shaped pastas)

2¼ to 2½ pounds (2 large bunches) **broccoli rabe**, ends trimmed, coarsely chopped

⅓ cup **extra-virgin olive oil** (EVOO)

6 to 8 **garlic cloves**, finely chopped

1 teaspoon **red pepper flakes**

½ cup freshly grated **Parmigiano-Reggiano**

Freshly ground black pepper

Place a pot of water on the stove to bring to a boil for the pasta. Cover the pot to bring water to a boil. Salt the water to season it and add the orecchiette. Cook al dente, with a bite to it. Heads up: Before draining the pasta, save a ladleful of the cooking water to add to the broccoli rabe.

Add the broccoli rabe and 2 to 3 cups water to a deep skillet. Cover the pan and bring the broccoli rabe to a boil. When the rabe wilts down into the pan, salt it. Simmer the rabe for about 7 minutes, until tender and no longer bitter. The color should remain deep green. Drain the rabe and reserve.

Return the deep skillet to the stove and place it over medium heat. Add the EVOO, garlic, and red pepper flakes and sauté for 2 to 3 minutes, stirring frequently. Add the broccoli rabe and turn to coat it in garlic oil. Add the ladleful of pasta water to the skillet; it will form a sauce as it emulsifies with the EVOO. Add the pasta, grated cheese, and salt and pepper to taste, and toss. Serve immediately.

Shrimp Primavera Pasta with Asparagus, Peas, and Leeks

Anytime is springtime. As the title suggests, this dish can transform the lousiest days and worst weather into a perfect spring evening. The light, bright flavors make for an easy, elegant meal any time of the year.
2 SERVINGS

Salt

½ pound **spaghetti**

1 **leek**

2 tablespoons **EVOO** (extra-virgin olive oil)

2 **garlic cloves**, thinly sliced

½ pound **shiitake mushrooms**, stemmed and sliced

1 cup **chicken or vegetable stock**

2 teaspoons **lemon zest**

½ pound medium to large **shrimp**, peeled and deveined

¾ to 1 pound **asparagus** (1 bundle), trimmed to 4 inches then cut into thirds

1 cup **frozen peas**

2 tablespoons **butter**, cut into small pieces

Black pepper

1 cup shaved or grated **Romano cheese**

Handful of fresh **flat-leaf parsley** leaves, chopped

Place a large covered pot of water on the stove and bring it up to a boil for the pasta. Salt the water and cook the spaghetti to al dente.

While the pasta is working, trim the tough green tops and the roots from the leek. Halve the leek lengthwise and dice it thin. Place the leeks in a colander and rinse them vigorously to release any grit. Drain the leeks well.

Heat the EVOO in a large, deep skillet over medium heat, add the garlic, and cook for a minute. Add the leeks and shiitakes and cook until they are tender, 3 to 4 minutes. Add the stock, raise the heat a little, and bring it up to a bubble. Once the stock bubbles, add the zest and the shrimp and cook it for 2 minutes, then add the asparagus and peas to the pan and cook them for 2 minutes more.

Melt the butter into the sauce, add the drained pasta to the pan, and toss to combine the shrimp and vegetables with the spaghetti. Season with a little pepper, adjust the salt to taste, and garnish with the cheese and parsley.

Ground Turkey Paprikash-Goulash with Macaroni

Reading this recipe makes my mouth water. Something about the ground turkey and spices combined with macaroni. Mmmmmm, delish!

4 SERVINGS

½ pound **rigate** (ribbed elbow macaroni)

Salt

1 tablespoon **extra-virgin olive oil** (EVOO)

1 tablespoon **butter**

2½ pounds ground **lean white-meat turkey**

4 **garlic cloves**, chopped

1 medium **onion**, chopped

1 **red bell pepper**, cored, seeded, and chopped

2 tablespoons **sweet paprika**

2 teaspoons **ground cumin**

2 teaspoons **dried marjoram**

2 teaspoons **freshly ground black pepper** (⅔ palmful)

2 cups **chicken stock** or broth

1 cup **sour cream**

2 tablespoons finely chopped fresh **dill**

2 tablespoons finely chopped fresh **flat-leaf parsley** (a generous handful)

Bring a pot of water to a boil for the pasta. When it comes to a boil, add the pasta and salt to season the cooking water. Cook the pasta for 6 minutes, al dente.

While the water comes to a boil and the pasta cooks, heat a deep skillet over medium-high heat. Add the EVOO, then butter, then ground meat. Break up the meat and crumble, 2 to 3 minutes. Add the garlic, onion, bell pepper, and seasonings to the turkey. Cook for 5 or 6 minutes, then add the chicken stock and sour cream. Bring to a bubble and reduce heat to low. Add the cooked pasta and stir. Let the pasta absorb some sauce, a minute or so. Adjust the seasonings and serve. Garnish with chopped parsley and dill.

White Beans, Pancetta, and Pasta

This is a mix-up of pasta e fagioli and minestra. Again, my indecisiveness is at play. 4 SERVINGS

---

3 tablespoons **extra-virgin olive oil** (EVOO)

⅓ pound **pancetta**, chopped

½ teaspoon **red pepper flakes**

4 **garlic cloves**, crushed

6 sprigs fresh **thyme**

3 sprigs fresh **rosemary**

2 **carrots**, chopped

1 medium **yellow onion**, chopped

2 **celery ribs** with greens, chopped

Salt and **freshly ground black pepper**

½ cup **dry white wine**

3 cups chopped fresh **dandelion greens** (1 small bunch)

1 head of **escarole**, chopped

2 15-ounce cans small **white beans** or cannellini, drained

1 15-ounce can **diced tomatoes** in juice, San Marzano variety if available

6 cups **chicken stock** or broth

2 cups **penne pasta**

Grated **Parmigiano-Reggiano** or Romano cheese, to pass at the table

Heat a soup pot over medium-high heat. Add the EVOO and the pancetta. Cook the pancetta for 3 to 4 minutes, then add the red pepper flakes, garlic, and herb sprigs. Add the vegetables as you chop: carrots, onions, and celery. Season with salt and pepper and cook until the carrots begin to soften, 7 to 8 minutes.

Add the wine and deglaze the pan, scraping up any good bits. Wilt in the greens and escarole in bunches. Add the beans, tomatoes, and stock and place a lid on the pot, raise the heat, and bring to a boil. Add the pasta and cook for 6 to 7 minutes, until cooked al dente. Serve the very thick soup in shallow bowls with lots of cheese.

Cowboy Spaghetti

Eat this meal in front of the TV. Invite Clint Eastwood and the cast of your favorite spaghetti western (mine's The Good, the Bad, and the Ugly).   4 SERVINGS

Salt

1 pound **spaghetti**

1 tablespoon **EVOO** (extra-virgin olive oil)

3 slices **smoky bacon**, chopped

1 pound **ground sirloin**

1 medium **onion**, chopped

3 to 4 **garlic cloves**, chopped

Black pepper

2 teaspoons **hot sauce**

1 tablespoon **Worcestershire sauce**

1 14-ounce can chopped or crushed **fire-roasted tomatoes**

1 8-ounce can **tomato sauce**

8 ounces sharp **Cheddar** cheese

4 **scallions**, trimmed, chopped

Bring a large pot of water to a boil. Salt the water and add the spaghetti. Cook the pasta to al dente, with a bite to it. Drain the spaghetti.

Heat a deep skillet over medium-high heat. Add the EVOO and bacon. Brown and crisp the bacon for 5 minutes, then remove with a slotted spoon to a paper-towel-lined plate. Drain off a little excess fat from the skillet if necessary, leaving just enough to coat the bottom. Add the beef and crumble it as it browns, 3 to 4 minutes. Add the onions and garlic and stir into the meat. Season the meat with salt and pepper, hot sauce, and Worcestershire. Cook for 5 to 6 minutes more, then stir in the tomatoes and tomato sauce.

Add the hot spaghetti to the meat and sauce and combine. Adjust the seasonings and serve up the pasta in shallow bowls. Grate some cheese over the pasta and sprinkle with the scallions.

Cacio e Pepe (Cheese and Pepper Pasta) and Spinach with White Beans

This Roman dish is as old as the city's seven hills. It doesn't get any easier, really. As a side, I fry up some garlic in oil and toss it with chopped defrosted spinach and some rinsed canned white beans.

4 SERVINGS

Salt

1 pound **spaghetti**

3 tablespoons **unsalted butter**, cut into small pieces

5 tablespoons **EVOO** (extra-virgin olive oil)

2 teaspoons **coarse black pepper**

1 cup grated **Pecorino Romano** cheese, 3 rounded handfuls

1 10-ounce box **frozen chopped spinach**

3 to 4 **garlic cloves**, chopped

1 14-ounce can **cannellini beans**, rinsed and drained

¼ teaspoon freshly grated **nutmeg**

Bring a large pot of water to a boil for the pasta and salt it. Add the pasta and cook to al dente. Heads up: You'll need to use a ladle or two of the cooking water (about ½ cup) for the sauce right before you drain the pasta.

Place a large skillet over low heat with the butter, 1 tablespoon of the EVOO, and pepper. Let it hang out until the pasta is done.

When the pasta is ready, take a ladle of the starchy cooking water and add it to the butter-pepper mixture. Drain the pasta and toss it in the pan with the sauce. Turn off the heat. Add the cheese in small handfuls, then toss the pasta with tongs, until all the cheese is incorporated into the creamy sauce. Add another ladle of cooking water if needed, then season the pasta to taste with salt and drizzle with 2 tablespoons of the EVOO.

While the pasta works, defrost the spinach in the microwave for 6 minutes on high. Place the spinach in a clean kitchen towel and wring the water out. Heat a small skillet over medium heat. Add the remaining 2 tablespoons of EVOO, twice around the pan, then the garlic. Cook the garlic for 2 minutes, and then add the beans. Add the spinach to the beans, breaking it up as you drop it into the pan. Season the spinach and beans with nutmeg, salt, and pepper. Serve the spinach and beans alongside the hot pasta.

Mega Meat-Stuffed Shells

My grandpa Emmanuel was the head cook in his house. My mama was the eldest of ten, so she got to help out a lot. This is the kind of supper I envision the kids having back in the day, made a little easier with short-cuts like frozen chopped spinach.   2 SERVINGS

1 10-ounce box **frozen chopped spinach**

Salt

8 **jumbo pasta shells**

2 tablespoons **EVOO** (extra-virgin olive oil), plus some for drizzling

1 pound **meatloaf mix** (ground beef, pork, and veal)

3 **garlic cloves**, 2 chopped, 1 crushed and halved

1 small **onion**, finely chopped

Black pepper

⅛ teaspoon freshly grated or ground **nutmeg**

1 **egg**, beaten

¼ cup **Italian-style bread crumbs** (a handful)

½ cup grated **Romano or Parmigiano-Reggiano cheese** (2 handfuls)

¼ teaspoon **red pepper flakes**

1 8-ounce can **tomato sauce**

A few fresh **basil** leaves, torn

Place the frozen spinach on a plate and defrost it in the microwave on High for 6 minutes. Wring the spinach dry in a clean towel.

While the spinach is in the microwave, preheat the oven to 425°F and, in a large covered pot, bring the water to a boil for the shells. Salt the boiling water and cook the shells for 6 to 7 minutes; they should still be firm at the center. Drizzle them with EVOO and set aside in a shallow baking dish.

While the pasta is working, brown the meat over medium to medium-high heat in 1 tablespoon of the EVOO (once around the pan). Add the chopped garlic and onions to the meat; season them with salt, pepper, and nutmeg; and cook the mixture for 5 minutes more. Transfer the meat to a bowl. Add the spinach and mix them together. Add the egg, bread crumbs, and half the cheese and combine. Fill the shells with the meat mixture and sprinkle the rest of the cheese on top, then bake for 11 to 12 minutes to set the filling in the shells and crisp the pasta at the edges.

While the shells bake, heat the remaining tablespoon of EVOO in a small pot over low heat with the halved garlic clove and cook for 3 to 4 minutes. Remove the garlic, add the red pepper flakes, and cook for a minute more, then stir in the tomato sauce and simmer for 5 minutes. Stir in the basil.

Pour ½ cup of sauce on each dinner plate and top it with 4 shells.

Mac-n-Cheddar with Broccoli

There is something so comforting about the classic mac 'n' cheese.
I make mine with broccoli.   4 SERVINGS

Coarse salt

1 pound **elbow macaroni** or cavatappi (corkscrew-shaped pasta)

2½ cups **broccoli florets**

1 tablespoon **extra-virgin olive oil** (EVOO)

2 tablespoons **unsalted butter**

1 small **onion**, finely chopped

3 tablespoons all-purpose **flour**

½ teaspoon **cayenne pepper**

1 teaspoon **paprika**

3 cups **whole milk**

1 cup **chicken stock** or broth

3 cups grated **sharp yellow Cheddar**

1 tablespoon **Dijon mustard**

Freshly ground black pepper

Bring a large pot of water to a boil. Add salt to season the cooking water, then add the pasta. Cook for 5 minutes, then add the broccoli and cook for 3 minutes more or until the pasta is cooked al dente and the florets are just tender. Drain well and return to the pot.

While the pasta cooks, heat a medium sauce pot over medium-low heat. Add the EVOO and heat with the butter until it melts. Add the onions and cook for 3 to 5 minutes to sweat them out and turn the juices sweet. Raise the heat a bit, then whisk in the flour, cayenne, and paprika. Whisk together until the roux bubbles up, then cook for 1 minute more. Whisk in the milk and stock and raise the heat a bit higher to bring the sauce to a quick boil. Once it bubbles, drop the heat back to a simmer and cook until the sauce thickens, 3 to 5 minutes.

Add the cheese to the thickened sauce and stir to melt it, a minute or so. Stir in the mustard and season the sauce with salt and pepper. Pour over the broccoli and cooked pasta and toss to combine. Adjust the seasonings, transfer to a large platter, and serve.

Southwestern Pasta Bake

Your favorite kid classic, mac 'n' cheese, picks up some ingredients along the way and heads Southwest.   4 SERVINGS

Coarse salt

1 pound **penne rigate** (ridged penne) or cavatappi (ridged corkscrew pasta)

2 tablespoons **vegetable oil**

4 6-ounce boneless, skinless chicken breast halves, cut into bite-size pieces

1 tablespoon **ground cumin**

1 tablespoon **ground coriander**

2 tablespoons **chili powder**

Coarse black pepper

1 large **yellow onion**, chopped

3 **garlic cloves**, chopped

1 **jalapeño pepper**, seeded and chopped

2 tablespoons **unsalted butter**

2 tablespoons all-purpose **flour**

2 cups **milk**

¾ pound **sharp yellow Cheddar cheese**, shredded (about 2½ cups)

¼ cup fresh **cilantro** leaves (a generous handful), chopped

½ cup fresh **flat-leaf parsley** leaves (a few handfuls), chopped

Preheat the broiler to high and position the rack 8 inches from the heat.

Bring a large pot of water to a boil. Salt the boiling water and cook the pasta until slightly undercooked—a little chewy at the center.

While the water is coming up to a boil, preheat a large skillet over medium-high heat with the vegetable oil. Season the chicken with cumin, coriander, chili powder, salt, and pepper. Add the seasoned chicken to the hot skillet and cook until lightly brown, about 4 to 5 minutes. Add the onions, garlic, and jalapeños and continue to cook for 5 minutes. While the chicken is cooking with the onions, make the Cheddar sauce.

In a medium sauce pot, melt the butter and add the flour to it. Cook for 1 to 2 minutes over moderate heat, then whisk in the milk. When the milk comes to a bubble, stir in the cheese, cilantro, and parsley with a wooden spoon. Season with a little salt and pepper and remove the cheese sauce from the heat.

Once the pasta is cooked, drain it and add it back into the large pot, add the contents of the chicken skillet and all of the Cheddar sauce, and stir to combine. Transfer to a baking dish and place under the broiler to lightly brown.

Eggplant and Wild Mushroom Pasta with Ricotta Salata

Leaving a little skin on the eggplants will add color and texture to the dish. The small eggplants are not too bitter and when they are firm, they will not soak up as much oil, so they do not need to be salted and pressed. This is a hearty meal—no sides necessary!   4 SERVINGS

2 ounces **dried porcini mushrooms**

1 cup **chicken stock** or broth

Salt

2 medium vine-ripe **tomatoes** (½ pound)

½ pound **cavatappi** (cork-screw-shaped hollow pasta), or other shaped pasta

2 pounds (4 or 5) baby **eggplants**

3 tablespoons **extra-virgin olive oil** (EVOO)

3 **garlic cloves**, chopped

Freshly ground black pepper

⅓ pound **ricotta salata cheese**, chopped and crumbled into small pieces (in specialty cheese case of market, among Italian selections)

1 cup (20 leaves) fresh **basil**, torn or shredded

Combine the porcinis and chicken stock in a small pot and bring up to a boil. Reduce the heat to lowest setting and let the mushrooms soften and steep for 10 to 15 minutes, until very tender.

Place a pot of water on the stove to boil for the pasta. When it boils, salt the water to season it. Cut a small x into the bottom of the tomatoes and plunge them into the boiling pasta water for 30 seconds, then remove to a cutting board to cool. Add the cavatappi to the water and cook to al dente, or with a bite to it.

While the porcinis and pasta cook, trim half of the skin from the eggplant.

Heat a large nonstick skillet over medium-high heat. Cut the eggplant into 1- by ½-inch bite-size pieces. Add the EVOO to the pan, followed by the garlic and eggplant. Turn and toss the eggplant and season it with salt and pepper. Let it brown lightly at the edges, about 5 minutes, then reduce the heat to medium low and continue to cook.

tidbit >> If your market has no ricotta salata (ricotta cheese that's been dried out a little), then use the same amount of feta but go easy on the salt because it is saltier. If you use goat cheese instead, toss and serve the dish and then garnish the individual plates with some crumbles, 2 ounces per portion. (Goat cheese is too delicate to mix.)

Pull the skins off the cooled tomatoes and cut them in half. Seed the tomatoes by gently squeezing them over the sink or a garbage bowl. Dice the tomatoes and add them to the cooking eggplant. Adjust seasoning with salt and pepper.

Remove the tender porcinis from the cooking broth and coarsely chop them. Add the broth and chopped mushrooms to the eggplant and tomatoes. Drain the pasta well and add the hot pasta to the pan. Toss to combine and coat and give the pasta a minute to soak in some juice. Add the ricotta salata and the basil; turn to wilt the basil, check the seasoning one last time, and serve.

Seafood

I never met a fish I didn't like—I LOVE
seafood. Fancy or not, there's something
here for everyone.

GO FISH!

*Tuna with Everything-but-the-Kitchen-Sink, Hold-the-Mayo,
    Stuffed Bread*
Italian Tuna Casserole
Sesame-Crusted Red Snapper with Ginger-Dressed Snappy Veggies
Salmon Burgers with Caesar Slaw
*Lime-and-Honey Glazed Salmon with Warm Black Bean and
    Corn Salad*
Tuna Skewers with Orange and Rosemary on Bitter Greens Slaw
Cornmeal-Crusted Catfish and Green Rice Pilaf
Sweet Lemon Salmon with Mini Carrots and Dill
Quick Cioppino
Baked Sole and Roasted Asparagus with Sesame

WHO YA CALLIN' "SHRIMP"?

*Pumpkin-Peanut Curry Noodles with Five-Spice Seared Scallops
    and Shrimp*
Spicy Shrimp and Bok Choy Noodle Bowl
*Crispy Fried Sesame Shrimp, Zucchini, and Mushroom Caps with a
    Ginger-Soy Dipping Sauce*
Lemon-Thyme Succotash with Garlic-Parsley Shrimp
Greek-Style Shrimp Scampi and Linguine
Grilled Shrimp and Chorizo Skewers with Piquillo Pepper Gazpacho
Iceberg Salad with Shrimp
Seafood au Gratin with Sautéed Artichokes and Spinach
Thai-Style Shrimp and Veggies with Toasted Coconut Rice
Shrimp and Pork Balls with Spicy Lime Dipping Sauce

SEAFOOD FOR A STEAL

Linguine with Rach's Cupboard Red Clam Sauce
Serrano-Wrapped Halibut with Tortillas and Savoy Cabbage
Chorizo-Cod-Potato Stew
Crab and Corn Chowda-Mac
Seafood Newburg Stoup with Cayenne-Chive-Buttered Corn Toasties
*Lemon and Brown Butter Fish Fillets with Seared Red and Yellow
    Grape Tomatoes*
Crab Cakes with a Creamy, Grainy Mustard Sauce
Crab Salad Bites on Endive
Fish Tacos with Avocado Dressing
Sweet Sea Scallops in a Caper-Raisin Sauce

Tuna with Everything-but-the-Kitchen-Sink, Hold-the-Mayo, Stuffed Bread

I usually have these ingredients on hand, in the cupboard, fridge, or freezer. Feel free to swap away based on the things you keep around. This is perfect for any too-tired night of the year. **4 SERVINGS**

1 **baguette** or other crusty loaf (day-old is fine)

1½ cups (2 small cans) **Italian tuna in oil**, drained

1 15-ounce can **artichoke hearts**, whole or quartered, drained and chopped or sliced

6 soft **sun-dried tomatoes**, dry or drained if packed in oil, thinly sliced

A handful of fresh **flat-leaf parsley**, chopped

A handful of **olives**, any or all varieties are fine, chopped

¼ **red onion**, chopped or thinly sliced

3 tablespoons **capers** or a couple of caper berries, drained and chopped

2 cups **arugula** or other greens, chopped

4 **anchovy fillets**, finely chopped, or a little anchovy paste (optional but recommended)

A couple of sprigs of **fresh herbs:** rosemary, thyme, tarragon, or basil—whichever you have—chopped

Coarse black pepper

Zest and juice of 1 lemon

3 tablespoons **extra-virgin olive oil** (EVOO)

Preheat the oven to 200°F.

Crisp the bread in the oven. Remove, split, and hollow out some of the soft insides.

Place the tuna in a bowl and flake it with a fork. Add the remaining salad ingredients, dress with pepper, lemon zest and juice, and EVOO, and work the salad together with a rubber spatula. Overfill the bottom of the loaf, mounding the salad. Set the top in place and press down to set the creation. Cut into quarters. Wrap each sandwich in wax paper or paper towels at one end to limit dripping as you crunch and munch.

tidbit >> I always have bread, always. Keep a well-wrapped baguette in the freezer and you'll always be ready to crisp and fill at will.

Italian Tuna Casserole

Tuna casserole was a classic back in the day when I was a kid. I'm bringing it back—Mediterranean style! 4 SERVINGS

1 10-ounce box **frozen chopped spinach**

Salt

1 pound medium or large **shell pasta** or other short-cut pasta with ridges

1 tablespoon **EVOO** (extra-virgin olive oil)

2 tablespoons **butter**, cut into pieces

1 medium **onion**, finely chopped

5 **garlic cloves**, finely chopped

3 tablespoons all-purpose **flour**

½ cup **dry white wine**, a couple of glugs

1 cup **chicken stock** (about ¼ of a quart-size box—the rest can go right in the fridge)

2 cups **milk**

¼ teaspoon freshly **grated nutmeg**, or to taste

1 teaspoon **hot sauce**

1 teaspoon **Dijon mustard**

Black pepper

2 6-ounce cans **white tuna in water**, drained, or 3 4-ounce cans Italian tuna in oil, drained

1 cup grated **Parmigiano-Reggiano** or Pecorino Romano cheese, 3 very generous handfuls

A handful of chopped fresh **flat-leaf parsley**

Place the spinach on a plate and microwave it for 6 minutes on High to defrost it. Place it in a clean kitchen towel and wring it dry, then reserve.

While the spinach is defrosting, get a large pot of water on the stove for the pasta. Bring to a boil, then salt the water liberally and cook the shells to al dente.

While the pasta works, heat a deep, large skillet over medium heat. Add the EVOO, then melt the butter into the oil. When the butter melts, add the onions and garlic and cook until tender, 4 to 5 minutes. Sprinkle the flour around the pan and cook for a minute, then whisk in the wine—it will cook off and the mixture will thicken almost immediately. Whisk in the stock, then whisk in the milk and bring it to a bubble. Reduce the heat a bit. Season the sauce with the nutmeg, hot sauce, and mustard, then season with salt and pepper to taste. Simmer for 2 to 3 minutes to thicken, then add the spinach, separating it as you add it to the sauce.

Preheat the broiler.

Back to the sauce: Add the tuna, flaking it as you go, then stir to combine. Heat the spinach and tuna through for a minute or so. Drain the pasta and toss with the sauce. Transfer the tuna to a casserole dish and cover it with the Parm or Romano. Place the casserole under the broiler for 2 minutes to brown the edges and the cheese. Top with the parsley and serve.

Sesame-Crusted Red Snapper with Ginger-Dressed Snappy Veggies

Snapper is so versatile, and in this recipe, I'm headed to Asia.

4 SERVINGS

2-inch piece **fresh ginger,** peeled and grated or minced

1 small **jalapeño pepper,** seeded and finely chopped

3 tablespoons **rice wine vinegar** or white wine vinegar

Salt and **freshly ground black pepper**

5 tablespoons **vegetable oil**

10 **radishes,** thinly sliced

1 **English (seedless) cucumber** (the one wrapped in plastic), thinly sliced

1 **yellow bell pepper,** seeded, quartered, and cut into thin strips

4 8-ounce portions **red snapper** fillet, skin on

½ cup **sesame seeds,** untoasted (available on spice aisle)

1 bunch **watercress,** trimmed of thick stems

1 cup (about 20 leaves) **fresh basil,** coarsely chopped

¼ cup toasted **unsalted peanuts,** coarsely chopped

In a salad bowl combine the ginger, jalapeño, vinegar, salt, and pepper. In a slow steady stream, whisk in 3 tablespoons of the vegetable oil. Add the radishes, cucumber, and bell pepper and toss to coat. Let the veggies marinate at room temperature while you prepare the sesame-crusted snapper.

With a sharp paring knife, score the skin side of the snapper fillets: Slash 3 ⅛-inch-deep cuts across the width of the fish. Season both sides of the fish with salt and pepper. Sprinkle and then gently press the sesame seeds onto both sides of the fish. Heat a large nonstick skillet over medium-high heat with the remaining 2 tablespoons of vegetable oil (twice around the pan). When the pan is hot, add the seasoned fish to the skillet skin side down. Sauté the snapper for 4 minutes, and if you find that the fillets bubble up in the center section, carefully press each fillet down with a fish spatula. Flip the fillets and continue to cook on the second side for 3 minutes, or until the fish is cooked through and opaque. While the fish is cooking on the second side, finish off the ginger-dressed snappy veggies.

To the marinating vegetables add the watercress, basil, and peanuts. Toss to combine.

To serve, distribute the snappy veggies among four plates and top with the sesame-crusted snapper.

Salmon Burgers with Caesar Slaw

Wild Alaskan canned salmon is a great staple to keep on hand—it's packed with good nutrition and calcium. This is my favorite way to use it.   4 SERVINGS

1 14-ounce can **Alaskan salmon**, drained and flaked

2 **egg whites**, lightly beaten

A handful of fresh **flat-leaf parsley**, finely chopped

Zest and juice of 1 lemon

3 **garlic cloves**, finely chopped

¾ cup **Italian bread crumbs**, 3 generous handfuls

Black pepper and **salt**

4 **anchovies**, finely chopped (optional)

2 teaspoons **Dijon mustard**

1 tablespoon **Worcestershire sauce**

¼ cup **EVOO** (extra-virgin olive oil), plus 2 tablespoons

A couple of handfuls of **grated Parmigiano-Reggiano** or Pecorino Romano cheese

2 **romaine lettuce** hearts, shredded

1 head **radicchio**, shredded

In a bowl, combine the flaked salmon, egg whites, parsley, the lemon zest, two thirds of the chopped garlic, the bread crumbs, and lots of black pepper and a little salt. Form 4 large patties or 8 mini patties.

Juice the lemon into a salad bowl—get it all! Add the remaining garlic, the chopped anchovies, Dijon mustard, and Worcestershire. Whisk in about ¼ cup EVOO and the cheese. Add lots of black pepper, no salt. Add the shredded lettuces to the bowl and toss to coat evenly. Now, season the slaw with salt to taste, if necessary.

Preheat the 2 tablespoons of EVOO, twice around the pan, in a nonstick skillet over medium to medium-high heat. Cook the salmon patties for 2 to 3 minutes on each side for mini patties, 4 minutes on each side for large patties.

Serve the salmon burgers atop a mound of the Caesar slaw.

Lime-and-Honey Glazed Salmon with Warm Black Bean and Corn Salad

Lime and honey may seem like an unlikely pair, it's a match made in heaven! This sweet-and-savory Southwestern recipe is a fantastic way to dish up big flavor in an even bigger serving of veggies.   4 SERVINGS

4 tablespoons **extra-virgin olive oil** (EVOO)

1 medium **red onion**, chopped

2 large **garlic cloves**, chopped

½ to 1 teaspoon **red pepper flakes** (medium heat to extra spicy)

1 teaspoon **ground cumin**

Salt and **freshly ground black pepper**

Juice of 2 limes

3 tablespoons **honey** (3 gobs)

1 teaspoon **chili powder** (⅓ palmful)

4 6-ounce **salmon fillets**

1 **red bell pepper**, cored, seeded, and chopped

1 10-ounce box **frozen corn kernels**, defrosted

tidbit >> If fresh corn is in season, by all means cut the kernels from 4 fresh ears instead of using frozen.

½ cup **chicken stock** or broth

1 15-ounce can **black beans**, rinsed and drained

2 to 3 tablespoons fresh **cilantro** leaves, chopped

6 cups **baby spinach**

Preheat a medium skillet over medium heat with 2 tablespoons of EVOO. Add the onions, garlic, red pepper flakes, cumin, salt, and pepper. Cook, stirring occasionally, for 3 minutes.

Meanwhile, preheat a medium nonstick skillet over medium-high heat with the remaining 2 tablespoons of EVOO. In a shallow dish, combine the juice of 1 lime, honey, chili powder, salt, and pepper. Add the salmon fillets to the lime-honey mixture and toss to coat. Add the seasoned salmon to the hot skillet and cook until just cooked through, about 3 to 4 minutes on each side.

To the cooked onions, add the bell peppers and corn kernels and cook for 1 minute. Add the chicken stock and continue to cook for another 2 minutes. Add the black beans and cook until the beans are just heated through. Remove the skillet from the heat and add the juice of the second lime, the cilantro, and spinach. Toss to wilt the spinach, then taste and adjust the seasoning. Serve the salmon on top of the warm black bean and corn salad.

Tuna Skewers with Orange and Rosemary on Bitter Greens Slaw

This is such a flavorful meal on a stick.   4 SERVINGS

2 pounds **tuna steak**, cubed

2 tablespoons **balsamic vinegar**

3 to 4 tablespoons **fresh rosemary**, finely chopped

Zest and juice of 1 large navel orange

1 tablespoon **grill seasoning**, such as McCormick's Montreal Steak Seasoning

Extra-virgin olive oil (EVOO) for drizzling, plus 2 tablespoons for dressing

2 heads **radicchio**, shredded

2 heads **Belgian endive**, shredded

½ **red onion**, very thinly sliced

1 **red bell pepper**, halved, cored, seeded, and very thinly sliced

2 tablespoons **red wine vinegar**

Salt and **freshly ground black pepper**

Preheat an outdoor grill, grill pan, or tabletop grill to high. Pile the cubed tuna onto metal skewers. Place them on a baking sheet or large shallow dish. Rub the balsamic vinegar into the fish. Combine the rosemary with the orange zest and grill seasoning. Drizzle EVOO over the skewers, then liberally coat the kabobs with the spice and herb mix. Cook the skewers a minute or so on each side, making quarter turns, for medium-rare fish; cook 2 minutes on each quarter turn for opaque, well-cooked fish.

While the fish cooks, mix the slaw by combining the shredded radicchio and endive with the onion and bell pepper. Juice the orange over the salad, then add the vinegar, followed by 2 tablespoons EVOO. Toss and season the slaw with salt and pepper.

Remove the fish from the skewers and serve on top of the bitter greens slaw.

Cornmeal-Crusted Catfish and Green Rice Pilaf

If you've never crusted seafood in cornmeal, try this recipe. Not only will you love it, you'll be coating everything in cornmeal—from catfish to calamari to snapper.   4 SERVINGS

5 tablespoons **extra-virgin olive oil** (EVOO)

1 tablespoon **unsalted butter**

1 large **shallot**, finely chopped

1 tablespoon fresh **thyme** leaves, chopped (from 4 sprigs)

Salt and **freshly ground black pepper**

1½ cups **long-grain rice**

½ cup **dry white wine**

3 cups **chicken stock** or broth

½ cup fresh **flat-leaf parsley** leaves (a couple of generous handfuls)

½ pound fresh **spinach** leaves, trimmed and cleaned

20 fresh **basil** leaves

1 **lemon**, ½ juiced, the other half cut into wedges

4 6- to 8-ounce **catfish fillets**

1 cup **yellow cornmeal**

Preheat the oven to 400°F.

Bring a medium sauce pot filled three-quarters full with water to a boil.

Heat a second medium saucepan or pot over moderate heat. Add 1 tablespoon of the EVOO (once around the pan), the butter, shallots, thyme, salt, and pepper. Sauté the shallots for 2 minutes, then add the rice and lightly brown, 3 to 5 minutes. Add the wine and allow it to evaporate entirely, 1 to 2 minutes. Add the chicken stock and bring to a boil. Cover the rice and reduce the heat. Cook for 18 to 20 minutes, until tender.

Salt the boiling water in the other pot and add the parsley, spinach, and basil. Stir to submerge the greens for 30 seconds, then carefully take the pot to the sink. Use a slotted spoon or a spider to remove the greens to a colander. Discard the water. Rinse the greens under slow-running cold water to stop the cooking process. Give the greens a gentle squeeze to get rid of the excess water. Transfer the cooled, drained greens to a blender or food processor. Add about 2 tablespoons of EVOO and the lemon juice. Puree until completely smooth. Reserve the puree for finishing the cooked rice.

Preheat a large oven-safe nonstick skillet over medium-high heat. Add the remaining 2 tablespoons of EVOO. Season the catfish with salt and pepper and coat evenly and completely in the cornmeal. Add the coated fish to the hot skillet and sear for 2 minutes on each side, then transfer the skillet with the fish to the oven and continue to cook for 8 to 10 minutes, until the fish is firm to the touch and opaque.

Once the rice is cooked, add the reserved greens puree and stir with a fork to combine and fluff the rice. Pile the rice onto dinner plates and serve the cornmeal-crusted catfish on top. Pass the lemon wedges at the table.

Sweet Lemon Salmon with Mini Carrots and Dill

Lemon . . . salmon . . . dill . . . what's there not to like?   4 SERVINGS

3 tablespoons **light brown sugar**

Zest and juice of 1 lemon

2 tablespoons **vegetable oil**

4 6-ounce **salmon fillets**

Salt and **freshly ground black pepper**

1 18-ounce bag of **"baby" carrots** (really, these are big carrots cut by machine into baby carrots), the larger babies cut in half on a long diagonal

2 tablespoons **unsalted butter**

¼ cup fresh **dill** (a generous handful), chopped

Preheat the oven to 400°F.

For the mini carrots with dill, fill a medium skillet with 1½ inches of water and bring up to a simmer.

For the sweet lemon salmon, in a small sauce pot, combine the brown sugar, 2 tablespoons water, and the lemon juice. Place over medium heat and bring up to a simmer while stirring to dissolve the sugar. Once at a simmer, cook for 1 minute, then reserve in a warm place.

To cook the salmon, preheat an ovenproof nonstick skillet over medium-high heat with the vegetable oil. Season the salmon fillets with salt, pepper, and the lemon zest. Add to the hot skillet, and cook for 3 to 4 minutes on the first side. Flip the salmon over, brush with the brown sugar–lemon mixture, transfer to the oven, and cook for 4 to 5 more minutes, or until cooked through.

While the salmon is cooking, add the baby carrots to the boiling water, season with salt, and simmer for 3 to 4 minutes, or until tender. Drain the carrots, then return them to the skillet and place back over the heat. Add the butter, dill, salt, and pepper and stir the carrots until the butter has melted. Transfer the carrots to a serving platter and serve alongside the sweet lemon salmon.

Quick Cioppino

My version of this classic Italian fish stew (pronounced chuh-PEE-noh) is speedy and spicy. This hearty dish is easy to whip up after a long day of work and is perfect all year 'round.   4 SERVINGS

3 tablespoons **extra-virgin olive oil** (EVOO)

4 sprigs **fresh thyme**

4 **garlic cloves**, smashed

1 teaspoon **red pepper flakes**

2 medium **onions**, quartered and thinly sliced

2 **celery ribs** with leafy tops from the heart, chopped

Salt and **freshly ground black pepper**

⅔ cup **white vermouth** or 1 cup dry white wine

1 15-ounce can **chunky-style crushed tomatoes**

2 cups **chicken stock** or broth

2 pounds **cod**

A wedge of fresh **lemon**

24 **mussels**, debearded and scrubbed

½ cup fresh **flat-leaf parsley** (a couple of handfuls), coarsely chopped

Heat a large, deep skillet over medium-high heat. Add the EVOO, thyme sprigs, garlic, and red pepper flakes and stir for 30 seconds, then add the onions and celery and season with salt and pepper. Cook for 5 minutes, then add the vermouth to deglaze the pan. Reduce the liquid by half, a minute or two. Add the tomatoes and stock and bring to a bubble. Dress the cod with a little lemon juice and salt and cut it into large chunks. Nestle the cod chunks into the bubbling pot so the liquids surround the fish. Cook the cod for 3 minutes, then add a layer of mussels to the pan and cover. Cook for 5 minutes longer, or until the mussels open. Discard any unopened mussels. Carefully stir the parsley in and remove the thyme stems. Ladle the stew into shallow bowls and serve.

Baked Sole and Roasted Asparagus with Sesame

Not only does my hubby have soul on stage, he digs this baked sole dish. I think you will, too.   4 SERVINGS

---

2 cups **chicken stock** or broth

1 tablespoon **vegetable oil**, plus some for drizzling

1 cup **white rice**

2 inch piece of **fresh ginger**, peeled and grated

4 tablespoons **tamari** (dark aged soy sauce, found on the international aisle)

2 **garlic cloves**, chopped

Juice of 1 lemon

6 **scallions**, thinly sliced

2 teaspoons **toasted sesame oil**

4 6- to 7-ounce **sole fillets**

2 pounds **asparagus**, trimmed to 4- to 5-inch tips

3 tablespoons **sesame seeds**

Salt and **freshly ground black pepper**

Preheat the oven to 400°F.

Bring the stock and a drizzle of vegetable oil to a boil. Add the rice and stir. Return to a boil, then lower the heat, cover, and simmer for about 18 minutes, until tender.

In a shallow baking dish, combine the ginger, tamari, garlic, lemon juice, scallions, 1 teaspoon of the toasted sesame oil, and a drizzle of vegetable oil. Add the sole fillets to the shallow dish and coat in the mixture. Let the fish sit while you prepare the asparagus.

Place the asparagus on a rimmed cookie sheet and drizzle with the tablespoon of vegetable oil, the remaining teaspoon of sesame oil, the sesame seeds, salt, and pepper. Toss the asparagus around to make sure it is thoroughly coated. Transfer the fish and the asparagus to the oven and roast for 12 to 14 minutes, or until the fish is cooked through and the asparagus is tender.

When the rice is tender, fluff it with a fork and remove from the heat.

Serve the baked sole alongside the roasted asparagus with the white rice.

Pumpkin-Peanut Curry Noodles with Five-Spice Seared Scallops and Shrimp

This is perfect for the fall—even on Halloween!   4 SERVINGS

Salt

1 pound **spaghetti**

8 tablespoons **vegetable oil** or peanut oil (Don't worry! You're not gonna wind up eating all that oil!)

3 **garlic cloves**, finely chopped

2-inch piece of **fresh ginger**, peeled and minced or grated

1 **red bell pepper**, thinly sliced

½ teaspoon **red pepper flakes**

¼ cup **creamy peanut butter**

¼ to ⅓ cup **tamari** (dark aged soy sauce; eyeball it)

1 15-ounce can **cooked pumpkin**

2 rounded tablespoons **mild or hot curry paste**, such as Patak's, found on the international foods aisle

3 tablespoons **five-spice powder**

12 large **sea scallops**, trimmed and patted dry

12 **jumbo shrimp**, 6 to 8 count, peeled and deveined

4 **scallions**, cut into 2-inch pieces, then thinly sliced lengthwise into matchsticks

Heat a large covered pot of water for the pasta. When the water boils, salt it, drop in the pasta, and cook to al dente. Heads up: you'll need to reserve a cup or so of the cooking water before you drain the pasta.

While the pasta cooks, heat a large, deep skillet over medium heat with 2 tablespoons of the vegetable or peanut oil. Add the garlic, ginger, red bell peppers, and red pepper flakes to the pan and cook them together for a couple of minutes, then add the peanut butter and stir until it melts. Whisk the tamari into the peanut butter, then stir in the pumpkin and curry paste—the sauce should now be very thick. Turn the heat down to low. Add a ladle or two of the boiling pasta cooking water to thin the sauce a bit, and simmer the sauce over low heat. Adjust the salt to taste.

Heat a large skillet over high heat. Pour the five-spice powder onto a plate with some salt. Press both sides of the scallops and shrimp into the spices. Add 3 tablespoons of the remaining oil to the hot skillet. Add the shrimp and sear on both sides, until opaque. Remove to a plate and reserve. Wipe the skillet out and add the last 3 tablespoons of oil to the skillet. Make sure the pan gets super hot again before you add the scallops, and sear on both sides until opaque. Remove to the same plate as the shrimp.

Drain the pasta, and return it to the pot. Add the pumpkin-peanut sauce to the pasta pot and toss until the pasta is thoroughly coated. Top the noodles with the scallions and seafood, then serve.

Spicy Shrimp and Bok Choy Noodle Bowl

Eat this bowl quick before the spicy shrimp jump right out of the bowl. This noodle bowl is quite the meal.   4 SERVINGS

3 tablespoons **vegetable oil**

2 teaspoons **red pepper** or **chili flakes**

4 **garlic cloves**, chopped

2 inch piece of **fresh ginger**, peeled and cut into very thin matchsticks or grated

½ pound **shiitake mushroom caps**, sliced (a couple of cups)

1 medium **bok choy**, trimmed and cut into 3-inch pieces, then cut lengthwise into sticks

Salt and **freshly ground black pepper**

1 quart **chicken stock** or broth

1 cup **seafood stock** (available on soup aisle) or clam juice

1½ pounds medium peeled and deveined **shrimp**

½ pound **vermicelli** (thin spaghetti)

4 **scallions**, cut into 3-inch pieces, then sliced lengthwise into thin sticks

Heat a medium soup pot over medium-high heat. Add the vegetable oil, red pepper flakes, garlic, ginger, mushrooms, and bok choy, then season with salt and pepper. Add the chicken stock and seafood stock. Put a lid on the pot and bring the soup to a boil. Add the shrimp and noodles and cook for 3 minutes; add the scallions and cook for 2 minutes. Turn off the heat and let the soup sit for 2 to 3 minutes more. Adjust the seasoning and serve.

Crispy Fried Sesame Shrimp, Zucchini, and Mushroom Caps with a Ginger-Soy Dipping Sauce

Here's my take on Japanese tempura—it's perfect as an appetizer or an easy summer meal.   4 SERVINGS

⅓ cup **tamari** (dark aged soy sauce)

1 **garlic clove,** crushed

1-inch piece of **fresh ginger,** peeled and grated

1 tablespoon **sugar**

Juice of 1 lime

Toasted sesame oil, for drizzling

1 teaspoon **hot sauce,** such as Tabasco

Vegetable oil, for frying

2½ cups **complete pancake mix,** any brand, divided

2 tablespoons **sesame seeds**

1 pound medium **shrimp,** peeled and deveined

1 medium **zucchini,** cut ½ inch thick on a bias

8 **shiitake mushrooms,** stems removed

In a small bowl, combine the tamari, ⅓ cup water, the garlic clove, ginger, sugar, lime juice, and a drizzle of sesame oil. Mix to dissolve the sugar, then add the hot sauce. Reserve the dipping sauce.

Heat a layer of vegetable oil, about 1½ inches deep, over medium to medium-high heat in a deep-sided skillet. To test the oil, add a 1-inch cube of bread to the hot oil. If it turns deep golden brown in a count of 40, the oil is ready.

While the oil is heating, in a bowl combine 2 cups of the pancake mix, 1¼ cups water, and the sesame seeds. Place the remaining plain pancake mix in another mixing bowl. Arrange the batter and the bowl of plain pancake mix near the cooktop and the heating oil. Line a plate with a few sheets of paper towels and keep within reach.

Once the oil is ready, toss the shrimp, zucchini, and shiitake mushroom caps in the plain pancake mix, coat evenly, and shake off any excess. The plain dry pancake mix will help the batter stick to the shrimp and veggies. Plan to work in 3 or 4 batches to coat and fry the shrimp and veggies. Use a fork to toss some of the shrimp and veggies into the batter. Remove the first batch from the batter, shaking off some of the excess batter as you add the coated pieces to the hot oil. Fry for 2 to 3 minutes, or until deeply golden brown, then flip and fry for 2 minutes more. Remove from the oil and drain on the lined plate. Repeat with the remaining shrimp and veggies.

Arrange the shrimp and veggies on a platter along with the dipping sauce. Serve immediately.

Lemon-Thyme Succotash with Garlic-Parsley Shrimp

Here's a healthy dish bursting with bright flavors and textures, from crunchy red bell pepper and celery to plump shrimp and cannellini beans. And don't forget . . . two people with garlic breath cancel each other out!   4 SERVINGS

4 tablespoons **extra-virgin olive oil** (EVOO)

1 medium **onion**, chopped

1 **red bell pepper**, cored, seeded, and chopped

2 **celery ribs** and greens, chopped

Salt and **freshly ground black pepper**

2 tablespoons **unsalted butter**, cut into small pieces

6 **garlic cloves**, minced

1½ pounds medium **shrimp**, peeled and deveined

2 cups frozen **corn kernels**

1 15-ounce can **cannellini beans**, drained

3 tablespoons fresh **thyme** leaves (from 5 to 6 sprigs), chopped

1 **lemon**, zested and cut into wedges

⅓ cup chopped fresh **flat-leaf parsley**

½ cup **dry white wine** or ⅓ cup white vermouth

Heat two skillets: one over medium heat, the other over medium-high heat. To the hotter pan, add 2 tablespoons of the EVOO, then the onions, bell peppers, celery, salt, and pepper. Give the pan a shake.

To the second skillet, add the remaining 2 tablespoons of EVOO and the butter, melting it into the oil. Add the garlic and cook for 1 minute, then add the shrimp and season with salt and pepper. Sauté the shrimp, tossing them around in the garlic butter until they become pink and firm, 3 to 5 minutes.

Add the frozen corn and cannellini beans to the succotash in the first pan. Adjust the salt and pepper and add the thyme and lemon zest. Once the beans and corn have warmed through, turn off the heat.

Add the parsley and wine to the shrimp and toss for 1 minute. To serve, pile the succotash onto plates and top with the garlic-parsley shrimp. Pass the lemon wedges at the table. Squeeze lemon juice over the shrimp and succotash before eating.

Greek-Style Shrimp Scampi and Linguine

Get a shot of ouzo ready and try a Greek spin on this Italian classic.

4 SERVINGS

Salt

1 pound **linguine**

1 pound medium to large **shrimp**, peeled and deveined, tails removed

Black pepper

⅓ cup **EVOO** (extra-virgin olive oil)

4 **garlic cloves**, thinly sliced

½ teaspoon **red pepper flakes**

2 fresh **oregano** sprigs, finely chopped

Handful of pitted **kalamata olives**, chopped

½ cup **white wine**

Zest and juice of 1 lemon

Handful of fresh **flat-leaf parsley** leaves, chopped

1 cup **feta cheese crumbles**

Place a large covered pot of water on the stove to boil. Salt the water and cook the pasta to al dente. Heads up: You'll need some of the pasta cooking water before you drain the pasta.

Season the shrimp with salt and pepper.

While the pasta cooks, heat the EVOO in a deep skillet and brown the garlic slices. Remove the garlic and reserve. Add the shrimp and cook for 3 to 4 minutes. Add the red pepper flakes, oregano, olives, wine, and lemon zest and cook together for a couple more minutes. Remove from the heat. Add a ladle of the starchy pasta cooking water to the sauce, then add the lemon juice. Add the drained pasta to the skillet. Let the pasta absorb the juices for a minute, then toss with the parsley, feta, and reserved garlic slices. Use tongs to pull the pasta from the skillet, giving it a turn to twist in as many ingredients as possible. Then, use the tongs to remove and arrange the shrimp and ingredients that may remain in the pan, distributing them evenly among the portions.

Grilled Shrimp and Chorizo Skewers with Piquillo Pepper Gazpacho

I love Spain! Have a hot night in Barcelona, baby!   4 SERVINGS

---

4 **wooden skewers**

1 **lemon**

16 extra-large **shrimp**, peeled and deveined

Coarse salt

EVOO (extra-virgin olive oil), for liberal drizzling

1¾-pound package fully cooked **chorizo**, such as Gaspar's brand, cut into 16 thick slices on an angle

A generous handful of fresh **flat-leaf parsley** leaves

A generous handful of fresh **cilantro** leaves

2 **garlic cloves**, cracked from their skins

1 jar **roasted Spanish piquillo peppers**, available in most markets (roasted red peppers may be substituted, about 1 cup packed, drained peppers)

1 28-ounce can **fire-roasted tomatoes**, diced or crushed

1 small **yellow onion**, coarsely chopped

½ **seedless cucumber**, peeled, chopped

2 **celery ribs** from the heart, chopped

2 thick slices **crusty bread**, crusts trimmed, chopped

1 tablespoon **hot sauce**, such as Tabasco, for medium to spicy heat level, to taste

Preheat a grill or grill pan over medium-high heat. Soak the skewers in cold water for 10 minutes to prevent them from burning.

Zest the lemon and reserve the zest on a cutting board.

Place the shrimp in a shallow dish and season it with salt, the juice of half the zested lemon, and a liberal drizzle of EVOO—just enough to coat the shrimp. Thread 4 shrimp alternately with 4 slices of chorizo onto each skewer.

Place the parsley leaves on the cutting board with the lemon zest. Add ½ palmful of cilantro leaves to the pile as well as 1 clove of garlic. Finely chop this mixture and reserve.

Place the remaining herbs and garlic in the food processor or in a large blender with the peppers, tomatoes, chopped vegetables, bread, and hot sauce. Process the gazpacho until smooth.

Grill the shrimp and chorizo for 3 to 4 minutes on each side until the shrimp are firm and opaque. Sprinkle small bowls of gazpacho with the reserved zest and herb mixture. Rest a shrimp skewer across the top of each bowl for dipping and dunking.

Iceberg Salad with Shrimp

I love iceberg lettuce. I like gourmet fare, too, but I'm no aristocrat—food snobs lose out on comfort foods and home-cooking gems like icy iceberg salad. Here, I dress up this old favorite.   4 SERVINGS

1 head of **iceberg lettuce**

½ cup prepared **cocktail sauce**

A few drops of **hot sauce**

2 teaspoons **lemon zest plus juice of 1 lemon**

¼ cup **mayonnaise**

1 cup small cooked **shrimp**, 100 count

Salt and **black pepper**

2 to 3 tablespoons snipped fresh **chives**

Slam the core of the head of lettuce on the counter, then twist and remove it. Quarter the head of lettuce lengthwise.

In a medium bowl, combine the cocktail sauce, hot sauce, lemon zest and juice, and mayo. Stir the shrimp into the dressing and spoon it evenly over the lettuce quarters. Season the salads with a little salt and pepper, sprinkle with the chives, and serve.

Seafood au Gratin with Sautéed Artichokes and Spinach

Bubbling, brown, and bursting with flavor, this dish will knock your socks off! 4 SERVINGS

¼ cup plus 1 tablespoon **extra-virgin olive oil (EVOO)**

4 tablespoons **butter**

1 **bay leaf**, fresh or dried

1½ pounds **cod**, cut into chunks

1 pound large raw **shrimp**, peeled, deveined, and tails removed, coarsely chopped

1 **lemon**

1 large **shallot**, finely chopped

2 tablespoons **all-purpose flour**

½ cup **chicken stock** or broth

1 cup **heavy cream**

3 tablespoons **dry sherry**

¼ teaspoon **grated nutmeg**

Salt and **freshly ground black pepper**

3 **garlic cloves**, chopped

2 15-ounce cans quartered **artichoke hearts** in water, drained

1 pound triple-washed **spinach**, stems discarded, coarsely chopped

2 cups (8 ounces) shredded **Gruyère cheese**

1 teaspoon **sweet paprika**

2 tablespoons chopped fresh **flat-leaf parsley**

2 to 3 tablespoons grated **Parmigiano-Reggiano** or Parmesan cheese

Preheat a broiler to high.

To a large skillet over medium heat add 1 tablespoon of the EVOO, 2 tablespoons of the butter, and the bay leaf. Add the fish and shrimp and cook for 2 to 3 minutes on each side, turning carefully with a fish spatula. Remove the fish and shrimp to a plate, squeeze lemon juice on the cooked fish, and reserve. Add 2 tablespoons more butter to the pan and the shallot. Sauté the shallot for 2 minutes, then add the flour and cook another minute. Whisk in the stock and thicken for a minute. Add the cream to the sauce and bring to a bubble. Stir in the sherry, then season the sauce with nutmeg, salt, and pepper. Slide the seafood back into the pan and cook together over medium-low heat to reduce the sauce and finish cooking the seafood, 5 to 6 minutes.

Heat a second skillet over medium-high heat. Add the remaining EVOO, the garlic, and drained artichokes. Fry for 2 minutes, then wilt in the spinach and season with salt and pepper to taste. Turn the pan off and reserve.

Pour the seafood into a shallow casserole and top with the Gruyère cheese, paprika, parsley, and Parm. Brown the casserole and serve. Pile the spinach and artichokes alongside the seafood.

Thai-Style Shrimp and Veggies with Toasted Coconut Rice

Good-bye Thai takeout, hello Thai-style shrimp. These flavors go great with the subtly sweet taste of coconut rice. 4 SERVINGS

2½ cups **chicken stock** or broth

1½ cups **sweetened shredded coconut**

1 cup **long-grain rice**

4 tablespoons **vegetable oil**

1½ pounds large **shrimp**, peeled and deveined

Salt and **freshly ground black pepper**

1 small **yellow onion**, sliced

8 **napa cabbage** leaves, thinly shredded

1 cup store-bought **shredded carrots**, or 1 medium **carrot**, cut into matchsticks

1 teaspoon **red pepper flakes**

3 large **garlic cloves**, chopped

3-inch piece of **fresh ginger**, peeled and grated

1 **red bell pepper**, cored, seeded, and thinly sliced

3 tablespoons **tamari** (dark aged soy sauce)

5 **scallions**, thinly sliced

20 fresh **basil** leaves, chopped or torn

¼ cup fresh **cilantro** leaves (a handful), chopped

Juice of 1 lime

In a sauce pot, combine 1½ cups of the chicken stock with 1 cup of the sweetened shredded coconut; bring the mixture up to a simmer, and add the rice. Return to a simmer over low heat and place a tight-fitting lid on the pot. Cook the rice for 18 minutes.

Heat a small skillet over medium heat, add the remaining ½ cup of shredded coconut, stir frequently, and toast until golden, about 2 to 3 minutes. Heads up: Once the coconut starts to brown it will go from golden to burnt quickly, so keep an eye on it. Remove the toasted coconut from the pan and reserve.

Heat a large skillet over medium-high heat with 2 tablespoons of vegetable oil. Season the shrimp with salt and pepper and add to the hot skillet. Sauté the shrimp for 2 minutes on each side, until they turn pink but are not yet firm, then remove from the pan and reserve. Return the skillet to the heat and add the remaining 2 tablespoons of vegetable oil. Add the onions, cabbage, carrots, red pepper flakes, garlic, ginger, and bell peppers to the pan. Cook, stirring frequently, for 3 to 4 minutes. Add the tamari and the remaining cup of stock, then toss the shrimp back into the pan and stir to combine. Cook the shrimp and veggies for 2 more minutes, until the shrimp are cooked through. Add the scallions, basil, half of the cilantro, and lime juice and taste for seasoning.

Add the reserved toasted coconut to the cooked rice. Fluff the rice with a fork to distribute the toasted coconut. Serve the Thai shrimp on top of the toasted coconut rice, sprinkled with the remaining cilantro.

Shrimp and Pork Balls with Spicy Lime Dipping Sauce

A lower-carb alternative to pot stickers and other dumplings.

24 BALLS, UP TO 4 SERVINGS OF 6 BALLS EACH

4 **scallions**, green and white parts, coarsely chopped

2-inch piece **fresh ginger**, peeled and grated or minced

1 **serrano or jalapeño pepper**, seeded and finely chopped, divided

2 **garlic cloves**, crushed

¼ cup plus 3 tablespoons **tamari** (dark aged soy sauce, found on the international aisle), divided

¼ cup fresh **cilantro leaves**

Zest and juice of 2 limes

½ pound medium **shrimp**, shelled and deveined, tails removed

1 pound **ground pork**

2 to 3 tablespoons **vegetable oil**

1 teaspoon toasted **sesame oil**

1 tablespoon **honey**

Toothpicks

In the bowl of a food processor combine the scallions, half of the ginger, half of the chopped chile pepper, the garlic, 3 tablespoons of the tamari, the cilantro, and the lime zest. Pulse for 30 seconds, scrape down the bowl, and then continue to process for 1 minute or until finely ground. Add the shrimp and pork and process until the shrimp are ground into small pieces and the mixture is well combined but not so fine that it becomes a paste, about 1 minute. Roll the shrimp and pork mixture into 24 balls about the size of large walnuts. If you dip your hands in water before rolling the mixture, the rolling goes a little easier.

Preheat a large nonstick skillet with the vegetable oil over medium heat. Add the balls and don't move them until they are browned on one side, about 2 minutes. Turn the balls and continue to cook, browning on all sides until cooked through, about 3 to 4 minutes longer.

While the balls are cooking, make the spicy lime dipping sauce: In a bowl combine the remaining ginger and chile pepper, the remaining tamari, the lime juice, sesame oil, honey, and 2 tablespoons of water. Taste and adjust the seasoning; if you find it to be too salty, add a little more water and a smidgen more honey.

Arrange the shrimp and pork balls on a platter with a bowl of the spicy lime dipping sauce and a bunch of toothpicks. Spear a ball with a toothpick, dip in the sauce, and eat.

Linguine with Rach's Cupboard Red Clam Sauce

Anchovies work magic here, tasting more like salted nuts. Plus, anchovies in any seafood sauce I serve are the secret ingredient that makes the eaters go "Hmm, what is that?" (Don't tell anyone my secret, k?)

4 SERVINGS

Salt

1 pound **linguine**

3 tablespoons **EVOO** (extra-virgin olive oil)

1 tin **flat anchovy fillets,** 2 ounces, drained

½ teaspoon **red pepper flakes**

¼ teaspoon **dried oregano leaves,** a couple of pinches

1 teaspoon **dried thyme leaves,** ⅓ palmful

5 to 6 **garlic cloves,** finely chopped

1 small **onion,** finely chopped

½ cup **dry red wine,** a couple of glugs

2 14-ounce cans **whole baby clams in juice**

1 28-ounce can **crushed tomatoes**

Black pepper

2 handfuls of chopped fresh **flat-leaf parsley**

Lemon zest, for garnish

Bring a large pot of water to a boil for the pasta. Salt the water, add the pasta, and cook to al dente.

Heat a large, deep skillet over medium-low heat. Add the EVOO, then add the anchovies and melt them into the oil. Next, add the red pepper flakes, oregano, thyme, and garlic. Cook the garlic for a minute, then add the onions, raise the heat to medium, and cook, stirring frequently, for 3 to 4 minutes, until the onions begin to get soft. Add the wine and cook it for a minute, then stir in the clams, adding the juice from one can (drain the other before you add the clams). Stir to combine and cook down the juice a minute or so to concentrate the flavor. Stir in the crushed tomatoes and season with salt and pepper (there's so much anchovy and clam in this sauce you may not need salt at all—taste to test it).

Drain the linguine well and add it to the sauce in the skillet. Add half the parsley and toss the pasta with the sauce. Adjust the salt and pepper and plate the pasta, garnishing it with the extra parsley and a little lemon zest.

Serrano-Wrapped Halibut with Tortillas and Savoy Cabbage

Serrano ham is similar to prosciutto. Wrapped around halibut it is delicious.   2 SERVINGS

8 small, **soft flour tortillas**

3 tablespoons **EVOO** (extra-virgin olive oil)

½ head **Savoy cabbage,** shredded

¾ small **onion**, thinly sliced

Salt

1 teaspoon ground **coriander**

½ tablespoon ground **cumin**

1 teaspoon **lime zest**

2 6-ounce **halibut fillets**

Black pepper

½ teaspoon **smoked sweet paprika**

4 very thin slices **Serrano ham** or proscuitto

¼ cup all-purpose **flour,** for dredging

2 tablespoons **butter**

Juice of 1 lime

tidbit >> These tortillas would be delicious with Warm Cinnamon-Chipotle Tomato Salsa, page 139.

Preheat the oven to 250° F. Dampen a clean kitchen towel and stack the tortillas in the center. Wrap the tortillas in the towel and place into a small pie or cake pan of a similar size, cover the dish with foil, and heat the tortillas for 20 minutes.

Heat a tablespoon of the EVOO (once around the pan) in a medium skillet over medium-high heat and add the cabbage and onions. Season the cabbage with salt, the coriander, cumin, and lime zest. Cook the cabbage for 10 minutes, turning frequently.

Season the fish fillets with salt, pepper, and the smoked paprika. Overlap 2 slices of Serrano to measure the length of the fillet. Place the fish on top. Wrap the sides up and over the fillet to enclose it completely. Repeat with the remaining ham and halibut. Spread a little flour on a cutting board or plate and dredge the ham-covered fish. Discard the remaining flour.

Heat the remaining 2 tablespoons of EVOO in a medium nonstick skillet over medium-high heat. Add the fish to the pan and cook for 2 to 3 minutes, then turn the fillets and reduce the heat to medium-low. Cook the fish a minute or so, add the butter, and as it melts, begin basting the fish with it. Turn off the heat and let the fish stand for 1 minute more. Slice each fish fillet into ½-inch slices and fan them out on 2 dinner plates. Squeeze some lime juice over the cabbage and pile it alongside the fish. Place the tortillas on a trivet in the towel and hot dish to keep them soft. As you dine, wrap the fish, cabbage, and sauce in tortillas and eat.

Chorizo-Cod-Potato Stew

This stew is easy to make, is good for you, and has a big satisfying flavor. 4 SERVINGS

2 tablespoons **EVOO** (extra-virgin olive oil)

½ pound **chorizo** or andouille sausage, thinly sliced

5 red or white **boiling potatoes**, cut in half, then thinly sliced into half moons

1 large **onion**, chopped

1 **carrot**, peeled, cut in half lengthwise, and sliced into half moons

4 **garlic cloves**, chopped

Salt and **black pepper**

1 cup **dry white wine**

1 14-ounce can diced **fire-roasted tomatoes**

1 quart **chicken stock**

2 jarred **roasted red peppers**, chopped

1½ pounds **fresh cod**, cut into 2-inch chunks

½ cup fresh **flat-leaf parsley**, a couple of generous handfuls, chopped

Preheat a soup pot over medium-high heat with the EVOO. Add the sliced chorizo and cook, stirring frequently, for 2 minutes. Add the potatoes and continue to cook for 2 minutes. Add the onions, carrots, and garlic, season with salt and pepper, and cook, stirring frequently, for 5 minutes. Add the white wine and cook for 3 minutes. Add the fire-roasted tomatoes, chicken stock, and roasted red peppers, bring up to a simmer and cook for 5 minutes. You want the soup to be at a gentle simmer before you add the fish so, if necessary, turn the heat down a little. Add the cod. Gently simmer for 3 to 4 minutes, or until the fish is cooked through. Finish the soup with the parsley, taste for seasoning, and serve.

Crab and Corn Chowda-Mac

Though I haven't lived on Cape Cod since I was eight, this dish proves I'm a true New England Patriot. With chowda and mac 'n' cheese in one dinner, you can get to Massachusetts in 30 minutes or less, regardless of where you live.   4 SERVINGS

Salt

1 pound **large shell pasta**

1 tablespoon **EVOO** (extra-virgin olive oil)

3 **bacon slices**, chopped

1 medium **onion**, chopped

2 **celery ribs** with greens, chopped

½ small **red bell pepper**, cored, seeded, and chopped

2 tablespoons all-purpose **flour**

1 cup **chicken stock**

1 cup **milk**

1 6-ounce tub **fresh lump crab meat**, flaked

1 cup **frozen corn kernels**

2 cups shredded sharp white **Cheddar cheese**

2 tablespoons fresh **thyme**, chopped

A couple of pinches **cayenne pepper**

3 tablespoons chopped or snipped fresh **chives**, for garnish

Bring a large pot of water to a boil for the pasta and salt it. Cook the pasta to al dente.

While the pasta cooks, heat a large, deep skillet over medium to medium-high heat. Add the EVOO and the bacon. Cook the bacon for 3 minutes. Add the onions and celery and cook for 3 minutes more. Add the bell peppers and cook for another minute or two. Add the flour and cook for 1 to 2 minutes. Whisk in the stock, then the milk. When the milk bubbles, add the crab and corn to heat through, another minute. Stir in the cheese, thyme, and cayenne pepper and heat until the cheese melts into the sauce. Drain the pasta and toss with the cheese, crab, and corn sauce. Adjust the seasonings. Ladle into bowls and garnish with the chives.

Seafood Newburg Stoup with Cayenne-Chive-Buttered Corn Toasties

This is an absolutely delish stoup.   4 SERVINGS

2 tablespoons **extra-virgin olive oil** (EVOO)

4 tablespoons **unsalted butter**

1 large starchy **potato**, peeled and chopped

2 **celery ribs** with their greens, chopped

1 medium **yellow onion**, chopped

1 **bay leaf**, fresh or dried

Salt and **freshly ground black pepper**

1 tablespoon **Old Bay Seasoning**

3 tablespoons all-purpose **flour**

¼ cup **dry sherry**

3 cups **chicken or seafood stock**

1½ pounds **cod, scrod, or haddock**, cut in chunks

1 pound medium **shrimp**, peeled and deveined, coarsely chopped

3 cups whole **milk** or half-and-half

½ teaspoon **cayenne pepper**

4 **corn toaster pastries**, such as Thomas' brand

2 tablespoons chopped fresh **chives**

Heat a medium soup pot over medium-high heat. Add the EVOO and 2 tablespoons of cold butter, cut into small pieces. Add the veggies as you get them chopped, then season them with the bay leaf, salt, pepper, and Old Bay Seasoning. Cook for 5 minutes to begin to soften, then add the flour and cook for a minute longer. Next, add the sherry and cook for 1 minute. Whisk in the stock and bring it up to a bubble, then arrange the seafood in an even layer around the pan. Cover the pan and cook until the fish is opaque and the shrimp is pink, 4 minutes. Remove the lid and add the milk and cook for 2 to 3 minutes longer to thicken. Add about ¼ teaspoon cayenne pepper, then adjust the seasonings. Discard the bay leaf.

Melt the remaining 2 tablespoons of butter and ¼ teaspoon of cayenne pepper. Toast the corn pastries, brush with cayenne butter, and sprinkle with the chopped chives. Serve alongside the stoup.

Lemon and Brown Butter Fish Fillets with Seared Red and Yellow Grape Tomatoes

This is a very healthy fish dinner with great color on the plate.

4 SERVINGS

4 tablespoons **extra-virgin olive oil** (EVOO)

½ pint **red grape tomatoes**

½ pint **yellow grape tomatoes**

½ cup fresh **flat-leaf parsley** leaves (a couple of handfuls), chopped

Salt and **freshly ground black pepper**

4 6-ounce **tilapia, skate,** or **Dover sole fillets**

All-purpose flour, for dredging

4 tablespoons cold **unsalted butter**

Juice of 1 lemon

Crusty bread

Preheat a large skillet over high heat with 2 tablespoons of the EVOO (twice around the pan). Add the grape tomatoes in an even layer and let them sear for 2 minutes without moving them. Add half of the parsley and season with salt and pepper, then continue to cook for 1 to 2 more minutes, or until all of the tomatoes start to burst. Remove them from the pan to a plate and cover with some aluminum foil to keep warm.

Thoroughly wipe out the skillet and return to the cooktop over medium-high heat. Season the fish with salt and pepper and then dredge in the flour. Add the remaining 2 tablespoons EVOO to the skillet. Once the oil is hot, shake the excess flour from the fish and add to the skillet. Cook the fish for 4 to 5 minutes on each side, or until firm to the touch and cooked through. Once cooked, transfer the fish to a serving platter and cover with aluminum foil to keep warm.

Wipe the skillet clean again and return to the cooktop over medium-high heat. Melt the butter; but keep your eye on it. It will go from melted to brown pretty quickly. Once the butter is brown and smells slightly nutty, add the lemon juice and the remaining parsley. Pour the brown butter over the fish and then top with the seared grape tomatoes. Serve with crusty bread, for mopping.

Crab Cakes with a Creamy, Grainy Mustard Sauce

Crab cakes are one of the most popular starters but they also make a great dinner, any night of the week. Also, thanks to ever-improving supermarket fish departments, great-quality lump crab meat is available any time of the year. Treat yourself to a rich supper of these cakes every now and then and it'll be even more fun to share them in their mini version next time you're having the gang over.   2 SERVINGS

4 tablespoons **EVOO** (extra-virgin olive oil; eyeball it)

½ small **onion**, finely chopped

1 **garlic clove**, chopped

Salt and **black pepper**

2 heaping tablespoons **grainy mustard**

¾ cup **chicken stock**

¼ cup **heavy cream** or half-and-half

7 slices **white sandwich bread**

½ cup **mayonnaise**

4 **scallions**, finely chopped

¼ cup fresh **flat-leaf parsley** leaves, a generous handful, chopped

1 teaspoon **hot sauce**

½ small **red bell pepper**, finely chopped

1 pound **fresh lump crab meat**, available in tubs at the fish counter

2 tablespoons **butter**

Preheat a small sauté pan or sauce pot over medium-high heat with 1 tablespoon of the EVOO, once around the pan. Add the onions and garlic and season with salt and pepper. Cook, stirring frequently, for 3 to 4 minutes. Add the grainy mustard, chicken stock, and cream and bring the sauce up to a simmer. Cook until thick, 2 to 3 minutes. Turn the sauce off and reheat it when you're ready to serve. If it thickens up too much, add a splash more of the chicken stock or water to loosen it up.

Place the bread in a food processor and use the pulse button to break it up, then let 'er rip and make fine bread crumbs.

In a bowl, combine the mayonnaise, scallions, parsley, hot sauce, red bell peppers, salt, and pepper. Gently run your fingers through the crab meat, feeling for any shells or cartilage while trying not to break up the meat too much. Add the crab meat to the mayonnaise mixture with a quarter of the fresh bread crumbs and gently fold the mixture to combine. Place the remaining bread crumbs on a plate; divide the crab mixture into 4 equal portions. Transfer the 4 crab portions to the plate with the bread crumbs and coat each one, gently pressing to adhere the bread crumbs and forming 1- to 1½-inch-thick cakes.

Preheat a medium nonstick skillet over medium heat

with the remaining EVOO, 3 times around the pan, and the butter. Once the butter melts, add the crab cakes and cook them for about 4 minutes on each side or until they are golden brown and heated through.

Divide the sauce between 2 plates, top with the crab cakes, and serve.

tidbit >> Fresh crab meat is a better value than the canned stuff because canned crab meat is packed with lots of water.

Crab Salad Bites on Endive

I love the slight bitterness of endive and here I combine it with sweet crab to be the perfect party starter.   24 PIECES, 6 TO 8 SERVINGS

6 ounces **lump white crab-meat**

¼ **red bell pepper,** finely chopped

1 **shallot,** finely chopped

Zest of 1 orange

3 **radishes,** grated

3 tablespoons chopped **celery leaves**

Salt and **freshly ground black pepper**

¼ cup **mayonnaise**

3 tablespoons **heavy cream**

24 leaves **Belgian endive**

Chopped fresh **flat-leaf parsley** or chives, for garnish

Place the crab in a medium bowl and use your fingertips to break it into small pieces. Add the bell pepper, shallot, orange zest, grated radish, celery greens, and salt and pepper. Combine the mayonnaise and heavy cream in a small bowl. Add the dressing to the crab and mix well. Mound a rounded spoonful of the crab salad onto the root end of each endive and fill the leaves to half their length. Arrange the stuffed endive on a platter and garnish with chopped parsley or chives.

Fish Tacos with Avocado Dressing

This dish is preventative medicine; it prevents one from ordering and pigging out on bad Mexican-style take-out food. If you make this instead you won't end up feeling too fat or too full.   4 SERVINGS

9 tablespoons **EVOO** (extra-virgin olive oil)

1 teaspoon **chili powder**, ⅓ palmful

Zest and juice of 2 limes

Salt

4 fresh **halibut steaks** or fillets, 6 to 8 ounces each

1 large yellow **onion**, chopped

3 large **garlic cloves**, chopped

1 **jalapeño pepper**, seeded and chopped

Black pepper

1 10-ounce box **frozen corn kernels**

½ cup **chicken stock**

1 **romaine heart**, shredded

¼ cup fresh **cilantro leaves**, a generous handful, coarsely chopped

2 ripe **Hass avocados**

2 tablespoons **red wine vinegar**

A couple shakes of **hot sauce**, to taste (optional)

12 6-inch soft **flour tortillas**

In a shallow dish, combine 2 tablespoons of the EVOO, the chili powder, the juice of 1 lime, and a little salt. Add the halibut and coat with the mixture. Let the fish marinate while you start the corn.

Preheat a large skillet over medium-high heat with 2 tablespoons of the EVOO, twice around the pan. Add the onions, garlic, jalapeño, and a little salt and pepper. Cook for about 3 minutes, stirring frequently. Add the corn and chicken stock, bring it up to a bubble, then continue to cook for 2 minutes. Put the romaine and cilantro in a salad bowl, transfer the hot corn mixture to the bowl, and mix them together so the heat from the corn wilts the romaine. Wipe the skillet clean and return it to the stovetop over medium-high heat with 2 tablespoons of the EVOO. Once hot, add the halibut to the skillet and cook it on each side for 4 to 5 minutes, or until cooked through. Flake the fish into large chunks with a fork, then add it to the bowl with the corn and romaine.

While the fish is cooking, make the avocado dressing. Cut all around the ripe avocados down to the pit. Twist and separate the halved fruit. Remove the pit with a spoon, and then use a spoon to scoop the flesh into the bowl of a food processor. Add the zest of the 2 limes and the remaining juice of 1 lime to the food processor. Add the red wine vinegar and some salt. With the machine running, stream in the remaining 3 tablespoons of EVOO and a couple of shakes of hot sauce. Stop the processor, taste the dressing, and adjust the seasonings with more salt, pepper, and hot sauce to taste.

Wipe out the skillet you cooked the halibut in. Place

it over high heat and blister the tortillas in the dry pan for a few seconds on each side. As you remove them from the pan have a clean kitchen towel handy to wrap them in and help keep them warm and soft. You can also simply wrap the tortillas in a barely damp kitchen towel and heat them in the microwave until they are warm and supple.

To assemble, arrange a pile of the halibut-corn-romaine mixture on a warm tortilla, top it with a spoonful of the avocado dressing, wrap, and roll it up. Eat and enjoy.

Sweet Sea Scallops in a Caper-Raisin Sauce

Serve with a green salad.   4 SERVINGS

3 tablespoons **extra-virgin olive oil** (EVOO)

2 **shallots**, chopped

Salt and **freshly ground black pepper**

¼ cup fresh **flat-leaf parsley** leaves (a generous handful), chopped

3 tablespoons **capers**, drained

¾ cup **dry white wine**

½ cup **golden raisins**

16 **sea scallops**, drained and trimmed

Juice of 1 lemon

2 tablespoons **unsalted butter**

Crusty bread, to pass at the table

Heat a large nonstick skillet over medium-high heat. Add 2 tablespoons of the EVOO (twice around the pan) and the chopped shallots. Cook the shallots for a minute or so, season with salt and pepper, and add the parsley and capers. Add the wine and golden raisins. Simmer for 3 minutes, then transfer to a bowl and reserve.

Wipe out the pan and return to the heat, raising the heat to high. Season the scallops with salt and pepper. Add the remaining tablespoon of EVOO to the very hot pan and immediately place the scallops in the pan. Sear the scallops in a single layer, allowing them to caramelize, 2 minutes on each side. Add the reserved caper-raisin mixture along with the lemon juice. Turn the heat back a bit and cook for 1 to 2 minutes. Remove the scallops from the pan and arrange on a serving platter. Remove the pan from the stove, add the butter, and shake the skillet until the butter has completely melted. Pour the sauce over the scallops and serve with the bread.

7

One-Pot Meals

There's nothing quite like a big ol' pot of chili simmering on the stove or a casserole bubbling in the oven. And the best part—at least I think so—are the leftovers the next day. Check out more Family Faves; Potluck Picks; and Soups, Stoups, and Chilis for simple ways to feed one or many!

FAMILY FAVES

Italian Sub Stoup and Garlic Toast Floaters
Stuffed Cabbage Stoup
Spicy and Sweet Chicken and Couscous Pot
Renaissance of Tuna Casserole
Hearty Sausage and Mushroom Stew Over Polenta
Mexican Fondue
Veggie Chickpea and Couscous Salad with Yogurt Dressing
Big Beef and Garlic Italian Stir-Fry
Bacon, Spinach, and Cream Potatoes
Cacio e Pepe (Cheese and Pepper) Spaghetti Squash

POTLUCK PICKS

Italian Chicken Pot Pie from the Boot
Double Eggplant Parm Fake-Baked Ziti
Spanakopita Chicken Meatballs with Spicy Cucumber Yogurt Sauce
Turkey Noodle Casserole
Wild Cream of Mushroom Egg Noodle Bake, Hold the Canned Soup
BLT Pasta Bake: Bacon, Leeks, and Tomatoes
Bresaola Salad
Ginger Vegetable Chicken Noodle Bowl
Grilled Chicken Pasta Salad
Grilled Eggplant and Capicola Parmigiana

SOUPS, STOUPS, AND CHILIS

Oktoberfest Stoup
Sausage and Tortellini Soup
Cream of Cheddar Soup and Lime Chicken Avocado Salad
Thai Chicken Noodle Soup
*Chorizo Chicken Spinach Stoup with Roasted Red Pepper and
    Manchego Toasts*
Taco Stoup with a Taco Toppings Salad
Polenta with Chunky Chicken and Chorizo Chili
Green and White Lightning Chunky Chicken Chili
Caution-Flag Chili with Flat-Tire Corn and Black Bean Toppers
Chicken Dumpling and Noodle Stoup

Italian Sub Stoup and Garlic Toast Floaters

Thicker than soup, thinner than stew, this stoup combines sausage, ham, pepperoni, veggies, and arugula. It tastes like a giant Italian sub!

4 SERVINGS

STOUP

2 tablespoons **extra-virgin olive oil** (EVOO)

¾ pound (3 links) **hot** or **sweet Italian sausage**, removed from casings

¼ pound piece **pepperoni**, diced

1 **ham steak**, ½ to ¾ pound, diced

1 **green bell pepper**, cored, seeded, quartered, and sliced

1 medium **yellow onion**, quartered and sliced

1 28-ounce can **diced tomatoes**

Salt and **freshly ground black pepper**

6 cups **chicken stock** or broth

1 cup **gemelli pasta** or other shaped pasta

CROUTONS

¼ cup **EVOO**

3 large **garlic cloves**, cracked from skins

5 cups **crusty bread**, cubed

1 teaspoon **red pepper flakes**

½ teaspoon dried **oregano**

½ cup grated **Parmigiano-Reggiano**

4 cups **arugula** (2 bunches), trimmed and coarsely chopped

Place a soup pot on the stovetop and preheat to medium high. Add the EVOO and the sausage. Brown and crumble the sausage, drain off excess fat if necessary, then add the pepperoni and ham. Cook for 2 minutes, then add the bell peppers and onions and cook for 2 or 3 minutes more. Add the tomatoes and season with salt and pepper. Add the chicken stock and bring to a boil. Stir in the pasta and cook for 8 minutes.

While the pasta cooks, heat the ¼ cup of EVOO in a large skillet over medium heat. Add the garlic and cook for 1 minute. Add the bread cubes, toss, and toast the cubes for 5 or 6 minutes. Season the toasty cubes with the red pepper flakes, oregano, and grated cheese.

Stir the arugula into the stoup just before you serve it up. Float several bread cubes in each bowl.

Stuffed Cabbage Stoup

A fan of 30-Minute Meals wrote in and asked me to come up with a stoup based on stuffed cabbage, so I did. It's quite a warm-up for any chilly night.   4 SERVINGS

2 tablespoons **EVOO** (extra-virgin olive oil)

1½ pounds **ground meatloaf mix** (a combination of beef, pork, and veal)

½ teaspoon **allspice**

½ tablespoon ground **coriander**, half a palmful

2 teaspoons **smoked sweet paprika**

Salt and **black pepper**

1 **bay leaf**

1 **onion**, chopped

2 **garlic cloves**, minced

1 **carrot**, thinly sliced with a vegetable peeler into strips, then finely chopped

1 pound **Savoy cabbage**, thinly sliced (1 small or ½ to ¾ larger head)

1 28-ounce can **diced tomatoes**

1 cup **tomato sauce**

1 quart **chicken stock**

1 cup **white rice**

Handful of fresh **flat-leaf parsley** leaves, chopped

3 tablespoons fresh **dill**, finely chopped

Heat a deep pot over medium-high heat. Add the EVOO, twice around the pan, then add the meat and brown it for 2 to 3 minutes. Season the meat with the allspice, coriander, smoked paprika, salt, and pepper, then add the bay leaf, the onions, garlic, and carrots. Cook the veggies for 2 to 3 minutes to begin to soften them, then add the cabbage and wilt it down a bit. Add the tomatoes, tomato sauce, and stock and cover the pot. Raise the heat to bring the stoup to a boil, then add the rice and reduce the heat to a simmer. Cook for 16 to 18 minutes, until the rice is just tender. Stir in the parsley and dill, discard the bay leaf, adjust the salt and pepper, and serve.

Spicy and Sweet Chicken and Couscous Pot

Exotic, easy, and healthy, too, this simple dish is just delish.   4 SERVINGS

2½ cups **chicken stock**

½ cup **mango chutney**

Salt and **black pepper**

2 tablespoons **EVOO** (extra-virgin olive oil)

½ tablespoon **ground coriander**

1 teaspoon **ground cumin**, ⅓ palmful

½ teaspoon **red pepper flakes**

4 boneless, skinless **chicken breasts**, cut into large bite-size pieces

1 large **onion**, thinly sliced

1 **red bell pepper**, cored, seeded, and thinly sliced

3 **garlic cloves**, finely chopped

3-inch piece **fresh ginger**, peeled and grated

Zest and juice of 1 lemon

1½ cups plain **couscous**

½ cup **plain yogurt**

10 fresh **mint** leaves, from several sprigs

¼ cup fresh **cilantro leaves**, a generous handful

3 **scallions**, trimmed, coarsely chopped

Juice of 1 lime

In a sauce pot over medium-low heat, combine 2 cups of the chicken stock with the mango chutney and a little salt and pepper, bring it up to a bubble, and then turn down the heat to low to just keep warm.

Heat a large skillet with high sides or a soup pot over medium-high heat with the EVOO. Once the oil is hot, add the coriander, cumin, and red pepper flakes to the oil and "toast" the spices, stirring constantly for about 15 seconds. Add the chicken and toss it in the spices until well coated. Spread the chicken out in an even layer and season it with salt and pepper. Cook the chicken pieces for 2 minutes on each side to brown, then add the onions, red bell pepper, garlic, and three fourths of the grated ginger. Cook for about 3 minutes, stirring frequently. Add the remaining ½ cup of chicken stock and continue to cook until almost all of the liquids have evaporated, about 2 to 3 minutes.

Scoot the chicken and veggies to the sides of the skillet, creating a crater in the center of the pan. Add the chicken stock–chutney mixture and the lemon zest and juice, bring up to a bubble, and then add the couscous to the crater. Give the skillet a shake to get the couscous to settle into the liquids but still try to keep it in the crater. Use the back of a spoon to spread it out into the liquids if the shaking doesn't do the trick. Cover it with a tight-fitting lid or with a piece of aluminum foil (if you are using foil, really wrap the top of the pan; you need to hold in the steam) and then turn off the heat and let it sit for about 5 minutes to cook the couscous.

While the couscous is cooking with the chicken and the veggies, make the minty cilantro sauce. In a blender combine the yogurt, mint, cilantro, scallions, lime juice, the remaining grated ginger, and a small splash of water. Turn the blender on and puree until the mixture is smooth. If it doesn't get going right away, add another splash of water to get it moving. Season the sauce with a little salt and pepper.

To serve, with a fork mix the couscous with the chicken and veggies, serve up a couple of heaping spoonfuls in shallow bowls, and give each serving a generous drizzle of the minty cilantro sauce.

Renaissance of Tuna Casserole

You can't beat this yum-o casserole for a one-pot meal.   4 SERVINGS

Salt

1 pound **fettuccine**

3 tablespoons **EVOO** (extra-virgin olive oil)

4 **garlic cloves,** finely chopped

1 small **onion,** chopped

2 6-ounce cans **Italian tuna in water or oil,** drained

½ cup tender **sun-dried tomatoes** (available in small pouches in the produce department), thinly sliced

½ cup **dry white wine**

½ cup **heavy cream**

½ cup grated **Parmigiano-Reggiano,** a few generous handfuls

Black pepper

1 cup **frozen peas,** a couple handfuls

1 cup shredded **fresh basil,** 20 leaves

Bring a large covered pot of water to a boil for the pasta. Salt the water, then add the pasta and cook to al dente.

While the pasta cooks, heat a deep skillet over medium heat with the EVOO. Sauté the garlic and onions until tender, 4 to 5 minutes. Add the tuna and sun-dried tomatoes and stir to heat them through, another minute or two. Add the wine and cook it down for a minute, then add the cream. When it comes to a bubble, stir in the cheese and season the sauce with salt and pepper. Stir in the peas and heat through. Toss the drained hot pasta with the sauce. Serve topped with shredded basil.

Hearty Sausage and Mushroom Stew Over Polenta

Polenta is as cheap as pasta, and quick-cooking polenta is five times faster to make. Need I explain further? It is simply a great go-to when you have people coming over.   6 SERVINGS

---

4 cups **chicken stock**

2 cups **milk**

5 **garlic cloves**, 2 crushed from their skins, 3 chopped

Salt and **black pepper**

1 cup **beef stock**

1 2-ounce package **dried porcini mushrooms**

4 tablespoons **EVOO** (extra-virgin olive oil)

1 pound **bulk hot Italian sausage**

2 pounds small **button mushrooms**, wiped clean with a damp towel, left whole if small, halved if larger

4 large **portobello mushroom caps**, thickly sliced (don't be precious about it, just run your knife through them)

1 pound fresh **shiitake mushrooms**, stemmed, caps halved

6 to 8 fresh **sage** leaves, chopped

1 large **onion**, finely chopped

¾ cup **dry red wine**

2 cups **quick-cooking polenta**, found in the Italian or specialty food aisles

1 cup grated **Parmigiano-Reggiano** cheese

3 tablespoons **butter**

1½ cups fresh **basil**, about 25 leaves, coarsely chopped or torn

Combine the chicken stock, milk, crushed garlic cloves, and a little salt and pepper in a large sauce pot. Bring it up to a simmer and then lower the heat until you are ready to add the polenta.

In a small sauce pot, bring the beef stock to a boil over high heat. Add the dried mushrooms, turn the heat off, and let them steep to rehydrate while you get the fresh mushrooms going.

Preheat a large skillet over medium-high heat with 2 tablespoons of the EVOO, 2 times around the pan. Add the sausage and break it up into little bits, using a wooden spoon. Brown it, stirring every now and then, for 5 minutes. Once it is brown, remove the sausage from the skillet and drain it on a paper-towel-lined plate. Drain all but about 2 tablespoons of the fat from the skillet, return the skillet to the stove over high heat, and add the remaining 2 tablespoons of EVOO. Add the fresh mushrooms, sage, and some pepper. Cook the mushrooms without stirring for 3 to 4 minutes, then give them a stir and cook for another 10 minutes, stirring every now and then. Add the chopped garlic, onions, and a little salt and continue to cook for 3 or 4 minutes. Add the wine and let it cook down for about a minute. Use a slotted spoon to remove the rehydrated porcini mushrooms from the beef stock and add them to the sautéed mushrooms. Line a small strainer or the corner of a colander with a paper coffee filter and pour all of the fortified beef stock through it and into the skillet. (Sometimes the dried mushrooms contain a little grit; you're removing it without giving up a drop of that fortified stock.) Return the sausage to the skillet, bring the mixture up to a bubble, and cook it until the liquids have reduced by half.

Back to the polenta: Remove the crushed garlic cloves from the chicken stock and milk, whisk in the polenta in a slow and steady stream, and cook, stirring frequently, for about 5 minutes. Turn the heat off and add the cheese, stirring it to combine. If the polenta gets a little too thick for your liking, add a little more stock or milk and that will loosen it up. Polenta is very understanding and forgiving.

Once the liquids in the stew have reduced by half, turn the heat off, add the butter and basil, and stir the stew until the butter has melted.

Serve each helping of the sausage and mushroom stew over a portion of the polenta.

Mexican Fondue

Here's where sombreros meet the Swiss Alps! This recipe injects serious south-of-the-border flavor into a classic European dish. It's a world of taste in just one pot!   4 SERVINGS

---

8 ounces **Pepper Jack cheese,** shredded

4 ounces **Gruyère cheese,** shredded

4 ounces **Cheddar cheese,** shredded

1 tablespoon **cornstarch**

1 cup **Mexican beer**

2 teaspoons **hot sauce,** such as Tabasco

Zest of 1 lime plus 1 table-spoon fresh lime juice

3 tablespoons canned **green chili peppers,** finely chopped

3 tablespoons **green salad olives** with pimientos, finely chopped

2 tablespoons chopped **fresh cilantro,** for garnish (optional)

SERVE WITH . . .

Grilled chicken or steak, cubed

Grilled, chopped linguiça sausage

Sliced zucchini

Chunks of bell peppers

In a small bowl combine the cheeses and cornstarch. Add the beer to a small pot and bring up to a bubble over medium heat. Reduce the heat to simmer and add the hot sauce, lime zest and juice, then the cheese mixture in handfuls. Stir constantly in a figure-eight pattern with a wooden spoon, melting the cheese in batches. When the cheese has been incorporated fully, stir in the chili peppers and olives with pimientos. Transfer the fondue to a fondue pot and garnish with cilantro, if using, then serve.

Veggie Chickpea and Couscous Salad with Yogurt Dressing

Any meat eater is going to love this veggie dish. The cool yogurt dressing blends the couscous and veggies together and also makes for a great side dish.   8 SERVINGS

4 cups **chicken or vegetable stock**

2 ¼ cups **couscous**

Salt and **black pepper**

2 tablespoons **EVOO** (extra-virgin olive oil)

1 small **red onion**, thinly sliced

2 **seedless European cucumbers**, cut in half lengthwise, then sliced into half moons

1 **red bell pepper**, chopped

1 cup fresh **flat-leaf parsley** leaves, 4 generous handfuls, chopped

1 pint **grape tomatoes**, halved

2 15-ounce cans **chickpeas**, drained, rinsed, then thoroughly dried

¾ cup **plain yogurt** (look for thick, creamy Greek-style yogurt)

3 tablespoons **red wine vinegar**

2 tablespoons **honey**

Hot sauce

15 fresh **mint** leaves (give or take a leaf), chopped

Bring the stock to a boil. Pour the couscous into a large heat-proof bowl, add some salt and pepper and the EVOO, and stir with a fork to coat the couscous in the oil. Once the stock is boiling, pour it over the couscous and then wrap the bowl tightly with plastic wrap and let it sit for 5 minutes.

While the couscous is steeping, combine the red onions, cucumbers, red bell peppers, parsley, grape tomatoes, chickpeas, salt, and pepper in a large salad bowl. To make the dressing, combine the yogurt, red wine vinegar, honey, a few dashes of hot sauce to taste, the mint, and some salt and pepper. Pour the dressing over the veggies and stir it up.

Fluff the couscous with a fork and add it to the dressed veggies. Toss thoroughly, taste, and adjust the seasonings with more salt and pepper.

Big Beef and Garlic Italian Stir-Fry

Whip up this healthy meal in a flash—it's easy to make, full of flavor, and sure to please the whole family.   4 SERVINGS

Coarse salt

1 bunch of **broccoli rabe**, coarsely chopped

4 tablespoons **extra-virgin olive oil** (EVOO)

5 large **garlic cloves**, carefully cracked from the skins and very thinly sliced

2 pounds **flank steak**, thinly sliced against the grain

Coarse black pepper

1 medium **yellow onion**, thinly sliced

1 **red bell pepper**, cored, seeded, and thinly sliced

½ teaspoon crushed **red pepper flakes**

2 tablespoons **balsamic vinegar**

A handful of fresh **flat-leaf parsley**, chopped

½ cup shaved **Parmigiano-Reggiano**, shaved from a wedge of Parm using a vegetable peeler

Crusty bread, warmed, to pass at the table

Bring a medium sauce pot of water to a boil, salt it, then add the broccoli rabe and cook for 5 minutes. Drain in a colander, scatter on a cookie sheet or large plate to quick-cool, then reserve.

Add the EVOO to a large nonstick skillet and arrange the sliced garlic in an even layer. Turn the heat on medium low and slowly brown the garlic, about 3 to 4 minutes. Keep an eye on it; the garlic can go from golden brown to burned very quickly. Once the garlic is golden brown, remove it with a slotted spoon to a plate lined with a paper towel.

Turn the heat up to high. Once the oil ripples and begins to smoke, add the beef to the pan in an even layer and season it with salt and pepper. Do not move the beef for at least 2 to 3 minutes. Give it time to caramelize. If you force it, you will rip the meat and make it tough. Once it is well browned on one side, stir the beef and continue to cook for 1 more minute. Remove the beef from the skillet with a slotted spoon and reserve it on a plate.

Return the skillet to the heat and add the onions, bell peppers, red pepper flakes, salt, and pepper. Cook, stirring frequently, for 3 minutes, or until the onions and peppers are tender. Add the reserved broccoli rabe, toss, and stir to combine. Season with salt and pepper and continue to cook for 2 minutes. Add the reserved beef and the golden garlic. Add the balsamic vinegar and cook for 1 to 2 more minutes to finish cooking the beef. Turn off the heat and add the parsley. Toss it all together and serve immediately, garnishing each serving with shaved Parmigiano curls. Serve with hot crusty bread.

Bacon, Spinach, and Cream Potatoes

Any mashed potato lover is going to freak out over this version with smoky bacon and spinach.   6 SERVINGS

---

3 pounds **Idaho potatoes**, peeled and sliced

Salt

EVOO (extra-virgin olive oil), for drizzling

4 center-cut **bacon** strips, chopped

1 medium **onion**, quartered and thinly sliced

2 10-ounce boxes **frozen chopped spinach**, defrosted and wrung out in a kitchen towel

1 cup **heavy cream**

Black pepper

¼ teaspoon freshly grated or ground **nutmeg**

Place the potatoes in a pot and cover with water. Bring up to a boil, salt the water, and cook until the potatoes are tender, 12 to 15 minutes.

To a small skillet over medium heat add a little EVOO and the bacon and cook until the bacon is browned, 7 to 8 minutes. Add the onions and cook until soft, 5 minutes more.

Drain the potatoes and place back in the hot pot. Add the bacon and onions and defrosted spinach to the potatoes, and mash to combine, then add the cream. Mash until smooth and season the mixture with salt, pepper, and the nutmeg.

Cacio e Pepe (Cheese and Pepper) Spaghetti Squash

This is an awesome dish. Your family will love it.   4 SERVINGS

1 4-pound **spaghetti squash**

2 tablespoons **extra-virgin olive oil** (EVOO)

1 cup grated **Romano cheese**

Salt and lots of **coarse ground black pepper**

To microwave squash: Cut in half and seed. Place ¼ inch water in a microwave-safe dish. Place the squash in the dish, the cut sides down—the sides will overlap. Cover with plastic wrap and microwave on High for 13 minutes. Reserve ¼ cup of the cooking liquid in a bowl. Shred the squash and add the "spaghetti" to the bowl with the reserved liquid.

To boil squash: Cut in half and seed. Boil the squash until tender, 15 to 20 minutes. Place ¼ cup, a ladleful, of cooking water into a bowl, then drain and shred the squash. Transfer to the bowl with the reserved liquid.

Toss the squash with the reserved liquid and dress with EVOO, lots of cheese, salt to taste, and lots of black pepper and serve.

Italian Chicken Pot Pie from the Boot

What if a pot pie got a Eurail pass and came back home to the States speaking Italian? It might taste something like this; it's one rich meal AND it's a one-pot wonder.   8 SERVINGS

2 tablespoons **EVOO** (extra-virgin olive oil)

3 tablespoons **butter**

1 pound **button mushrooms**, trimmed and halved

1 1 pound bag **frozen pearl onions**, defrosted, then drained on a kitchen towel to remove excess liquid

4 large **garlic cloves**, finely chopped

2 large **carrots**, peeled and thinly sliced

3 **celery ribs**, thinly sliced

1 teaspoon **red pepper flakes**

Salt and **black pepper**

1 24-ounce log prepared plain or flavored **polenta** (on the refrigerator aisle)

1 1-pound ball fresh **mozzarella cheese**

3 tablespoons all-purpose **flour**

1 cup **dry white wine**

1 quart **chicken stock**

½ cup **heavy cream** or half-and-half

2 cooked **rotisserie chickens**

1 pint **red grape tomatoes**

1 10-ounce box **frozen peas**

1½ cups **fresh basil**, about 25 leaves, coarsely chopped or torn

¾ cup fresh **flat-leaf parsley** leaves, about 3 generous handfuls, chopped

1 cup grated **Parmigiano-Reggiano** cheese, 3 overflowing handfuls

Preheat the broiler. Place the rack at the center position or drop the lower or upper broiler pans as far from the heat source as possible.

Preheat a large pot over medium-high heat with the EVOO, 2 times around the pan. Add the butter and, once it melts, add the mushrooms and cook for 4 to 5 minutes, to give them a little color. Add the pearl onions, garlic, carrots, celery, red pepper flakes, and a little salt and pepper. Cook, stirring occasionally, 5 minutes longer.

While the veggies are cooking, slice the polenta log into ¼-inch-thick disks. One log should yield 20 to 22 disks. Halve the ball of mozzarella, then slice each half into ¼-inch-thick half moons and reserve alongside the polenta disks.

Sprinkle the flour into the veggies and stir to combine, then continue to cook for another minute or two. Add the white wine, scraping up any bits on the bottom of the pot with a wooden spoon. Add the chicken stock

recipe continued

and cream and bring up to a bubble, then simmer for 10 minutes.

Remove all the meat from the rotisserie chickens, tearing it into large bite-size pieces and discarding the skin. Add the chicken meat to the simmering sauce as you break it up. Once all of the meat is in the pot, add the tomatoes and peas and cook for another 2 minutes. Add the basil and parsley; taste to adjust the seasoning. Transfer the mixture to a large oval or rectangular baking dish, casserole, or lasagna pan. (Disposable pans are fine as well but buy two and double them up for sturdiness and to keep the bottom of the pot pie from scorching.) Shingle the polenta disks and the mozzarella half moons over the top of the chicken and vegetables, distributing the cheese evenly among the polenta. Sprinkle the top of the assembled dish with the grated cheese and transfer to the broiler several inches from the heat. Broil until the polenta is warm and the cheeses have browned.

tidbit >> The pot pie can be assembled ahead of time if you like; bake it for 25 minutes, or until browned. It also reheats well.

Double Eggplant Parm Fake-Baked Ziti

Nothing pleases like baked ziti, the universal carried dish that is welcome at any occasion. It's always the empty chafing dish on any buffet and the first request when Mom asks you what you want for dinner. This is one of my best: In 30 minutes, you can turn out eggplant baked ziti with both breaded eggplant and eggplant sauce. It is a hands-down winner.   6 SERVINGS

2 medium **eggplants,** 1 peeled and chopped, 1 thinly sliced

½ cup plus 2 tablespoons **EVOO** (extra-virgin olive oil)

Salt and **black pepper**

2 **eggs**

¼ to ⅓ cup **milk** or cream

1 pound **ziti rigate** or rigatoni

1½ cups grated **Parmigiano-Reggiano cheese**

1 cup **Italian-style bread crumbs,** 4 generous handfuls

3 tablespoons fresh chopped **rosemary** leaves, from 4 to 5 sprigs

2 **garlic cloves,** crushed from their skins

1 teaspoon **red pepper flakes**

1 28-ounce can **crushed tomatoes or crushed fire-roasted tomatoes**

Handful of fresh **flat-leaf parsley** leaves, chopped

2 cups shredded **provolone cheese**

Heat the oven to 500° F.

Place a large covered pot of water on to boil.

Spread the chopped eggplant on a nonstick rimmed baking sheet. Pour about ¼ cup of the EVOO in a small dish, then, using a pastry brush, coat the eggplant with oil and season liberally with salt and pepper. Roast the eggplant for 20 minutes, or until the eggplant pieces are dark and tender.

Preheat about ¼ cup of the EVOO in a large nonstick skillet over medium heat.

Beat the eggs with the milk or cream in a wide, shallow dish and season the mixture with salt and pepper.

When the water comes to a boil, salt it liberally and add the pasta. Cook the pasta to al dente (with a bite to it). Drain the pasta and reserve.

In a wide, shallow dish combine about ½ cup of the grated cheese with the bread crumbs and rosemary. Coat the eggplant slices in the egg mixture then the bread crumbs and cook in the hot EVOO for 3 to 4 minutes on each side. Work in two batches if necessary. Drain the eggplant on paper towels.

Preheat another large skillet over medium heat. Add the remaining 2 tablespoons of EVOO and the garlic.

recipe continued

Cook for a couple of minutes, then remove the garlic and add the red pepper flakes, tomatoes, parsley, and salt.

When the roasted eggplant is done, switch the oven to broil. Scrape the roasted eggplant pieces into a food processor and process them until they're smooth. Add the pureed eggplant to the tomato sauce and stir to combine.

Toss the drained hot pasta with half of the sauce and the remaining 1 cup of grated Parmigiano cheese. Spread the pasta in a baking dish and top it with the eggplant slices, the remaining sauce, and all of the provolone. Place the fake-baked ziti under the broiler for 2 to 3 minutes to brown the cheese.

Spanakopita Chicken Meatballs with Spicy Cucumber Yogurt Sauce

The Olympics only come around every few years, but there's always a game on somewhere. Have some fellow sports spectators over and serve this fantastic meatball dish.   6 SERVINGS

2 10-ounce boxes **frozen chopped spinach**, defrosted

¾ cup crumbled **feta cheese**

1 pound **ground chicken**

1 small **onion**, finely chopped

3 **garlic cloves**, finely chopped

1 tablespoon **grill seasoning**, such as McCormick's Montreal Steak Seasoning

EVOO (extra-virgin olive oil), for liberal drizzling

1½ cups **Greek-style plain yogurt**

⅓ **seedless cucumber**, peeled and chopped

3 tablespoons chopped **fresh dill**

½ tablespoon ground **cumin**

½ tablespoon ground **coriander**

Juice of ½ **lemon**

Salt

Preheat the oven to 400° F.

Wring out the spinach completely dry. Separate the spinach as you add it to a mixing bowl. Add the feta, chicken, onions, two thirds of the chopped garlic, the grill seasoning, and a liberal drizzle of EVOO to the bowl. Mix the meat with the veggies and feta and form eighteen 1½-inch meatballs. Place the meatballs on a rimmed non-stick baking sheet and bake them for 10 to 12 minutes, until they are golden and the juices run clear.

While the meatballs bake, place the yogurt, remaining chopped garlic, the cucumbers, dill, cumin, coriander, lemon juice, and a little salt in a food processor and process until smooth. Adjust the seasonings and transfer the sauce to a serving bowl. Serve the meatballs with a bowl of the sauce and toothpicks for dipping.

> **tidbit >>** Greek yogurt is widely available and is much thicker and richer than regular yogurt. Substitute plain yogurt if you must, but do try to find the Greek kind.

Turkey Noodle Casserole

Here's an upscale spin on the classic Tuna Noodle Casserole—it'll knock their socks off at your next potluck supper!   4 SERVINGS

Coarse salt

½ pound **extra-wide egg noodles**

1 tablespoon **extra-virgin olive oil** (EVOO)

3 slices **bacon** or turkey bacon, chopped

1 package (about 1⅓ pounds) **ground turkey breast**

1 pound **white mushrooms**, wiped, trimmed, and sliced

1 medium **onion**, chopped

Freshly ground black pepper, to taste

2 teaspoons **ground thyme** or poultry seasoning

½ cup **dry white wine**

1 cup **chicken stock** or broth

½ cup **heavy cream**

¼ teaspoon **freshly grated nutmeg**

2 tablespoons **unsalted butter**, softened

2 cups grated **Gruyère cheese** (about an 8-ounce brick)

1 cup **plain bread crumbs**

2 to 3 tablespoons chopped fresh **flat-leaf parsley**

Bring a large pot of water to a boil for the egg noodles. When it boils, salt the water and cook the noodles al dente. Drain well and return to the pot.

Preheat a large, deep skillet over medium-high heat. Add the EVOO and the bacon. Cook for 2 to 3 minutes, until the fat is rendered and the bacon begins to brown at the edges. Add the turkey and brown it, crumbling it with a wooden spoon. Move the meat over to one side of the pan and add the mushrooms and onions to the opposite side. Cook the mushrooms and onions for 3 to 5 minutes, then stir the meat and veggies together. Season the mixture liberally with salt and pepper, and sprinkle in the ground thyme or poultry seasoning. Cook for another 5 minutes. Add the wine and deglaze the pan, using a wooden spoon to scrape up pan drippings and browned bits. Stir in the stock and bring to a bubble, then stir in the cream and reduce the heat to low. Add the nutmeg and stir. Taste and adjust seasonings if necessary.

Preheat the broiler to high. Combine the noodles with the turkey and sauce. Grease a casserole dish with a little softened butter. Transfer the turkey-noodle mixture to the dish and top with Gruyère cheese and then bread crumbs. Place the casserole 8 to 10 inches from the broiler and brown for 2 to 3 minutes, or until the cheese is melted and the crumbs are brown. Garnish the casserole with the parsley.

Wild Cream of Mushroom Egg Noodle Bake, Hold the Canned Soup

Serve with a green salad and you're all set.   4 SERVINGS

CREAM OF MUSHROOM SAUCE

1 tablespoon **extra-virgin olive oil** (EVOO)

2 tablespoons **unsalted butter**

12 **button mushrooms,** brushed off with a damp towel and chopped

2 tablespoons all-purpose **flour**

1 cup **chicken stock** or broth

1 cup **whole milk** or cream

⅛ teaspoon freshly **grated** or **ground nutmeg**

Salt and **freshly ground black pepper**

CASSEROLE

2 tablespoons **EVOO**

1 **shallot,** thinly sliced

2 **portobello mushroom caps,** halved and thinly sliced

½ pound fresh **mixed wild mushrooms,** such as shiitakes, oysters, and wood-ears, stems trimmed and caps thinly sliced

1 tablespoon fresh **thyme** leaves, finely chopped (from 4 sprigs)

Salt and **freshly ground black pepper**

⅓ cup **dry white wine,** or more stock

1 pound extra-wide **egg noodles**

1 to 2 tablespoons **unsalted butter,** softened

¾ pound **Gruyère** or Emmentaler cheese, shredded

3 tablespoons chopped fresh **chives** (12 to 15 chives)

Bring a large pot of water to a boil for the egg noodles.

To make the mushroom sauce, heat a medium sauce pot over medium heat. Add the EVOO and the butter. When the butter melts, add the chopped button mushrooms and cook for 5 minutes, until just tender. Sprinkle in the flour and cook for 1 minute. Whisk in the chicken stock and bring to a bubble, then stir in the whole milk. Reduce the heat to low and gently simmer. Season the sauce with nutmeg, salt, and pepper.

To make the casserole, heat a nonstick skillet over medium-high heat. Add the 2 tablespoons of EVOO, then the shallots and mushrooms. Cook the mushrooms for 8 minutes, or until tender. Season with the thyme, salt, and pepper, and deglaze the pan with the wine or a little stock. Reduce the heat to medium low and let the liquid cook off.

Preheat the broiler to high.

While the mushrooms cook, drop the egg noodles into the boiling water, salt the water, and cook the noodles al dente, with a bite to them. Drain the noodles and return

recipe continued

them to the hot pot. Add the creamy sauce to the pot and toss the noodles to coat in the sauce.

Lightly coat a casserole dish with the softened butter, then transfer the cream of mushroom noodles to the dish and top with the mushroom ragout and the shredded cheese. Place the casserole under the broiler and melt and bubble the cheese until brown at the edges. Garnish with chives and serve.

BLT Pasta Bake: Bacon, Leeks, and Tomatoes

Tender leeks, crispy bacon, and tangy tomatoes—this pasta bake is bursting with flavor!   4 SERVINGS

Coarse salt

1 pound **elbow macaroni** or cavatappi (corkscrew-shaped pasta)

1 tablespoon **extra-virgin olive oil** (EVOO)

8 slices **bacon**, coarsely chopped

2 large **leeks**, trimmed of roots and dark green tops

Coarse black pepper

3 tablespoons **unsalted butter**

3 tablespoons all-purpose **flour**

½ teaspoon **cayenne pepper**

1 teaspoon **paprika**

3 cups **whole milk**

1 cup **chicken stock** or broth

3½ cups grated **Gruyère cheese**

1 tablespoon **Dijon mustard**

1 pint **cherry tomatoes**

¾ cup **plain bread crumbs**

Place a pot of water on to boil for the pasta. When the water reaches a boil, add some salt and the pasta and cook until al dente.

While the pasta cooks, heat a large skillet over medium heat. Add the EVOO and chopped bacon and cook until crisp. While the bacon is cooking, split the trimmed leeks in half lengthwise, lay the leeks cut side down, and thinly slice into half-moons. Fill a large bowl with water and mix the leeks into the water. Allow the water to settle and the dirt and grit to settle on the bottom of the bowl. Using your hands, draw the leeks from the water, taking care to not unsettle the dirt. Drain the cleaned leeks on a kitchen towel, pat dry, and then add to the pan with the bacon. Season the leeks with salt and pepper. Cook the leeks until tender, about 3 to 4 minutes.

To start the cheese sauce, heat a medium sauce pot over medium heat. Add the butter and melt, then add the flour, cayenne, and paprika and whisk together over the heat until the roux bubbles; cook for 1 minute more. Whisk in the milk and stock and raise the heat a little. Bring the sauce to a quick boil and simmer to thicken, about 5 minutes. Remove the sauce from the heat and whisk in 3 cups of the grated cheese and the mustard. Set aside.

Add the cherry tomatoes to the leeks and continue to cook for 2 minutes. Remove from the heat and reserve.

Preheat the broiler.

Drain the pasta and add it back to the pasta pot.

recipe continued

Combine the reserved leek mixture and the cheese sauce with the pasta. Season with salt and pepper to taste.

Transfer the pasta to a baking dish. Combine the remaining ½ cup of grated cheese with the bread crumbs. Top the pasta with the mixture. Place the dish under the broiler until the cheese melts and the bread crumbs are brown.

Bresaola Salad

High in protein, with practically no carbs—this salad rocks and makes a great lunch or dinner! 4 SERVINGS

8 cups **arugula**

Juice of 1 lemon

Extra-virgin olive oil (EVOO), for drizzling

Coarse salt

6-ounce chunk of **Parmigiano-Reggiano**

1 pound **bresaola** (cured beef, like prosciutto; available at deli counter)

1 15-ounce can **artichoke hearts** in water, drained

4 sprigs **fresh rosemary**

A handful of fresh **flat-leaf parsley**

½ cup **capers**, drained

Aged **balsamic vinegar**, for drizzling (look for 6-plus years of age, widely available in many markets)

Place the arugula in a bowl and dress with lemon juice, EVOO, and salt. Divide the arugula among 4 dinner plates or place on a serving platter and mound the greens. Use a vegetable peeler to shred some cheese on top of the arugula. Arrange the bresaola in a thin layer all around the plate, draping it over the arugula. The plates or platter should look like a mound of beef. Thinly slice the artichokes, finely chop the rosemary and parsley, and slice the capers. Decoratively arrange the artichokes, chopped herbs, and capers all over the meat. Drizzle the completed salad with aged balsamic vinegar and serve.

Ginger Vegetable Chicken Noodle Bowl

I love noodle bowls! What's not to like? This one makes plain chicken noodle soup seem, well, really plain. The next time you want either take-out Asian food or just a bowl of chicken noodle soup, make this instead. It rules!   4 SERVINGS

2 tablespoons **vegetable oil**

1 pound boneless, skinless **chicken tenders** (white meat) or thighs (dark meat), cut into bite-size pieces

4 **garlic cloves,** finely chopped

1 2-inch piece of **fresh ginger,** peeled and cut into thin matchsticks or grated

1 cup shredded **carrots** (available in pouches in the produce department)

Salt and **freshly ground black pepper**

2 teaspoons **ground cumin**

2 teaspoons **Chinese five-spice powder**

6 cups **chicken stock** or broth

½ pound **vermicelli** (thin spaghetti)

4 **scallions,** trimmed and cut into 2½-inch lengths, then cut lengthwise into matchsticks

2 cups fresh crisp **bean spouts**

Heat a medium pot over medium-high heat. Add the vegetable oil, then add the chicken and lightly brown it, about 3 minutes. Add the garlic and ginger, stir, add the carrots, season with salt and pepper, and add the cumin and five-spice powder. Add the stock and bring the soup to a boil. Add the vermicelli and reduce the heat to a simmer. Cook for 3 minutes, then add the scallions and bean sprouts and turn off the heat. Let the soup stand for 5 minutes, adjust the seasonings, and serve.

Grilled Chicken Pasta Salad

Talk about flexible, this chicken is a cheerleader. Yes, it's equally good steaming hot or icebox cold. Eat this dish four seasons of the year, hot or not, indoors or out. It's G-R-E-A-T . . . great!   4 SERVINGS

Salt

½ pound **short-cut pasta**

3 **garlic cloves**, chopped

2 tablespoons **grill seasoning**, such as McCormick's Montreal Steak Seasoning, 2 palmfuls

2 teaspoons **hot sauce**

3 tablespoons **Worcestershire sauce**

5 tablespoons **red wine vinegar**

½ cup **EVOO** (extra-virgin olive oil)

2 large **onions**, sliced 1 inch thick

6 thin-cut **chicken breast cutlets**

2 tablespoons **Dijon mustard**

Black pepper

¼ cup grated **Parmigiano-Reggiano** or Pecorino Romano cheese, a handful

2 bunches **arugula**, thoroughly washed and coarsely chopped

1 small head **radicchio**, cored and coarsely chopped

2 cups fresh **basil**, 20 leaves, coarsely chopped

¼ cup fresh **flat-leaf parsley**, a generous handful, chopped

3 **celery ribs**, thinly sliced

1 ball **fresh mozzarella cheese**, cut into bite-size pieces

1 pint **grape tomatoes**, left whole if small, cut in half if large

Heat a grill pan or outdoor grill to high heat.

Bring a large pot of water with a tight-fitting lid to a boil over high heat. Once the water boils, add some salt and the pasta, and cook until al dente.

In a small bowl, mix the garlic, grill seasoning, hot sauce, Worcestershire sauce, and 2 tablespoons of the vinegar. Whisk in ¼ cup of the EVOO. Divide the mixture between two shallow bowls. Add the sliced onions to one and the chicken cutlets to the other. Toss to coat both thoroughly and marinate for a few minutes.

In a salad bowl, combine the mustard and the remaining 3 tablespoons of vinegar with a little salt and pepper. In a slow, steady stream, whisk in the remaining ¼ cup of EVOO, then add the grated cheese. Once the pasta is cooked, drain it thoroughly and add it to the salad bowl with the dressing; toss to coat.

Grill the onion slices, cooking them on each side until well marked, about 2 to 3 minutes. Grill the chicken cutlets for 3 to 4 minutes on each side. Remove the onions and the chicken from the grill to a cutting board to rest and cool off for about 5 minutes. Coarsely chop the grilled onions and cut the chicken into thin strips. Add them to the dressed pasta. Add the arugula, radicchio, basil, parsley, celery, mozzarella, and grape tomatoes. Season with a little salt and pepper and toss thoroughly.

Grilled Eggplant and Capicola Parmigiana

No bread crumbs, plus it's not deep-fried! You could eat a mountain of this eggplant Parm and not have to loosen your belt.   4 SERVINGS

1 cup **extra-virgin olive oil (EVOO)**

4 **garlic cloves**, crushed

2 medium **eggplant**, ends cut off, sliced crosswise, ¾ inch thick

Salt

1 teaspoon **coarse black pepper**

1 medium **yellow onion**, finely chopped

1 28-ounce can **crushed tomatoes**

1 teaspoon **ground cumin** (⅓ palmful)

¼ teaspoon **ground cinnamon**

A handful of fresh **flat-leaf parsley**, finely chopped

½ pound deli-sliced **capicola hot ham**

½ cup grated **Parmigiano-Reggiano**

6 pieces sharp deli-sliced **provolone**

6 cups **mixed greens**, any variety

2 tablespoons **red wine vinegar**

Preheat the oven to 450°F.

Combine the EVOO and garlic in a small pot over medium-low heat. When the garlic simmers, reduce heat to low.

Brush the eggplant on both sides with the garlic infused EVOO and arrange on a baking sheet. Season the eggplant with salt and the pepper and place in the oven to roast. Roast the eggplant for 15 to 18 minutes, turning once, until browned at the edges, lightly golden, and just tender to the touch. While it roasts, prepare the sauce.

From the remaining EVOO, fish out the garlic and chop it up. Heat a small to medium pot over medium heat. Add about 2 tablespoons of the garlic-infused EVOO and the chopped garlic. Add the onion and cook for 10 minutes, stirring frequently. Add the tomatoes, salt, pepper, cumin, and cinnamon and heat through. Simmer for 5 minutes. Stir in half of the parsley. Remove the eggplant from the oven and switch the broiler on high.

To make your casserole, ladle a little of the tomato sauce in the bottom of a casserole and add a layer of eggplant, then a layer of capicola, then the remaining eggplant, remaining sauce, Parmigiano, provolone, and the remaining parsley. Broil until the cheese is brown and bubbly, about 3 minutes.

Place the salad greens in a bowl and toss with the vinegar, then 3 tablespoons of EVOO (use remaining garlic oil if you still have some left), and season the salad with salt and pepper to taste.

Serve the eggplant parm alongside a little green salad.

Oktoberfest Stoup

This is perfect for fall. And don't forget to add the bottle of beer!

4 SERVINGS

2 tablespoons **vegetable oil**

2 tablespoons **butter**, cut into pats

3 **knockwursts**, diced into 1-inch cubes

3 **bratwursts**, diced into 1-inch cubes

1 **red onion**, quartered and thinly sliced

2 pounds **red cabbage**, quartered and shredded

1 teaspoon **caraway seeds**

Salt and **freshly ground black pepper**

1 12-ounce bottle **dark beer**

1 quart **veal or chicken stock**

2 cups **tomato sauce**

2 tablespoons **Worcestershire sauce**

1 **bay leaf**, fresh or dried

3 tablespoons finely chopped **flat-leaf parsley**

2 **Red or Golden Delicious apples**, peeled and diced

Juice of ½ lemon

Heat a big soup pot over medium-high heat. Add 1 tablespoon of the vegetable oil and half the butter. When the butter melts into the oil, add the cubed wursts and brown them on all sides, 5 minutes. Remove the browned sausages and add the remaining tablespoon each of oil and butter. When the butter melts into the oil, add the onion and cook for 2 minutes. Add the cabbage and caraway, season with salt and pepper, and stir. Cook the cabbage for 10 minutes, stirring frequently. Add the beer and cook down 1 minute. Add the stock, tomato sauce, Worcestershire, and bay leaf and stir to combine. Add the wursts back to the pot. Cover the pot and bring the stoup up to a boil, 2 or 3 minutes. Remove the lid and simmer for 5 to 10 minutes longer, until the cabbage is tender. Remove the bay leaf. Combine the parsley, apple, and lemon juice in a small bowl. Ladle the stoup into shallow bowls and top with generous spoonfuls of the flavored apples to stir into the stoup as you eat it.

Sausage and Tortellini Soup

Let your guests munch on a few store-bought items like mixed olives, cheese, and salamis while you're throwing this dinner together. If your company is impatient for the main course, shave a few more minutes off the soup's cook time by heating up the chicken stock in a separate pot while you start cooking up the sausage. 8 SERVINGS

2 tablespoons **EVOO** (extra-virgin olive oil)

1 pound bulk **sweet Italian sausage**

2 large **onions**, chopped

3 **celery ribs**, with green leafy tops, finely chopped

4 large **garlic cloves**, chopped

1 small **fennel bulb**, cored and chopped, a handful of the green fronds reserved

2 large pinches of **red pepper flakes**

Salt and **black pepper**

1 28-ounce can **diced tomatoes**

2 quarts **chicken stock**

2 9-ounce packages **fresh tortellini** (cheese, spinach, or mushroom)

1½ cups fresh **basil**, about 25 leaves, chopped

½ cup fresh **flat-leaf parsley** leaves, about 2 generous handfuls, chopped

Grated **Parmigiano-Reggiano** cheese, for passing at the table

Preheat a large soup pot over medium-high heat with 2 tablespoons of the EVOO, 2 times around the pan. Add the sausage to the hot pot and break it up with a wooden spoon into little pieces as it cooks, 3 to 4 minutes. Add the onions, celery, garlic, chopped fennel, red pepper flakes, and a little salt and pepper. Cook, stirring frequently, for 5 minutes. Add the tomatoes and continue to cook for a minute, then add the chicken stock. Put a lid on the pot to bring the soup up to a simmer and cook for 10 minutes. Uncover the pot, add the tortellini, and cook for 5 minutes. Once the pasta is cooked through, add the basil and parsley, then taste and re-reason with a little more salt and pepper if you think it needs it. Chop up the reserved fennel fronds, stir them in, and serve. Pass the cheese at the table.

Cream of Cheddar Soup and Lime Chicken Avocado Salad

The zesty lime chicken and cooling avocado, along with the Cheddar soup, are a match made in heaven.   4 SERVINGS

2 tablespoons **butter**

1 large **yellow onion**, chopped

3 **garlic cloves**, chopped

1 teaspoon **red pepper flakes**

Salt and **freshly ground black pepper**

2 tablespoons **ground cumin**

2 tablespoons **all-purpose flour**

1 quart **chicken stock** or broth

1 cup **heavy cream**

5 tablespoons **extra-virgin olive oil** (EVOO)

5 thin **chicken breast cutlets**

1 tablespoon **ground coriander**

2 **limes**

1 ripe **Hass avocado**

½ head **iceberg lettuce**, shredded

½ pint **cherry tomatoes**, cut in half

¼ cup fresh **cilantro leaves**, chopped

4 cups good-quality **aged Cheddar cheese**, grated

Heat a soup pot over medium heat with the butter. When the butter melts, add the onion, garlic, red pepper flakes, salt, pepper, and 1 tablespoon of the cumin (a palmful). Cook for 3 minutes. Add the flour and cook for 1 minute more. Whisk in the chicken stock and heavy cream, bring up to a simmer, and cook for 10 minutes.

Preheat a large skillet over medium-high heat with 2 tablespoons of the EVOO. Season the chicken breasts with the remaining tablespoon of cumin, the coriander, and salt and pepper; add to the hot skillet and cook for 2 to 3 minutes on each side, or until cooked through. Remove the chicken to the cutting board, squeeze the juice of 1 lime over the chicken, and allow it to cool slightly.

Cut the avocado in half lengthwise, cutting around the pit. Separate the halves and using a spoon, scoop out the pit and then scoop the avocado from its skin. Chop the avocado flesh into bite-size pieces. Add to a mixing bowl. To the avocado add the shredded iceberg lettuce, tomatoes, and cilantro. Cut the chicken into thin strips and add to the bowl. Squeeze the juice of the remaining lime over the salad and drizzle with the remaining 3 tablespoons of EVOO. Season with salt and pepper and toss to coat.

To finish the soup, turn the heat off. While whisking, add the grated Cheddar cheese in 3 additions. Serve the Cheddar soup immediately alongside the lime chicken avocado salad.

> **tidbit >>** The cheese is the big flavor in this soup, so look for good-quality Cheddar that has a super-sharp, deep Cheddar flavor.

Thai Chicken Noodle Soup

Here's a Thai spin on an old standby comfort food—perfect for a chilly day!   4 SERVINGS

2 tablespoons **vegetable oil**

1 medium **yellow onion,** quartered and thinly sliced

3 **garlic cloves,** finely chopped

2 **poblano or Anaheim peppers,** seeded and thinly sliced

Salt and **freshly ground black pepper**

1 cup shredded **carrots** (in pouches on the produce aisle)

6 cups (1½ quarts) **chicken stock** or broth

2 pounds **chicken tenders,** cut into bite-size chunks

1 small bundle from a 3.75-ounce package of **bean thread noodles** (there are usually 3 bundles in 1 package; recommended brand Kame)

3 tablespoons fresh **cilantro leaves,** chopped

15 fresh **basil leaves,** roughly chopped

Juice of 1 lime

Heat a large, heavy-bottomed soup pot with the vegetable oil over high heat. Once you see the oil ripple, add the onion, garlic, and sliced peppers. Season the vegetables with salt and pepper and cook, stirring frequently, for 2 minutes. Add the carrots and chicken stock. Cover with a lid and bring up to a simmer. Once simmering, add the chicken and noodles and simmer for 10 minutes more. Remove the soup from the heat and add the cilantro, basil, and the lime juice.

Chorizo Chicken Spinach Stoup with Roasted Red Pepper and Manchego Toasts

Here's a killer dinner that a charging Pamplona bull would brake for.

4 SERVINGS

---

2 tablespoons **EVOO** (extra-virgin olive oil)

½ pound **chorizo**, cut in quarters lengthwise, then thinly sliced

1 large yellow **onion**, chopped

3 **garlic cloves**, chopped

Salt and **black pepper**

2 10-ounce boxes **frozen chopped spinach**

1 quart **chicken stock**

½ cup **heavy cream** or half-and-half

¾ pound **chicken tenders**, cut into bite-size pieces

8 **baguette** slices, cut ½ inch thick on an angle

⅓ pound **manchego cheese**, rind removed, grated

1 jarred **roasted red pepper**, chopped

¼ cup fresh **flat-leaf parsley**, a generous handful, chopped

Heat a medium soup pot over medium-high heat with the EVOO. Add the chorizo and cook for about 2 to 3 minutes, stirring it frequently. Remove it from the pot to drain on a paper towel. To the hot soup pot add the onions, garlic, salt, and pepper. Cook while stirring frequently for about 4 or 5 minutes, or until the onions are tender.

Defrost the spinach in the microwave on High for 6 minutes. Place the spinach in a kitchen towel and wring out the liquid. Add the spinach to the onions and continue to cook for about 2 minutes. Transfer the onions and spinach to a blender or food processor with ½ cup of the chicken stock. Puree it until somewhat smooth. (If the pureeing gives you any trouble, add some more stock.) Add the pureed spinach back to the soup pot and stir in the remaining 3½ cups of chicken stock and the cream. Bring it to a simmer and add the reserved chorizo and chicken pieces. Simmer them gently for 8 to 10 minutes, or until the chicken is cooked through and the flavors have come together.

Preheat the broiler and place a rack on the second groove. While the soup is simmering, toast the baguette slices until they are golden brown under the broiler. Mix the grated manchego with the roasted red pepper and the parsley on your cutting board. Once the toast is golden, top each with a little of the cheese mixture and return them to the broiler to melt and lightly brown the cheese.

Transfer the stoup to serving bowls and serve 2 roasted pepper and manchego toasts alongside.

Taco Stoup with a Taco Toppings Salad

It's like a taco in a bowl. Does it get any better than that?   4 SERVINGS

4 tablespoons **extra-virgin olive oil** (EVOO), divided

1½ pounds **ground sirloin**

1 tablespoon **ground cumin**

1 tablespoon **ground coriander**

1 tablespoon **chili powder**

½ tablespoon **dried oregano**

1 large **yellow onion**, chopped

3 **garlic cloves**, chopped

Salt and **freshly ground black pepper**

1 15-ounce can **stewed tomatoes**

1 quart **chicken stock** or broth

3 **limes**

⅓ cup **mild taco sauce**

1 head **iceberg lettuce**, shredded

½ pint **cherry or grape tomatoes**, cut in half

1 handful fresh **cilantro leaves**, chopped

1 handful fresh **flat-leaf parsley**, chopped

1 cup good-quality **sharp Cheddar cheese**, shredded

Sour cream, for garnish

Heat a medium soup pot over medium-high heat with 2 tablespoons EVOO (twice around the pan). Add the ground sirloin. Brown the meat, breaking it up with a wooden spoon. Season it with the cumin, coriander, chili powder, oregano, onion, garlic, salt, and pepper. Stir to combine and continue to cook for 5 minutes. Add the stewed tomatoes and chicken stock, then bring the stoup up to a boil. Reduce the heat and simmer for 10 minutes. While the stoup is cooking, prepare the taco toppings salad.

In a small bowl combine the juice of 2 limes, the taco sauce, salt and pepper. Whisk in 2 tablespoons of EVOO. Reserve the dressing.

In a salad bowl combine the shredded lettuce, tomatoes, half of the chopped cilantro, the parsley, and grated Cheddar cheese. Pour the dressing over the salad and toss to combine.

Squeeze the juice of the remaining lime into the stoup. Ladle the stoup into serving bowls and garnish with a small dollop of sour cream and a sprinkle of cilantro.

Polenta with Chunky Chicken and Chorizo Chili

A lot of people are intimidated by polenta, but it's also one of the easiest things to prepare! The trick is to whisk quickly and continuously as you add the polenta to the liquid, avoiding lumps. It's ready in minutes and absorbs the taste of whatever you stir in to it! It can be served hot, cold, room temp, creamy, baked, grilled, or fried crisp. It truly is the Renaissance Man of ingredients! This polenta is the foundation for a killer meaty chili. It's perfect for a cold winter night.   6 SERVINGS

1 tablespoon **EVOO** (extra-virgin olive oil)

¾ pound packaged **chorizo** (not smoked), chopped

2 pounds **ground chicken**

3 tablespoons **chili powder**

1 tablespoon ground **cumin**

1 **onion**, chopped

3 **garlic cloves**, finely chopped

1 **red bell pepper**, chopped

1 15-ounce can **red kidney beans**, drained

1 12-ounce bottle of **beer**

1 28-ounce can diced **fire-roasted tomatoes**

Salt

6 cups **chicken stock**

2 cups **quick-cooking polenta**

2 tablespoons **butter**

2 **scallions**, finely chopped

2 tablespoons fresh chopped **thyme**

Heat a big, deep skillet over medium-high heat with the EVOO, once around the pan. Add the chorizo and cook to render its fat, 2 minutes. Push the chorizo off to the side of the pot and add the chicken meat. Brown and crumble the chicken, 5 to 6 minutes, seasoning the chicken with the chili powder and cumin while it cooks. Add the onions, garlic, peppers, and beans to the skillet and cook for another 5 to 6 minutes. Stir the beer into the chili, cook for a minute to reduce the liquid, then add the tomatoes and heat through. Season the chili with salt and reduce the heat to low.

Bring the stock to a boil in a medium pot, then stir in the polenta. Keep stirring until the polenta masses and thickens enough to mold to the sides of a bowl, 2 to 3 minutes. Stir in the butter, scallions, and thyme and season it with salt.

Fill 6 bowls halfway with polenta and make a well in the center, pushing the polenta up the sides. Top the polenta with chili and serve.

Green and White Lightning Chunky Chicken Chili

You won't believe what the tomatillo salsa does for this recipe.

4 SERVINGS

---

2 tablespoons **vegetable or canola oil**

6 6-ounce **boneless, skinless chicken breasts**, cut into bite-size pieces

Salt and **freshly ground black pepper**

1 medium **yellow onion**, thinly sliced

5 **garlic cloves**, finely chopped

1 **jalapeño pepper**, seeded and finely chopped

2 tablespoons **ground cumin**

1 tablespoon **ground coriander** (a palmful)

1 cup **mild or hot tomatillo salsa** (green salsa on Mexican foods aisle)

4 cups **chicken stock** or broth

1 15-ounce can **cannellini or Great Northern beans**

1 handful fresh **cilantro**, roughly chopped

1 handful fresh **flat-leaf parsley**, roughly chopped

Juice of 1 lime

Shredded **Monterey Jack** or **Pepper Jack cheese**, for garnish

1 individual lunch-box-size bag of **corn chips**, optional and not that dangerous

Heat a medium soup pot over medium-high heat with the vegetable oil. Add the chicken to the hot oil and season liberally with salt and pepper. Cook for 2 to 3 minutes, stirring frequently. Add the onion, garlic, jalapeño, cumin, and coriander and cook for 3 to 4 minutes, continuing to stir. Add the tomatillo salsa and the chicken stock. Bring the chili up to a simmer. Add half of the beans. With a fork thoroughly mash the other half of the beans, then add to the chili. This method will help to thicken the chili. Simmer the chili for 10 minutes. Remove the chili from the heat and add the cilantro, parsley, and lime juice.

Serve each bowl of chili with a little shredded Monterey Jack cheese on top. Oh, and go ahead, have a chip or two! I crush up a small bag and stir them right in!

Caution-Flag Chili with Flat-Tire Corn and Black Bean Toppers

NASCAR has become HUGE. If you're into racing or just a fan of fiery foods, this one is for you! Serve with plenty of cold beer.   6 SERVINGS

2 tablespoons **EVOO** (extra-virgin olive oil)

2 **poblano peppers**, seeded and thinly sliced

2 pounds **ground sirloin**

1 medium **onion**, chopped

3 to 4 **garlic cloves**, chopped

2 tablespoons **grill seasoning**, such as McCormick's Montreal Steak Seasoning, a couple palmfuls

2 tablespoons **Worcestershire sauce**

2 **chipotles in adobo**, chopped, plus 1 tablespoon adobo sauce

½ cup **steak sauce**, such as Peter Luger or A1

1 cup **beer** (⅔ bottle)

1 cup **beef stock**

1 28-ounce can **crushed fire-roasted tomatoes**

1 package **corn muffin mix**, preferably Jiffy, batter made according to package directions for corn pancakes

1 15.5-ounce can **black beans**, rinsed, drained, and patted dry with paper towels

½ tablespoon ground **cumin**

2 **scallions**, finely chopped

Softened **butter**, for greasing a griddle

Heat the EVOO in a medium soup pot over medium-high to high heat. When the oil smokes, add the sliced poblanos and char them for a couple of minutes, then scoot them off to the side of the pan and add the meat. Break up the beef and brown it for a couple of minutes, then add the onions and garlic. Season the meat with the grill seasoning, Worcestershire, chipotles, and adobo sauce. Cook until the onions are tender, 5 to 6 minutes more, then stir in the steak sauce and beer. Cook the beer off for 1 minute, then add the stock and tomatoes and reduce the heat to low.

Prepare the corn pancake batter according to the package instructions. Finely chop the beans in a food processor and stir them into the corn batter. Season the batter with the cumin, and stir in the scallions.

Heat a nonstick griddle pan over medium heat. Butter the griddle, then pour three 3- to 4-inch corn pancakes. Flip the cakes when the bottoms are deeply golden and cook them for another minute or two on the second side. Repeat with the remaining batter to make 6 cakes.

Top each bowlful of the chili with a corn and black bean pancake; these are your flat-tire toppers!

Chicken Dumpling and Noodle Stoup

If you have a mini meatball in your house (or you're just a kid at heart) this one will feed you well, stomach and soul!   4 SERVINGS

Salt

½ pound **short-cut pasta**, such as ditalini or penne

2 tablespoons **EVOO** (extra-virgin olive oil)

1 large **yellow onion**, ¾ of it thinly sliced, ¼ of it grated

¼ teaspoon **red pepper flakes**, a couple of pinches

3 **garlic cloves**, chopped

Black pepper

5 cups **chicken stock**

1½-pound package **ground chicken breast meat**

1 cup fresh **basil**, 20 leaves, chopped

¼ cup fresh **flat-leaf parsley**, a generous handful, chopped

1 **egg white**

Zest of 1 lemon

½ cup grated **Parmigiano-Reggiano** or Pecorino Romano cheese, a couple of handfuls, plus some to pass at the table

1 pint **grape tomatoes**

1 12-ounce sack triple-washed **baby spinach**

¼ cup store-bought **pesto**

Bring a medium pot of water to a boil, salt it, and cook the pasta just shy of al dente—about 5 minutes. Drain and reserve.

While the pasta works, preheat a large soup pot with the oil over medium high heat. Add the sliced onion, red pepper flakes, garlic, salt, and pepper and cook, stirring frequently, for 4 to 5 minutes, until the onions are tender and golden. Add the chicken stock and bring it up to a boil, then turn down the heat to medium low and simmer while you make the chicken dumplings.

In a mixing bowl, combine the ground chicken, basil, parsley, egg white, grated onion, lemon zest, grated cheese, and a little salt and pepper. Mix well. Using a serving spoon, scoop out a walnut-size spoonful of the chicken mixture, then use a second serving spoon to push the chicken mixture off the first spoon into the simmering stock. Repeat this with the rest of the chicken mixture, working as quickly as you can to get all the balls into the stock. Shake the pan in order to settle the chicken dumplings into the stock. Cover and cook the dumplings for 5 minutes. Add the tomatoes, pasta, and spinach to the soup and cook for 2 minutes more. Ladle the soup into serving bowls and top each bowl with a dollop of the pesto and more grated cheese.

Chicken

If you're anything like me, chicken is a staple in your house. Why not take that same old chicken and jazz it up a bit? Get your little helpers cooking and clearing their plates with my top ten Kids' Picks. Or, you can go All-American or even transport yourself with some International flare.

KIDS' PICKS

Chicken with White and Wild Rice Soup
Honey Chicken Over Snow Pea Rice
BBQ Drumsticks and Mustardy Mustard Greens
Chicken Parm Pizza
Orange-Cashew Chicken with Broccoli
*Double-Dipped Buttermilk Chicken Fingers on Spinach Salad with
    Blue Cheese Dressing*
Honey Nut Chicken Sticks
Turkey or Chicken Croquettes with Spinach Mashers and Pan Gravy
*Chicken Cutlets on Buttermilk-Cheddar-Chorizo Biscuits with
    Tomato-Olive Salsa Mayo*
Grilled Chicken Parmigiana

ALL-AMERICAN

Balsamic Chicken with White Beans and Wilted Spinach
Cajun Jumble-laya Stoup
*Caesar Salad to Go: Shrimp or Chicken Lettuce Wraps with
    Creamy Caesar Dressing*
Chipotle Chicken Rolls with Avocado Dipping Sauce
Creamy Chicken and Asparagus on Toast
Pretzel-Crusted Chicken Breasts with a Cheddar-Mustard Sauce
Tex-Mex Mixed Crunchy Fry
Noodle-Free Chicken Soup
Spiced Grilled Chicken and Veggie Pockets
For Neil Diamond: Tangy Cherry Chicken

INTERNATIONAL

Chicken and Sweet Potato Curry-in-a-Hurry
Chicken Greek-a-Tikka Salad with Parsley-Feta Pesto
Mediterranean Chicken and Sausage Couscous Pot
Thai Chicken Pizza
Asian-Style Cashew Chicken
Teriyaki Chicken with Warm Ginger-Carrot Slaw
Ginger-Soy Chicken on Shredded Lettuce
Montalcino Chicken with Figs and Buttered Gnocchi with Nutmeg
White Burgundy Chicken Over Buttered Egg Noodles
*Spanish-Style Chicken with Mushroom-Chorizo Sauce
    and Butter-Herb Spani-Spuds*

Chicken with White and Wild Rice Soup

This one will get your kids up off the couch. They're going to love this take on classic chicken soup. Pack the leftovers in a Thermos for lunch the next day.   4 SERVINGS

---

1 5.5- to 7-ounce package **white and wild rice blend**, such as Near East brand, either chicken or herb flavor

2 tablespoons **extra-virgin olive oil** (EVOO)

1 large **yellow onion**, chopped

3 **garlic cloves**, chopped

2 medium **carrots**, peeled and thinly sliced

2 **celery ribs**, thinly sliced

1 **bay leaf**

1 tablespoon fresh **thyme** leaves, chopped

Salt and **freshly ground black pepper**

1 quart **chicken stock** or broth

2 pounds **chicken tenders**, cut into bite-size pieces

½ cup fresh **flat-leaf parsley** leaves (a few handfuls), chopped

¼ cup fresh **dill** (a generous handful), chopped

Juice of 1 lemon

Hot sauce, such as Tabasco

Cook the rice according to the package directions.

Preheat a large soup pot over medium-high heat with the EVOO. Add the onions, garlic, carrots, celery, bay leaf, and thyme, season with salt and pepper, and cook, stirring frequently, for 5 minutes. Add the chicken stock, bring up to a simmer, and cook for 5 minutes. Add the chicken and continue to cook for 10 minutes. Add the parsley, dill, the lemon juice, and hot sauce to taste. Remove the bay leaf.

Divide the cooked white and wild rice among 4 serving bowls; ladle the soup over the rice, making sure to distribute the chicken and veggies evenly among the bowls.

Honey Chicken Over Snow Pea Rice

Your little honey will love this chicken dish with the natural sweet kick.

4 SERVINGS

3 tablespoons **vegetable oil**

1 tablespoon **unsalted butter**

1½ cups **long-grain rice**

Salt and **freshly ground black pepper**

½ cup **dry white wine** (a couple of glugs)

4½ cups **chicken stock** or broth

Zest and juice of 1 lemon

2 large handfuls **snow peas**, thinly sliced across the width

2 pounds **chicken tenders**, cut into bite-size pieces

½ teaspoon **red pepper flakes**

1 large **onion**, sliced

3 large **garlic cloves**, chopped

3-inch piece of **fresh ginger**, peeled and grated

3 tablespoons **honey**

1 tablespoon **cornstarch**

5 **scallions**, thinly sliced

Heat a medium saucepan or pot over medium-high heat. Add 1 tablespoon of the vegetable oil and the butter to the pot. Once the butter melts, add the rice, season with salt and pepper, and lightly brown the rice for 3 to 5 minutes. Add the wine and allow it to evaporate entirely, 1 to 2 minutes. Add 3 cups of the chicken stock and the lemon zest to the rice. Bring the liquid to a boil. Cover and reduce the heat. Cook the rice for 18 to 20 minutes, or until tender. Once the rice only has about 3 more minutes of cook time, remove the lid and add the sliced snow peas. Don't stir the rice; just add the snow peas on top and put the lid on. The steam will lightly cook the snow peas. Once cooked, fluff the rice with a fork and stir in the snow peas. They should still have some crunch to them.

While the rice is cooking, preheat a large skillet over medium-high heat with the remaining 2 tablespoons of vegetable oil (twice around the pan). Add the chicken, season with salt and pepper, and brown for about 3 minutes. Add the red pepper flakes, onions, garlic, ginger, and honey. Stir frequently and continue to cook for 3 to 4 minutes, or until the onions are tender. Add the remaining 1½ cups of chicken stock to the pan and bring up to a simmer. Once at a simmer, combine the cornstarch with a splash of water, and mix to create a thin paste. Add the cornstarch mixture to the simmering chicken, mix thoroughly, and continue to cook for 2 minutes, or until the liquid is thickened. Add the sliced scallions and the lemon juice to the chicken and stir to combine.

Serve the honey chicken over the snow pea rice.

BBQ Drumsticks and Mustardy Mustard Greens

Toss that bottle of BBQ sauce that's been sitting in your fridge and surprise your kids with this homemade version. Nothin' like a good drumstick. 4 SERVINGS

12 **chicken drumsticks**

Salt and **freshly ground black pepper**

2 tablespoons **vegetable oil**, plus some for drizzling

1 large **sweet onion**, such as Vidalia, chopped

6 **garlic cloves**, chopped

3 tablespoons **chili powder**

1 teaspoon **ground cinnamon**

3 tablespoons **honey**

4 tablespoons **tomato paste**

¾ cup **yellow mustard**

¾ cup **cider vinegar**

3 tablespoons **Worcestershire sauce**

1¼ to 1½ cups **chicken stock** or broth

4 slices **bacon**, chopped

6 to 8 cups chopped **mustard greens** (2 bundles), trimmed and chopped

Preheat a broiler to high and situate the rack 6 to 8 inches from heat source.

Place the drumsticks on a slotted broiler pan and season them liberally with salt and pepper. Drizzle the drumsticks with a little vegetable oil and place under the broiler for 6 minutes. Flip the drumsticks and place them back under the broiler for another 6 minutes. While the drumsticks are broiling, start the BBQ sauce.

Heat a small saucepan with 1 tablespoon vegetable oil over high heat. Add half of the onion, 2 of the chopped garlic cloves, salt, pepper, the chili powder, and cinnamon. Cook for 1 minute, stirring frequently. Add the honey, tomato paste, ½ cup of the yellow mustard, ½ cup of the cider vinegar, the Worcestershire sauce, and ¾ cup of the chicken stock. Bring the sauce up to a simmer; turn down the heat to medium and cook for 5 to 8 minutes, or until thickened.

While the sauce is working, heat a large skillet over medium-high heat with 1 tablespoon of vegetable oil. Add the chopped bacon and cook until crisp, about 3 minutes. Remove the bacon to a plate lined with a paper towel to drain. Raise the heat to high and add the remaining half of the onion and 4 chopped garlic cloves. Cook them together, stirring frequently, for 1 to 2 minutes. Add the chopped mustard greens, tossing to coat. Add the remaining ¼ cup mustard and ¼ cup cider vinegar. Stir to distribute. Season the greens with salt and pepper, and stir until the mustard greens begin to wilt, a minute or two. Add the remaining ½ cup chicken stock, bring it up to a simmer, and then lower the heat to medium. Cook the greens for 8 to 10 minutes, until tender and spicy but no longer bitter. If all the stock cooks away before they are done, add a little more as you go.

To finish off the drumsticks, remove them from the broiler and pour the BBQ sauce over them. Using tongs, coat the drumsticks completely in the sauce. Place the coated drumsticks back under the broiler and broil for 2 to 3 minutes. Flip and broil for another 2 to 3 minutes. Using a paring knife, have a peek inside the drumsticks to ensure that they are cooked through before serving.

Transfer the "mustardy" mustard greens to a platter and garnish with the reserved crispy bacon. Serve alongside the BBQ drumsticks.

tidbit >> The BBQ drumsticks are a great ready-to-go snack that can be munched while on the move.

Chicken Parm Pizza

This is a real kid-pleaser. Whether you have kids of your own or not, cooking with a kid rocks! Kids are more honest, funny, and self-effacing than almost any of my grown friends, and kids today are really getting into good food. They love to cook and to watch food-related TV. If you don't have one of your own, borrow a kid tonight; enjoy a laugh and a tasty meal, together.   4 SERVINGS

Cornmeal or flour, to handle dough

1 **pizza dough**, store-bought or from your favorite pizzeria

2 tablespoons **EVOO** (extra-virgin olive oil), plus a drizzle

1 pound **ground chicken**

3 **garlic cloves**, chopped

1 small **onion**, chopped

Salt and **black pepper**

Handful of fresh **flat-leaf parsley** leaves, chopped

A couple pinches of **red pepper flakes**

A couple pinches of **dried oregano**

1 8-ounce can **tomato sauce**

1 cup grated **Parmigiano-Reggiano** cheese

1½ cups shredded **provolone cheese**

5 or 6 fresh **basil leaves**, shredded or torn

Preheat the oven to 425°F.

Coat your hands and the work surface with a little cornmeal or flour and, using your hand or a rolling pin, form a 14-inch round pizza. Place the pizza on a pizza baking tray and prick the dough with the tines of a fork in several places. Drizzle a little bit of EVOO over the dough and place it in the oven. Bake it for 10 minutes.

Meanwhile, heat a deep skillet over medium-high heat with the 2 tablespoons of EVOO, 2 times around the pan. Add the meat and brown it, breaking it up with a wooden spoon. To the browned meat, add the garlic and onions and season them with salt and pepper. Cook them together for 5 to 6 minutes, then add the parsley, red pepper flakes, oregano, and tomato sauce. Heat the sauce through.

Remove the pizza from the oven after 10 minutes and top it with the meat sauce, then scatter the cheeses over all. Return it to the oven and bake it until it's golden and bubbly, another 10 to 12 minutes. Top the pizza with shredded basil, cut, and serve.

Orange-Cashew Chicken with Broccoli

Maybe this will sound familiar to you: You go to a Chinese restaurant and order Cashew Chicken. When it comes, you can count the number of cashews you get on one hand. You eat your precious cashews sparingly so as to make them last to the end of your meal. How irritating is that? I say put as many fistfuls of cashews in this dish as you like when you make this orange-flavored version of an old favorite at home. Your friends will hug you for it!   8 SERVINGS

5 tablespoons **vegetable oil**

7 boneless, skinless **chicken breasts**, 6 ounces each, cut into large bite-size pieces

Salt and **black pepper**

1 large **onion**, thinly sliced

4 large **garlic cloves**, chopped

2 **red bell peppers**, seeded and sliced

1 16-ounce bag of **broccoli florets**

1 rounded teaspoon **red pepper flakes**

½ tablespoon **ground coriander**, ½ palmful

Zest and juice of 2 oranges

½ cup **tamari** (dark aged soy sauce)

3 tablespoons **honey**

3 cups **chicken stock**

1 tablespoon **cornstarch**

1, 2, or 3 cups—as many cups of **roasted, unsalted cashews** as you like

½ cup fresh **cilantro leaves**, 2 generous handfuls, chopped

Preheat a large, deep skillet over high heat with 3 tablespoons of the oil, 3 times around the pan. Season the chicken with some salt and pepper and brown the meat; brown it in 2 batches if necessary. Once the meat has browned, remove it to a plate and reserve. Return the skillet to the heat and add the remaining 2 tablespoons of oil, the onions, garlic, red bell peppers, broccoli, red pepper flakes, and coriander. Cook, stirring frequently, for 3 to 4 minutes, or until the veggies start to get tender. Add the orange zest and juice, tamari, and honey; stir, scraping up any brown bits on the bottom of the pan. Add the chicken stock and bring up to a simmer, then return the browned chicken to the pan and cook for another 5 minutes, or until the chicken is cooked through. Mix the cornstarch with a little splash of water in a small bowl and add to the pan to thicken up the sauce a bit. Add the cashews—AS MANY AS YOU WANT! Garnish with the chopped cilantro.

Double-Dipped Buttermilk Chicken Fingers on Spinach Salad with Blue Cheese Dressing

Double dipping may be a no-no at parties, but not in my kitchen! Adding an extra coating of flour and buttermilk makes for extra crispy and delicious chicken fingers that no kid can resist!   4 SERVINGS

Zest and juice of 2 lemons

A few dashes of **hot sauce**

1 cup **blue cheese crumbles**

½ cup **sour cream**

1 **celery rib**, finely chopped

Salt and **black pepper**

Vegetable oil, for frying

3 cups **all-purpose flour** (eyeball it—I scoop mine out with a coffee cup)

2 cups **buttermilk**

1 teaspoon **paprika**, ⅓ palmful

1½ to 2 pounds **chicken tenders**

1 pound triple-washed **spinach**, stemmed and chopped

½ small **red onion**, thinly sliced

10 **button mushrooms**, stemmed and thinly sliced

In a small mixing bowl, combine the lemon juice, hot sauce, crumbled blue cheese, sour cream, celery, salt, and pepper. Mix the dressing well and reserve.

Preheat 1½ inches of vegetable oil in a large deep skillet. While the oil is heating, set up a breading assembly line near the stove. Put the flour in a large, wide bowl; pour the buttermilk into a second large, wide bowl; then stir in the lemon zest and paprika. Season the chicken tenders with salt and pepper. Working in 2 or 3 batches, dust the chicken tenders in the flour, shake off the excess, then coat in the buttermilk. Transfer them back to the flour and coat them thoroughly, then back to the buttermilk, and then back into the flour for one last coating.

To test the oil temperature, add a 1-inch cube of bread to the hot oil. If it turns deep golden brown by a count of 40, the oil is ready. If the bread cube browns too quickly, turn down the heat and wait a few minutes for it to cool down. Carefully place the first batch of coated tenders in the hot oil. Fry the tenders in small batches for 6 to 7 minutes, turning when the first side has become golden brown. Once cooked, remove from the oil to a paper-towel-lined plate and immediately sprinkle them with a little salt. Repeat until all the tenders are fried.

After the last batch of tenders goes into the oil, combine the spinach, red onion, and sliced mushrooms in a large salad bowl. Pour half of the dressing over the salad and toss it to coat. Top the salad with the fried chicken tenders, whole or chopped, your choice, and serve the remaining dressing on the side for dipping.

Honey Nut Chicken Sticks

Serve with vegetable sticks.   4 SERVINGS

2 pounds **chicken tenders**

Salt and **freshly ground black pepper**

1 cup all-purpose **flour**

3 **eggs**

A splash of **milk**

2 cups **Honey Nut Corn Flakes**

1 cup **bread crumbs**

1 tablespoon **sweet paprika**

1 tablespoon **poultry seasoning**

2 tablespoons **grill seasoning**, such as McCormick's Montreal Steak Seasoning

¼ cup **vegetable oil**

Preheat the oven to 400°F.

Season the chicken tenders with salt and pepper. Place the flour in a large, shallow dish. Coat the chicken in the flour. Beat the eggs and milk in a shallow dish. Combine the cereal, bread crumbs, paprika, poultry seasoning, grill seasoning, and vegetable oil in a food processor. Transfer the breading to a shallow dish.

Place a nonstick baking sheet near the chicken breading station. In batches, dip the flour-coated chicken into the egg mixture and then in the breading and place on the nonstick cookie sheet. When all the tenders have been coated, bake them for 15 minutes, or until evenly browned and cooked through. Cool enough to handle and serve, or pack up for a picnic! This chicken may be served hot or cold.

Turkey or Chicken Croquettes with Spinach Mashers and Pan Gravy

Crispy on the outside and delicious on the inside—you can't go wrong with these tasty bites!   4 SERVINGS

3 large starchy **potatoes,** peeled and cubed

Coarse salt

1 package (about 1⅓ pounds) **ground turkey breast** or ground chicken

2 **celery ribs** and their greens, finely chopped

1 small **yellow onion**, finely chopped

2 teaspoons **poultry seasoning**

3 tablespoons chopped fresh **thyme** (from 5 to 6 sprigs)

3 tablespoons chopped fresh **flat-leaf parsley**

Coarse black pepper

1 **egg yolk**

2 cups **plain bread crumbs**

⅓ cup **vegetable oil**

4 tablespoons **unsalted butter**

2 tablespoons all-purpose **flour**

2½ cups **chicken stock** or broth

½ cup **cream** or half-and-half

1 pound triple-washed **baby spinach leaves**

Prepared whole-berry cranberry sauce, to pass at the table

Place the potatoes in a pot and cover with cold water. Put a lid on the pot and bring the water to a boil. Salt the water and cook the potatoes until tender, about 15 minutes.

While the potatoes cook, make the croquettes. Place the turkey or chicken in a bowl. Add the celery, onions, poultry seasoning, thyme, parsley, salt, pepper, and egg yolk. Combine and form 8 patties. Coat both sides of the patties in the bread crumbs. Heat the vegetable oil in a large nonstick skillet over medium to medium-high heat. Cook the patties for 5 minutes on each side. Remove the croquettes to a plate and cover loosely with foil to keep warm. Reduce the heat under the skillet. Add 2 table-spoons of the butter to the skillet and melt, then whisk in the flour. Cook the roux for a minute or two. Whisk in 2 cups of the chicken stock and bring to a bubble. Thicken for a minute or so and turn off the heat. Season the sauce with a little salt and pepper.

Drain the cooked potatoes and return to the hot pot. Add the remaining 2 tablespoons of butter, the remaining ½ cup of chicken stock, and the cream. Mash and season the potatoes with salt and pepper. Fold in the spinach leaves until they all wilt into the potatoes.

To serve, pile the spinach mashers on plates and top each portion with 2 croquettes and a spoonful of gravy. Pass the cranberry sauce at the table.

Chicken Cutlets on Buttermilk-Cheddar-Chorizo Biscuits with Tomato-Olive Slasa Mayo

This one is good for B, L, D: brunches, lunches, or dinners.   4 SERVINGS

1 8-ounce package **buttermilk biscuit mix,** such as Jiffy brand

½ cup shredded **extra-sharp Cheddar cheese**

¼ pound packaged (not fresh) Spanish **chorizo,** casing removed, finely chopped

2 **plum tomatoes,** seeded and chopped

3 tablespoons fresh **flat-leaf parsley** or cilantro leaves (a handful), finely chopped

¼ small **red onion,** finely chopped

10 large **green olives,** cracked away from the pits and coarsely chopped

Juice of 1 lime

1 to 2 dashes of **hot sauce,** such as Tabasco

½ cup **mayonnaise**

Salt and **freshly ground black pepper**

2 tablespoons **vegetable oil**

4 thin-cut **chicken cutlets,** 3 to 4 ounces each

½ tablespoon **ground coriander**

4 **romaine lettuce** leaves

Preheat the oven to 450°F.

Place the buttermilk biscuit mix in a bowl. Add the shredded Cheddar and the chorizo and mix with a fork to distribute. Add water according to the package directions. Once combined, dump the biscuit mix out on a lightly floured cutting board. Using your fingertips, press out the dough into a 1-inch-thick square. Divide the square with a knife into 4 squares. Arrange the jumbo-size biscuits on a foil-lined cookie sheet and bake for 12 to 15 minutes, or until the biscuits are cooked through and the bottoms are golden brown. Remove from the oven and let cool.

To make the tomato, olive, and salsa mayo, in a bowl, combine the tomatoes, parsley or cilantro, onions, olives, half of the lime juice, dash of hot sauce, and the mayonnaise. Season with salt and pepper and reserve.

Preheat a large skillet over medium-high heat with the vegetable oil. Season the chicken with salt, pepper, coriander, and the remaining half of the lime juice. Add the seasoned chicken to the skillet and cook on each side for 3 to 4 minutes, or until cooked through.

Split the Cheddar-chorizo biscuits in half. Slather the

recipe continued

tidbit >> Spanish-style chorizo is made with smoked pork and comes already cooked in the package. Mexican-style chorizo is made with fresh (uncooked) pork and must be thoroughly cooked.

tops and bottoms of the biscuits with the tomato, olive, and salsa mayo. Cut each cooked chicken cutlet in half; arrange the halved cutlets on the bottoms of the biscuits, garnish with a folded leaf of romaine lettuce, and finish with the biscuit top. Open wide!

Grilled Chicken Parmigiana

No bread crumbs and it's not fried. Eat two portions. Life is good.

4 SERVINGS

2 pounds thin **chicken breast** cutlets

Salt and **freshly ground black pepper**

Extra-virgin olive oil (EVOO), for drizzling, plus 5 tablespoons

3 to 4 **garlic cloves**, chopped

1 teaspoon **red pepper flakes**

1 small **yellow onion**, finely chopped

1 28-ounce can **fire-roasted diced tomatoes**, such as Muir Glen brand

20 **fresh basil** leaves (1 cup), shredded or torn

½ cup grated **Parmigiano-Reggiano**

½ pound **smoked mozzarella**, thinly sliced

6 cups **mixed greens**, any variety

2 tablespoons **red wine vinegar**

Heat an outdoor grill or indoor grill pan to high. Season the chicken with salt and pepper and drizzle with EVOO to keep it from sticking to the grill. Cook for 3 to 4 minutes on each side and transfer to a foil-covered platter to hold. If you are using a grill pan, cook the chicken in 2 batches if necessary. While the chicken cooks, make the sauce.

Place a medium pot on the stove over medium heat. Add 2 tablespoons of the EVOO (twice around the pan). Add the garlic, red pepper flakes, and onion. Cook for 10 minutes, stirring often. Add the tomatoes and heat through, 2 minutes. Wilt in the basil and season the sauce with salt and pepper.

Preheat the broiler to high.

Layer the chicken with the tomato sauce in a casserole dish. Top the casserole with Parmigiano and mozzarella. Brown the chicken parm casserole under the broiler for 3 minutes. Meanwhile, prepare the salad.

Place the greens in a salad bowl. Dress with the vinegar and the remaining 3 tablespoons of EVOO. Season with salt and pepper to taste.

Serve the chicken parm alongside a little salad.

Balsamic Chicken with White Beans and Wilted Spinach

Another easy chicken dinner: good for you, a good go-to, and good to go!   4 SERVINGS

2 tablespoons **balsamic vinegar**

4 tablespoons **EVOO** (extra-virgin olive oil)

1 tablespoon **grill seasoning** such as McCormick's Montreal Steak Seasoning, a palmful

4 boneless, skinless **chicken breast halves**

2 medium **onions**, thinly sliced

4 large **garlic cloves**, chopped

1 teaspoon **dried thyme**, ⅓ palmful

¼ teaspoon **red pepper flakes**

Salt and **black pepper**

1 **bay leaf**

¾ cup **white wine**

2 cups **chicken stock**

1 14-ounce can **cannellini beans**, drained

1 12-ounce sack **baby spinach** or ¾ pound from bulk bins, washed and patted dry

½ cup fresh **flat-leaf parsley**, a couple of generous handfuls, chopped

Juice of 1 lemon

In a shallow dish, combine the balsamic vinegar, about 2 tablespoons of the EVOO, and the grill seasoning. Coat the chicken breasts in the mixture and set aside to marinate while you start the white beans and wilted spinach.

Heat a large skillet over medium-high heat with the remaining 2 tablespoons of EVOO, twice around the pan. Add the onions, garlic, thyme, red pepper flakes, salt, pepper, and bay leaf. Cook, stirring frequently, until the onions are a little brown, 3 to 4 minutes. Add the white wine and chicken stock, bring up to a bubble, and cook for 5 minutes.

Heat another large skillet over medium-high heat. When it is hot, add the chicken breasts and cook for 5 to 6 minutes on each side. Remove the chicken to a plate, cover loosely with foil, and let rest a few minutes.

Add the cannellini beans to the skillet with the onions and stir to combine. Cook for about 2 minutes or until the beans are heated through. Turn off the heat and discard the bay leaf. Stir in the spinach, parsley, and lemon juice. Toss and stir until the spinach wilts.

To serve, place a portion of the white beans and wilted spinach on each serving plate. Thickly slice each chicken breast on an angle and arrange over the beans and spinach.

Cajun Jumble-laya Stoup

This jumble is a lot like jambalaya, so I call it a Jumble-laya. You can substitute turkey or tender cuts of pork and beef for the chicken. Or go all seafood by bumping up the amount of shrimp and adding crabmeat at the end to just heat it through.

Is okra not your thing? Substitute defrosted frozen French-cut green beans.   4 SERVINGS

2 tablespoons **vegetable oil**

1 pound **andouille sausage**, sliced on an angle into ½-inch-thick slices (found in packaged meats near kielbasa)

2 pounds **chicken tenders**, cut into bite-size pieces

Salt and **freshly ground black pepper**

1 medium **yellow onion**, sliced

3 large **garlic cloves**, chopped

3 **celery ribs**, chopped

1 **green bell pepper**, quartered, then sliced into thin strips

1 **red bell pepper**, quartered, then sliced into thin strips

4 sprigs **fresh thyme**

2 cups **chicken stock** or broth

1 cup **tomato sauce** or V-8 juice

¼ cup **hot sauce**, such as Frank's Red Hot

1 pound raw medium **shrimp**, peeled and deveined

8 ounces (½ bag) whole or chopped **frozen okra**, defrosted

A handful of fresh **flat-leaf parsley**, chopped

4 **scallions**, green and white parts, thinly sliced

tidbit >> Andouille sausage is a spicy, smoky sausage with a flavor that packs a punch. It is used in Cajun-style food and is a staple in gumbo and jambalaya.

Heat a large, deep skillet over high heat with the vegetable oil. Add the andouille sausage and brown for 2 to 3 minutes. Move the andouille sausage to one side of the pan and add the chicken tenders. Season the meat with salt and pepper. Continue to cook for another 3 minutes, until the chicken starts to brown. Stir to combine the chicken with the andouille sausage, then add the onion, garlic, celery, green and red bell peppers, and thyme sprigs. Cook, stirring frequently, for 5 minutes. Add the chicken stock, tomato sauce, and hot sauce and bring up to a boil. Add the shrimp and okra, cover the pot, and simmer for 5 minutes or until the shrimp are firm and pink. Uncover the stoup and stir. Turn the heat off, stir in the parsley and scallions, and serve.

Caesar Salad to Go: Shrimp or Chicken Lettuce Wraps with Creamy Caesar Dressing

This recipe requires no cooking and is served cold, so it makes a perfect low-carb on-the-go lunch. Pack the dressing with an ice pack to keep it chilled.   4 SERVINGS

2 **romaine lettuce** hearts

1 pound fully cooked jumbo **shrimp** (from the seafood counter)

1 **rotisserie chicken** (available in many markets)

4 heaping tablespoons **reduced-fat mayonnaise**

1 **garlic clove**, crushed

Zest and juice of 1 lemon

2 tablespoons **anchovy paste** (optional—but the salad tastes better with it in)

½ cup grated **Parmigiano-Reggiano** or Parmesan (a few handfuls)

2 teaspoons **Worcestershire sauce**

1 teaspoon **coarse black pepper**

3 tablespoons **extra-virgin olive oil** (EVOO)

Cut the bottoms off the romaine and cut the hearts in half lengthwise. Wash the lettuce and separate the leaves. Let it dry in the dish draining rack while you prepare the rest of the menu.

Remove the tails from the shrimp and place the shrimp in a bowl or, if this is a picnic meal, pack for travel.

To remove the chicken meat from the chicken, cut the chicken breasts off first. Cut the legs and thighs off using kitchen scissors. Slice the meat up on an angle. Arrange on a plate or in a plastic container.

Place the mayo, garlic, lemon zest and juice, anchovy paste, cheese, Worcestershire, and pepper in the blender and turn it on. Stream the EVOO into the dressing through the center of the lid. When the dressing is combined, use a rubber spatula to remove the thick dressing to a bowl or a plastic container.

Place the lettuce on a serving platter or pack in a large plastic bag or container to travel.

To assemble, spread some dressing onto a lettuce leaf. Fill the leaf with a large shrimp or sliced cold chicken, like a lettuce taco, and eat!

Chipotle Chicken Rolls with Avocado Dipping Sauce

The spicy chipotle and cooling avocado go together beautifully!

4 SERVINGS

CHIPOTLE CHICKEN ROLLS

1 package (1⅓ pounds) **ground chicken breast**

6 **scallions,** thinly sliced, then chopped

1½ cups grated **sharp Cheddar cheese**

1 **garlic clove,** finely chopped

1 **chipotle pepper in adobo sauce,** finely chopped, or 3 tablespoons of a chipotle-flavored salsa

Salt and **freshly ground black pepper**

6 sheets frozen **phyllo dough,** defrosted

4 tablespoons **unsalted butter,** melted

DIPPING SAUCE

1 ripe **Hass avocado**

Juice of 3 limes

A handful of fresh **cilantro** leaves (2 tablespoons)

1 teaspoon **coarse salt**

3 tablespoons **extra-virgin olive oil** (EVOO)

Bibb lettuce, to serve rolls on

Preheat the oven to 400°F.

In a bowl, combine the ground chicken, scallions, Cheddar cheese, garlic, and chipotles and season with salt and pepper. Transfer the mixture to a sealable plastic bag. To turn the sealable plastic bag into a homemade pastry bag, trim 1½ inches off one of the bottom corners of the plastic bag. Push the chicken mixture to the cut corner without pushing it through the hole. Reserve while you prepare the phyllo.

Arrange 1 sheet of phyllo dough with the long side closest to you on your kitchen counter, brush liberally from edge to edge with the melted butter, and season with salt and pepper. Place another sheet of phyllo on top, again brush liberally with butter, and season with salt and pepper. Repeat with the third sheet of phyllo.

Place the trimmed end of the pastry bag ½ inch in from the left side and ½ inch up from the bottom of the phyllo sheet. Squeeze half of the chicken mixture from the bag while moving along in a straight line from left to right. Roll the front edge of the phyllo sheet away from you, encasing the chicken mixture. Continue until you have completed a long roll. Tuck the ends in and then brush the entire outside of the phyllo log with more melted butter. Transfer the first log to a rimmed cookie sheet, putting the seam side down. Repeat this process to make the second log with the remaining half of the chicken mixture. Bake for 15 minutes, or until the logs feel firm to the touch.

While the phyllo-wrapped chicken is in the oven, cut the avocado in half lengthwise, cutting around the pit.

Separate the halves and scoop out the pit with a spoon, then use the spoon to scoop the avocado from its skin. Place the avocado in a food processor bowl and combine with the lime juice, cilantro, coarse salt, and about 3 tablespoons of water. Process until the avocado mixture is smooth, then stream the EVOO into the dressing. Taste and adjust the seasonings.

Once the chipotle chicken rolls are cooked, remove from the oven and let them cool just enough to handle. Cut each roll in half, then cut each half into 3 equal pieces. Serve 3 chicken rolls per person on a bed of Bibb lettuce with a small bowl or ramekin of the dipping sauce.

tidbit >> Chipotles in adobo sauce are sold in 7-ounce cans in the international foods aisle.

Creamy Chicken and Asparagus on Toast

All the food groups are covered in this quick and filling dish.

4 SERVINGS

4 tablespoons **extra-virgin olive oil** (EVOO)

1 large **yellow onion**, thinly sliced

1 tablespoon fresh **thyme** leaves, chopped (from 4 sprigs)

3 **garlic cloves**, chopped

Salt and **freshly ground black pepper**

6 tablespoons softened **unsalted butter**

4 6-ounce boneless, skinless **chicken breast halves**

1 **French baguette**

1 cup fresh **flat-leaf parsley** leaves, chopped

2 tablespoons all-purpose **flour**

½ cup **dry white wine**

1 cup **chicken stock** or broth

¼ cup **half-and-half** or cream

1 bunch of thin "pencil" **asparagus**, ends trimmed off, then cut into 1-inch lengths

1 cup grated **Gruyère cheese**

2 tablespoons **plain bread crumbs**

4 thin slices **Black Forest ham** or other good-quality ham, chopped

Preheat the oven to 400°F.

Preheat a large skillet over medium-high heat with 2 tablespoons of the EVOO (twice around the pan). Add the onions, thyme, and garlic, season with salt and pepper, and cook, stirring frequently, until nice and brown, about 5 to 8 minutes. Remove the onions from the pan, add the remaining 2 tablespoons of EVOO and 1 tablespoon of the butter, add the chicken, season with salt and pepper, and cook until lightly browned, about 3 to 4 minutes on each side.

While the chicken is cooking, split the French bread in half lengthwise, just shy of cutting it completely through. Dig out some of the insides of the bread and discard. Push the bread open and flatten out to keep it open. In a small bowl, combine the remaining 5 tablespoons of butter, a little salt and pepper, and 3 tablespoons of the parsley, and evenly spread the butter mixture on the inside of the bread. Cut the buttered loaf into 4 portions, arrange on a cookie sheet, and transfer to the oven and bake until golden brown, about 5 minutes. Remove the toasted bread from the oven, set aside on the cookie sheet, and switch the broiler on.

Add the browned onions back to the skillet with the chicken, dust with the flour, and continue to cook for 1 minute. Whisk in the white wine, stock, and half-and-half and bring up to a simmer. Add the asparagus and continue to cook for 2 to 3 minutes, or until the asparagus are tender and the sauce is thick. In a small bowl, combine the grated Gruyère with the bread crumbs; toss to coat the cheese evenly with the bread crumbs. Stir the remaining chopped parsley and the chopped ham into the chicken and sauce. Divide the creamy chicken into 4 portions in the pan, then transfer each portion to top the toasted bread. Sprinkle a little of the cheese on top of the chicken, then transfer the cookie sheet to the broiler to melt and brown the cheese.

Pretzel-Crusted Chicken Breasts with a Cheddar-Mustard Sauce

Yup, this was a really good idea. Serve with oil-and-vinegar dressed slaw salad. 4 SERVINGS

4 medium (quart-size) **plastic food storage bags**

4 6- to 8-ounce boneless, skinless **chicken breast halves**

1 5-ounce bag of **salted pretzels**, any shape

1 tablespoon fresh **thyme** leaves, chopped

Freshly ground black pepper

2 **eggs**

Vegetable oil, for frying

2 tablespoons **unsalted butter**

2 tablespoons all-purpose **flour**

2 cups **milk**

2 cups grated **extra-sharp Cheddar cheese**

2 heaping tablespoons **spicy brown mustard**, such as Gulden's

Coarse salt

¼ cup fresh **flat-leaf parsley** leaves (a generous handful), chopped

¼ small **yellow onion**, finely chopped

1 large **sour dill pickle**, finely chopped

1 **lemon**, cut into wedges

Sprinkle a little water into the food storage baggies. Place 1 chicken breast in each bag and seal it up, pushing out excess air. Use a mallet or the bottom of a heavy pot or pan and pound each breast until flat, just shy of busting out of the bag. Repeat with the other 3 chicken breasts.

Place the pretzels in a food processor or blender and grind until fine. Transfer the ground pretzels to a shallow dish and add the thyme and some pepper. Crack and beat 2 eggs in a second shallow dish with a splash of water. Working with 1 pounded chicken breast at a time, coat the breast in the ground pretzels, then in the eggs, then in the pretzels again. Preheat a large skillet with ¼ inch of vegetable oil; add the pretzel-coated chicken breasts to the hot oil. Cook in a single layer, in 2 batches if necessary, about 3 or 4 minutes on each side, until the cutlets' juices run clear and the breading is evenly browned.

While the chicken is frying, in a medium sauce pot over medium heat, melt the butter and add the flour to it. Cook for 1 minute, then whisk in the milk. When the milk comes to a bubble, stir in the cheese and mustard with a wooden spoon. Season with a little salt and pepper and remove the cheese sauce from the heat.

Transfer the fried pretzel-crusted chicken breasts to serving plates, drizzle with the cheddar-mustard sauce, and then sprinkle with a little parsley, finely chopped onions, and finely chopped pickles. Serve immediately, with lemon wedges alongside.

Tex-Mex Mixed Crunchy Fry

I double coat the chicken and veggies in this mixed fry, making good use of the thick and tangy buttermilk. The results are a super-crunchy and satisfying crust that's full of flavor.   4 SERVINGS

Vegetable oil, for frying

3 cups all-purpose **flour**

1 tablespoon **ground cumin,** a palmful

1 tablespoon **chili powder,** a palmful

2 cups **buttermilk**

2 **limes**, zested, then cut into wedges

2 pounds **chicken tenders**

Salt and **black pepper**

A very generous handful of fresh **cilantro** or flat-leaf parsley leaves, chopped

1 large **red onion**, cut into ¼-inch-thick slices, rings separated

1 large **red bell pepper**, seeded and cut into ¼-inch-thick rings

Ranch salad dressing, for dipping

Preheat the oven to 250°F.

Preheat 1½ inches of vegetable oil in a high-sided, large skillet over medium to medium-high heat. To test the oil, submerge a wooden spoon handle in the oil and see if bubbles rise out and away from it—that says you're good to go.

While the oil is heating, set up a breading station right near the stove. Combine the flour, cumin, and chili powder in a large, wide bowl. In a second large, wide bowl, mix the buttermilk and lime zest. Season the chicken tenders with a little salt and pepper and toss them with all of the chopped cilantro or parsley.

Working in small batches, run the chicken tenders through the flour, shake off the excess, and then coat them in the buttermilk. Transfer them back to the flour and coat them thoroughly, then back into the buttermilk. Dip them back into the flour for a third and final coating. Carefully place the first batch of coated tenders in the hot oil. Fry the tenders for 6 to 7 minutes, turning when the first side is golden brown. Remove them from the oil to a paper-towel-lined plate and immediately sprinkle them with a little salt. Repeat with the remaining chicken pieces. Transfer them to a cookie sheet and keep them warm in the oven while you fry the veggies.

Sprinkle the red onion rings and red bell pepper rings with a little bit of water, and toss them around a bit; the water will help the first coating of flour stick to the veggies. Repeat the same flour-buttermilk, flour-buttermilk-flour process with the veggie rings. Cook the veggies for

recipe continued

4 to 5 minutes then drain on paper towels. As you are frying and draining the veggie rings, transfer the fried items to a second cookie sheet and keep them warm in the oven while you continue to fry.

Serve the chicken, onions, and peppers with the lime wedges and ranch salad dressing.

Noodle-Free Chicken Soup

This is a great late-night snack or easy lunch. It's my version of stracciatelle or "rag" soup. Basically, it's an Italian egg-drop soup. It's best to eat this really fresh and hot, so if you're cooking for one or two, just cut the recipe in half.   4 SERVINGS

2 quarts chicken **stock** or broth

8 **eggs**

½ teaspoon **grated nutmeg**

1 teaspoon **freshly ground black pepper**

¼ cup grated **Parmigiano-Reggiano**, plus some to pass at table

3 tablespoons finely chopped fresh **flat-leaf parsley**

Bring the stock to a boil in a medium soup pot, then reduce heat to medium to have a good strong simmer going on. Beat the eggs with the nutmeg, pepper, and cheese. Add the eggs to the soup pot and stir them in with a whisk, swirling in a figure-eight pattern, making the eggs into rags in the soup. Ladle into shallow bowls and garnish with generous sprinkles of parsley and more cheese.

tidbit >> Buy stock or broth in asceptic boxes rather than cans. They might cost a little more, but the stocks especially have great slow-cooked flavor that really makes fast-cooked food taste rich. Plus, whatever you don't use can go directly into the refrigerator, without having to transfer it from a can. If I know I am not going to use my remaining stock within the next few days, I will transfer it to a resealable plastic bag and freeze it flat.

Spiced Grilled Chicken and Veggie Pockets

Here's my All-American spin on Middle Eastern shwarma.

4 SERVINGS

1 cup **plain yogurt**

½ teaspoon **ground cinnamon**

1 tablespoon **ground cumin**

1 tablespoon **ground coriander**

½ teaspoon **red pepper flakes**

Juice of 1 **lemon**

¼ cup fresh **cilantro** leaves (a handful), finely chopped

2 pounds **chicken tenders**

½ **English** or **seedless cucumber**, finely chopped

3 **plum tomatoes**, finely chopped

½ cup crumbled **feta cheese**

10 **kalamata olives**, pitted and coarsely chopped

4 **scallions**, thinly sliced

1 **red** or **yellow bell pepper**, cored, seeded, and finely chopped

2 cups shredded **carrots** (available in pouches in the produce department)

½ cup fresh **flat-leaf parsley** leaves (a couple of generous handfuls), chopped

2 tablespoons fresh **dill**, chopped

2 cups shredded **red leaf lettuce**

1 heaping tablespoon **Dijon mustard**

2 tablespoons **red wine vinegar**

¼ cup **extra-virgin olive oil (EVOO)**

4 **pita pockets**

Salt and **freshly ground black pepper**

Preheat a grill pan or outdoor grill to high.

In a shallow bowl, combine the yogurt, cinnamon, cumin, coriander, red pepper flakes, lemon juice, and cilantro. Add the chicken tenders and coat evenly. Marinate for 10 minutes. Shake off any excess marinade, then grill the chicken for about 4 to 5 minutes on each side, until charred at the edges and firm and cooked through.

While the chicken is working, in a large bowl combine the cucumbers, tomatoes, feta cheese, olives, scallions, bell peppers, carrots, parsley, dill, and shredded red leaf lettuce.

For the dressing, in a small bowl, combine the mustard and red wine vinegar. In a slow, steady stream, whisk in the EVOO.

When you remove the chicken from the grill, place the pitas on the grill to blister and warm through. Chop the grilled chicken into bite-size pieces and add to the veggies along with the dressing; season with salt and pepper, and toss to coat thoroughly. Cut the pitas in half; fill the pockets with the chicken and veggies.

For Neil Diamond: Tangy Cherry Chicken

You got the way to move me, Baby! Serve with a green salad and boiled baby potatoes.   4 SERVINGS

3 tablespoons **extra-virgin olive oil** (EVOO)

4 6-ounce boneless, skinless **chicken breast halves**

1 tablespoon fresh **thyme** leaves, chopped (from 4 sprigs)

Salt and **freshly ground black pepper**

1 small **red onion**, finely chopped

2 **celery ribs**, finely chopped

¼ teaspoon **red pepper flakes**

¼ teaspoon **freshly grated** or **ground nutmeg**

½ cup **dry white wine**

1 cup **chicken stock** or broth

½ cup **dried cherries**

3 tablespoons cold **unsalted butter**

Preheat a large nonstick skillet over medium-high heat with 2 tablespoons of the EVOO (twice around the pan). Season the chicken liberally with half of the thyme and salt and pepper and add to the hot skillet. Cook the chicken for 5 to 6 minutes on each side until cooked through. Remove the chicken from the pan and cover with foil to keep warm.

Return the skillet to the burner over medium-high heat, add the remaining 1 tablespoon of EVOO, and add the onions, celery, red pepper flakes, nutmeg, salt, and pepper. Cook for 3 to 4 minutes, or until the celery and onions are tender. Add the white wine and cook until the pan is almost dry, 1 minute. Add the chicken stock, dried cherries, and remaining thyme and continue to cook for about 4 to 5 minutes, or until there is only about ¼ cup of liquid left in the pan. Turn the heat off under the pan. Add the butter and whisk until it has completely melted.

Serve the chicken breasts whole or sliced with cherry sauce poured over them.

Chicken and Sweet Potato Curry-in-a-Hurry

This was the first dish with an actual garnish sent to outer space. Yep, that's right . . . they were eating this recipe on a NASA Space Shuttle.

4 SERVINGS

1 cup **white rice**

2 tablespoons **vegetable oil**

1 medium-size **sweet potato**, peeled, cut in half lengthwise, then thinly sliced into half moons

Salt and **freshly ground black pepper**

1 rounded tablespoon **mild curry paste** or 2 tablespoons curry powder

2 pounds **chicken tenders**, cut into bite-size chunks

1 large **yellow onion**, thinly sliced

1 **red bell pepper**, cored, seeded, and thinly sliced

1 tablespoon all-purpose **flour**

2½ cups **chicken stock** or broth

½ cup **heavy cream** or half-and-half

¼ cup prepared **mango chutney** (a couple of heaping tablespoons)

1 10-ounce box **frozen peas**

¼ cup fresh **cilantro** leaves chopped

Heat 2 cups of water to a boil in a pot, then add the rice, stir, and return to a simmer. Reduce the heat to medium-low and cook for 18 minutes, or until tender.

Preheat a large, deep skillet over medium-high heat with the vegetable oil. Add the sweet potatoes to the skillet, season with salt, pepper, and curry paste or powder, and cook, stirring frequently, for 3 to 4 minutes, or until lightly browned. Scoot the potatoes over to one side of the pan and add the chunks of chicken, season with salt and pepper, and cook, browning slightly, for 3 minutes. Add the onions and bell peppers and toss to combine. Add the flour and continue to cook for 1 minute. Add the chicken stock, cream, and mango chutney, bring to a simmer, and cook for 10 minutes, or until the chicken and potatoes are cooked through and the sauce has thickened.

Add the peas and cilantro and simmer for 1 minute to heat the peas through. Serve over the rice.

Chicken Greek-a-Tikka Salad with Parsley-Feta Pesto

Greek pesto adds Mediterranean flare to this tikka-tasty salad!

4 SERVINGS

1 cup **plain yogurt**

1 teaspoon **ground coriander**

1 teaspoon **ground cumin**

1 teaspoon **dried oregano**

1 tablespoon **grill seasoning**, such as McCormick's Montreal Steak Seasoning

2 to 2½ pounds **white-meat chicken**, cut into bite-size cubes

1 **romaine lettuce** heart, chopped or torn

2 vine-ripe **tomatoes**, chopped

½ **English (seedless) cucumber** (the one wrapped in plastic), chopped

½ **red onion**, chopped

3 **celery ribs**, chopped

½ cup pitted **kalamata olives**

6 **pepperoncini** hot peppers, chopped

Juice of 1 lemon

Extra-virgin olive oil (EVOO), for drizzling

Salt and **freshly ground black pepper**

PARSLEY-FETA PESTO

1 cup fresh **flat-leaf parsley**

½ cup **crumbled feta**

1 **garlic clove**

1 teaspoon **coarse black pepper**

3 tablespoons **chopped walnuts**

¼ cup EVOO

Preheat a grill pan to high heat.

In a bowl, combine the yogurt, coriander, cumin, oregano, and the grill seasoning. Coat the chicken in the mixture, then thread the meat onto metal skewers. Brush the grill pan with oil and grill the meat for 5 to 6 minutes on each side.

Combine the chopped veggies, olives, and hot peppers on a large platter or in a serving bowl. Dress the salad very lightly in lemon juice, EVOO, and salt and pepper.

Place all ingredients for the pesto in the food processor except the EVOO. Turn the processor on and stream in the EVOO until all is incorporated.

Place the grilled meat on the salad and top liberally with the pesto, streaming it back and forth over the salad and the meat.

Mediterranean Chicken and Sausage Couscous Pot

If you've met your pork quota for the day, try a flavored chicken or turkey sausage instead of the Italian sausage. Or, if you are suffering from chicken overload, then omit the chicken and the Italian sausage and go for a good-quality seafood sausage. Bump up the total amount of sausage, figuring about 3 seafood sausages per person.   4 SERVINGS

2 tablespoons **extra-virgin olive oil** (EVOO)

4 **hot Italian sausage links**

4 6-ounce **boneless, skinless chicken breasts**, cut into ½-inch-thick slices

Salt and **freshly ground black pepper**

2 teaspoons **poultry seasoning** (⅔ palmful)

1 medium **yellow onion**, thinly sliced

4 **garlic cloves**, finely chopped

2 **celery ribs**, chopped

1 small **red bell pepper**, cored, seeded, diced

1 10-ounce box **frozen French-cut green beans**, defrosted

1 cup **chicken stock** or broth

½ cup pitted **kalamata olives**

1 tablespoon **capers**, drained

2 **oranges**, zest reserved, peel and pith removed, cut into disks

⅓ cup **plain couscous**

2 handfuls fresh **flat-leaf parsley** leaves, coarsely chopped

Heat a large soup pot with the EVOO over medium-high heat. Add the sausage and brown all over for about 5 minutes. Move the sausage to one side of the pot and then add the sliced chicken. Season liberally with salt and pepper and add the poultry seasoning. Brown the chicken for about 3 minutes, then turn to brown the opposite side. Add the onion, garlic, celery, and bell pepper. Cook for 2 minutes, stirring frequently. Add the defrosted green beans and the chicken stock. Bring the liquid up to a simmer, then add the olives, capers, orange slices, and orange zest, and stir to distribute. Stir in the couscous and cover the pot with a tight-fitting lid. Turn the stove off and let the pot sit covered for 5 minutes. Remove the lid and add the parsley while fluffing the dish with a serving fork. Serve immediately, making sure everyone gets a sausage link.

tidbit >> Stocks especially add long-cooked flavor to any quick-cooking dish!

Thai Chicken Pizza

Do you have trouble making up your mind? How does this sound: grilled meat, salad, take-out Thai food, and pizza, all in one meal? There are no special ingredients required and you can have this pizza on the table in less time than it would take the delivery man to get to your door.   2 TO 4 SERVINGS

---

1 **pizza dough**

½ cup **duck sauce** or plum sauce

½ teaspoon **red pepper flakes**

1 10-ounce sack (2 cups) shredded **provolone** or Monterey Jack cheese

½ **red bell pepper**, cored, seeded, and thinly sliced

1 tablespoon **vegetable oil**

2 tablespoons **tamari** (dark aged soy sauce)

1 rounded tablespoon smooth **peanut butter**

2 teaspoons **hot sauce**

2 teaspoons **grill seasoning**, such as McCormick's Montreal Steak Seasoning

4 **chicken breast cutlets**, ½ pound total

2 tablespoons **honey**

2 tablespoons **cider vinegar** or any white vinegar on hand

¼ seedless **cucumber**, peeled and cut into matchsticks

4 **scallions**, white and green parts, chopped

1 cup **bean sprouts**, a couple of handfuls

A palmful of fresh **cilantro leaves**, chopped

¼ cup **chopped roasted peanuts**

Preheat the oven to 425°F. Form the pizza crust on a pizza pan or cookie sheet. Top it with duck or plum sauce, spreading it around like you would pizza sauce. Sprinkle the pizza with some red pepper flakes, then top it with the cheese and bell peppers. Bake until golden and bubbly, 15 to 17 minutes.

In a small bowl, combine the vegetable oil, tamari, and peanut butter with the hot sauce and grill seasoning. Use the microwave to loosen up the peanut butter if it is too cold to blend into sauce; 10 seconds ought to do it. Coat the chicken evenly with the mixture and let it stand for 10 minutes. Preheat a grill pan or nonstick skillet over medium-high heat. Cook the chicken cutlets for 2 to 3 minutes on each side, or until firm. Slice the chicken into very thin strips.

While the chicken cooks, mix the honey and vinegar in a medium bowl. Add the cucumber and turn to coat in the dressing.

When the pizza comes out of the oven, top it with the chicken, scallions, sprouts, and cilantro. Drain the cucumbers and scatter them over the pizza. Garnish the pizza with peanuts, cut it into 8 wedges, and serve.

Asian-Style Cashew Chicken

Your family and friends will love this super simple stir-fry.   4 SERVINGS

3 tablespoons **vegetable oil**

1 tablespoon **unsalted butter**

1 large **onion**, ¼ finely chopped, ¾ thinly sliced

1½ cups **brown rice**

3 cups **chicken stock** or broth

1 teaspoon **red pepper flakes**

1½ pounds **chicken tenders**; boneless, skinless chicken breasts; or boneless, skinless thighs, cut into 2-inch pieces

2 tablespoons **grill seasoning**, such as McCormick's Montreal Steak Seasoning

4 **garlic cloves**, chopped

1 **red bell pepper**, cored, seeded, and thinly sliced

1 cup **pea pods**, chopped

2 cups **bean sprouts**

4 **scallions**, sliced on the diagonal in 2-inch lengths

⅓ cup **tamari** (dark aged soy sauce, found on the international aisle)

½ cup **duck sauce** (found on the international aisle)

2 to 3 tablespoons chopped fresh **cilantro** or flat-leaf parsley, your preference

1 cup **raw cashews**

In a medium pot over medium heat, combine 1 tablespoon of the vegetable oil (once around the pan) and the butter. When the butter melts into the oil, add the chopped onions and cook for 2 minutes, then add the rice and cook for 3 minutes more. Add the stock and cover the pot. Raise the heat to bring the stock to a rapid boil. Once the stock boils, reduce the heat to low and cook, stirring occasionally, until the rice is tender, about another 30 minutes.

While the rice cooks, make the chicken. Heat a large skillet over high heat. Add the remaining 2 tablespoons of vegetable oil, the red pepper flakes, and then the chicken. Season the chicken with the grill seasoning. Lightly brown the chicken on both sides, then move off to one side of the pan. Add the remaining onions, the garlic, bell peppers, pea pods, bean sprouts, and scallions. Cook for 2 to 3 minutes, then mix the vegetables and meat together and add the tamari and duck sauce. Toss to coat. Turn off the heat and add the chopped cilantro or parsley and the nuts.

Top the rice with the cashew chicken and serve.

Teriyaki Chicken with Warm Ginger-Carrot Slaw

This dinner is full of antioxidants, low in fat, high in fiber, and huge on flavor. Can you get anything better for you than that? Plus, you won't find this one on any take-out menu.   4 SERVINGS

1½ pounds **chicken breast cutlets**

⅓ cup **teriyaki sauce**

4 tablespoons **vegetable oil**

1 rounded tablespoon **grill seasoning**, such as McCormick's Montreal Steak Seasoning

1 small **Savoy cabbage**, about 1½ pounds

1 bunch **scallions**, trimmed

1 cup **snow peas**, a couple of handfuls

¼ cup **honey**

3 tablespoons **cider vinegar**

3 tablespoons **pickled ginger**, drained and thinly sliced (found on the Asian foods aisle)

2 cups shredded or julienned **carrots**

Salt and **black pepper**

In a large plastic food storage bag, combine the chicken cutlets with the teriyaki sauce, 2 tablespoons of the oil, and the grill seasoning. Close the bag and press to coat the chicken evenly. Let the chicken stand for 15 minutes.

Preheat an outdoor grill or indoor grill pan or skillet to medium high.

Cut the cabbage into quarters and cut away the core. Shred the cabbage with a knife and set it aside. Cut the scallions into 3-inch lengths, then pile them lengthwise and julienne them into thin strips. Pull the threads from the ends of the snow peas and julienne them into thin strips, lengthwise, like the scallions.

Drizzle the honey into a small bowl. Add the vinegar and combine with a fork. Pat the chicken cutlets dry and place them on the grill or grill pan (or into a hot skillet) and cook for 3 minutes on each side.

Heat a nonstick skillet over high heat. Add the remaining 2 tablespoons of oil, twice around the pan. Add the pickled ginger and the carrots and stir-fry for 2 minutes. Add the cabbage and stir-fry for 2 minutes more. Fluff and toss the veggies with tongs so they stay dry and crisp while cooking. Add the scallions and snow peas and stir-fry for another minute. Add the honey and vinegar combination, pouring it all around the pan in a slow stream. Cook the liquids down for 30 seconds, then turn off the heat. Continue to toss the slaw and season it up with salt and pepper to taste.

Thinly slice the chicken on the diagonal. Mound up

one fourth of the slaw on each plate and place the sliced chicken alongside, edging its way up the slaw salad. Serve immediately.

Ginger-Soy Chicken on Shredded Lettuce

Here's a low-carb-lover's delight! Have two servings—it's good for you!
4 SERVINGS

3 tablespoons **vegetable oil**

1¼ pounds **chicken breast cutlets**, cut into thin strips

Salt and **coarse black pepper**

2-inch piece of **fresh ginger**, peeled and minced

4 large **garlic cloves**, chopped

½ teaspoon **red pepper flakes**

6 **scallions**, cut into 2-inch lengths, then cut lengthwise into thin matchsticks

¼ cup **tamari** (dark aged soy sauce, found on the international aisle)

3 tablespoons **honey**

1 head of **iceberg lettuce**, core removed, shredded

Heat a large nonstick skillet over high heat. Add the vegetable oil. It should smoke up a bit. Add the chicken and season with a little salt and lots of black pepper. Stir-fry for a minute to sear the meat at the edges, then add the ginger, garlic, and red pepper flakes and cook for 2 minutes more. Add the scallions and stir fry for another minute, then add the tamari and honey to form a sauce and glaze the chicken. Remove the pan from the heat. Cover a platter with shredded lettuce, top with the chicken, and serve.

Montalcino Chicken with Figs and Buttered Gnocchi with Nutmeg

Montalcino, Italy, is the city I married in. I will make this dish for John every September 24, for our wedding anniversary. The way to anyone's heart, forever and ever, is through his or her stomach! This is not your average chicken dinner.   4 SERVINGS

¼ cup **EVOO** (extra-virgin olive oil)

⅓ pound thick-cut (¼-inch thick) **pancetta**, cut into sticks

2 pounds **boneless, skinless chicken, breasts and thighs**, cut into large chunks

Salt and **black pepper**

All-purpose **flour**, for dredging

1 large **onion**, thinly sliced

4 garlic **cloves**, crushed

14 to 16 **dried black mission figs**, quartered

⅓ bottle **Rosso di Montalcino wine**

1 cup **chicken stock**, plus up to ½ cup more if needed

¼ cup fresh **flat-leaf parsley**, a generous handful, chopped

Zest of 1 lemon

1 tablespoon chopped fresh **thyme**, 4 sprigs

1 12- to 16-ounce package fresh or frozen **gnocchi**

3 tablespoons **butter**

¼ teaspoon freshly **grated nutmeg**

3 tablespoons chopped or snipped **chives**, 10 blades

Place a pot of water on the stove to boil for the gnocchi.

Heat a deep skillet over medium-high heat. Add the EVOO and the pancetta. Brown the pancetta, 3 to 4 minutes, then remove it with a slotted spoon and reserve.

While the pancetta browns, season the chicken chunks with salt and pepper and dredge them in a little flour. After removing the pancetta from the pan, add the chicken. Brown the pieces for a few minutes on each side over high heat, then scoot the meat to the edges of the pan and add the onions, garlic, and figs. Sauté 5 minutes, combine the chicken with the onions and figs, then add the wine and cook it down for 5 minutes or so until only about ⅓ cup of liquid remains. Add 1 cup of the chicken stock, the parsley, lemon zest, and thyme to the chicken and stir to combine. Reduce the heat to a simmer and cook for another 10 minutes, while you make the gnocchi.

Add salt and gnocchi to the boiling water and cook them according to package directions, 4 minutes for fresh gnocchi, 6 minutes for frozen. Drain. Heat a medium nonstick skillet over medium-low heat. Melt the butter and brown it. Add the drained gnocchi to the browned butter. Raise the heat to medium high and lightly brown the gnocchi. Season the gnocchi with salt, pepper, and nutmeg, turn to coat, and add the chives, toss, and remove from the heat.

Adjust the seasonings on the chicken with figs. If you would like a little more sauce, add another half cup of stock to the pan. Serve the chicken and figs in shallow dishes, the gnocchi piled in the center of the bowl on top of the chicken. Garnish it with the crisp pancetta sticks.

tidbit >> Look for plump, tender dried figs in the bulk section of the market or buy the figs in packages. Check for tough stem tops and trim them off if necessary.

This dish uses Rosso di Montalcino wine (an affordable, younger version of Brunello—I call it "Baby Brunello") but you can substitute any dry red wine you like from your on-hand supply.

White Burgundy Chicken Over Buttered Egg Noodles

The key to achieving great flavor in this style of French country cooking is getting the ingredients nice and brown and caramelized. The full flavor is worth every minute of cooking.   6 SERVINGS

Salt

1½ pounds **wide egg noodles**

6 tablespoons (¾ stick) **butter**

½ cup fresh **flat-leaf parsley** leaves, 2 generous handfuls, coarsely chopped

Black pepper

4 tablespoons **EVOO** (extra-virgin olive oil), plus a little more as necessary

6 boneless, skinless **chicken breasts**, 6 ounces each, cut into bite-size pieces

2 cups **white burgundy wine**

1 16-ounce bag **frozen pearl onions**, defrosted and patted dry on kitchen towels

4 **garlic cloves**, smashed

½ pound **baby carrots**

5 **celery ribs**

6 **fresh thyme** sprigs

2 **bay leaves**, fresh or dried

3 tablespoons all-purpose **flour**

3 cups **chicken stock**

1 10-ounce box **frozen peas**, defrosted

Fill a large covered pot with water and bring to a boil over high heat. Once it's at a boil, add some salt and the egg noodles and cook them according to the package directions. Drain the noodles really well, then transfer them to a large bowl. Add 3 tablespoons of the butter, the parsley, and a little salt and pepper. Keep warm.

While the water is coming up to a boil, preheat a large nonstick skillet with 2 tablespoons of the EVOO, 2 times around the pan, over medium-high to high heat. Preheat a second pan, a large Dutch oven or heavy-bottomed soup pot, over medium heat. Season the chicken liberally with salt and pepper, add half of the chicken to the skillet, and brown it for about 2 minutes on each side. Remove the browned chicken to a plate and return the skillet to the heat. Add a little more oil and the remaining chicken, and brown it on both sides. Combine all the browned meat and deglaze the pan with 1 cup of the wine, using a wooden spoon to scrape up all the brown bits. Remove from the heat.

While the first batch of chicken is cooking, add the remaining 2 tablespoons of EVOO and 3 tablespoons of butter to the Dutch oven or soup pot. Once the butter starts to bubble, add the pearl onions and garlic cloves and brown them for 4 to 5 minutes, until they are nice and brown all over. Cut the baby carrots in half lengthwise and cut the celery into 1½- to 2-inch pieces, about the same length as the carrots. Strip the leaves off the thyme sprigs and chop, then add the baby carrots, celery, thyme, and bay leaves to the pearl onions and season them with salt and pepper. Cook the vegetables, stirring them frequently, for 2 minutes more. Sprinkle them with the flour and cook them for 1 minute, then add the remaining cup of wine and the liquid from the chicken skillet. Add the chicken stock and bring everything up to a bubble, then add the reserved chicken and simmer everything together for 10 minutes. Add the peas and cook them until they're heated through, about 1 minute. Discard the bay leaves.

Serve over the buttered egg noodles.

Spanish-Style Chicken with Mushroom-Chorizo Sauce and Butter-Herb Spani-Spuds

This is a real-deal, square meal (that is, one you might find in a restaurant on a square in Barcelona!).   4 SERVINGS

---

2 pounds **boiling potatoes**

3 tablespoons chopped or snipped **chives**, about 10

2 tablespoons cold **butter**, cut into pieces

½ cup fresh **flat-leaf parsley**, a couple of handfuls, chopped

Salt and **black pepper**

A few shakes of **hot sauce**, such as Tabasco

¼ cup **EVOO** (extra-virgin olive oil)

4 boneless, skinless **chicken breast halves**

1 teaspoon **dried thyme**

2 teaspoons **paprika**

½ pound **chorizo** sausage, cut into quarters lengthwise, then finely chopped

½ pound **button mushrooms**, stemmed and thinly sliced

2 **portobello mushroom caps**, thinly sliced

½ pound **shiitake, oyster, or cremini mushrooms**, or whichever funky mushrooms your store carries, stemmed and thinly sliced

1 medium yellow **onion**, chopped

4 large **garlic cloves**, chopped

½ cup **dry sherry**

1 cup **chicken stock**

Put the potatoes in a sauce pot, cover them with water, and place the pot over high heat to bring them to a boil. Cook them for about 12 minutes, or until they are fork tender. Once cooked, drain the potatoes and return them to the pot, then place them over medium heat for about 1 minute to dry them out a bit. Turn the heat off and add the chives, butter, half of the parsley, salt, pepper, and hot sauce to taste. Stir the potatoes until the butter has melted, then transfer to a serving platter.

While the potatoes are cooking, preheat a large skillet over medium-high heat with 2 tablespoons of the EVOO, twice around the pan. Season the chicken with salt, pepper, the thyme, and the paprika. Add the chicken to the skillet and cook it on each side for 5 to 6 minutes, or until it is cooked through. Remove the chicken from the skillet to a plate and cover it loosely with foil to keep it warm. Return the skillet to the cooktop over medium-high heat. Add the remaining 2 tablespoons of EVOO and the chorizo and cook, stirring it frequently, for about 2 minutes. Remove the chorizo from the skillet to a plate using a slotted spoon and reserve.

Turn the heat up to high and add the mushrooms to the skillet. Spread them out in an even layer and resist the temptation to stir for a couple of minutes so that the mushrooms can start to brown. Once they are brown, go ahead and shake the pan up, stir, and continue to cook them for 2 minutes more, then add the onions, garlic, and reserved chorizo and season with salt and pepper. Continue to cook, stirring every now and then, for about 3 minutes, or until the onions start to look tender. Add the sherry and cook for 1 minute more, then add the chicken stock and bring it up to a bubble. Simmer for about 2 minutes. Add the remaining parsley and stir it to combine, then taste and adjust the seasonings with salt and pepper.

To serve, arrange the cooked chicken breasts on serving plates, top with the mushroom-chorizo sauce, and serve the butter and herb spuds alongside.

tidbit >> Sherry is a great thing to have on hand in the wine rack. You can use it in Marsalas, dressings, soups, or any chicken dish. One of my favorite appetizers is mushrooms cooked in garlic, butter, and sherry.

Meat

John enjoys a SWM (Steak with Men) night out on the town each month with his buddies. Why not do your own at home with some of these recipes? We cook (and eat) a lot of meat. You'll forget you're eating at home with these classics!

GRILL GREAT

Ginger Flank Steak with Wasabi Smashed Potatoes and
    Seared Savoy Cabbage
Pork or Veal Chops with Caramelized Onion Sauce
Spanish Pork Chops with Linguica Corn Stuffing and Wine Gravy
Cumin and Lime Roasted Pork Tenderloin with Spicy Creamed Corn
Baby Lamb Chops with Artichoke and Tarragon Dip
Steaks with Tangy Corn Relish and Smashed Spuds
Super-Grilled Steak Sandwich with Horseradish-Dijon Cream
Big Bistro Burgers with Shallots and Beet and Goat Cheese Salad
Broiled Lamb Chops with Mediterranean Potato-Veggie Mix
Grilled Flank Steak Sandwich with Blue Cheese Vinaigrette–
    Dressed Arugula and Pears

$10 MEALS

Uptown Down-Home Chili
Lion's Head (Pork Meatballs and Napa Cabbage)
Ham Wafflewiches
Rosemary Lemon-Pepper Pork Tenderloin with Greens
Pork Loin Chops with Sweet and Hot Peppers
Ham and Spinach Hash with Fried Eggs
Swedish Meatballs on Noodles
Flank Steak with Zucchini and Yellow Squash "Pappardelle"
Shish Kabob Salad
Involtini all'Enotec'Antica with Gnocchi

FOR COLD MONTHS

BLT Soup
Lemon Roast Pork Tenderloins with Warm Beets, Chicory,
    and Goat Cheese
Saucy Buttered, Smothered Steaks with Spinach Gratin
Beans and Greens Soup with Pancetta
Thai-Style Grilled Beef in Broth with a Lot o' Noodles
Quick Cassoulet Stuffed Bread Melts
London Broil with Steak Sauce Gravy, Smashed Cauliflower with
    Cheese, and Red Chard with Ham
Croque Monsieur with Greens
Beef Stroganoff Over Buttered Parsley-Cauliflower "Noodles"
Chili-Rubbed Roast Pork Tenderloins with Crunchy, Chunky Black
    Bean and Jicama Salad

Ginger Flank Steak with Wasabi Smashed Potatoes and Seared Savoy Cabbage

This is not your average steak and baked dinner; it's about meat and potatoes in a whole new way. Try the same recipe with beef cut for London broil or skirt steaks. All of these cuts are affordable, but with this recipe they become way above average.   4 SERVINGS

3-inch piece of **fresh ginger**, peeled and grated

¼ cup **tamari** (dark aged soy sauce)

Zest and juice of 2 limes

5 tablespoons **vegetable oil**

2 tablespoons **grill seasoning**, such as McCormick's Montreal Steak Seasoning

2 pounds **flank steak**

2½ to 3 pounds **Idaho potatoes** (4 large potatoes), peeled and cut into chunks

Salt

¼ to ⅓ cup **heavy cream**

1 to 2 tablespoons **wasabi paste**—how hot do ya like it?

4 **scallions**, root end trimmed

A handful of fresh **cilantro leaves**

1 small head **Savoy cabbage**, quartered, cored, and shredded

Black pepper

Preheat a grill pan or outdoor grill to high.

Combine the ginger, tamari, lime juice, 3 tablespoons of the oil, and the grill seasoning in a large shallow dish. Add the meat to the marinade and turn to coat it. Let it stand for 10 minutes, then grill the meat for 6 to 7 minutes on each side.

Place the potatoes in a pot and cover them with water. Bring them to a boil, salt the potatoes, and cook them until tender, 10 to 12 minutes. Drain the potatoes and return them to the hot pot. Mash the potatoes, adding the cream and wasabi to achieve the desired consistency and heat level. Adjust the salt to taste.

While the potatoes and meat cook, finely chop the scallions together with the cilantro and lime zest. Set aside.

Heat a large skillet over high heat. Add the remaining 2 tablespoons of vegetable oil, twice around the pan. Stir-fry the cabbage until it's wilted and just tender but still has a bite, 4 to 5 minutes. Season the cabbage with salt and black pepper.

Let the meat rest for 5 minutes, then thinly slice it on an angle against the grain. Serve the meat on mounds of mashed potatoes and garnish with a generous sprinkling of the chopped scallion-cilantro-lime zest. Pile the seared cabbage alongside.

Pork or Veal Chops with Caramelized Onion Sauce

This might sound like a fancy-pants meal but don't let it fool you. Chicken breasts will do if chops aren't what you're into tonight.

2 SERVINGS

4 tablespoons **EVOO** (extra-virgin olive oil)

1 large **onion** or 2 medium onions, chopped

5 or 6 **fresh thyme** sprigs

Salt and **black pepper**

2 large **garlic cloves**, chopped

3 tablespoons **balsamic vinegar**

1 cup **chicken stock**

2 tablespoons **butter**

¼ cup fresh **flat-leaf parsley leaves**, a handful, chopped

2 bone-in **veal rib chops** or bone-in loin pork chops, 1 to 1½ inches thick

tidbit >> If you are using veal chops, you can reduce the cooking time slightly if you prefer them a bit pink inside. For chicken breasts, cook for 6 minutes on each side.

For the caramelized onion sauce, preheat a large skillet over medium heat with 2 tablespoons of the EVOO. Add the onions and thyme sprigs, then season them with salt and pepper. Cook, stirring every now and then, for 10 to 12 minutes, or until golden brown. Add the garlic and continue to cook for 1 minute, then add the vinegar and chicken stock. Bring to a simmer over high heat and cook until the liquids have reduced by half, 3 to 4 minutes more. Turn the heat off, remove the thyme twigs (all the flavorful leaves will have fallen off by now), and add the butter and parsley. Stir until the butter melts.

Once the onions are on their way, preheat a second skillet over medium-high heat with the remaining 2 tablespoons of EVOO. Season the chops liberally with salt and pepper and add them to the hot skillet. Cook the chops for 5 minutes on the first side. Resist the temptation to move the chops around in the pan, as it will slow down the browning. Flip the chops and reduce the heat to medium. Cook them on the second side for 8 to 10 minutes, or to the desired doneness. Transfer them to a plate and cover loosely with aluminum foil to rest for a couple of minutes. Serve the chops topped with some of the caramelized onion sauce.

Spanish Pork Chops with Linguica Corn Stuffing and Wine Gravy

This is actually my version of a fantabulous meal I enjoyed at a late-night hot spot in Vancouver, north of the border. It's good because you get salty, sweet, and savory in each and every bite. I serve these with green beans.   4 SERVINGS

4 thick **boneless center-cut pork chops**, about 2 pounds

Salt and **black pepper**

3 tablespoons **EVOO** (extra-virgin olive oil)

2 tablespoons **butter**

2 tablespoons all-purpose **flour**

1 cup **dry red wine** (about ¼ bottle)

½ cup **black cherry preserves** or all-fruit spread

2 cups **beef stock**

½ pound **linguica** or chorizo, chopped

2 **celery ribs**, chopped

1 medium **onion**, chopped

2 **garlic cloves**, chopped

1 small **red bell pepper**, cored, seeded, and chopped

4 **corn muffins**, crumbled

1 teaspoon **smoked paprika**, ⅓ palmful

2 tablespoons chopped fresh **thyme leaves**, from 4 to 5 sprigs

1 pound **green beans**, stem ends trimmed

A handful of fresh **flat-leaf parsley**, chopped

Preheat the oven to 350°F.

Heat a skillet over medium-high heat. Season the pork chops with salt and pepper. Add 2 tablespoons of the EVOO, twice around the pan. Add the chops and caramelize the meat for 2 minutes on each side. Transfer the chops to a baking sheet and put in the oven to finish cooking through, 12 to 15 minutes. Add the butter to the same skillet and reduce the heat a bit. Add the flour and cook for 1 minute. Whisk the wine into the pan and cook for 1 minute, then whisk in the preserves and 1 cup of the stock. Season with salt and pepper and let the gravy thicken over low heat.

Heat a medium nonstick skillet over medium-high heat with the remaining tablespoon of EVOO. When the oil smokes, add the linguica or chorizo and brown it for 2 minutes. Add the celery, onions, garlic, and bell peppers, and season them with salt and pepper. Cook for 5 minutes, then crumble the muffins into the skillet and combine with the vegetables. Dampen the stuffing with the remaining cup of stock and season with the paprika and thyme. Reduce the heat to low and keep the stuffing warm until it is ready to serve.

Heat 1 inch of water in a skillet and add salt and the beans. Cook for 4 to 5 minutes, until the beans are tender, then drain.

Remove the meat from the oven and whisk the drippings into your gravy. Pile the stuffing on plates with the chops alongside and ladle the gravy over both. Scatter the parsley over the meat and stuffing. Serve with the green beans.

Cumin and Lime Roasted Pork Tenderloin with Spicy Creamed Corn

Sweet, smoky, zingy. YUM, this dish is tasty!   4 SERVINGS

2¼ pounds **pork tenderloin** (sometimes sold 2 tenderloins per package)

Juice of 2 limes

4 tablespoons **extra-virgin olive oil** (EVOO)

2 tablespoons **ground cumin** (2 palmfuls)

1 tablespoon **ground coriander** (1 palmful)

Salt and **freshly ground black pepper**

6 **garlic cloves** (4 cloves cracked and 2 cloves chopped)

2 tablespoons **unsalted butter**

1 large **yellow onion**, chopped

2 **jalapeño peppers**, seeded and chopped

1 small **red bell pepper**, cored, seeded, and finely chopped

2 10-ounce boxes **frozen corn kernels**, or kernels cut from 5 ears of fresh corn

1 tablespoon all-purpose **flour**

1½ cups **chicken stock** or broth

½ cup **heavy cream**

¼ cup fresh **flat-leaf parsley** leaves (a generous handful), chopped

2 tablespoons chopped fresh **cilantro** leaves (a small handful)

Preheat the oven to 500°F.

Trim the silver skin or connective tissue off the tenderloins with a very sharp, thin knife.

Place the tenderloins on a rimmed nonstick cookie sheet and coat them with the lime juice, rubbing the juice into the meat. Drizzle EVOO over the tenderloins, just enough to coat, about 2 tablespoons. Season the meat with the cumin, coriander, salt, and pepper. Cut small slits into the meat and disperse chunks of the cracked garlic cloves into the slits. Roast for 20 minutes. Remove from the oven and let rest for a few minutes, tented loosely with foil.

While the pork is cooking, preheat a skillet over medium-high heat with 2 tablespoons of the EVOO (twice around the pan) and the butter. Add the onions, jalapeños, bell peppers, chopped garlic, corn kernels, salt, and pepper. Cook for 4 to 5 minutes, or until the onions are tender. Sprinkle with the flour, and continue to cook for 1 minute. Whisk in the chicken stock and heavy cream. Bring the corn up to a simmer and then lower the heat to medium low and cook until it is thick and creamy, about 5 minutes. Finish the spicy creamed corn with the parsley and cilantro. Taste and adjust the seasoning with salt and pepper.

Slice the rested roasted pork and serve alongside the spicy creamed corn.

Baby Lamb Chops with Artichoke and Tarragon Dip

Hello, perfect party starter! These baby lamb chops with a little spoonful of artichoke and tarragon dip are sure to get your taste buds jumping.   24 CHOPS, 6 TO 8 SERVINGS

---

1 15-ounce can quartered **artichoke hearts** in water, drained

1 6-ounce jar **marinated baby mushrooms** and their liquid

1 **shallot,** coarsely chopped

4 sprigs **fresh tarragon,** stripped, plus a few sprigs for garnish

3 tablespoons **white wine vinegar**

Salt and **freshly ground black pepper**

½ cup **extra-virgin olive oil** (EVOO), plus some for drizzling

24 **baby lamb chops** (get the butcher to cut them)

½ pound **baby cut carrots** (available in produce department)

½ pound **sugar snap peas**

4 **radishes,** cleaned and trimmed but left on greens, halved lengthwise

Preheat a broiler or grill pan to high.

In a food processor, combine the artichokes, marinated mushrooms, shallot, tarragon, and vinegar. Season with salt and pepper and turn the processor on; stream in about ½ cup of the EVOO until a spoonable, fairly smooth dip forms, about 1 minute. Scrape the dip into a serving bowl and place a demitasse (small) spoon in the dip so it can be easily dolloped onto each individual lamb chop when they're served.

Drizzle the chops with a few teaspoons of EVOO and season with salt and pepper. Grill or broil for 2 minutes on each side and remove to rest.

To serve, place the dip on a large platter or cutting board and surround with the cooked chops and piles of baby cut carrots, sugar snap peas, and halved radishes for dipping and topping. Garnish the platter with additional sprigs of tarragon.

Steaks with Tangy Corn Relish and Smashed Spuds

This is a gut-bustingly delicious twist on steak and bakers.

4 SERVINGS

---

2 to 2¼ pounds red or white **boiling potatoes** (if larger than a golf ball, cut them in half)

4 tablespoons **EVOO** (extra-virgin olive oil)

2 medium **onions**, thinly sliced

4 **garlic cloves**, chopped

1½ tablespoons **chili powder**, 1½ palmfuls

1 teaspoon **ground cumin**, ⅓ palmful

1 tablespoon **sugar**

Salt and **black pepper**

4 1-inch-thick **Delmonico steaks**

Grill seasoning, such as McCormick's Montreal Steak Seasoning, to taste

1½ cups **chicken stock**

1 10-ounce box **frozen corn kernels**

2 ounces **cream cheese**, at room temperature

2 cups shredded **Cheddar cheese**

4 **scallions**, thinly sliced

2 **limes**, both zested, one juiced, the other cut into quarters

¼ cup fresh **cilantro leaves**, a generous handful, coarsely chopped

Place the potatoes in a medium-size sauce pot, add enough water to cover them by an inch or two, and place over high heat to bring it up to a boil. Boil the potatoes for about 12 minutes, or until they are fork tender.

To start the corn relish, preheat a medium-size skillet over medium-high heat with 2 tablespoons of the EVOO, twice around the pan. Add the onions, garlic, chili powder, cumin, sugar, salt, and pepper. Cook for 4 to 5 minutes, stirring frequently, until the onions start to take on a golden color and are nice and tender.

While the onions for the corn relish are cooking, preheat a large skillet over medium-high heat with the remaining 2 tablespoons of EVOO. Pat the steaks dry with a paper towel, and season liberally with the grill seasoning. Add the steaks to the hot skillet and cook on each side for 4 to 5 minutes for rare; 5 to 6 minutes for medium. Remove them from the skillet and let the steaks rest, loosely covered with foil, for about 5 minutes.

Once you have the steaks going, get back to the corn relish. Add the chicken stock and bring the liquid up to a bubble. Add the corn and continue to cook for about 2 to 3 minutes, or until the liquids have reduced by half.

Check on the boiling potatoes. If tender, drain and return them to the hot pot. Smash the potatoes with a masher and combine them with the cream cheese, Cheddar cheese, and scallions. Season with a little salt and pepper. Resmash, taste, and adjust the seasonings.

To the corn relish add the lime zest and juice and the cilantro. Stir to combine and taste the relish to adjust the seasoning with salt and pepper.

Squeeze a quarter of a lime over each of the rested steaks. Serve the steaks with a large helping of the tangy corn relish and a big mound of the super smashed spuds.

Super-Grilled Steak Sandwich with Horseradish-Dijon Cream

When measuring Worcestershire sauce, pop that plastic thing-a-ma-bob off the top of the bottle before you pour! 4 SERVINGS

2 pounds **flank steak**

¼ cup **Worcestershire sauce**

3 **garlic cloves**, chopped

Salt and **freshly ground black pepper**

Extra-virgin olive oil (EVOO), for drizzling

4 **plum tomatoes**, sliced into thirds lengthwise

1 large **red onion**, sliced into ½-inch-thick disks

1 **baguette**

1 cup whole or reduced-fat **sour cream**

3 tablespoons **prepared horseradish**

1 heaping tablespoon **Dijon mustard**

¼ cup fresh **flat-leaf parsley** leaves chopped

1 bunch of **arugula** or watercress, cleaned and trimmed (a couple of cups)

Preheat a grill pan or outdoor grill on high.

Season the steak with 2 tablespoons of the Worcestershire, the garlic, salt, and pepper, drizzle with some EVOO, and marinate for 5 minutes.

Drizzle the tomatoes and red onion slices with a little EVOO, the remaining 2 tablespoons of Worcestershire, and some salt and pepper. Place on the grill and cook until well marked on both sides, 2 to 3 minutes. Remove from the grill and reserve.

Grill the flank steak for 6 to 7 minutes on each side. Remove the steak from the grill to a cutting board to rest for 5 minutes.

Split the baguette lengthwise without cutting it all the way through, then cut into 4 equal sub-style rolls. Drizzle EVOO over the inside and season with salt and pepper. Place the open-faced cut rolls on the grill, oiled insides exposed. Place a heavy pan atop the bread to keep it flat on the grill. Grill until well marked, 1 to 2 minutes.

In a bowl, combine the sour cream, horseradish, mustard, and parsley and season with salt and pepper.

Thinly slice the flank steak on an angle, cutting the meat against the grain.

To assemble the sandwiches, slather the inside of the grilled bread with the horseradish-Dijon cream. Divide the sliced steak, grilled red onions, and tomatoes among the 4 grilled baguette rolls. Pile some arugula or watercress on each sandwich and serve.

Big Bistro Burgers with Shallots on Grilled Bread and Beet and Goat Cheese Salad

All of our favorite bistro flavors in a burger! Does it get any better than that?   4 SERVINGS

5 tablespoons **extra-virgin olive oil** (EVOO), plus some for drizzling

4 large **shallots**, thinly sliced

Salt and **freshly ground black pepper**

4 tablespoons **sherry vinegar**

2 pounds **ground sirloin**

2 tablespoons fresh **thyme** leaves, chopped (from 4 sprigs)

2 tablespoons **Worcestershire sauce**

1 tablespoon **grill seasoning**, such as McCormick's Montreal Steak Seasoning (a palmful)

2 tablespoons **Dijon mustard**

4 thick slices **crusty country-style bread**

1 8¼-ounce can **sliced beets**, drained and sliced

6 cups **frisée, arugula, watercress,** or **baby spinach**

1 cup crumbled **goat cheese**

Preheat a grill pan or outdoor grill to high.

Preheat a small skillet over medium-high heat with 2 tablespoons of EVOO. Add the shallots, season with salt and pepper, and cook, stirring frequently, for 5 to 6 minutes, or until lightly brown. Add 2 tablespoons of the sherry vinegar and continue to cook for 1 minute, then remove from the heat and reserve.

While the shallots cook, in a large bowl, combine the beef, thyme, Worcestershire, grill seasoning, and Dijon mustard. Form the meat into 4 large patties about 1¼ inches thick. Coat the beef patties with a drizzle of EVOO. Grill for 5 to 6 minutes per side for medium rare, 7 to 8 minutes per side for medium well to well.

Drizzle or brush EVOO onto both sides of the bread slices, season with salt and pepper, and add to the grill. Cook until well marked on both sides, remove from the grill, and wrap in foil to keep warm.

In a bowl, combine the beets and greens, the remaining 2 tablespoons of sherry vinegar, the remaining 3 tablespoons of EVOO, and a little salt and pepper. Add the crumbled goat cheese and toss to distribute.

To serve, divide the grilled bread among 4 serving plates. Top the bread with the beet and goat cheese salad, letting it overflow onto the plates. Transfer the burgers to top the salad and then pile each burger with some of the caramelized shallots. Attack your big bistro burger with a fork and knife, please. This *is* a bistro!

Broiled Lamb Chops with Mediterranean Potato-Veggie Mix

Lamb chops are quick cooking. If you are the type who only indulges in leg of lamb once a year at holidays, pick up some chops and try this one at home tonight.   4 SERVINGS

4 tablespoons **EVOO** (extra-virgin olive oil)

1 large **baking potato**, scrubbed clean

Salt and **black pepper**

¼ teaspoon **dried thyme**

1 large **fennel bulb**, cut in quarters, cored, and thinly sliced, a few fronds reserved

1 large **onion**, thinly sliced

3 large **garlic cloves**, chopped

¼ teaspoon **red pepper flakes**

1½ cups **chicken stock**

2 pounds **rack of lamb**, cut into individual chops, 3 to 4 chops per person

1 tablespoon **balsamic vinegar**

10 **kalamata olives**, pitted and coarsely chopped, ½ cup

10 fresh **mint leaves**, a few sprigs, chopped

¾ cup fresh **basil**, 15 leaves, chopped

Preheat the broiler to high. Place the rack about 6 inches from the heat.

Preheat a large nonstick skillet over medium-high heat with 2 tablespoons of the EVOO, twice around the pan. Quarter the potato lengthwise, then thinly slice it across into small, thin bite-size pieces. Add the potatoes to the hot skillet and spread them out in an even layer across the pan. Season the potatoes with salt, pepper, and thyme. Resist the temptation to shake or stir the pan for a few minutes, until the potatoes start to brown up. Once they are a little brown on the first side, turn them and continue to cook them until they are evenly golden and cooked through, about 8 to 10 minutes. Turn the heat down a little if the potatoes start browning faster than they are cooking through.

While the potatoes are working, preheat a second skillet over medium-high heat with the remaining 2 tablespoons of EVOO. Add the sliced fennel, onions, garlic, red pepper flakes, salt, and pepper. Cook until both the onions and the fennel are tender, about 4 to 5 minutes, stirring frequently. Add the chicken stock and bring up to a bubble, then simmer for 3 minutes or until there is very little liquid left in the pan, less than ½ cup.

Arrange the chops on a broiler pan. Season both sides of the lamb chops with salt and pepper and broil them for 4 minutes on each side for medium rare.

Add the balsamic vinegar and olives to the skillet with the fennel, tossing to combine them. Turn the heat down to low while the chops finish broiling. Once the chops are ready to come out of the broiler, add the mint and basil to the fennel, add the cooked browned-up potatoes, and toss to combine. Serve the chops alongside the fennel and potatoes and garnish with the fennel fronds.

Grilled Flank Steak Sandwich with Blue Cheese Vinaigrette–Dressed Arugula and Pears

This sandwich has it all: hearty pieces of charred meat, creamy flavorful cheese, peppery greens, and a crisp, bright bite from the pears to round it all off! 4 SERVINGS

2 **lemons**

2 tablespoons fresh **thyme** leaves (from about 4 sprigs), stripped and chopped

Salt and **freshly ground black pepper**

1½ pounds **flank steak**

1 tablespoon **Dijon mustard**

2 tablespoons **white wine vinegar**

5 tablespoons **extra-virgin olive oil** (EVOO)

¼ cup crumbled **blue cheese**

4 **kaiser rolls**, split

1 **garlic clove**, crushed

1 ripe **Bartlett, Anjou, or Bosc pear**

8 slices **prosciutto di Parma**

1 large bunch of **arugula**, cleaned and trimmed (2 to 2½ cups)

Preheat a grill pan or outdoor grill on high.

In a shallow bowl, combine the juice of 1½ lemons, the thyme, salt, and pepper. Add the steak and toss to coat. Marinate the steak for 5 to 10 minutes.

Grill the steak for 6 to 7 minutes on each side. Remove to a plate and loosely tent with foil to let the juices redistribute before slicing.

In a small bowl, combine the Dijon mustard with the vinegar, salt, and pepper. Whisk in 3 tablespoons of the EVOO, then the blue cheese. Toast the rolls. Rub the toasted cut sides with the garlic clove.

Thinly slice the pear, and toss in a salad bowl with the juice of the remaining half lemon. Slice the prosciutto into strips. Add the arugula leaves and prosciutto to the salad bowl and toss with the vinaigrette.

Thinly slice the steak against the grain and on an angle. Layer half of the steak slices onto the rolls and top with the arugula-pear salad. Add the remaining steak and roll tops.

Uptown Down-Home Chili

Chili is a hearty and delicious way to stretch a buck. This super fast recipe gets jazzed up with smoked Gouda and imported beer to bring a little uptown flare to an affordable down-home dish! **4 SERVINGS**

3 tablespoons **extra-virgin olive oil** (EVOO)

2 pounds **ground sirloin**

2 tablespoons **grill seasoning**, such as McCormick's Montreal Steak Seasoning

½ pound **baby portobello mushrooms**, chopped

¼ pound **shiitake mushroom caps**, sliced

1 medium **yellow onion**, chopped

3 **celery ribs**, chopped

1 large **red bell pepper**, cored, seeded, and chopped

4 to 6 **garlic cloves**, chopped

2 tablespoons **Worcestershire sauce**

2 canned **chipotle peppers in adobo**, chopped, with their juices, or 1 generous palmful ground chipotle chili powder (about 2 tablespoons)

1 tablespoon **ground cumin**

1 bottle **imported beer**, such as Stella Artois (imported just 'cause we're Uptown and that's all they drink here)

1 15-ounce can **black beans**, drained

1 15-ounce can **crushed tomatoes**

1 cup **beef stock** or broth

2 to 3 tablespoons fresh **thyme** leaves

8-ounce piece of **smoked Gouda**, shredded

1 small **white onion**, finely chopped

Heat a deep, large skillet or a pot over high heat. Add 2 tablespoons of the EVOO (twice around the pan) and the meat. Season it with the grill seasoning and sear it, browning and crumbling it, for 3 to 5 minutes. Transfer the meat to a plate and return the pot to the stove.

Reduce the heat to medium high and add the remaining tablespoon of EVOO. Add the mushrooms and begin to brown them before adding the other veggies. After 2 or 3 minutes the mushrooms will begin to shrink and soften. Push the mushrooms off to one side of the pot and add all the remaining veggies to the opposite side of the pot. Once the onions, celery, bell peppers, and garlic have been working for a few minutes, mix the veggies with the mushrooms. Return the meat to the pan, and season with the Worcestershire sauce, chipotle, and cumin. Add the beer to deglaze the pot, scraping up all the pan drippings. Reduce the beer by half, 2 minutes. Add the black beans, tomatoes, stock, and thyme to the chili and simmer for 10 minutes to let the flavors combine. Taste to adjust the seasonings. Top bowlfuls of the chili with shredded smoked Gouda and finely chopped raw onions.

Lion's Head (Pork Meatballs and Napa Cabbage)

The wonderful actress Ming Na taught me this recipe. It was handed down to her from her parents, who owned a successful Chinese restaurant for twenty-five years. It's not fair! Ming Na is gorgeous and talented and she can cook, too! But, we can console ourselves with these Chinese meatballs. The chopped cabbage is served in a pile, the meatballs in the middle: a head surrounded by a mane . . . a lion's head.   4 SERVINGS

Coarse salt

1 cup **short-grain white rice**

Vegetable oil, for drizzling and frying

½ pound **shiitake mushrooms,** stems removed and finely chopped

6 **garlic cloves,** finely chopped

2 pounds **ground pork**

⅓ cup **tamari** (dark aged soy sauce found on the international aisle), plus more for serving

1 **egg,** lightly beaten

½ cup plus 1 tablespoon **cornstarch**

1 teaspoon finely ground **black pepper**

1 cup **chicken stock** or broth

1 medium to large head of **Napa cabbage,** cut into large dice

Bring 2 cups of water to a boil. Add salt and the rice. When the water returns to a boil, reduce the heat to a simmer and cover the pot. Simmer for 20 minutes, or until the water is absorbed. Set aside.

Drizzle some oil in a small nonstick skillet preheated to medium-high heat, then cook the mushrooms and garlic for 3 to 4 minutes. Season with a little salt. Remove from the pan and cool for 5 minutes.

Pour 2 inches of the oil in the bottom of a large wok or wok-shaped skillet and heat over high heat.

Place the pork in a bowl. Add the mushrooms and garlic. Add the tamari, the egg, a few spoonfuls of the cornstarch, and the pepper. Use a pair of chopsticks to mix the meat, stirring only in one direction until combined. The mixture will be wet. Place all but one tablespoon of the remaining cornstarch on a plate. Form 10 to 12 large, soft meatballs and dust them lightly but evenly in the cornstarch.

When the oil smokes, add the balls and flash-fry them for 2 minutes on each side, or until deep golden in color. Drain the balls on paper towels.

In a deep pot heat the chicken stock to a bubble. Add half of the cabbage, then layer in all of the balls and the remaining cabbage. The pot should be filled to the top. Place a lid on the pot and simmer for 10 minutes. The cabbage will cook down and add to the broth. Remove a ladleful of broth to a small bowl and dissolve a tablespoon of cornstarch in it, then return it to the pot. Simmer with the lid off for a minute or two to thicken the broth. Serve with the rice and extra tamari.

Ham Wafflewiches

The Monte Cristo, a ham, turkey, and cheese sammie on French toast, is a fave of mine. This guilty pleasure is a fun-and-tasty twist on the traditional 'Cristo.   MAKES 4 SAMMIES

2 tablespoons softened **butter**

4 tablespoons **honey mustard**

8 **waffles,** such as Eggos, lightly toasted

½ pound deli-sliced **ham**

½ pound deli-sliced **smoked turkey** or honey roast turkey

½ pound deli-sliced **Swiss cheese**

¾ cup prepared **cranberry sauce**

Heat a large nonstick skillet over medium heat. Add the butter and melt it. Assemble the sandwiches by spreading honey mustard on 4 of the waffles, then topping with equal amounts of ham, turkey, and Swiss cheese. Spread cranberry sauce liberally on the remaining 4 waffles and place them atop the sandwiches. Fry the assembled sandwiches in the melted butter and cook for a few minutes on each side until they are deeply golden in color and the cheese melts.

Rosemary Lemon-Pepper Pork Tenderloin with Greens

If you like the smell of rosemary, you're gonna love the taste of it on this pork dish.   4 SERVINGS

2 ¼ pounds **pork tenderloins** (1 package with 2 tenderloins)

Zest and juice of 2 lemons

½ tablespoon **coarsely ground black pepper**, plus some for seasoning

4 **garlic cloves**, chopped

2 sprigs fresh **rosemary**, leaves stripped and finely chopped

7 tablespoons **extra-virgin olive oil** (EVOO)

Coarse salt

3 thick slices **country-style bread**, cut into 1-inch cubes

3 heaping tablespoons **mayonnaise**

½ cup grated **Parmigiano-Reggiano**

2 large **romaine lettuce** hearts, chopped, or 8 to 10 cups mixed greens

Preheat the oven to 500°F.

Trim the silver skin or connective tissue off the tenderloins with a very sharp thin knife.

Place the tenderloins on a rimmed nonstick cookie sheet. In a bowl, mix together all of the lemon zest, the juice of 1 lemon, the coarse ground black pepper, 3 cloves of the chopped garlic, the rosemary, 2 tablespoons of the EVOO, and some salt. Thoroughly coat the tenderloins in the rosemary-lemon-pepper mixture, rubbing it into the meat. Roast in the hot oven for about 20 to 22 minutes. Once roasted, remove from the oven to a cutting board to rest for a few minutes, loosely tented with aluminum foil.

To make the croutons, preheat a medium skillet over medium-high heat with 2 tablespoons of the EVOO and add the cubed bread; toss to coat in the oil. Add the remaining 1 clove of chopped garlic, salt, and pepper and toast the bread cubes, stirring frequently, until golden brown, about 4 to 5 minutes. Remove from the heat and reserve.

While the croutons are toasting, in a bowl, combine the mayo and the juice of the remaining lemon. Whisk in 3 tablespoons of EVOO, season with pepper, and stir in the grated cheese.

Once the pork is out of the oven and resting, put the salad together. In a salad bowl, combine the homemade garlic croutons with the greens. Pour the dressing over the salad and toss to coat. Thinly slice the rested pork tenderloin and serve alongside the salad.

Pork Loin Chops with Sweet and Hot Peppers

Serve these chops with the Wilted Spinach with Garlic Chips (page 129).   4 SERVINGS

---

4 **center-cut pork loin chops,** 1 inch thick

Salt and **freshly ground black pepper**

2 tablespoons **extra-virgin olive oil** (EVOO)

1 **yellow bell pepper,** cored, seeded, and sliced

1 **orange bell pepper,** cored, seeded, and sliced

4 jarred red **hot Italian cherry peppers,** sliced

½ cup **white wine** or chicken stock

2 tablespoons chopped fresh **flat-leaf parsley** (a handful)

Heat a large skillet over medium-high heat. Season the chops with salt and pepper. Add 1 tablespoon of the EVOO to the pan (once around the pan). Add the chops and cook for 5 minutes on each side.

After the chops have cooked through, transfer to a platter and cover with foil. Return the pan to the heat and add the remaining tablespoon of EVOO and the bell peppers. Sauté the peppers, stirring frequently, for 5 minutes. Add the hot cherry peppers and a splash of their brine to the pan, and cook for 1 minute. Add the wine or stock and scrape up the pan drippings. Arrange the peppers over the chops and sprinkle with parsley.

Ham and Spinach Hash with Fried Eggs

This is a B, L, or D: breakfast, lunch, or dinner recipe.   4 SERVINGS

2 tablespoons **extra-virgin olive oil** (EVOO)

4 tablespoons **unsalted butter**

8 small **red potatoes**

Salt and **freshly ground black pepper**

1 tablespoon fresh **thyme** leaves, chopped (from 4 sprigs)

¼ teaspoon crushed **red pepper flakes**

1 medium **red onion**, chopped

1 large **ham steak**, finely chopped

4 extra-large **eggs**

2 cups **baby spinach** leaves, chopped

10 fresh **basil** leaves, chopped or torn

½ cup grated **Parmigiano-Reggiano**

2 **plum tomatoes**, seeded and chopped

Preheat a large nonstick skillet over medium-high heat with the EVOO and 2 tablespoons of the butter. While the pan is getting hot and the butter is melting, cut the potatoes in half and then thinly slice them. Add them to the hot skillet and season with salt, pepper, the thyme, and the red pepper flakes. Cook, stirring every now and then, for about 10 minutes, or until the potatoes have browned and are tender. Add the onions and ham and continue to cook for 3 to 4 minutes.

Preheat another skillet over medium-high heat with the remaining 2 tablespoons of butter. Once the butter has melted and the bubbles have subsided, crack the eggs into the pan, season with salt and pepper, and fry to the desired doneness.

While the eggs are frying, finish off the hash by adding the spinach and basil to the potatoes. Toss to wilt the spinach. Sprinkle the hash with the cheese and remove from the heat. Transfer the ham and spinach hash to plates. Top each portion with some tomatoes and a single fried egg.

Swedish Meatballs on Noodles

I love the cuisine of Italy, but I decided to cross the European borders and give traditional spaghetti and meatballs a new bite! The Italian favorite gets revamped with this fast, affordable, and Swedish-inspired meal even your Nona will love!   4 SERVINGS

1¾ pounds **ground sirloin**

1 large **egg**, beaten

¼ cup **plain bread crumbs**

½ small **yellow onion**, chopped

A healthy grating of **nutmeg**

½ cup fresh **flat-leaf parsley** leaves (3 handfuls), chopped

Salt and **freshly ground black pepper**

2 tablespoons **extra-virgin olive oil** (EVOO)

2 cups **beef stock**

1 tablespoon **red currant or grape jelly**

1 cup **heavy cream** or sour cream

½ pound **wide egg noodles**

2 tablespoons **butter**

8 **cornichons** or 6 baby gherkins, chopped, for garnish

Place the ground sirloin in a large mixing bowl and punch a well into the center. Fill the well with the egg, bread crumbs, onion, nutmeg, half of the chopped parsley, and a little salt and pepper. Mix up the meatball ingredients until well combined, yet not overmixed. Divide the mix into 4 equal parts. Roll each part into 6 balls. Heat a large nonstick skillet over medium-high heat with the EVOO. Add the meatballs and brown on all sides, about 5 minutes, giving the pan a good shake now and then. Add the stock, jelly, and heavy cream or sour cream. Bring it up to a bubble, then reduce the heat to a simmer and cook for 8 to 10 minutes.

Place a large pot of water on to boil. Add the noodles and season the water with salt. Cook until just tender, 5 to 6 minutes. Drain the egg noodles and shake dry. Put the noodles back in the hot pot and add the remaining chopped parsley and the butter and season with salt and pepper. Stir until the butter has melted. Top the noodles with the meatballs, their sauce, and pickles.

Flank Steak with Zucchini and Yellow Squash "Pappardelle"

I've got zucchini and squash stepping in as a fun, flavorful, and fancy replacement for pasta. This veggie "pappardelle" is a perfect bed for a nice piece of meat and won't have you missing the carbs! 4 SERVINGS

Salt

6 **garlic cloves**, chopped

6 tablespoons **extra-virgin olive oil** (EVOO), divided

2 tablespoons fresh **thyme leaves**, chopped

2 pounds **flank steak**

Freshly ground black pepper

2 medium **zucchini**

2 medium **yellow squash**

1 teaspoon **red pepper flakes**

Zest and juice of 1 lemon

½ cup **chicken stock** or broth

2 tablespoons **butter**

A handful of fresh **flat-leaf parsley**, chopped

¾ cup grated **Parmigiano-Reggiano**

Preheat a charcoal grill, grill pan, or large skillet (if using a large skillet for the steak, you might have to cut the steak in half to make it fit in the pan).

For the zucchini and yellow squash "pappardelle," in a large skillet bring 1 inch of salted water to a boil. Cover the skillet with a lid or a piece of foil so it comes to a boil quickly.

In a large shallow dish, combine half of the garlic, 3 tablespoons of the EVOO, and the thyme. Add the flank steak and coat completely in the mixture, allowing it to marinate for 5 to 10 minutes, depending on how much of a rush you are in. Season the flank steak with salt and pepper, place on the hot grill, and cook for 5 to 6 minutes per side. Remove from the grill and let rest for 5 minutes. While the steak is cooking, prepare the squash pappardelle.

Trim the ends off the zucchini and yellow squash, then slice lengthwise into ⅛-inch-thick slices. Assemble the long slices into a few stacks and then cut in half lengthwise to create the pappardelle, that is, large, wide ribbon shapes. Add the squash to the boiling water, cook for 1 minute, drain in a colander, and run cold water over them to stop the cooking. Transfer the squash ribbons to a clean kitchen towel and pat dry. Set aside.

Return the skillet to the stove and heat the remaining 3 tablespoons of EVOO over medium-high heat. Add the remaining garlic and the red pepper flakes and cook for 1 minute, or until the garlic starts to turn slightly brown. Be careful not to burn the garlic, but if you do, it will only take a minute or two to start over. Add the cooled dry squash pappardelle to the garlic and red pepper flakes and season with salt and pepper. Toss to combine and then add the lemon juice and chicken stock and continue to cook for 2 minutes, frequently and gently tossing but trying not to break up the squash pappardelle. Turn off the heat and add the butter, parsley, grated cheese, and lemon zest. Gently toss to melt the butter.

Thinly slice the flank steak on an angle and against the grain. Serve with the hot squash pappardelle.

tidbit >> Pappardelle is a wide ribbon-shaped pasta, but in this recipe it is the shape of the zucchini and yellow squash.

Shish Kabob Salad

I'm a fan of any food on a stick. This salad brings together two of my favorite things . . . a shish kabob and chopped veggies.   4 SERVINGS

2 pounds **boneless leg of lamb**, cubed

Zest and Juice of 1 lemon

Zest and Juice of 1 orange

2 tablespoons **grill seasoning**, such as McCormick's Montreal Steak Seasoning

4 **garlic** cloves, finely chopped

1 teaspoon **red pepper flakes**

1 tablespoon **ground cumin**

2 teaspoons **sweet paprika**

½ teaspoon **ground allspice**

A handful of fresh **cilantro leaves**, finely chopped

3 tablespoons **extra-virgin olive oil** (EVOO)

1 cup **plain yogurt**

A few drops of **hot sauce**, such as Tabasco

2 teaspoons **ground coriander**

Salt and **freshly ground black pepper**

½ **English (seedless) cucumber**, cut in bite-size pieces

2 vine-ripe **tomatoes**, seeded and chopped

1 **green bell pepper**, cored, seeded, and diced into bite-size pieces

½ **red onion**, chopped

2 tablespoons chopped **fresh dill** or cilantro, for garnish

Preheat an outdoor grill or a grill pan to medium-high heat.

Thread the meat cubes onto metal skewers. In a shallow dish that will hold the skewers, combine the lemon zest and juice, orange zest and juice, grill seasoning, garlic, red pepper flakes, cumin, paprika, allspice, cilantro, and EVOO. Slather the marinade all over the kabobs. Let the kabobs hang out for 10 minutes, then grill for 8 to 10 minutes for medium rare, 12 to 15 minutes for medium well. Give them a quarter turn every couple of minutes as they cook.

While the meat is on the grill, prepare the salad. In a medium bowl, combine the yogurt, hot sauce, coriander, and salt and pepper to taste. Add the veggies to the bowl and toss to coat them in the spiced yogurt. Taste to adjust the seasonings.

Slide the meat off the skewers and serve the hot spiced lamb alongside the cool, chunky vegetable salad. Garnish the salad with your choice of chopped dill or some more cilantro.

Involtini all'Enotec'Antica with Gnocchi

I had these mini versions of stuffed cabbage, meatballs in radicchio, in Rome, near the Spanish Steps at Enotec'Antica (Ancient Wine Bar), which is a real haunt of mine when in the city.   4 SERVINGS

1¼ pounds **ground sirloin**

2 handfuls of grated cheese, such as **Parmigiano-Reggiano** or Romano cheese, plus more for sprinkling

A handful of fresh **flat-leaf parsley**, chopped

10 fresh **basil** leaves, shredded or torn

3 **garlic cloves**, chopped

1 **egg**, beaten

A couple of handfuls of **Italian-style bread crumbs**

Salt and **freshly ground black pepper**

1 tablespoon **extra-virgin olive oil** (EVOO), plus more for drizzling

1 tablespoon **unsalted butter**, cut into pieces

3 tablespoons all-purpose **flour**

½ cup **dry red wine**

2 cups **beef stock** or broth

1 cup **tomato sauce**

1 head of **radicchio**, leaves separated

1 pound frozen **gnocchi** (potato dumplings)

Bring a large pot of water to a boil for the gnocchi.

Mix the beef with the cheese, parsley, basil, garlic, egg, bread crumbs, salt, pepper, and a drizzle of EVOO.

Preheat a large, deep skillet over medium heat. Add the tablespoon of EVOO and the butter. When the butter melts, add the flour and cook for 1 minute. Whisk in the wine and stock and bring to a bubble. Add the tomato sauce. Return the sauce to a bubble and reduce the heat to medium low.

Form about 20 large meatballs, slightly oval in shape, and wrap in the radicchio leaves. Set them into the hot sauce in an even layer. Spoon a little of the sauce over the tops. Cover and simmer for 10 to 12 minutes.

Drop the gnocchi into the boiling water and salt the water to season it. Cook until the gnocchi are tender and floating, 5 to 6 minutes or according to the package directions. Drain well.

Arrange 5 wrapped meatballs on each plate. Spoon a touch of sauce over each. Add the gnocchi to the remaining sauce in the skillet. Coat the gnocchi in the remaining sauce and season with a little grated cheese, salt, and pepper, then serve alongside the meatballs in red lettuce wraps.

BLT Soup

Bacon, Leek, and Tomato Soup is so easy and too delicious; you'll make this in the chilly months, year after year. It is especially welcome on rainy nights.   4 SERVINGS

EVOO (extra-virgin olive oil), for drizzling

6 slices lean, smoky good-quality **bacon**, chopped into ½-inch pieces

3 small **celery ribs** from the heart of the stalk, finely chopped

2 small to medium **carrots**

3 **leeks**, rough tops and roots trimmed

1 **bay leaf**

Salt and **black pepper**

3 medium starchy **potatoes**, such as Idaho, peeled

8 cups **chicken stock**

1 14-ounce can **petite-diced tomatoes**, drained

A handful of fresh **flat-leaf parsley**, finely chopped

Crusty bread, for dunking and mopping

Heat a medium soup pot or deep-sided skillet over medium-high heat. To the hot pan add a drizzle of EVOO and the bacon. Cook the bacon until brown and crisp. Remove the bacon to a paper towel–lined plate and reserve. Drain off all but 2 tablespoons of the remaining fat and add the chopped celery. While the celery cooks over medium heat, peel the carrots, then lay them flat on a cutting board. Hold each carrot at the root end and use the vegetable peeler to make long, thin strips. Chop the thin slices into small carrot bits or chips ½-inch wide. Add the chips to the celery and stir. Cut the leeks lengthwise and then into ½-inch half moons. Place the sliced leeks in a colander and run them under cold water, separating the layers to wash away all the trapped grit. When the leeks are clean, shake off the water and add to the celery and carrots. Stir the veggies together, add the bay leaf, and season with salt and pepper. While the leeks cook until wilted, 3 to 4 minutes, slice the potatoes.

Cut each potato into thirds crosswise. Stand each potato third upright and slice it thinly. The pieces will look like raw potato chips.

Add the stock to the vegetables and bring to a boil. Reduce the heat and add the potatoes and tomatoes. Cook for 8 to 10 minutes or until the potatoes are tender and starting to break up a bit. Add the reserved bacon and parsley and stir. Adjust the seasonings. Serve immediately with the crusty bread.

Lemon Roast Pork Tenderloins with Warm Beets, Chicory, and Goat Cheese

If you like goat cheese, you're going to love this dish. The flavors will have you cuddling up in front of the fireplace craving more.

4 SERVINGS

4 tablespoons **extra-virgin olive oil (EVOO)**, divided

1 tablespoon **dry mustard** or 2 tablespoons prepared Dijon mustard

3 **garlic cloves**, chopped

Juice and zest of 2 lemons

2 **pork tenderloins** (2 to 2¼ pounds), trimmed of silver skin and connective tissue

Salt and **freshly ground black pepper**

4 slices **bacon**, chopped

1 small **yellow onion**, thinly sliced

1 tablespoon fresh **thyme leaves**, chopped

1 15-ounce can sliced **beets**, drained of all but about 4 tablespoons juice

1 head **chicory**, washed, dried, and torn into bite-size pieces (see Tidbit)

20 fresh **basil leaves**, chopped

1 handful fresh **flat-leaf parsley**, chopped

½ cup **crumbled goat cheese**

Preheat the oven to 450°F.

In a small bowl combine 2 tablespoons of the EVOO, the mustard, garlic, and half the lemon juice and reserve. Toss the tenderloins in the lemon mixture. Place the tenderloins on a nonstick baking sheet with a rim. Season them with salt and pepper and roast for 25 minutes, then remove and let rest.

While the pork is roasting, preheat a medium-size skillet with the remaining 2 tablespoons of EVOO over medium-high heat. Add the chopped bacon and cook until crisp, about 3 minutes. Add the onion and thyme and cook for 2 to 3 minutes, stirring occasionally. Add the sliced beets and the reserved beet juice, salt, and pepper and cook for 2 more minutes, or until the beets are warmed.

Meanwhile, in a salad bowl combine the chicory, lemon zest, the remaining lemon juice, the basil, and parsley. Transfer the warm beets to the salad bowl and toss to combine and wilt the chicory.

Slice the pork thin on an angle. Serve the sliced pork with the warm beets and chicory alongside. Top the warm vegetables with goat cheese crumbles.

tidbit >> Chicory is great raw or cooked. It has a big flavor that trumps regular lettuce any day.

Saucy Buttered, Smothered Steaks with Spinach Gratin

Cancel your reservation at the steakhouse and try this tasty recipe.

4 SERVINGS

4 tablespoons **extra-virgin olive oil** (EVOO)

1 large **Spanish onion**, finely chopped

3 **garlic cloves**, chopped

¼ teaspoon **grated or ground nutmeg**

Salt and **freshly ground black pepper**

2 10-ounce boxes **frozen chopped spinach**, defrosted, squeezed dry of excess liquid

¾ cup **chicken stock** or broth

4 ounces **cream cheese**

1 cup (4 to 6 ounces) shredded **Swiss cheese**

2 tablespoons **plain bread crumbs** (optional)

3 tablespoons **Worcestershire sauce**

1 tablespoon **hot sauce**, such as Tabasco

8 ounces (1 stick) **unsalted butter**, softened

4 10-ounce **sirloin strip steaks**, 1 inch thick

Preheat the oven to 450°F.

For the spinach gratin, heat a medium skillet with 2 tablespoons of the EVOO over medium-high heat. Add the onion, garlic, nutmeg, salt, and pepper and cook for 2 minutes. Remove and reserve in a small mixing bowl 3 tablespoons of the cooked onion mixture to use in your saucy butter. To the remaining onion in the skillet, add the squeezed spinach, stirring to distribute the onion in the spinach. Next, add the chicken stock and continue to cook for 2 minutes. Add the cream cheese, stirring to distribute. Transfer the mixture to a small baking dish. Mix the shredded Swiss cheese with the plain bread crumbs. Top the spinach with the Swiss cheese mixture and transfer to the oven for 10 to 12 minutes, or until the top is golden brown.

For the saucy butter, add the Worcestershire sauce, hot sauce, salt, and pepper to the reserved onion mixture. Mix to combine, then add the soft butter. Mix to combine again and reserve in the refrigerator.

For the steaks, heat a large skillet over medium-high heat with the remaining 2 tablespoons of EVOO. Liberally season both sides of the steaks with salt and pepper. Add the steaks to the pan and cook for 5 to 6 minutes on each side. Remove from heat to a platter and top each steak with a rounded tablespoon of saucy butter. Allow the meat to rest and the butter to melt for 3 to 5 minutes. Serve steaks with the spinach gratin.

tidbit >> Leftover butter can be frozen, well wrapped, for up to 6 months.

Beans and Greens Soup
with Pancetta

Pancetta gives the soup its deep flavor. It is rolled cured pork that is similar to bacon, but not smoked. It is widely available at the deli counter in larger supermarkets or small Italian import shops.   4 SERVINGS

---

1 loaf **Italian semolina bread**

3 tablespoons **extra-virgin olive oil** (EVOO)

¼ pound **pancetta**, available at the deli, sliced the thickness of bacon, chopped

4 to 5 **garlic cloves**, chopped

½ teaspoon **red pepper flakes**

1 medium **white** or **yellow onion**, chopped

2 large heads of **escarole**, washed, dried, and coarsely chopped

½ teaspoon **freshly grated** or **ground nutmeg**

Salt and **freshly ground black pepper**

1 quart **chicken stock** or broth

2 15-ounce cans **white beans** or cannellini

Grated **Parmigiano-Reggiano** or Romano cheese, to pass at the table

Preheat the oven to 200°F.

Place the bread in the oven to heat and crust it up.

Heat a medium soup pot or a large, deep-sided skillet over medium-high heat. Add the EVOO, then add the pancetta, separating the pieces as you drop it in.

Brown the pancetta lightly, about 2 minutes or so, then add the garlic, red pepper flakes, and onions, and reduce the heat a bit. Cook for 3 to 4 minutes, then start turning and wilting piles of the greens into the pan. Once the greens are all in the pan, season them with nutmeg, salt, and pepper. Add the chicken stock and beans and turn the heat back up to medium high to bring the soup to a boil. Once the soup boils, reduce the heat back down to simmer and cook for 10 minutes. Adjust the salt and pepper and serve the soup in shallow bowls with lots of cheese and crusty hunks of bread for mopping up the bowl.

ai-Style Grilled Beef in Broth with a Lot o' Noodles

Thai-style food made with ingredients available in any grocery store. If you're not into beef, try it with pork or chicken, instead.   4 SERVINGS

Salt

½ pound **thin pasta**

3-inch piece of **fresh ginger**, peeled and grated

2 tablespoons **Worcestershire sauce**

4 tablespoons **vegetable oil**

2 teaspoons **hot sauce**

4 ½-inch-thick **shell steaks**

1 teaspoon **ground coriander**, ⅓ palmful

½ teaspoon **ground cumin**

1 large **onion**, thinly sliced

4 **garlic cloves**, finely chopped

1 medium **carrot**, peeled and grated

2 **celery ribs**, thinly sliced

1 **jalapeño or serrano pepper**, seeded and finely chopped

12 **shiitake mushrooms**, stems removed and discarded, caps thinly sliced

Black pepper

5 cups **chicken stock**

¼ cup fresh **cilantro leaves**, chopped, a generous handful

¾ cup fresh **basil**, chopped, about 15 leaves

Juice of 1 lime

Preheat an outdoor grill or grill pan over high heat.

Bring a large pot of water with a tight-fitting lid to a boil over high heat to cook the pasta. Once it comes to a boil, add some salt and the pasta. Cook the pasta according to the package directions until it is al dente, drain, and run it under cold water to rinse off some of the starch. Let the noodles sit in the colander for a few minutes to dry off.

While the water is coming up to a boil, in a shallow dish combine half of the ginger, the Worcestershire sauce, 2 tablespoons of the vegetable oil, and the hot sauce. Add the shell steaks and let them marinate while you get everything else working.

Preheat a soup pot over medium-high heat with the remaining 2 tablespoons of vegetable oil, twice around the pan. Add the coriander and cumin and toast them for about 30 seconds, stirring constantly. Add the onions, garlic, carrots, celery, the remaining ginger, the jalapeño or serrano pepper, shiitake mushrooms, salt, and a little pepper; cook, stirring every now and then, for 3 to 4 minutes. Add the chicken stock and bring it up to a bubble; reduce the heat and then let it simmer for 10 to 15 minutes.

While the broth is cooking away, get the steaks cooking. Season the steaks with a little salt, transfer them to the hot grill, and cook on each side for about 2 minutes. Remove them from the grill and let them rest for a few minutes. Thinly slice the steaks on a sharp angle (this is always easier to do when you are using a sharp knife). Cut the thin slices in half.

Once the broth is simmering, add the cooked drained

noodles, the cilantro, and basil. Reheat the noodles, 1 minute. Add the lime juice to the pot and then taste for seasoning; add salt and pepper accordingly. To serve, use kitchen tongs to transfer 4 servings of the noodles and veggies to soup bowls. Top each noodle pile with some of the grilled sliced steak, then ladle some of the broth over the top.

Quick Cassoulet Stuffed Bread Melts

This will warm you right up on a cold evening.   4 SERVINGS

---

1 **baguette** (day-old is fine)

½ pound **sausage** (choose from andouille, chorizo, Italian bulk hot or sweet, kielbasa)

2 tablespoons **extra-virgin olive oil** (EVOO)

1 **carrot**, chopped

1 small **yellow onion**, chopped

2 large **garlic cloves**, chopped

1 **bay leaf**

1 teaspoon **dried thyme** or 1 tablespoon fresh thyme leaves (a couple of sprigs)

1 can small **white beans** or cannellini, rinsed and drained

Salt and **freshly ground black pepper**

½ cup **white wine** or chicken stock

4 slices deli **Swiss cheese** or thinly sliced Cheddar, Fontina, Gouda, or Gruyère

A handful of chopped fresh **flat-leaf parsley**

Preheat the oven to 200°F.

Crisp the bread in the low oven, remove, and split lengthwise. Hollow it out and cut each half in half again across, making 4 bread boats. Switch the broiler on and place a rack 8 inches or so from the heat.

If you are using cooked sausage, finely chop it. For raw Italian, cut open a couple of links. Heat a large non-stick skillet over medium-high heat. Add the EVOO and the sausage; brown cooked sausage for 2 minutes, and brown and break up raw sausage into small bits, 5 minutes. Add the carrots, onions, garlic, bay leaf, and thyme and cook for 5 minutes more. Add the beans and stir to combine. Season the quick cassoulet with salt and pepper. Deglaze the pan with the wine or stock, scraping up the good bits. Reduce the heat to low and simmer over very low heat for 2 to 3 minutes to combine the flavors. If the mixture sticks at all, add a bit more wine or stock, but do not make the mixture wet. It should be starchy and thick.

Fill the bread boats with the cassoulet. Top with cheese, folding the slices to fit. Melt the cheese under the broiler and garnish each open-face stuffed sandwich with a little parsley. Serve with a fork and knife.

London Broil with Cauliflower and Red Chard with Ham

This hearty, well-rounded meal will satisfy all your taste buds. I'm sure you'll go back for seconds.   4 SERVINGS

---

1 large head **cauliflower**, cut into florets

1 cup **chicken stock** or broth

4 tablespoons **butter**, cut into pieces

1 cup shredded **white extra-sharp Vermont Cheddar cheese**, such as Cabot brand

¼ cup grated **Parmigiano-Reggiano** (a couple of handfuls)

Salt and **coarse black pepper**

A generous grating of **nutmeg**

1½ pounds **shoulder steak**, 1½ inches thick, for London broil

1 tablespoon **Worcestershire sauce**

2 tablespoons **vegetable oil** or olive oil

½ pound **ham**, chopped

6 cups chopped **red chard** (1 large bunch)

3 tablespoons **red wine vinegar**

1 tablespoon **honey**

1 **shallot**, finely chopped

2 tablespoons **flour**

2 cups **beef stock** or broth

¼ cup **steak sauce**, such as A1 or Lea and Perrins brands

Place the cauliflower in a medium shallow pot or pan. Add the beef stock, cover, and place the pot over high heat. When the liquid boils, reduce the heat to medium low and simmer, covered, for 8 minutes. Start the steak (see below) while the cauliflower cooks. After 8 minutes, remove the cover, raise the heat to medium high, and allow the broth and vegetable juices to reduce by half, 1 to 2 minutes. Add 2 tablespoons of the butter and the cheeses and smash the cauliflower with a masher to the same consistency as desired for mashed potatoes. Season the cauliflower with salt, pepper, and nutmeg to taste.

Turn the broiler on. Brush the meat with Worcestershire and season with salt and pepper. Broil the steak on the top rack for 6 minutes on each side, for medium-rare to medium doneness.

While the steak and cauliflower cook, heat a second large skillet over medium-high heat. Add the oil and the ham. Sear the ham and caramelize at the edges, 2 minutes.

Add the chard and wilt the greens into the pan, then season with salt, pepper, and a dash of nutmeg, if you like. Cook 5 to 7 minutes more, turning frequently with tongs, then add the vinegar to the pan and a drizzle of honey. Turn to coat the greens, adjust seasoning, and transfer to a serving dish.

Remove the meat from the broiler and let it rest 5 minutes under a foil tent.

Place a small skillet over medium heat. Melt the remaining 2 tablespoons of butter, add the shallot, and cook for 2 minutes, then whisk in the flour and cook for 1 minute. Add the beef stock to the pan and bring to a bubble. Reduce the stock for 2 minutes, then add the steak sauce and black pepper, to taste.

Very thinly slice the meat on an angle against the grain (the lines in the meat). The degree of thinness will determine how tender it is to cut and chew, so make sure the carving knife is sharp—the thinner the better!

Serve the sliced steak with the steak sauce gravy all over it and the smashed cauliflower and red chard with ham piled up alongside the meat.

tidbit >> London broil is a method of cooking, not a cut. You'll find both shoulder steak and top round packaged as "London Broil" and either works, but I prefer the shoulder cut. Bottom line: Both are cheap and very tasty if you cut them right.

Croque Monsieur with Greens

Ah, April in Paris! Word of advice: Pack a parka! I have been in France twice in April, once to Paris, once to Bordeaux. Twice I froze. Oh, well. The hot ham and cheese tastes better then.   4 SERVINGS

4 tablespoons softened **unsalted butter**

2 tablespoons all-purpose **flour**

1 cup **half-and-half** or whole milk

2 teaspoons **Dijon mustard**

⅛ teaspoon **freshly grated** or **ground nutmeg**

Salt and **freshly ground black pepper**

8 slices **sandwich bread**

¾ pound **baked ham**, thinly sliced

2 cups shredded **Gruyère cheese** (½ pound)

2 tablespoons **white wine vinegar**

1 teaspoon **apricot jam** or orange marmalade

2 tablespoons fresh **tarragon** leaves, chopped (from 2 stems)

3 tablespoons **extra-virgin olive oil** (EVOO)

6 cups **mixed baby greens**, any variety

Heat a heavy nonstick pan or a griddle over medium-low to medium heat.

Heat a small sauce pot over medium heat. Add 2 tablespoons of the butter and melt. Whisk the flour into the butter and cook for 1 minute, then whisk in the half-and-half. Season with 1 teaspoon of the Dijon mustard, the nutmeg, salt, and pepper and cook for 2 minutes to thicken. Remove from the heat. Spread the bread slices with the sauce and make sandwiches, using a couple of folded slices of ham per sandwich.

Spread the remaining 2 tablespoons of softened butter lightly across the outside faces of each sandwich. Spread the shredded cheese across a plate and gently press each side of the sandwiches into the cheese, then place on the hot pan or griddle. The cheese will brown and form a crisp coating as the sandwich cooks and heats through. Cook for 3 minutes on each side, or until evenly golden.

In a salad bowl, whisk together the remaining tea-spoon of mustard, the vinegar, apricot jam, and tarragon. Whisk in the EVOO in a slow stream. Add the greens to the bowl and toss to dress. Season the salad with salt and pepper and serve on large plates with the hot sandwiches alongside.

Beef Stroganoff Over Buttered Parsley-Cauliflower "Noodles"

If you are looking to save a few bucks and a little time, you can buy 2 pounds of pepper steak strips and cut that into bite-size pieces. The beef won't be quite as tender but the flavor will be great.   4 SERVINGS

4 tablespoons **vegetable oil**

2 pounds **beef tenderloin**

Salt and **freshly ground black pepper**

5 tablespoons **butter**

1 small **onion**, sliced

2 tablespoons **all-purpose flour**

2 cans (about 3 cups total) **beef consommé**

2 tablespoons **Dijon mustard**

1 small head **cauliflower**

½ cup **chicken stock** or broth

¾ cup chopped fresh **flat-leaf parsley**, divided

1 cup **sour cream**

6 **cornichons** or baby gherkins, chopped (optional)

Fill a large skillet with 1 inch of water. Place the skillet over high heat and bring to a boil for the cauliflower "noodles."

Preheat a large skillet with 2 tablespoons of the vegetable oil (twice around the pan) over high heat. You will be searing the meat in this pan, so you want it to be screaming hot.

Thinly slice the meat and cut into 2-inch-long very thin strips. Season the meat with salt and pepper and add to the hot oil, spreading the meat out in an even layer. Sear the meat, caramelizing it, for about 2 minutes without touching it, then toss and continue to cook for another 2 minutes.

Remove the meat from the pan and reserve on a plate. Reduce the heat on the burner to medium low. Cool the pan for a minute, then add 2 tablespoons of the butter to the skillet, melt, and add half of the sliced onion. Cook for 2 to 3 minutes, then add the flour, stirring to distribute. Cook the flour for 30 seconds. Whisk in the beef consommé and the Dijon mustard and turn the heat down to low, gently simmering for 10 minutes.

While the stroganoff sauce is cooking, prepare the cauliflower "noodles": With a paring knife, remove the stem of the cauliflower, trying to keep the head intact. With the cut side down on the cutting board, slice the cauliflower into ¼-inch-thick slices. Stack those slices and cut them in half, lengthwise. Add some salt and the cauliflower

recipe continued

"noodles" to the skillet with the boiling water. Cook for 2 minutes. Drain the cauliflower in a colander. Return the pan to the heat and add the remaining 2 tablespoons of vegetable oil, the remaining onion, salt, and pepper; cook for 1 minute.

Add the cauliflower and chicken stock to the onion, stir to coat, and cook for 3 minutes, or until the cauliflower is tender. Turn the heat off and add the remaining 3 tablespoons of butter and ½ cup of the chopped parsley. Toss to coat and reserve while you finish off the stroganoff.

Add the meat back to the pan with the stroganoff sauce. Add the sour cream, stirring to combine. Turn the heat back up to medium high and simmer for 2 to 3 minutes, to finish cooking the meat. Taste the dish, checking for seasoning, and arrange the beef stroganoff on a bed of the cauliflower "noodles." Garnish with the remaining ¼ cup chopped parsley and the chopped cornichons.

tidbit >> For easy slicing of raw meat, pop it into the freezer for 10 to 15 minutes before starting to prepare the meal. This firms up the meat and you'll find that it will be easier to control the thickness of the slices.

Chili-Rubbed Roast Pork Tenderloins with Crunchy, Chunky Black Bean and Jicama Salad

Jicama tastes both sweet and nutty, and the thing I love about it is that it is really crispy. I love it in all kinds of salads.   4 SERVINGS

2 **pork tenderloins** (2 to 2¼ pounds), trimmed of silver skin and connective tissue

2 tablespoons **chili powder**

1 tablespoon **ground cumin**

Salt and **freshly ground black pepper**

4 tablespoons **extra-virgin olive oil** (EVOO), plus more for drizzling

Juice of 2 limes

1 tablespoon **Dijon mustard**

1 1-pound **jicama**

1 ripe **Hass avocado**

1 small **red onion**, thinly sliced

1 **English (seedless) cucumber** (the one wrapped in plastic), cut into ¼-inch-thick disks

1 15-ounce can **black beans**, drained and thoroughly rinsed

A handful of fresh **cilantro**, chopped

A handful of fresh **flat-leaf parsley**, chopped

Preheat the oven to 450°F.

Place the tenderloins on a nonstick baking sheet with a rim. Combine the chili powder and cumin in a small bowl. Rub the seasoning mixture into the tenderloins, coating them completely. Season with some salt and pepper and then drizzle the tenderloins with of EVOO, just enough to coat. Roast for 25 minutes. Allow the meat to rest. While the pork is roasting, prepare the black bean and jicama salad.

In a small bowl combine the lime juice, mustard, salt, and pepper. Whisk in about 4 tablespoons of EVOO. With a paring knife, peel the light brown skin from the jicama. Slice it into ¼-inch-thick disks, stack the disks up, then cut into ¼-inch-wide strips and reserve. Cut all around the circumference of the ripe avocado, lengthwise and down to the pit. Twist and separate the halved fruit. Remove the pit with a spoon, then scoop the flesh out in one piece from both halves. Chop the avocado into bite-size pieces. In a salad bowl combine the jicama, avocado chunks, red onion, cucumber, black beans, cilantro, and parsley. Pour the dressing over the salad and toss to combine.

Slice the pork on an angle into ½-inch-thick slices. Serve the sliced pork with the salad piled on top.

10

Date Night/ Fake Outs

Dim the lights, get the music just right, and dish up a meal for you and your honey. And don't forget dessert! (These recipes are so good that you might even want to share them with company.)

SURF 'N' TURF

Olive and Anchovy–Slathered Beef Tenderloin Steaks

Grilled Surf 'n' Turf: Sirloin Burgers a with Grilled Shrimp

East Coast Surf 'n' Turf: Rocket-Style Clams Casino and New York
*   Strip Steaks with Roquefort-Watercress Salad*

Big Mussels with Chorizo and Saffron Rice

Shrimp Martinis and Manhattan Steaks

Thai Shrimp and Pork Balls Over Coconut Curried Noodles

Mashed Plantains with Oh, Baby! Garlic-Tomato Shrimp on Grilled
*   Flank Steak, and Quick Rice with Black Beans*

Surf 'n' Turf Salad

Sexy Surf 'n' Turf: Seared Scallops and Tenderloin Steaks

Chili-Rubbed Flank Steak with Shrimp and Guacamole

JOHN'S FAVES

Balsamic-Glazed Pork Chops with Arugula-Basil Rice Pilaf

Venetian Calamari with Spicy Sauce and Egg Fettuccine

Rosemary-Lemon Broiled Lamb Chops with Gremolata and White
*   Beans, Prosciutto, and Greens*

Sweet and Savory Stuffed Veal Rolls with a Mustard Pan Sauce

Veal Saltimbocca with Spinach Polenta

Black Pepper and Coriander–Crusted Tuna with Potato Salad

Hazelnut-Crusted Chicken with Gorgonzola Sauce

Chicken Marvalasala and Pappardelle with Rosemary Gravy

T-Bone Steaks with Arugula and Tomatoes

Pepper-Crusted Tenderloins with Mushroom Marsala Cream

CHEAP DATES

Pasta with a Lot of Mussel

Honey-Orange–Glazed Ham Steaks with Spicy Black Bean,
*   Zucchini, and Corn Salad*

Spicy Shrimp and Penne with Puttanesca Sauce

Ham and Swiss Crepes with Chopped Salad

Prosciutto and Spinach Bucatini

Poached Eggs on Potato, Spinach, and Smoked Salmon Salad

Chicken with Sweet Raisins and Apricots on Couscous

Sea Bass with Puttanesca and Potatoes

Broiled Haddock with Bacon-Fried Greens

Pasta with Swiss Chard, Bacon, and Lemony Ricotta Cheese

Olive and Anchovy–Slathered Beef Tenderloin Steaks

Calling all salty flavor fans . . . this one's for you.   4 SERVINGS

Coarse salt

½ pound **orzo** pasta

2 tablespoons **extra-virgin olive oil** (EVOO), plus some for drizzling

2 medium to large **yellow onions**, chopped

3 **garlic cloves**, chopped

Salt and **coarse black pepper**

¼ cup **white vermouth** or ½ cup dry white wine

4 tablespoons **unsalted butter**, softened

3 tablespoons store-bought **green** or **black olive tapenade**, any brand

2 rounded tablespoons **anchovy paste** from a tube

8 1-inch-thick **beef tenderloin steaks**

¼ cup fresh **flat-leaf parsley** (a generous handful), chopped

½ cup grated **Parmigiano-Reggiano** (a couple of overflowing handfuls)

2 **beefsteak tomatoes**, sliced and seasoned with salt

Bring a large pot of water to a boil for the orzo. Add a generous amount of salt to the water and cook the orzo al dente, with a bite to it.

Preheat the broiler to high.

Preheat a large skillet over medium-high heat with the 2 tablespoons of EVOO. Add the onions, garlic, salt, and pepper. Cook, stirring occasionally, for about 15 minutes, or until the onions are caramelized. Deglaze the pan with the vermouth or wine.

Combine the soft butter with the olive tapenade and anchovy paste and reserve in the refrigerator.

Arrange the steaks on a slotted broiler pan. Drizzle EVOO over the steaks and season with salt and pepper. Broil the steaks for 3 minutes on each side for medium rare, 5 minutes for well done.

Add the cooked drained orzo to the browned onions, then stir in the parsley and grated cheese. Toss to distribute.

Remove the steaks from the broiler and the butter from the refrigerator. Top each steak with a little olive-anchovy butter. Adjust the salt and pepper, then serve the steaks with the caramelized onion, orzo, and sliced tomatoes alongside.

Grilled Surf 'n' Turf: Sirloin Burgers with Grilled Shrimp

This burger is fancy enough to entertain with and much more affordable than steaks and lobster for your crew!   4 SERVINGS

1½ pounds **ground sirloin**

1 large **shallot**, finely chopped

2 tablespoons fresh **thyme leaves**, chopped

1 tablespoon **Worcestershire sauce**

1 teaspoon **smoked Hungarian paprika** or 2 teaspoons ground cumin

2 teaspoons **grill seasoning**

Extra-virgin olive oil (EVOO), for drizzling

8 raw jumbo **shrimp**, peeled and deveined

1 tablespoon chopped fresh **flat-leaf parsley**

1 **lemon**, zested and then cut into wedges

2 **garlic cloves**, finely chopped

½ head **iceberg lettuce**, cored and quartered

2 rounded tablespoons **prepared horseradish**

1 cup bottled **chili sauce**

4 slices of toasted **bread**

Preheat a grill pan or outdoor grill to high.

In a large bowl combine the beef, shallot, thyme, Worcestershire, smoked paprika or cumin, and grill seasoning. Divide the meat into 4 portions and form large patties about 1¼ inches thick. Coat the beef patties with a drizzle of EVOO. Cook for 3 to 4 minutes on each side for medium rare, 6 minutes per side for medium-well to well done.

Cut the shrimp along the deveining line and "butterfly" them open a little. Be careful not to cut all the way through the shrimp and to leave the tails intact. Place the shrimp in a shallow dish and coat in EVOO. Sprinkle with the grill seasoning or salt and pepper. Add the parsley, lemon zest, and garlic and turn the shrimp to coat evenly in flavorings. Grill the shrimp alongside the meat patties for 2 to 3 minutes on each side, until heads curl toward tails and the shrimp are pink.

While the meat and shrimp cook, arrange 4 beds of cut iceberg lettuce on a platter and combine the horseradish with the chili sauce in a small bowl. To serve, place the burgers on toast with lettuce "buns" as tops and dot with sauce, then top with 2 grilled shrimp. Pass the remaining sauce and the lemon wedges at the table.

East Coast Surf 'n' Turf: Rocket-Style Clams Casino and New York Strip Steaks with Roquefort-Watercress Salad

This uber-fancy combo will surely impress! **4 SERVINGS**

4 tablespoons **extra-virgin olive oil** (EVOO)

4 12-ounce **New York strip steaks**, 1 inch thick

Salt and **freshly ground black pepper**

Rock salt or pickling salt (available on spice aisle in boxes)

24 **cherrystone clams** (buy them scrubbed, split them, and loosen clam)

8 ounces (1 stick) **butter**, softened

2 **garlic cloves**, finely chopped

½ bunch **arugula** (AKA rocket lettuce), washed and finely chopped by hand or in the food processor

Several drops of **hot sauce** (2 teaspoons)

4 slices center-cut **bacon** (lean and thin), cut into 24 1-inch pieces

3 ounces **Roquefort cheese**, crumbled

¼ small **red onion**, thinly sliced

3 tablespoons **white wine vinegar**

2 bunches **watercress**, trimmed of thick stems and torn into bite-size pieces

Preheat the oven to 500°F.

For the steaks, heat a large nonstick skillet over high heat or use 2 pans if necessary. Add 1 tablespoon of the EVOO to the pan. Season the steaks with salt and pepper. Place the steaks in the skillet and sear for 2 minutes on each side. Reduce heat to medium and cook the steaks 6 minutes longer for medium rare, 8 for medium to medium well. Remove the steaks to a warm plate to rest for 5 minutes. While the steaks are cooking, start the clams.

Pour rock salt into a shallow baking pan or dish. Set the clams upright into the salt. The salt will steady them. Mix the butter with the garlic, arugula, and hot sauce. Dab each clam with 1 teaspoon of the mixture and top with a piece of bacon. Bake for 7 to 8 minutes, until the bacon is crisp and the butter is brown and bubbling. Once the clams are cooking away in the oven, start the salad for the steaks.

In a bowl, combine the Roquefort, red onion, white wine vinegar, the remaining 3 tablespoons of EVOO, and salt and pepper. With a fork, mash up the cheese slightly, then give the mixture a little whisking. Add the watercress and toss to coat.

Have the rocket clams casino as an appetizer or serve alongside the New York strip steaks and the Roquefort-watercress salad.

Big Mussels with Chorizo and Saffron Rice

This meal is a lazy-man's version of paella.   4 SERVINGS

---

2 cups **chicken stock** or broth

1 cup **seafood stock** or clam juice (available at the seafood counter or near the canned tuna)

¼ teaspoon **saffron threads**

2 tablespoons **extra-virgin olive oil** (EVOO), plus more for drizzling

1½ cups **short-grain white rice**

½ pound **chorizo** sausage, diced

3 **garlic cloves**, chopped

1 medium **onion**, chopped

1 **red bell pepper**, cored, seeded, and chopped

2 **celery ribs** with greens, chopped

1 **bay leaf**, fresh or dried

Salt and **freshly ground black pepper**

½ cup **dry white wine**

1 14-ounce can **diced tomatoes**

2 pounds cleaned **mussels** (Pull off the hairy "beards" with your fingers.)

½ cup fresh **flat-leaf parsley** (a couple of generous handfuls)

1 cup **frozen green peas**, defrosted

Crusty bread

In a medium saucepan, heat the combination of stocks and saffron to a boil, then add a generous drizzle of EVOO and the rice. Cover and cook until tender, stirring occasionally, about 17 minutes.

Heat a deep skillet over medium-high heat. Add the 2 tablespoons of the EVOO and the chorizo and cook for 2 minutes to render some of the chorizo's fat, then add the garlic, onions, bell peppers, celery, and bay leaf and season with salt and pepper. Cook the vegetables for 7 to 8 minutes, then add the wine and reduce for 1 minute. Add the tomatoes and stir. Add the mussels to the pan in an even layer, then cover the pan tightly. Cook for 3 to 4 minutes to open the mussels. Remove the lid and discard any unopened mussels. Also discard the bay leaf. Combine the parsley in the pan with a serious shake.

To serve, add the peas to the cooked rice and toss to combine. Arrange the cooked rice in shallow bowls or on a large, deep platter. Top with the mussels and sauce. Pass crusty bread for mopping.

tidbit >> Saffron powder is sometimes available in small, affordable envelopes near the fish counter. Saffron threads are more expensive, but a tin will last a long time—just remember to keep it in a cool place away from the heat of the stove!

Shrimp Martinis and Manhattan Steaks

I usually make the shrimp martinis while the steaks cook, but if you prefer you can make the shrimp first and let them chill in the fridge.

4 SERVINGS

Zest of 1 lemon plus 1 tablespoon lemon juice

1 celery rib, very finely chopped

Several drops of hot sauce, to taste

2 cups prepared cocktail sauce

¾ cup good-quality, well-chilled vodka

Salt and coarse black pepper

4 1- to 1¼-inch-thick New York strip steaks or porterhouse steaks, each 10 to 12 ounces

2 tablespoons extra-virgin olive oil (EVOO)

3 tablespoons grill seasoning, such as McCormick's Montreal Steak Seasoning

1 head of broccoli, cut in spears

2 tablespoons unsalted butter

1 large shallot, chopped

1 shot sweet vermouth (1½ ounces)

3 shots rye whiskey (4½ ounces)

4 slices white bread, toasted and cut into points

2 tablespoons finely chopped fresh flat-leaf parsley

20 cooked jumbo shrimp, cleaned and deveined

In a small pitcher, combine the lemon zest, celery, hot sauce, cocktail sauce, and vodka and season with salt and coarse black pepper. Place the sauce in the refrigerator to chill.

Drizzle the steaks with EVOO on both sides and coat them evenly with the grill seasoning. Heat a large nonstick skillet or heavy cast-iron skillet over high heat. Cook the meat for 5 minutes on each side for medium rare, 7 minutes per side for medium well, and remove to a platter to allow the meat to rest and the juices to redistribute. Loosely tent the steaks with foil to keep in some heat.

Bring 1 inch of water to a boil in a saucepan. Season the boiling water liberally with salt. Add the spears and simmer the broccoli for 5 minutes, until just fork-tender but still bright green.

Return the skillet to the stove and reduce the heat to medium. Add 1 tablespoon of the EVOO (once around the pan), plus 1 tablespoon of the butter and melt together. Add the shallots and cook for 2 minutes. Add the vermouth and whiskey and ignite to burn off the alcohol (don't you look impressive doing this!). Once the flame dies, turn off the heat, add the remaining tablespoon of butter, and gloss up the reduction of, essentially, a Manhattan cocktail and

recipe continued

the steaks' pan drippings. Place the toast points on dinner plates. Serve the steaks on the toast points and spoon the pan sauce over the meat. Garnish with parsley, and place broccoli spears alongside the steaks.

Chill 4 martini glasses by filling them with ice. Rinse the shrimp in cold water and pat dry. Squeeze the lemon juice over them and season with a bit of salt. Pour out the ice in the glasses and hook the shrimp, 5 per glass, over the edge of the martini glasses, tails hanging on the outside of the rim. Go get the chilled sauce, fill the glasses to the rim. Serve with the steaks for a very unusual surf 'n' turf!

Thai Shrimp and Pork Balls Over Coconut Curried Noodles

This dish is so good that if you ever share it with friends they'll each be calling you the next week for home delivery.   4 SERVINGS

Salt

1 pound of thin **long-cut pasta**

4 **scallions**, trimmed

3-inch piece of **fresh ginger**, peeled and grated

1 **serrano** or **jalapeño pepper**, seeded and finely chopped

4 **garlic cloves**, 2 crushed, 2 chopped

4 tablespoons **tamari** (dark aged soy sauce)

¼ cup fresh **cilantro leaves**

1 cup fresh **basil**, 20 leaves, coarsely chopped or torn

Zest and juice of 1 lime

1 pound medium **shrimp**, shelled and deveined

1 pound **ground pork**

6 tablespoons **vegetable oil**

1 teaspoon **ground coriander**, ⅓ palmful

½ teaspoon **ground cumin**

1 tablespoon **curry powder**, a palmful

1 medium **onion**, thinly sliced

1 small **carrot**, peeled and grated

1 large **red bell pepper**, cored, seeded, and thinly sliced

1 cup **chicken stock**

1 cup canned **unsweetened coconut milk**

Hot sauce (optional)

Place a large pot of water with a tight-fitting lid over high heat and bring it to a boil. Add some salt and the pasta and cook until al dente. Drain the pasta thoroughly and reserve.

While the water is coming up to a boil for the pasta, start the shrimp and pork balls. In the bowl of a food processor, combine the scallions, half of the grated ginger, half of the chopped serrano or jalapeño pepper, the crushed garlic, 3 tablespoons of the tamari, half of the cilantro and basil, and the lime zest. Pulse for 30 seconds, scrape down the bowl, and then process 1 minute, or until finely ground. Add the shrimp and pork and process until the shrimp are ground into small pieces and the mixture is well combined but not so fine that it becomes a paste, about 1 minute.

Preheat a large nonstick skillet with 4 tablespoons of the oil. With wet palms, roll the shrimp-pork mixture into walnut-size balls and add to the hot skillet as you go. Don't move the balls until they are brown on one side, about 2 minutes. Turn the balls and continue to cook, browning on all sides until cooked through, about 3 to 4 minutes.

While the shrimp and pork balls and pasta are cooking, start the coconut curry sauce for the noodles. Preheat a large skillet or soup pot over medium heat with the

recipe continued

remaining 2 tablespoons of oil. Add the coriander, cumin, and curry powder and toast the spices for about 30 seconds in the hot oil. Add the onions, carrot, bell pepper, the remaining ginger and serrano or jalapeño pepper, and the 2 chopped garlic cloves. Add a little more oil to the pan if it starts to look dry. Use a wooden spoon to scrape up any spices that might be sticking to the bottom of the pan. Cook the mixture for about 3 minutes, stirring frequently.

Add the chicken stock, coconut milk, and the remaining tablespoon of tamari and bring it up to a bubble, then gently simmer for 5 minutes. Add the lime juice and taste and adjust for seasoning with either more tamari or a little salt. If you want a bit more spice, hit it with some hot sauce. Add the cooked drained noodles and the remaining cilantro and basil. Toss to combine. Divide the coconut curried noodles among 4 shallow bowls and top with the shrimp and pork balls.

Mashed Plantains with Oh, Baby! Garlic-Tomato Shrimp on Grilled Flank Steak and Quick Rice with Black Beans

Gloria Estefan taught me how to cook plantains in the microwave and her husband, Emilio, gave me ideas for lightening up some Cuban-influenced dishes. The result is this interpretation of Metro-Retro Cuban cooking. This dinner is also delicious made with grilled thin-cut chicken breast, seasoned in the same manner as the steak. Plantains look like green bananas and are available in the produce department.

4 SERVINGS

7 tablespoons **extra-virgin olive oil** (EVOO), plus a little to drizzle

2 medium **yellow onions**, 1 finely chopped, 1 thinly sliced

1 tablespoon plus 2 teaspoons **ground cumin**

3 tablespoons fresh **thyme** (from 5 or 6 sprigs), chopped

3 cups **chicken stock** or broth

1½ cups uncooked **white rice**

1 15-ounce can **black beans**

Coarse salt

2 pounds **flank steak**

2 tablespoons **grill seasoning**, such as McCormick's Montreal Steak Seasoning

1 **lime**, zested, cut into wedges

3 **green plantains**

Wax paper

1 small **green bell pepper**, cored, seeded, and finely chopped

4 **garlic cloves**, finely chopped

1 pound small **shrimp**, peeled, deveined, and coarsely chopped

Coarse black pepper

Zest and juice of 1 lemon

1 8-ounce can **tomato sauce**

3 tablespoons finely chopped fresh **flat-leaf parsley** (a handful of leaves)

Hot sauce, such as Tabasco, to taste

Heat a medium pot over medium heat. Add 1 tablespoon of the EVOO (once around the pan), and half of the finely chopped onions. Sauté for 3 minutes, then season with 2 teaspoons of the cumin and the thyme leaves. Pour in 2½ cups of the chicken stock and raise the heat to bring to a boil. Add the rice and lower the heat to a simmer when a boil resumes. Cover the pot tightly. After 12 minutes, stir

recipe continued

in the black beans and replace the cover. Cook for another 6 to 7 minutes. Turn off the heat, season the rice and beans with salt, and stir to combine, then let stand until ready to serve. While the rice cooks, make the plantains with shrimp and the meat.

Preheat a grill pan over high heat. The meat can also be prepared in a hot large cast-iron or nonstick skillet if you do not have a grill pan.

Place the flank steak in a shallow dish and drizzle with EVOO to coat—about 2 tablespoons. Mix the grill seasoning with the tablespoon of cumin (eyeball the measurement in your palm). Add the lime zest to the grill seasoning and cumin. Rub the mixture over the steak evenly. Place the steak on the hot grill or in the hot pan and cook for 4 to 5 minutes, then turn and cook for 3 minutes longer. Remove from the heat and let the juices redistribute for 5 minutes.

Slit the skins of the plantains from end to end to vent them for microwave cooking. Wrap each in wax paper, twisting the paper at the ends. Microwave the plantains for 4 to 5 minutes together or 90 seconds individually on High.

While the plantains and steak cook, place a medium nonstick skillet on the heat over a high flame. Add 2 tablespoons of the EVOO and the sliced onions. Sear the onions and heat through, but leave a bite to them. Place on a serving platter and cover with foil to keep them warm. Return the pan to the stove and reduce the heat to between medium high and medium. Add 2 tablespoons of the EVOO and the remaining finely chopped onions, the bell peppers, garlic, and shrimp.

Season with salt and pepper and add the lemon zest. Cook until the shrimp are firm and the peppers begin to soften, 4 minutes or so. Add half of the lemon juice, the tomato sauce, and parsley. Turn off the heat. Adjust the seasoning with salt, pepper, and lemon juice.

Peel and mash the steaming hot plantains with the remaining ½ cup chicken stock and a drizzle of EVOO.

Season the plantains with salt and pile on a platter or dinner plates, then top with garlicky shrimp and tomatoes. Very thinly slice the cooked steak on an angle, working against the grain. Squeeze lime juice over the meat and arrange over the reserved cooked sliced onions on the serving platter. Fluff up the rice and black beans a bit, transfer them to a bowl, and pass at the table.

tidbit >> Gloria Estefan's favorite of her albums is one she shares with many great guest artists. It's called *Unwrapped*, and you might want to play it for mood music with this supper. It'll taste even better!

Surf 'n' Turf Salad

I love taking concepts and flavors of traditional dishes and turning them into something completely new. So why not take the dynamic duo of surf and turf and make a delicious salad? Enjoy.   4 SERVINGS

---

2 large **garlic cloves**, minced

1-inch piece of **fresh ginger**, peeled and minced or grated

3 tablespoons **tamari** (dark aged soy sauce)

1 teaspoon **coriander** (⅓ palmful)

2 teaspoons **ground cumin** (½ to ⅔ palmful)

1 teaspoon **turmeric** (⅓ palmful)

½ teaspoon **ground cayenne pepper**

1 tablespoon **grill seasoning**, such as McCormick's Montreal Steak Seasoning

Zest of 1 lemon

2 tablespoons **extra-virgin olive oil** (EVOO), plus some for drizzling

2 pounds **flank steak**

1 bunch **scallions**

16 raw medium **shrimp**, deveined

Salt and **freshly ground black pepper**

1 teaspoon **red pepper flakes**

2 **romaine lettuce** hearts, chopped

4 ounces **baby spinach leaves**

¼ cup fresh **flat-leaf parsley** (a couple of handfuls), chopped

½ **red onion**, chopped

DRESSING

Juice of 1 lemon

2 tablespoons **tomato paste**

2 teaspoons **Worcestershire sauce**

3 tablespoons **extra-virgin olive oil** (EVOO)

Salt and **freshly ground black pepper**

Preheat a tabletop grill, grill pan, or outdoor grill to high.

Combine the first 10 ingredients in a shallow dish. Coat the flank steak in the mixture and set aside for 10 to 15 minutes.

Trim the ends and an inch of the tops off of the scallions. Remove the tails from the deveined shrimp. Drizzle EVOO over both the scallions and the shrimp and season with salt, pepper, and red pepper flakes. Grill the scallions and shrimp for 2 minutes on each side. Then remove and reserve.

Place the meat on the grill pan and cook for 3 to 4 minutes on each side. Remove the meat to a plate, tent with foil, and let the juices settle for 5 minutes.

Combine the greens, parsley, and onion on a large platter or individual plates. Cut the grilled scallions into 1-inch pieces, scatter over the greens, then evenly distribute the grilled shrimp over the greens. In a small bowl mix the lemon juice, tomato paste, and Worcestershire and whisk in the EVOO. Season the dressing with salt and pepper and drizzle it back and forth over the arranged greens and scallions and shrimp. Slice the steak very thin against the grain on an angle and arrange it over the salad.

Sexy Surf 'n' Turf: Seared Scallops and Tenderloin Steaks

We always have sweet vermouth on hand to make Manhattans, but we use it for nothing else—until now! (Who knew you could make such a sexy meal so simply? Hey, there are some things you should never be too tired for, wink-wink, nudge-nudge!)   4 SERVINGS

EVOO (extra-virgin olive oil), for drizzling, plus 1 tablespoon

4 **tenderloin steaks,** 1 inch thick

8 large **diver sea scallops**

Salt and **black pepper**

1 large **shallot,** chopped

2 **garlic cloves,** chopped

½ cup **sweet vermouth**

2 tablespoons **butter**

1 pound thin **asparagus,** tough ends trimmed

Juice of ½ **lemon**

2 tablespoons chopped or snipped **chives,** 10 blades, for garnish

tidbit >> Your scallops may still have the adductor muscle—a thin, tough strip that attaches the animal to its shell—intact. If so, nick it off with your fingers.

Drizzle some EVOO over the steaks to coat them lightly. Get a nonstick skillet screaming hot and add the meat. Cook for 3 minutes on each side for medium rare, 4 for medium to medium well. Transfer the steaks to a platter and pull the pan off the heat to cool for a minute.

Pat the scallops completely dry. Drizzle some EVOO over the scallops and season them with salt and pepper. Get a skillet screaming hot and cook the scallops for 2 to 3 minutes on each side, until they are well caramelized.

Bring 2 inches of water to a boil in a clean medium skillet for the asparagus.

Return the pan you cooked the meat in to the stove over medium heat and add 1 tablespoon of EVOO, once around the pan. Add the shallots and garlic and cook for 2 minutes. Add the sweet vermouth and cook until reduced by half, 30 seconds or so. Add the butter to the pan and swirl to incorporate to finish the sauce.

Add the asparagus to the boiling water. Cook for 2 to 3 minutes, or until just tender and bright green. Remove to a plate and dress the asparagus with the lemon juice, a drizzle of EVOO, and salt and pepper.

Place each tenderloin steak on a plate and drizzle the Manhattan sauce over the top. Arrange 2 scallops on top of each steak and garnish with the chives. Serve the asparagus spears alongside.

Chili-Rubbed Flank Steak with Shrimp and Guacamole Stacks

Mexican food doesn't have to be heavy and unhealthy. This is a delicious thinly sliced steak. It's a reason to throw a fiesta.   4 SERVINGS

1½ tablespoons **grill seasoning**, such as McCormick's Montreal Steak Seasoning, 1½ palmfuls

1 tablespoon **dark Mexican chili powder**, a palmful

Zest of 1 lime

2 to 2¼ pounds **flank steak**

2 tablespoons **butter**

1½ cups **long-grain white rice**

1 small **onion**, chopped

½ **red bell pepper**, chopped

1 **jalapeño pepper**, seeded and chopped

2 **garlic cloves**, chopped

3 cups **chicken stock**

2 tablespoons **tomato paste**

2 teaspoons **hot sauce**

1 pound small to medium **shrimp**, peeled and deveined

2 tablespoons finely chopped **fresh cilantro** or flat-leaf parsley

Salt

Cooking spray or oil to coat the grill or grill pan

2 ripe **beefsteak tomatoes**, sliced

2 **Hass avocados**, halved, scooped from skin, and sliced

Juice of ½ lemon

1 small **red onion**, thinly sliced

½ cup **crumbled queso asadero** (Mexican white mild cheese), goat cheese, queso fresco, or queso blanco

Preheat an outdoor grill or indoor grill pan over high heat. Combine the grill seasoning, chili powder, and lime zest and rub into both sides of the meat. Let the meat stand for 10 minutes while you get the rice going.

Heat a medium sauce pot over medium heat. Add the butter and when it melts add the rice and toast it for a couple of minutes. Add the onions, bell peppers, jalapeños, and garlic and cook for a few minutes to begin to soften the veggies. Add the stock and raise the heat to bring it up to a bubble. Stir in the tomato paste and the hot sauce. Reduce the heat to a simmer, cover the pot, and cook for 13 minutes. Add the shrimp to the pot so they can steam on top of the rice and cook until they are pink and firm, 5 minutes longer. Stir the shrimp and cilantro into the rice and season it with salt.

Oil the grill surface or grill pan and cook the meat for 7 to 8 minutes on the first side and 5 to 6 minutes on the flip side for medium doneness. Let the meat rest, covered loosely with aluminum foil.

Season the sliced tomatoes with salt and dress the

avocados with the lemon juice. Make 4 stacks, alternating the tomatoes with avocado and onion slices.

Slice the steak and serve the slices on a bed of shrimp rice, with the guacamole stacks alongside. Garnish the guacamole stacks with cheese crumbles.

Balsamic-Glazed Pork Chops with Arugula-Basil Rice Pilaf

This is one of John and my favorite date-night meals. The rich balsamic glaze gives the chops such a luxurious taste, and the best part? I don't have to spend all day in the kitchen!   4 SERVINGS

3 tablespoons cold **unsalted butter**

1 6-ounce box **rice pilaf mix**, such as Near East brand

3 tablespoons **extra-virgin olive oil** (EVOO)

4 1-inch-thick **center-cut pork loin chops**

Salt and **freshly ground black pepper**

1 small **onion**, chopped

1 tablespoon fresh **thyme** leaves (from a couple of sprigs), chopped

1 sprig of fresh **rosemary**, chopped

3 **garlic cloves**, chopped

¼ cup **balsamic vinegar**

2 tablespoons **honey**

1 cup **chicken stock** or broth

2 cups trimmed and chopped **arugula** (from 1 bunch)

15 to 20 fresh **basil** leaves, shredded or torn

In a medium pot over high heat, combine 1 tablespoon of the butter and 1¾ cups water. Cover and bring to a simmer. Add the rice and flavor packet to the water. Stir to combine, reduce the heat, and cook for 18 minutes, covered.

While the rice is cooking, heat a large skillet over medium-high heat for the chops. Add 2 tablespoons of the EVOO (twice around the pan). Season the chops with salt and pepper, then add to the hot skillet. Cook the chops for 5 minutes on each side.

Transfer the chops to a platter and cover with foil. Return the pan to the heat and add the remaining tablespoon of EVOO and the onions, thyme, rosemary, and garlic, then sauté for 4 to 5 minutes. Add the balsamic vinegar, honey, and chicken stock. Cook until the liquids have reduced by half.

While the glaze is reducing, finish the rice pilaf. Add the arugula and basil to the cooked rice, stirring with a fork to fluff the rice and combine the greens at the same time.

Once the balsamic glaze has reduced by half, turn off the heat and add the remaining 2 tablespoons of cold butter. Stir and shake the pan until the butter melts. Add the chops to the pan and coat them in the balsamic glaze. Serve the glazed chops alongside the arugula-basil rice pilaf.

Venetian Calamari with Spicy Sauce and Egg Fettuccine

I can make anything spicy for John and he'll like it, but this calamari sure is a winner.   4 SERVINGS

1 pound **calamari**, cut into thin rings

2 tablespoons **extra-virgin olive oil** (EVOO)

4 **garlic cloves**, chopped

1 teaspoon **red pepper flakes**

½ cup **dry white wine**

1 14-ounce can chunky-style **crushed tomatoes**

1 teaspoon **curry powder**

Pinch of **ground cinnamon**

Salt and **freshly ground black pepper**

A handful of chopped fresh **flat-leaf parsley**

¾ pound **egg fettuccine**, cooked al dente

10 fresh **basil** leaves, shredded or torn

Pat the calamari dry. Heat a large skillet over medium-high heat. Add the EVOO and calamari and cook for 3 minutes, turning frequently. Add the garlic and red pepper flakes and cook for 2 minutes more. Add the wine and cook off, 30 seconds. Add the tomatoes, curry, cinnamon, salt, pepper, and parsley. Toss the pasta with the calamari and sauce and turn out onto a large platter. Cover with the basil and serve.

Rosemary-Lemon Broiled Lamb Chops with Gremolata and White Beans, Prosciutto, and Greens

If you say the words rosemary and lamb in the same sentence, I'm sold.

4 SERVINGS

---

4 small sprigs or 1 long stem **fresh rosemary**, needles removed then finely chopped (3 tablespoons)

Zest and juice of 2 lemons

5 tablespoons **extra-virgin olive oil** (EVOO), divided

4 **garlic cloves**, chopped, divided

8 **loin lamb chops**

Salt and **freshly ground black pepper**

¼ cup fresh **flat-leaf parsley** (a handful)

1 teaspoon **red pepper flakes**

1 small **yellow onion**, chopped

1 15-ounce can **cannellini beans**, drained, well rinsed, and shaken dry

1 bunch **arugula**, washed and trimmed of thick stems

¼ pound **sliced prosciutto**, cut into strips

Preheat the broiler to high.

In a shallow dish combine the rosemary, lemon juice, about 3 tablespoons of the EVOO, and one quarter of the chopped garlic. Add the lamb chops and rub the mixture on both sides of all the chops. Season the chops with salt and pepper and arrange the chops on a broiler pan. Place the chops about 6 to 8 inches from the broiler and cook for 5 minutes on each side. Remove the chops from the broiler and let rest for 5 minutes. While the chops are cooking, prepare the gremolata.

Make a pile on your cutting board of the lemon zest, one quarter of the chopped garlic, and parsley leaves. Run your knife through the pile until well combined and finely chopped; reserve.

After you prepare the gremolata, move on to the white beans, prosciutto, and greens. Preheat a large skillet with the remaining 2 tablespoons of EVOO (twice around the pan). Add the remaining chopped garlic, the red pepper flakes, and onion. Cook for 2 minutes, then add the cannellini beans, salt, and pepper. Stir to combine and continue to cook for 3 minutes. Turn the heat off and fold in the arugula and prosciutto.

To serve, divide the cannellini bean mixture among 4 plates, and top that with 2 chops on each portion. Top each chop with a sprinkle of the gremolata.

Sweet and Savory Stuffed Veal Rolls with a Mustard Pan Sauce

This dish is sweet, savory, and even gets a little spice from the mustard; it'll please your whole palate!   4 SERVINGS

½ cup **pine nuts**, toasted

12 large **green olives**, pitted, coarsely chopped

¼ cup **golden raisins**

½ cup fresh **flat-leaf parsley**, chopped

Grated zest of 1 lemon

2 tablespoons grated **Parmigiano-Reggiano**

½ cup shredded **mozzarella cheese**

Salt and **freshly ground black pepper**

1⅓ pounds (8 pieces) **veal shoulder scallopini**

8 slices **prosciutto di Parma**

Toothpicks

2 tablespoons **extra-virgin olive oil** (EVOO)

1 tablespoon **unsalted butter**

2 **garlic cloves**, chopped

1 tablespoon fresh **thyme** leaves, chopped (from 4 sprigs)

1 rounded tablespoon **tomato paste**

½ small **yellow onion**, chopped

1 heaping tablespoon **Dijon mustard**

¾ cup **chicken stock** or broth

To make the filling, in a medium bowl, combine the pine nuts, olives, raisins, parsley, lemon zest, Parmigiano, and mozzarella. Season with a little salt and pepper. Taste and adjust the seasoning; this is your last chance to make sure the filling is up to par.

Lay the 8 pieces of scallopini out on the cutting board without overlapping any of the pieces. Season the meat with a little salt and pepper. Lay 1 slice of prosciutto on top of each scallopini. If necessary, fold the prosciutto so that it fits the veal pieces without an overhang. Place about 1 heaping tablespoon of the filling on the lower half of each slice. Starting at the point closest to you, roll each portion away from you into a cigar shape. Secure each veal roll with a toothpick.

Heat a large nonstick skillet over medium-high heat. Add the EVOO and the butter. Once the butter is no longer foaming, add the 8 veal rolls. Brown on all sides, 2 to 3 minutes. Move the veal rolls over a little, clearing a spot in the skillet to add the garlic, thyme, tomato paste, and onions. Season with salt and pepper and cook for 1 minute. Add the mustard and chicken stock and continue to cook for 4 minutes. Serve the rolls with the sauce poured over them.

Veal Saltimbocca with Spinach Polenta

Saltimbocca means "jump in the mouth" and that's exactly what this dish is going to do for you. 4 SERVINGS

3 cups **chicken stock** or broth

8 **veal cutlets**

Salt and **freshly ground black pepper**

16 fresh **sage** leaves

8 slices **prosciutto di Parma**

2 tablespoons **extra-virgin olive oil** (EVOO)

4 tablespoons **unsalted butter**

1 cup **instant or quick-cooking polenta** (found in Italian foods or specialty foods aisles)

1 10-ounce box frozen **chopped spinach**, defrosted and wrung dry in a clean kitchen towel

½ cup grated **Parmigiano-Reggiano** or Romano cheese (a couple of generous handfuls)

Freshly grated or **ground nutmeg**, to taste

2 **garlic cloves**, chopped

1 **shallot**, thinly sliced

1 tablespoon **all-purpose flour**

½ cup **dry white wine**

3 tablespoons fresh **flat-leaf parsley** leaves, chopped

Heat the chicken stock to a boil in a medium sauce pot.

Heat a large nonstick skillet over medium to medium-high heat and heat a platter in a warm oven. Season the cutlets with salt and pepper and place 2 leaves of sage on each of the cutlets. Wrap each cutlet in prosciutto. Add a tablespoon of the EVOO (once around the pan) and 2 tablespoons of the butter to the pan. Fry the saltimbocca for 3 minutes on each side and transfer to the warm platter. Cover with loose foil to keep warm.

Add the remaining tablespoon of EVOO and the polenta to the simmering chicken stock. Stir to mass the polenta, 2 minutes, and add the spinach, separating it into small bits. Stir in the cheese and season the mixture with salt, pepper, and nutmeg.

Add another tablespoon of butter to the skillet, then add the garlic and shallots. Cook for 2 minutes, add the flour, and cook for a minute more. Whisk in the wine and the remaining tablespoon of butter. Remove from the heat and whisk in the parsley.

Place the spinach polenta on plates and top with 2 pieces of saltimbocca. Spoon a healthy drizzle of sauce over the saltimbocca and serve.

tidbit >> You can also make this with thin chicken cutlets, cooking the saltimbocca a minute or two longer until opaque all the way through.

Black Pepper and Coriander-Crusted Tuna with Potato Salad

Here's a hipster menu for urbanites or just hicks from the sticks like me.   4 SERVINGS

2 pounds red or white **boiling potatoes**, washed

8 tablespoons **EVOO** (extra-virgin olive oil)

1 tablespoon **grill seasoning** such as McCormick's Montreal Steak Seasoning

1 **fennel bulb**, fronds trimmed and chopped, the bulb quartered, core removed and discarded, quarters thinly sliced lengthwise

½ small **red onion**, thinly sliced

10 fresh **basil leaves**, chopped, about ½ cup

¼ cup fresh **flat-leaf parsley**, a generous handful, chopped

Zest and juice of 1 orange

1 tablespoon **Dijon mustard**

Salt and **black pepper**

¼ cup **all-purpose flour**

1 tablespoon **ground coriander**

1 tablespoon **coarse black pepper**

4 1½-inch-thick **tuna steaks**

Preheat the oven to 450°F.

Cut the potatoes into wedges and drop them onto a cookie sheet. Coat the potatoes in 3 tablespoons of the EVOO. Season the spuds with the grill seasoning. Roast the potatoes, turning them once, for 25 minutes, until tender and brown at the edges and a bit crusty.

In a large salad bowl, combine the fennel fronds, thinly sliced fennel, red onion, basil, and parsley. In a small bowl, combine the orange zest and juice with the Dijon mustard and a little salt and pepper. In a slow steady stream, whisk in 3 tablespoons of the EVOO. Pour the dressing over the fennel salad, toss to coat, and reserve.

When the potatoes have about 10 more minutes to roast, start the tuna. In a shallow dish, combine the flour, coriander, and coarsely ground black pepper and a little salt. Pat the tuna steaks dry and then coat them in the flour mixture, pressing it in lightly. Preheat a large non-stick skillet over high heat with the remaining 2 tablespoons of EVOO, twice around the pan. When the pan is very hot, add the steaks. Sear and brown the tuna steaks for 2 minutes, then turn, and immediately reduce the heat to medium. Loosely tent the pan with aluminum foil and cook the steaks 5 minutes for rare, 7 minutes for medium. The steaks should be firm but have a little give, and some pink should remain at the center.

recipe continued

Remove the roasted potatoes from the oven and add them to the dressed fennel salad, tossing to combine. Taste them for seasoning and add a little salt and pepper if you want. Serve the tuna steaks alongside the orange and fennel–roasted potato salad.

Hazelnut-Crusted Chicken with Gorgonzola Sauce

I'll tell ya . . . the kick of the Gorgonzola sauce with the nut-crusted chicken is a heckuva one-two punch. You're gonna love it.   4 SERVINGS

2 tablespoons all-purpose **flour** (hey, there's no bread crumbs, get over the 2 tablespoons!)

1 teaspoon **poultry seasoning**

1 teaspoon **garlic powder**

2 large **egg whites**

1 cup chopped **hazelnuts**

4 6-ounce boneless, **skinless chicken breasts**

Salt and **freshly ground black pepper**

2 tablespoons **extra-virgin olive oil (EVOO)**

1 cup **whole milk**

½ cup **Gorgonzola cheese**

2 tablespoons chopped **fresh sage** or 1 teaspoon dried sage, for garnish

Preheat the oven to 325°F.

Mix the flour, poultry seasoning, and garlic powder on a dish. Beat the egg whites in a shallow plate or bowl. Place the hazelnuts on a piece of wax paper or plastic wrap spread on a cutting board or work surface.

Preheat a nonstick skillet with an oven-safe handle over medium to medium-high heat. Season the chicken with salt and pepper. Turn in flour to dust the breasts, then turn them in the egg whites, then press the breasts into the nuts on both sides. Wash hands. Add EVOO to the pan and add the chicken. Brown the nut-crusted chicken for 2 minutes on each side, then transfer to the oven and finish cooking the chicken through, 8 to 10 minutes.

Shortly before serving, warm the milk over medium heat in a small pot. Add the cheese and melt it into the milk. If using dried sage, stir it into the sauce. Simmer for 5 minutes.

To serve, place the chicken on plates and pour a couple of spoons of the Gorgonzola sauce over the center of each piece. Garnish with chopped fresh sage, if using.

Chicken Marvalasala and Pappardelle with Rosemary Gravy

I revisit classics and take them to a new level, raising the bar a bit; that's why I call this chicken Marvalasala—it's Chicken Marsala taken to divine new heights. The wide ribbon pasta I serve with the chicken in this menu is topped with my version of a wonderful, rich gravy created by chef Emeril Lagasse; he uses it to drown shrimp.   4 SERVINGS

Salt

¾ pound **pappardelle** pasta (you can substitute fettuccine)

4 large, thin boneless, skinless **chicken breast cutlets**

Black pepper

4 tablespoons **EVOO** (extra-virgin olive oil)

2 large **garlic cloves**, crushed

2 **portobello mushroom caps**, sliced

12 **shiitake mushrooms**, stemmed and sliced

4 tablespoons (½ stick) **butter**

2 tablespoons **tomato paste** (the kind in a tube stores easily in the refrigerator)

2 tablespoons minced fresh **rosemary** (a couple of sprigs)

2 tablespoons all-purpose **flour**

1½ cups **chicken stock**

1 tablespoon **Worcestershire sauce**

2 tablespoons **capers**, drained

½ cup **Marsala wine**

Grated **Pecorino Romano** cheese

A couple handfuls of **arugula** or baby spinach leaves, thinly sliced, for garnish

Put a large covered pot of water on to boil for the pasta. When it comes up to a boil, salt the water, drop in the pasta, and cook to al dente.

While the pasta is working, season the chicken with salt and pepper. Heat a large nonstick skillet with 2 tablespoons of the EVOO, 2 times around the pan, over medium to medium-high heat. Add the chicken to the pan and brown it lightly on both sides, then remove it to a platter and cover it with foil to hold in the heat. To the same skillet, add the remaining 2 tablespoons of EVOO and 1 clove of the garlic. Cook the garlic for a minute or so, then remove it and add the mushrooms. Cook until the mushrooms brown evenly and become tender, 8 to 10 minutes.

While the mushrooms work, start the gravy for the pasta. In a deep medium skillet, melt 2 tablespoons of the butter into the tomato paste over medium heat. Add the remaining garlic clove and cook it for a couple of minutes, then remove. Add the rosemary, cook for 1 minute, then add the flour and whisk it into the garlic-infused

recipe continued

tomato butter. Cook the flour for a minute, then whisk in the stock and Worcestershire sauce. Simmer to thicken, 5 minutes. Season the sauce with salt and pepper to your taste.

To the cooked mushrooms, add the capers and Marsala and reduce for a minute or so. Add the remaining 2 tablespoons of butter in small bits to finish the sauce, and shake the pan to incorporate it. Slide the chicken back into the sauce and warm it through.

Drain the pasta and toss it with the rosemary gravy and a handful of cheese. Serve the pasta alongside the Chicken Marvalasala, and scatter arugula or spinach across both the chicken and pasta to garnish.

T-Bone Steaks with Arugula and Tomatoes

T-bones are thin-cut porterhouse steaks. (Porterhouse steaks also have a larger cut of tenderloin.) If you use porterhouse steaks instead of the T-bones, have them cut 1 inch thick.   2 SERVINGS

2 large **T-bone steaks**, 1 inch thick

2 tablespoons **EVOO** (extra-virgin olive oil), plus more for coating the meat

2 tablespoons fresh **rosemary** leaves, from about 4 sprigs, finely chopped

Salt and **black pepper**

2 **Roma tomatoes**, seeded and thinly sliced

4 to 5 cups **arugula leaves**, cut into ½-inch strips

Juice of 1 lemon

Preheat an outdoor grill or indoor grill pan to high.

Use a pastry brush to coat the meat lightly on both sides with EVOO. Rub the meat with rosemary and season it with salt and pepper. Let the meat rest at room temperature for 15 minutes. Cook it for 4 minutes on each side for medium rare. Let the meat rest for 5 minutes before cutting it. Dress the tomatoes and arugula with lemon juice, the 2 tablespoons of EVOO, and salt and pepper. Top the meat with lots of tomatoes and arugula and serve.

Pepper-Crusted Tenderloins with Mushroom Marsala Cream

This meal is for a special night: Congratulations! Happy Anniversary! I'm sorry. I love you. Thank you for everything. Take your pick and say it with food.   2 SERVINGS

4 1-inch-thick **beef tenderloin steaks**, 3 to 4 inches round, about 1 pound total

2 tablespoons **EVOO** (extra-virgin olive oil)

Salt and **black pepper**

4 teaspoons **coarse black pepper**, a rounded palmful

2 tablespoons **butter**

6 **white mushroom caps**, very thinly sliced

⅓ cup **Marsala**

⅔ cup **heavy cream**

Chopped fresh **flat-leaf parsley** or chives, for garnish

Preheat the oven to 425° F. Set the meat on the counter to take the chill off.

Pour the coarse black pepper onto a small plate. Heat the 2 tablespoons of EVOO in a nonstick skillet over medium-high to high heat. When the oil smokes, press each steak into the pepper to coat it on one side, then place the peppered side of the meat down in the skillet. Sear and caramelize the meat for 3 to 4 minutes, then turn and cook for 2 minutes on the second side for rare, 3 minutes for pink.

While the meat cooks, heat a small skillet over medium heat and melt the butter. Add the mushrooms and lightly sauté them for 4 to 5 minutes. Season the mushrooms with salt and pepper and add the Marsala to the pan. Reduce the liquid by half (a minute or so), cooking off the alcohol and concentrating the flavor, then stir in the cream and warm it through. Reduce the heat a bit and let the sauce thicken for 2 to 3 minutes.

Spoon the sauce over the meat and serve.

Pasta with a Lot of Mussel

This dish is bound to make a mussel lover out of anyone. The spicy kick of the chorizo and the fire-roasted tomatoes bring this dish to a whole new level.   4 SERVINGS

Coarse salt

1 pound **spaghetti**

2 tablespoons **extra-virgin olive oil** (EVOO)

½ pound **chorizo**, cut in half lengthwise, then sliced into half-moons

1 small **red onion**, chopped

3 **garlic cloves**, chopped

1 **celery rib**, finely chopped

1 small **carrot**, peeled and finely chopped

1 tablespoon fresh **thyme** leaves, chopped

Coarse black pepper

1 cup **dry white wine**

1 15-ounce can **diced fire-roasted tomatoes**, such as Muir Glen brand

1 pound **mussels** (ask at the seafood counter to check that they have been scrubbed)

½ cup fresh **flat-leaf parsley** leaves (two handfuls), coarsely chopped

Crusty bread

Bring a large pot of water up to a boil to cook the spaghetti. Add salt to the boiling water, add the pasta, and cook al dente.

Heat a large, deep skillet with a tight-fitting lid over medium heat with the EVOO. Add the chorizo and cook for 2 minutes, add the onions, garlic, celery, carrots, and thyme, and season with salt and pepper. Cook for 5 minutes, add the wine and fire-roasted tomatoes, and bring up to a bubble. Add the mussels and cover with the tight-fitting lid or some aluminum foil; cook until the mussels open, 4 to 6 minutes.

Discard any unopened shells. Using a slotted spoon, transfer the mussels to a bowl and cover with foil to keep warm. Add the drained cooked pasta and the parsley to the skillet with the chorizo and tomatoes, toss to coat in the sauce, and cook for 1 minute.

Divide the pasta among 4 serving bowls and top each bowl of pasta with a portion of the mussels. Serve immediately with some crusty bread.

Honey-Orange–Glazed Ham Steaks with Spicy Black Bean, Zucchini, and Corn Salad

This sweet dish will be perfect to make for your sweety!   4 SERVINGS

Zest and juice of 2 oranges

1 tablespoon **ground coriander**

½ cup **honey**

1 tablespoon **chili powder**

Salt and **freshly ground black pepper**

1½ cups **chicken stock** or broth

3 tablespoons **extra-virgin olive oil** (EVOO)

1 large **red onion**, chopped

3 large **garlic cloves**, chopped

1 **jalapeño pepper**, chopped

1 small **zucchini**, thinly sliced into disks

1 10-ounce box **frozen corn kernels**

2 large **ham steaks**, cut in half

1 15-ounce can **black beans**, drained and rinsed

Zest and juice of 1 lime

¼ cup fresh **flat-leaf parsley** leaves (a generous handful), chopped

In a small sauce pot over high heat, combine the orange juice, coriander, honey, chili powder, salt, pepper, and 1 cup of the chicken stock. Bring the mixture to a boil and simmer until reduced by half, about 5 minutes. Keep warm.

Preheat a medium skillet over medium-high heat with 2 tablespoons of the EVOO (twice around the pan). Add the onions, garlic, jalapeños, zucchini, salt, and pepper. Cook, stirring frequently for about 3 minutes, or until the onions start to turn translucent. Add the frozen corn, stir to combine, and continue to cook for 2 more minutes.

While the corn is cooking with the veggies, preheat another skillet over medium-high heat with the remaining tablespoon of EVOO. Add the ham steaks and heat through and brown slightly, about 2 minutes on each side.

To the corn and veggie mixture add the black beans and the remaining ½ cup of chicken stock and cook until the beans are heated through.

To the ham steaks, add the reduced honey-orange glaze. Flip the ham steaks around in the glaze and continue to cook for about 1 minute.

Add the orange zest, lime zest and juice, and parsley to the veggie and black bean mixture. Toss to combine. Serve the glazed ham steaks with a helping of the warm black bean, zucchini, and corn salad.

Spicy Shrimp and Penne with Puttanesca Sauce

Puttanesca is a sauce named after streetwalkers. The ladies would make pots of a fishy-smelling mixture of tomatoes, anchovies, and garlic and leave the pots in brothel windows to attract fishermen like stray cats. After the business was done, the sauce was tossed with pasta and became their dinner, or breakfast.   4 SERVINGS

1 pound **penne** pasta

Coarse salt

¼ cup **extra-virgin olive oil** (EVOO)

8 **garlic cloves**, finely chopped

2 teaspoons **red pepper flakes**

8 to 10 whole **anchovy** fillets

½ cup cracked, pitted, good-quality **black olives**, such as kalamata, or ⅓ cup pitted oil-cured black olives (saltier taste), your choice, coarsely chopped

3 to 4 tablespoons **capers**, drained and coarsely chopped

1 14-ounce can **crushed tomatoes**

1 14-ounce can **diced tomatoes**

1 pound (24 count) peeled and deveined **shrimp**, tails removed

2 handfuls fresh **flat-leaf parsley** leaves, finely chopped

Place a large pot of water on to boil. When it comes up, add the penne pasta and salt.

While the pasta cooks, heat a large, deep skillet over medium heat. Add the EVOO, garlic, crushed red pepper flakes, and anchovies. Break up the fish with the back of a wooden spoon until they melt into the oil. The fish will develop a nutty, salty flavor; if you think you don't like anchovies, try this ONCE and you will! Add the olives, capers, and tomatoes. Bring the sauce to a bubble and add the shrimp, scattering them in a single layer. Cover the pan to cook the shrimp, 3 to 4 minutes. They will turn pink, opaque, and firm. Uncover the pan and add the parsley. Toss and adjust the seasonings to taste.

When the pasta is al dente, drain it well and add it to the sauce. Toss to combine and serve hot.

Ham and Swiss Crepes with Chopped Salad

A fancier version of ham and cheese sandwiches, these crepes are sure to impress.   4 SERVINGS

½ cup all-purpose **flour**

Coarse salt

3 **eggs**, beaten

¾ cup **milk**

2 tablespoons **brandy** (purchase a 2-ounce nip if you don't want a large bottle)

2 tablespoons melted **unsalted butter**

1 pint **red cherry tomatoes**

1 pint **yellow cherry tomatoes**

10 fresh **basil** leaves, chopped

½ cup fresh **flat-leaf parsley** leaves (a handful)

2 tablespoons **balsamic vinegar**

3 tablespoons **extra-virgin olive oil** (EVOO)

Coarse black pepper

½ seedless **cucumber**, quartered lengthwise and chopped into bite-size pieces

1 bunch of **watercress**, stemmed and coarsely chopped

1 small **red onion**, thinly sliced

Vegetable oil, for cooking crepes

2 cups shredded **Swiss cheese** (from an 8-ounce brick)

½ pound thinly sliced **Black Forest ham**, chopped into ribbons

For the crepe batter, combine the flour and a pinch of salt in a bowl and make a well in the center. Add the eggs, milk, and brandy to the well and whisk to combine. Stir in the melted butter. Cover the batter and set aside for 20 minutes.

While the batter is resting, halve the red and yellow cherry tomatoes and add them to a salad bowl. Add the basil, parsley, balsamic vinegar, EVOO, salt, and pepper. Toss to coat. Add the cucumbers, watercress, and onions.

Preheat a 10-inch nonstick skillet over medium-low heat with a drizzle of vegetable oil. Cover the bottom of the skillet with just enough batter to coat, lifting and shaking the skillet to help the batter along. Let the crepe cook and lightly brown on one side, just about 1 minute. Turn the crepe with a rubber spatula, lifting up the edges, then use a toothpick or your finger to flip it over. Once it is flipped, scatter some of the cheese and ham on top. Season with a little salt and pepper, then fold the crepe over and continue to cook until the cheese starts to melt. Transfer the crepe to a plate and cover with foil to keep warm. Repeat this 7 more times to serve 2 crepes per person.

Divide the 8 crepes among 4 serving plates; serve some salad next to the crepes.

Prosciutto and Spinach Bucatini

Bucatini is hollow spaghetti and makes slurping up your pasta even more fun. I make this dish with prosciutto and leafy greens.

2 SERVINGS

Salt

½ pound **bucatini** pasta

3 tablespoons **EVOO** (extra-virgin olive oil)

3 large **garlic cloves**, thinly sliced

1 teaspoon **red pepper flakes**

1 pound **fresh spinach**, stems removed, shredded

6 slices **prosciutto**, cut into thin strips

Zest and juice of 1 lemon

Black pepper

½ cup grated **Parmigiano-Reggiano**, a couple of generous handfuls, plus more to pass at the table

Place a large covered pot of water over high heat and bring it up to a boil to cook the pasta. Once the water boils, add some salt and the pasta and cook to al dente. Heads up: You'll need to reserve a couple of ladles of the cooking water just before you drain the pasta.

While the pasta cooks, heat a large skillet over medium-high heat with the EVOO. Add the sliced garlic and cook it until it's golden, about 1 minute. Add the red pepper flakes and a couple of ladles of the starchy pasta cooking water. Stand back: It will really bubble up! Add the drained pasta to the skillet and toss it around until the pasta has soaked up about three fourths of the liquid. Turn the heat off and add the spinach, prosciutto strips, lemon zest, and lemon juice, and season with a little salt and pepper. Toss to wilt the spinach and distribute the prosciutto. Sprinkle the pasta liberally with the Parmigiano, toss to coat the pasta, and serve.

Poached Eggs on Potato, Spinach, and Smoked Salmon Salad

Who says you can't have a brunch date? This is perfect for two—and easy on your wallet. Wash it down with crisp white wine or mimosas, and you'll be good to go!   2 SERVINGS

1 pound small **red potatoes,** cut into quarters

Salt

4 large handfuls of **baby spinach**

Zest and juice of 1 lemon

¼ cup pitted **kalamata olives,** coarsely chopped

Black pepper

1 tablespoon **Dijon mustard**

3 tablespoons **mayonnaise**

2 tablespoons **capers,** (drained and chopped

2 tablespoons chopped fresh **dill**

1 tablespoon **white vinegar**

4 **eggs**

3 or 4 slices **smoked salmon,** cut into strips

Place the potatoes in a sauce pot, cover them with water, place the pot over high heat, and bring the water to a boil. Once it is boiling, add some salt and cook until the potatoes are tender, 12 to 15 minutes. Drain the potatoes and spread out on a cookie sheet to cool, about 5 minutes.

When cool, transfer the potatoes to a bowl. Add the spinach, lemon zest, and olives and season them with salt and pepper.

In a bowl, combine the mustard, mayonnaise, capers, dill, lemon juice, and a little splash of cold water to loosen up the dressing—just enough to make it drizzle-able.

Fill a medium skillet with about 2 inches of water. Bring the water to a gentle simmer over high heat. Once the water is at a bubble, turn the heat down to medium low; you need a gentle simmer for poaching eggs. Pour the vinegar into the simmering water. Crack an egg into a small bowl, then gently slide the egg into the simmering water. Repeat this with the remaining 3 eggs. Cook the eggs for about 2 minutes for runny yolks, or about 4 minutes for solid yolks. Do not allow the water to boil. Use a slotted spoon to remove the eggs to a towel-lined plate to drain.

Add the salmon to the potato mixture, and toss to combine and then divide between two plates. Top each serving of salad with two poached eggs and then liberally drizzle each with the caper dressing.

Chicken with Sweet Raisins and Apricots on Couscous

Why go to Morocco when its cuisine can come to you? This dish is sure to impress any date with its authentic Moroccan flavors at a fraction of an airline ticket's price!   4 SERVINGS

3 tablespoons **extra-virgin olive oil** (EVOO)

4 6-ounce boneless, skinless **chicken breast halves**

Salt and **freshly ground black pepper**

1 tablespoon fresh **thyme** leaves (from a couple of sprigs), chopped

½ cup **sliced almonds** (2 2-ounce packages from the baking aisle of the market)

3½ cups **chicken stock** or broth, divided

1½ cups **plain couscous**

3 tablespoons chopped fresh **flat-leaf parsley** (a generous handful)

2 tablespoons **unsalted butter**

3 large **shallots**, thinly sliced

2 tablespoons all-purpose **flour**

12 dried, **pitted apricots**, halved

1 cup **golden raisins**

2 tablespoons **cider** or **white wine vinegar**

Preheat a large nonstick skillet over medium-high heat. Add 2 tablespoons of the EVOO (twice around the pan). Season the chicken breasts with salt, pepper, and chopped thyme. Add the chicken to the hot skillet and cook on each side for 5 to 6 minutes.

Toast the nuts in the bottom of a medium sauce pot over medium heat until golden. Transfer the toasted nuts to a dish and reserve. Return the pot to the stovetop. Add 1½ cups of the chicken stock and the remaining tablespoon of EVOO, cover the pot, and raise the heat; bring the broth to a boil. Remove the pot from the heat. Add the couscous and parsley to the stock, then stir. Cover and let the couscous stand for 5 minutes. Fluff the cooked couscous with a fork and toss with the toasted almonds. Cover to keep it warm while you make the sauce for the chicken.

Remove the chicken from the skillet to a plate and cover with foil. Return the skillet to the heat and add the butter and shallots. Cook for about 2 minutes. Dust with the flour and continue to cook for 1 minute. Add the apricots, golden raisins, and cider vinegar. Whisk in the remaining 2 cups of chicken stock and turn the heat up to high. Simmer the mixture until thick. Add the chicken back to the skillet, coat in the sauce, and heat the chicken, about 1 minute. Serve the chicken and some sauce over the almond couscous.

Sea Bass with Puttanesca and Potatoes

These simple foil packets are a roasted alternative to fish in parchment, steamy paper pouches of fish and veggies. The flavor produced by this method is pronounced; you'll be surprised at how much great grill flavor you can get even though the meal is cooked in a foil packet. With vegetable, starch, and protein piled together, this is a one-pouch meal with NO CLEANUP! Made on the grill, this is sure to become a three-season favorite.   2 SERVINGS

1 tablespoon **anchovy paste**

Juice of ½ lemon

¼ cup **EVOO** (extra-virgin olive oil), plus more for liberal drizzling

1 pound **fingerling, small white, or Yukon Gold potatoes**

4 **garlic cloves**, crushed

16 to 20 **cherry tomatoes**

A generous handful of fresh **flat-leaf parsley** leaves, chopped

¼ cup pitted **kalamata olives**, chopped

4 tablespoons **capers**, drained

½ to 1 teaspoon **red pepper flakes**

½ cup **white vermouth** or dry white wine

2 **sea bass fillets**, 6 to 8 ounces each

Salt and **black pepper**

Preheat a grill to medium temperature, about 375°F.

Rip off 4 pieces of foil, each 18 inches long, and make 2 double-thick stacks. In a bowl, combine the anchovy paste with the lemon juice, then stream in the ¼ cup of EVOO. Cut the potatoes into wedges and add them to a second bowl with the garlic. Halve most of the tomatoes and add them to the bowl. (You can leave small, grape-size tomatoes whole; they'll burst on their own during cooking.)

Add the parsley, olives, capers, and red pepper flakes to the potatoes; drizzle with the anchovy and oil dressing; and toss to combine. Divide the potatoes and tomatoes evenly between the two foil slabs. Bend the edges of the

recipe continued

tidbit >> To prepare this recipe in the oven, seal the ingredients in parchment-paper pouches and bake at 400°F for 20 minutes without turning, or until the fish is opaque. (Omit the vermouth or wine entirely as this method, essentially steaming the fish, produces more liquids in the packet.) The color and texture will be softer using this method, but the potent flavor of the sauce still hits its spicy mark on your palate.

foil up a bit and douse each packet with ¼ cup of white vermouth or wine. Drizzle some oil over the fish and season with salt and pepper. Place the fish atop the potatoes and tomatoes and seal the packets up. Grill them for 20 minutes, turning once. Open the packets carefully and serve.

Broiled Haddock with Bacon-Fried Greens

It's amazing what the right spices will do to the simplest (and most inexpensive) ingredients!   4 SERVINGS

1 tablespoon **extra-virgin olive oil** (EVOO)

4 slices **applewood-smoked bacon,** chopped

1 medium **red onion**, chopped

3 tablespoons **red wine vinegar**

6 cups (1½ pounds) **Swiss chard** or red Swiss chard, coarsely chopped

Salt and **freshly ground black pepper**

½ teaspoon **grated nutmeg**

5 tablespoons softened **butter**

2¼ to 2½ pounds **haddock fillets**, cut into 4 portions

Juice of ½ **lemon**

¼ cup **mayonnaise**

10 fresh **chive** blades, snipped or chopped

Preheat the broiler and preheat a skillet over medium-high heat.

To the skillet, add the EVOO and bacon. Render the bacon fat 3 minutes, then add the onion and cook together with the bacon for another 3 or 4 minutes. Deglaze the pan with the vinegar. Add the greens in bunches, wilting into the pan. Season the greens with salt, pepper, and nutmeg. Reduce the heat to medium low and let the greens cook for 10 minutes, tossing occasionally with tongs.

Grease a shallow broiler pan with 1 tablespoon of the butter. Set the fish into the pan, white, fleshy side up. Dress the fish with the lemon juice and some salt. Mix the 4 tablespoons of remaining butter with the mayonnaise. Broil the fish for 3 or 4 minutes, 3 or 4 inches from the heat, then remove from the oven and slather the combined mayo-butter evenly over the fish. If the pan looks dry, add a splash of water to it and return the fish to the oven. Broil the fish for 5 minutes more, or until the top of the haddock is bubbly and evenly browned. Top the cooked fish with the chives and carefully transfer it to dinner plates with a fish spatula. Serve with a pile of bacon-fried greens on the side.

Pasta with Swiss Chard, Bacon, and Lemony Ricotta Cheese

In this dish, the hot pasta is served atop a mound of lemon-flavored ricotta cheese. The heat from the pasta will warm the cheese and send the lemony scent straight to your nose.   4 SERVINGS

Coarse salt

1 pound **cellantani** (ridged corkscrew-shaped pasta) or other ridged short-cut pasta

2 tablespoons **extra-virgin olive oil** (EVOO)

5 slices **bacon**, coarsely chopped

3 or 4 **garlic cloves**, chopped

1 small **yellow onion**, chopped

Freshly ground black pepper

½ teaspoon **red pepper flakes**

1 bunch of **Swiss chard**, cleaned and coarsely chopped

1 cup **chicken stock** or broth

1 cup whole-milk **ricotta cheese**

Zest and juice of 1 lemon

1 cup grated **Parmigiano-Reggiano** (a few handfuls), plus some to pass at the table

Bring a large pot of water to a boil for the pasta. When the water comes to a boil, add salt and cook the pasta al dente.

While the pasta cooks, preheat a large, deep skillet over moderate heat. Add the EVOO and bacon and cook until the bacon crisps, about 3 minutes. To the bacon add the garlic, onions, salt, black pepper, and red pepper flakes and cook, stirring frequently, for 5 minutes, or until the onions are lightly caramelized. Add the chopped Swiss chard, toss to coat, and wilt the chard down. Turn the heat up to high and add the chicken stock and a couple of ladles, about a cup, of the starchy, boiling water from the cooking pasta. When the liquid comes up to a boil, reduce the heat and simmer for 6 to 7 minutes.

In a small bowl, combine the ricotta with the lemon zest and season with salt and pepper. Place ¼ cup of the ricotta mixture in the bottom of each of 4 pasta bowls and reserve.

Add the lemon juice to the Swiss chard. Drain the pasta well and toss with the greens for a minute or so to let the juices absorb into the pasta. Turn the heat off and add the grated Parmigiano cheese to the pasta and greens and continue to toss to distribute. Serve the pasta immediately, dishing it up on top of the ricotta cheese. Stir the lemony ricotta up in your bowl to mix with the pasta.

Boozy Berries and Biscuits

Is this a cocktail or a dessert? Your call. My call is YUM-O!

8 SERVINGS

½ pint **raspberries**

½ pint **blackberries**

2 pints **strawberries**, sliced

1 nip (2 ounces) **Frangelico**, Sambuca, or Amaretto—a couple generous shots

2 cups **heavy cream**

¼ cup **sugar**

2 packages of **anisette toasts**, such as Stella D'oro; cut into large bits with a serrated knife

1 3.5-ounce bar **bittersweet chocolate**, such as Ghirardelli (look for it on the baking aisle)

In a bowl, combine the berries with the liqueur of choice. Let the berries sit and macerate while you make dinner. Whip up the cream with the sugar, using a hand mixer, until soft peaks form; reserve the whipped cream in the refrigerator.

Once dinner starts winding down, arrange the bits of anisette toasts in a shallow serving dish with sides. Top with the booze-soaked berries, spreading them over the toasts. If the whipped cream has lost some of its air, give it a quick beat with a whisk. Top the berries with the whipped cream. Using a vegetable peeler, shave curls from the side of the chocolate bar, letting them cover the whipped cream.

Wine-Soaked Peaches with Ice Cream

A fancy dessert that's easy to make.   2 SERVINGS

1½ cups **red wine**

½ cup **sugar**

1 **cinnamon stick**

2 or 3 **whole peppercorns**

1 or 2 **strips of lemon zest**

2 large **ripe peaches**, halved and pitted

1 pint **vanilla bean ice cream**

Combine the wine, sugar, cinnamon, peppercorns, and zest in a sauce pot and reduce over medium-high heat to a syrup, 12 to 15 minutes. Remove the cinnamon, peppercorns, and zest with a slotted spoon and discard. Add the peach halves and turn to coat in the wine sauce. Spoon the winey peaches into dishes and top them with ice cream.

Tipsy Triple-Chocolate Shakes and Strawberries

Dunk large-stem berries and you're in for a divine treat.   4 SERVINGS

8 shots **chocolate cream liqueur**, such as Bailey's

12 scoops **chocolate ice cream**

4 cups **chocolate milk**

Whipped cream, from a canister (in the dairy case)

1 **dark chocolate bar**, for garnish

Working in 2 batches, combine the chocolate liqueur, ice cream, and chocolate milk in a blender and whir until it is thick but smooth. Pour the shakes into tall glasses and garnish them with whipped cream. Use a vegetable peeler to shave the dark chocolate over each. Serve them with straws and long spoons on plates to catch the drips.

Mascarpone Parfait
with Citrus Salad

Sweet, tart, crunchy, and creamy, this dessert is just about perfect, and low-carb to boot! This is great for Sunday brunch, or as a light and refreshing ending to a heavy winter meal. Try it with blood oranges when they're in season, or your favorite combination of citrus fruits.

4 SERVINGS

8 vanilla or plain **meringue cookies**

8 ounces **mascarpone cheese**

2 tablespoons **honey**

1 large **orange**

1 **ruby grapefruit**

Zest of 1 lime

1 tablespoon chopped **fresh mint**, plus sprigs for garnishing

Put the cookies into a food storage bag and crush them with a rolling pin or the back of a pan. Set aside. In a bowl, mix together the mascarpone and 1 tablespoon of the honey. Set this aside also as you make the citrus salad.

Slice the top and bottom off the orange and grapefruit so that the fruit sits upright. Remove the peel by slicing around the flesh, cutting deep enough to remove the outer membrane along with the peel. Cut the segments away from the membrane and transfer to a bowl. Squeeze a little of the juice from the remains of the orange and grapefruit over the segments. Stir in the lime zest, remaining tablespoon of honey, and mint.

To assemble the parfaits, divide the crushed meringue cookies among 4 tall, narrow glasses or ice cream dishes. Put ¼ cup of the mascarpone on top of the cookies in each glass, followed by one fourth of the citrus salad. Garnish with a mint sprig and serve immediately.

Very Berry Crumble

I like to use frozen berries for this crumble. Not only can I have it any time of year, but the juices left in the bag after thawing provide sweetness (without adding a lot of sugar) and sauce for the crumble.

4 SERVINGS

CRUMBLE TOPPING

¾ cup sliced **almonds**, lightly crushed

⅓ cup **quick-cooking oats**

2 teaspoons **sugar**

Hefty pinch of **ground cinnamon**

Pinch of freshly **grated nutmeg**

2 tablespoons **butter**, softened, plus more for greasing ramekins

FILLING

1 10-ounce bag **frozen raspberries**, thawed

1 10-ounce bag **frozen blueberries**, thawed

1 tablespoon **sugar**

1 tablespoon **cornstarch**

Preheat the oven to 375°F. Grease four 6-ounce ramekins and transfer them to a foil-lined baking sheet and set aside.

To make the topping, in a bowl combine the almonds, oats, sugar, and spices. Add the butter, and, with your fingers or a fork, rub the butter into the dry ingredients until large, coarse crumbs form. Set aside while you make the filling.

To make the filling, put the berries into a strainer set over a bowl to catch the juices. Add the sugar and cornstarch to the juices and whisk until smooth and the starch dissolves. Gently fold the berries back into their juices, and divide the mixture among the greased ramekins. Top each filled dish with one fourth of the crumble topping and place on the baking sheet. Bake until bubbling hot and the topping is golden, about 20 minutes. Allow the crumbles to cool for at least 10 minutes before serving.

Ginger-Poached Pears with Ricotta and Blueberries

This dish is so simple, yet it could be served at any elegant dinner party. It is equally good warm or cold and makes a great addition to a Sunday brunch.   4 SERVINGS

1 cup **water**

1-inch piece of **fresh ginger**, peeled and sliced

2 tablespoons **sugar**

Zest of 1 lemon

2 firm **pears**, such as Bosc or Anjou, peeled, cored, and coarsely chopped

¾ cup **whole-milk ricotta**

Dash of **ground cinnamon**

½ cup fresh **blueberries**

In a saucepan, bring the water, ginger, sugar, and lemon zest to a boil over medium-high heat. Add the pears, and when the pot returns to a boil, reduce the heat to medium-low to maintain the simmer. Cook the pears until very soft when pierced with a knife (but not falling apart), 12 to 15 minutes. Remove the pan from the heat and, using a slotted spoon, divide the pears among 4 dessert cups or ice cream dishes.

Add the ricotta and cinnamon to the warm syrup and stir gently until very smooth. Top the pears with the warm cheese mixture, then tumble some fresh blueberries over each serving.

Angel Food Cake with Sorbet Sauce and Berries

This is so angelic, you can have 2 slices.   16 SERVINGS

1 pint **lemon sorbet**

2 tablespoons **lemon zest**

1 pint **blackberries**

1 pint **strawberries**, sliced

½ pint **raspberries**

2 store-bought **angel food cakes**

In a small sauce pot, melt the sorbet with the zest over low heat. Stir in the berries. Cut the cake into wedges and pour the berries and sauce over the top.

Looking for Mr. Goodbar Sundaes

Surprise your date with this outstanding treat!   4 SERVINGS

2 pints **vanilla ice cream**

1 jar **chocolate fudge sauce**

1 cup **red-skinned salted peanuts**, available on the snack aisle of the market

¼ cup **honey**

Whipped cream, from a canister (in the dairy case)

8 **mini Mr. Goodbars**, for garnish (optional)

Get 4 sundae cups or goblets out and place a huge scoop of ice cream in each. Heat the fudge sauce for 30 seconds in a microwave, with the lid off the jar. Sprinkle a handful of nuts into each dish, then top each with a layer of fudge, another scoop of ice cream, and a spoonful more of fudge. Heat the honey in a microwave for 10 to 15 seconds. Top the sundaes with whipped cream and a drizzle of warm honey, then garnish them with a few more red peanuts and a couple of mini candy bars. Serve them on plates, to catch any overflow, and pass out the long sundae spoons.

Fired-Up Peaches and Cream

The flaming whiskey is a great way to end your meal!   6 SERVINGS

4 tablespoons (½ stick) **butter**, cut into small pieces

4 medium-ripe **peaches**, sliced

Pinch of ground **cinnamon**

¼ cup **brown sugar**

4 shots **whiskey**

2 pints **vanilla ice cream**

Whipped cream, from a canister (in the dairy case)

Heat a large skillet over medium heat. Add the butter, and when it melts, add the peaches. Season them with the cinnamon. Turn up the heat to medium high and cook the peaches for 3 minutes, then add the brown sugar and melt it into the butter. Pull the pan off the flame, add the whiskey, then return the pan to the stove and dip the skillet to set the whiskey aflame, or light it carefully with a kitchen match. When the flame dies out, scoop some ice cream into dishes, top them with peaches and sauce, add some whipped cream, and serve.

tidbit >> A shot, or jigger, is usually about 1½ ounces, but can be anything from 1 to 2 ounces (2 to 4 tablespoons).

Stuffed Roasted Strawberries

This is an inside-out version of chocolate-dipped strawberries. Roasting the fruit brings out even more flavor and juiciness. You'll never settle for plain old dipped berries again! You can use any type of chocolate (milk, white, or semisweet).   4 SERVINGS

12 extra-large **strawberries** (the bigger the better!)

1 to 2 ounces **bittersweet chocolate**, chopped

1 teaspoon **sugar** (optional)

Whipped cream, from a canister (in the dairy case)

Cocoa powder, for garnish

Preheat the oven to 400°F.

Slice the tops of the berries off just below the stem. Cut the tips off (about ¼ inch), so that the berries will sit upright. Next, use a small spoon or a melon-ball scoop to hollow out the strawberries, working from their tops, to create a cavity in each one. Stuff some chocolate into the cavity of each strawberry and place them upright in a baking dish. Lightly sprinkle the berries with sugar, if using. Roast the berries until soft and the chocolate is melted, 10 to 12 minutes.

To serve, place 3 strawberries on a dessert plate in a triangle. If the berries have given off liquid in the baking dish, spoon it over them. Spray a small mound of cream in the center of the berries, and top each berry with a rosette of cream. Sift a little cocoa powder over the plate, and serve!

INDEX